THE MUSIC FORUM

Volume II

THE MUSIC FORUM

Volume II

Edited by WILLIAM J. MITCHELL *and* FELIX SALZER

HEDI SIEGEL, EDITORIAL ASSISTANT

Columbia University Press 1970 New York and London

ISBN: 0–231–03153–x
Library of Congress Catalog Card Number: 67–16204
Printed in the United States of America

Foreword

RECEPTION of *The Music Forum*, Volume I, has been gratifying. We speak not merely of the number of copies distributed, but also of the volume of correspondence addressed to the editors and authors, and the large number of contributions received for future issues. Several of the articles planned for inclusion in Volume II proved to be of considerable length. Since the editors are committed to the publication of significant and timely papers, regardless of their length, it has not been possible to limit arbitrarily the size of this volume; it is considerably larger than Volume I.

Volume II, like Volume I, represents a broad spread of articles, both historically and topically. Of special interest in connection with Lewis Lockwood's article is a separate publication by the Columbia University Press of a full-size facsimile of the autograph of the first movement of Beethoven's Sonata for Violoncello and Piano, Opus 69. As in Volume I, linear-structural graphs accompany several articles. For guidance in the comprehending of these graphs, the reader is referred to the Glossary in Volume I, pages 260 to 268, where the procedures of linear-structural analysis are described and illustrated.

Plans for Volume III have been completed. It will include a translation of the theoretical tracts of Christoph Bernhard, prepared with extensive annotations by Walter Hilse. Plans for future issues include, among analytic papers, annotated translations of Heinrich Schenker's *Beitrag zur Ornamentik* and of his edition of Brahms' study of fifths, octaves, and unusual voice leading. As in Volumes I and II, however, our principal efforts will be directed toward a broad and varied coverage of music and musical topics representative of many styles and periods.

We observe with pride that the Columbia University Press was cited by the Production Quality Committee of the Association of American University Presses for the many distinguished features of its production of Volume I. To all those who contributed to this success, we express our sincerest thanks. We are also most grateful to Thames Hickman, who again provided the expert autography.

WILLIAM J. MITCHELL

FELIX SALZER

Contents

Contributors

Lewis Lockwood is Professor of Music at Princeton University

David Loeb teaches at the Mannes College of Music

Carl Schachter teaches at the Mannes College of Music

Saul Novack is Professor of Music at Queens College of the City University of New York

William J. Mitchell is Professor of Music at the State University of New York at Binghamton

Hedi Siegel is Editorial Assistant for *The Music Forum*

Felix Salzer is Professor of Music at Queens College of the City University of New York

Roy Travis is Professor of Music at the University of California at Los Angeles

THE MUSIC FORUM

Volume II

The Autograph of the First Movement of Beethoven's Sonata for Violoncello and Pianoforte, Opus 69

LEWIS LOCKWOOD

REMARKABLY few of the primary manuscript sources of Beethoven's works have yet been made accessible in reproduction, despite their acknowledged importance. Valued deeply and universally as artistic possessions, the Beethoven autographs have been coveted, hoarded, revered—and at times dismembered—but rarely published in the complete facsimile editions that would stimulate close study of their contents. It is true that a fair number of single pages are distributed widely through a thicket of Beethoven publications. But the entire group of complete manuscripts produced to date consists of eleven works: eight piano sonatas (Op. 26; 27, No. 2; 53; 57; 78; 109; 110; 111); two symphonies (the Fifth and the Ninth); and the *Kyrie* of the *Missa Solemnis*.[1]

For the sketches the situation is roughly comparable: apart from single leaves, three complete sketchbooks have so far been issued in full facsimile.[2]

[1] Op. 26, Erich Prieger, ed. (Berlin, Cohen, 1895); Op. 27, No. 2, Heinrich Schenker, ed., in "Musikalische Seltenheiten," Vol. I (Vienna, Universal-Edition, 1921); Op. 53, Dagmar Weise, ed. (Bonn, Beethoven-Haus, 1954); see also her article in *Beethoven Jahrbuch*, Jg. 1955/56, 102–11; Op. 57 (Paris, Piazza, 1927); Op. 78 (Munich, Drei Masken, 1923); Op. 109, O. Jonas, ed. (New York, Lehman Foundation, 1965); Op. 110, K. M. Komma, ed. (Stuttgart, Ichthys, 1967); Op. 111, (Munich, Drei Masken, 1922). Fifth Symphony, G. Schünemann, ed. (Berlin, Maximilian, 1942); Ninth Symphony (Leipzig, Kistner and Siegel, 1924); *Missa Solemnis: Kyrie*, W. Virneisel, ed. (Tutzing, Schneider, 1965).

[2] The "Engelmann" sketchbook of 1822–23, published as "Ludwig van Beethoven, Skizzenbuch" (Leipzig, Röder, 1913); the "Moscow" sketchbook of 1825, published by M. Ivanov-Boretzky in *Muzykalnoye Obrazovanie* (*Musikalische Bildung*), Nos. 1/2 of the 1927 volume; the "Wielhorsky" sketchbook of 1802–03, published by N. Fishman as *Kniga Eskizov Beethovena* . . . (3 vols.; Moscow, State Publishing House, 1962).

Yet even if these sketchbook publications have attracted less attention than they deserve, they nevertheless reinforce awareness of the great potential importance of their musical material, and a program for their publication is in course of realization. But outside of circles of specialists, the comparable documentary importance of the autographs has remained obscure and largely unsuspected, not only because of the absence of publications but because of the widespread and mistaken assumption that their contents probably represented the "finished" versions as supposedly translated into the "official" versions of the nineteenth-century Gesamtausgabe.[3]

THE AUTOGRAPH AND RELATED SOURCES

AGAINST this background, the present publication of the entire extant autograph of the first movement of the Sonata for Violoncello and Piano in A Major, Op. 69, marks a significant step forward.[4] With this facsimile, a complete autograph of a major Beethoven movement appears for the first time in a widely circulating serial publication, while at the same time an important Beethoven work for chamber ensemble is added to the small circle of published autographs.

By way of further preface to a description of the manuscript and the sources related to it, a word should be said about terms. "Autograph" is inevitably the basic term of this discussion. While everyone knows the common-sense meaning of the term, and while there is no reason to doubt that the musical document reproduced here is the only known source which

[3] Gesamtausgabe: *Ludwig van Beethoven's Werke* (Leipzig, Breitkopf and Härtel, 1864–90). Hereafter cited as GA. Even in the large specialized literature, studies of the autographs themselves have not been plentiful, despite the pioneering work of Heinrich Schenker in calling attention to their great value as musical documents. Schenker's own studies of Beethoven autographs, embodied in his *Erläuterungsausgaben der letzten Sonaten Beethovens* (Vienna, Universal-Edition, 1913–20) and in other writings, were followed by important studies by O. Jonas on Op. 61 (*Zeitschrift für Musikwissenschaft*, XIII [1931], 443–50) and Op. 93 (*Music and Letters*, XX [1939], 177–82), as well as more recent writings; see also Paul Mies, *Textkritische Untersuchungen bei Beethoven* (Munich, Henle, 1957) and Hubert Unverricht, *Die Eigenschriften und Originalausgaben von Werken Beethovens in ihrer Bedeutung für die moderne Textkritik* (Kassel, Bärenreiter, 1960); also recent studies by Alan Tyson, especially his painstaking and significant contributions to Beethoven textual criticism, in which the autographs naturally play a vital role. These include the important book, *The Authentic English Editions of Beethoven* (London, Faber and Faber, 1963) and numerous articles, including, most recently, "The Textual Problems of Beethoven's Violin Concerto," *The Musical Quarterly*, LIII (October, 1967), 482–502.

[4] I should like to thank Felix Salzer, owner of the manuscript, for repeatedly placing it at my disposal for the close examination of detailed problems.

corresponds to that meaning, there is good reason to recognize that the term in its customary usage is loose and somewhat ambiguous, at least for Beethoven's works.[5] The typical function of the term is that of an abbreviated designation (and that is its use here) for what might be termed "the last finished version of a work written down by its author"—the *Fassung letzter Hand*. But the conveniences of terminology should not obscure the complexities lurking in the concept framed by the words "last finished," and for complexities of this kind the material associated with Op. 69 forms a masterly example.

The earlier history of the manuscript is not fully documented but in its essential outline it is clear enough. According to Kinsky–Halm, its first owner after 1827 was the publisher Domenico Artaria,[6] but whether the manuscript as Artaria knew it consisted of the entire Sonata or only the first movement we do not know. By the end of the century, at all events, the separate existence of the first-movement autograph is an established fact, as is its change of owner. While the bulk of the Artaria collection of Beethoven manuscripts eventually passed to the Berlin Library, this manuscript became the property of Heinrich Steger of Vienna, an enthusiastic collector of Beethoven treasures.[7] Steger exhibited the first-movement autograph at an international exposition on music and theater that was held in Vienna in 1892, and the manuscript probably remained in his possession until the dispersal of his holdings between 1904 and 1907. At about this time it evidently passed to the Wittgenstein family of Vienna,[8] from whom in turn it came into the possession of Felix Salzer. Neither internal nor external evidence gives any clue to the earlier fate of the

[5] Further on this point see Unverricht, pp. 12–13.

[6] G. Kinsky and H. Halm, *Das Werk Beethovens* (Munich, Henle, 1955), p. 164.

[7] *Fachkatalog der Wiener Musikausstellung 1892*, p. 287, No. 20; "Sonate (A-Dur) für Pianoforte und Violoncell. Op. 69, Erster Satz. Autogr. (1807–08). Dr. Heinrich Steger, Wien." Steger was also the owner of the autographs of other Beethoven works, including Op. 28; 33; 53; 59, No. 3; 62; 96; 98; 102, No. 2; 120; and WoO 20. It seems that in this same year the manuscript (explicitly only the first movement) was given to Brahms for his scrutiny and, possibly, his acquisition. This is clear from a letter Brahms wrote to Joachim on April 2, 1892: "Der erste Satz der A-dur–Cello–Sonate von Beethoven liegt bei mir, und ich habe die heimliche Angst, dass mein bescheidenes Sträuben, ihn für ein Manuskript von mir(!) zu erwerben, mich schliesslich um den Schatz bringt!" For the entire letter see *Johannes Brahms im Briefwechsel mit Joseph Joachim*, Andreas Moser, ed. (Berlin, Deutsche Brahms–Gesellschaft, 1912) II, 275, Letter No. 506. For this reference I am indebted to Felix Salzer.

[8] Max Unger, "Die Beethoven-Handschriften der Familie W. in Wien," *Neues Beethoven Jahrbuch*, VII (1937), 160 f.

AUTOGRAPH OF THE FIRST MOVEMENT OF BEETHOVEN'S SONATA FOR VIOLONCELLO AND PIANOFORTE, OPUS 69

I recto (bars 1-17)

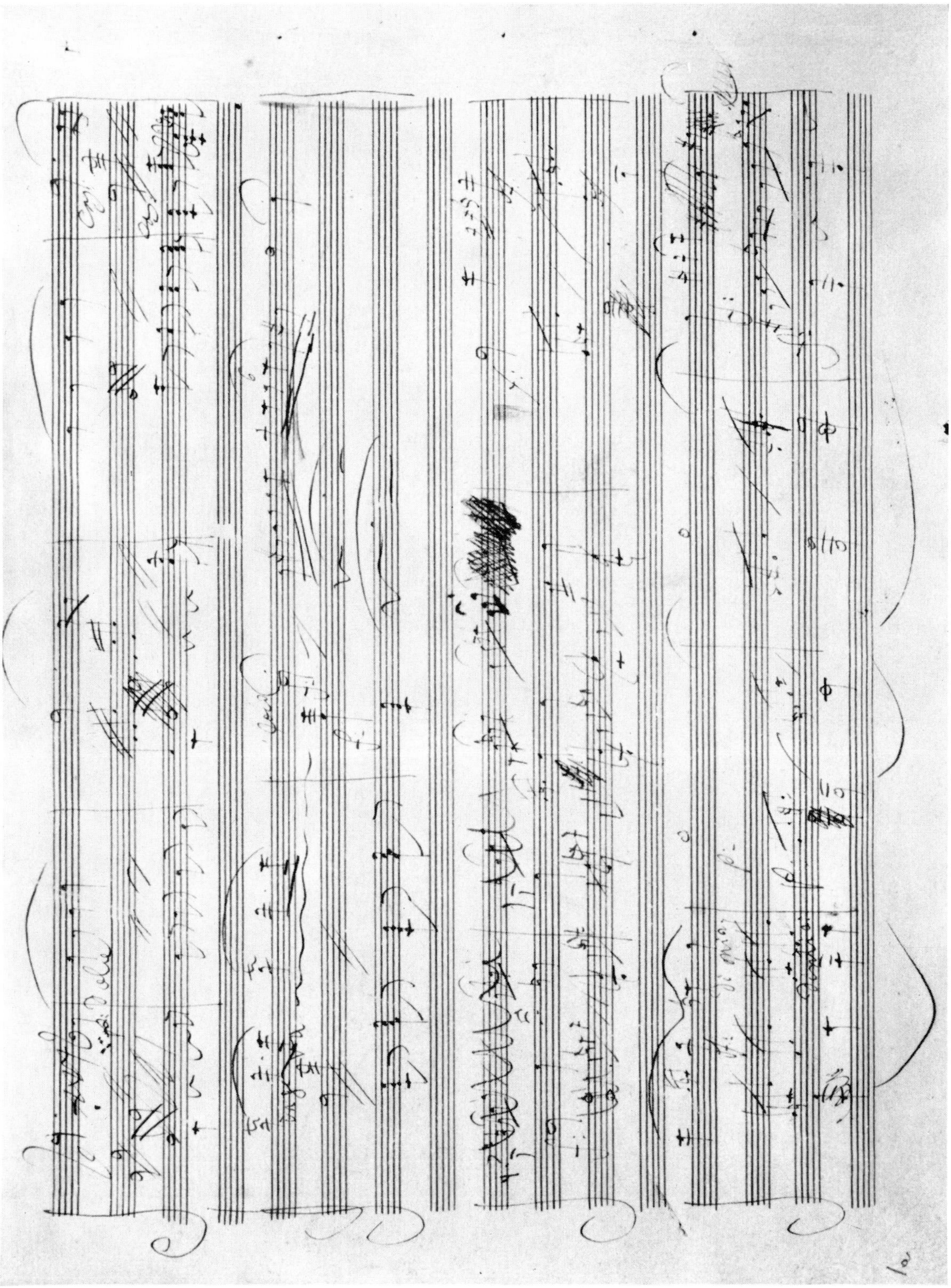

1 verso (bars 18–31)

2 recto (bars 32–46)

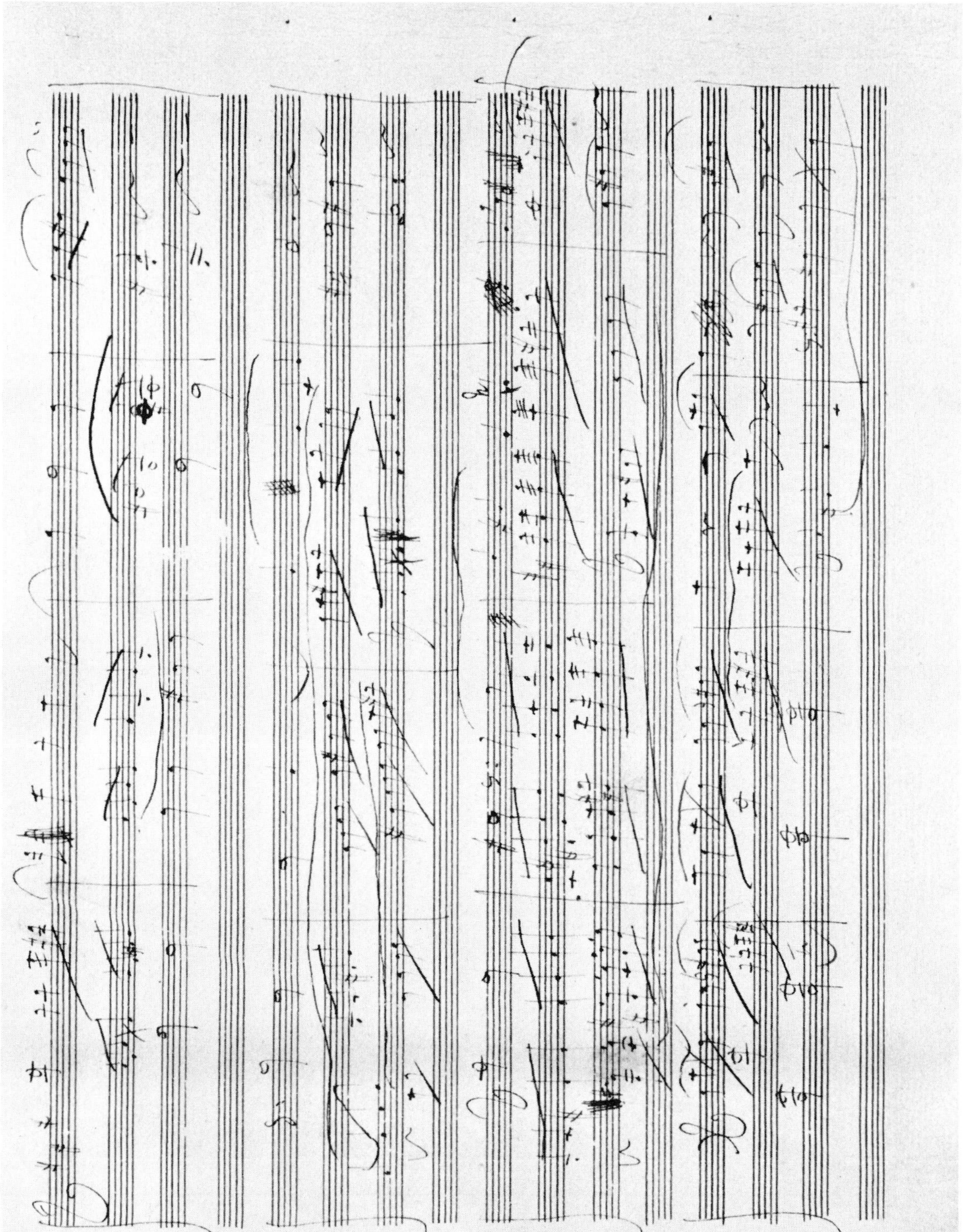

2 verso (bars 47–62)

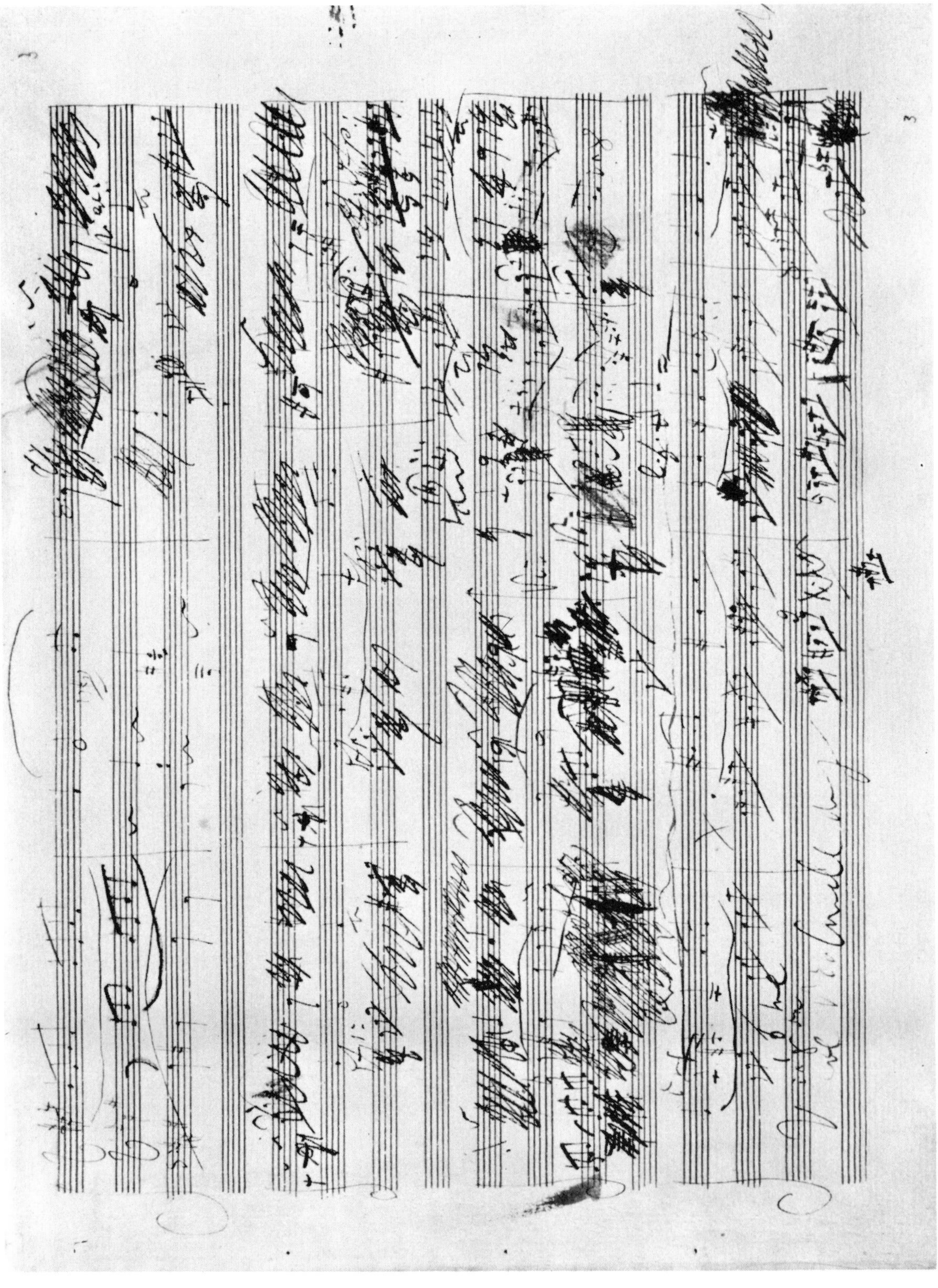

3 recto (bars 63–76)

3 verso (bars 77–90)

4 recto (bars 91–106)

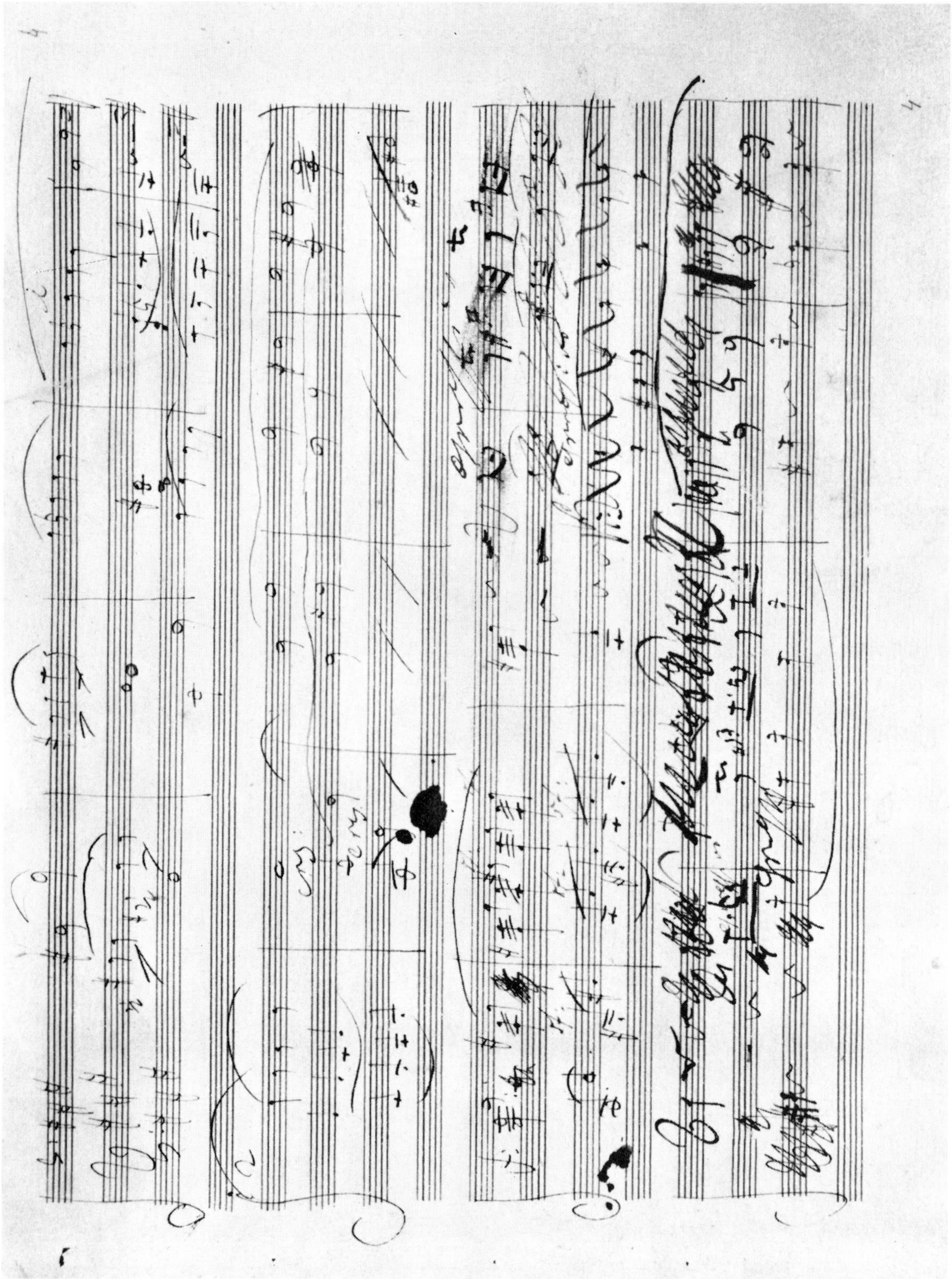

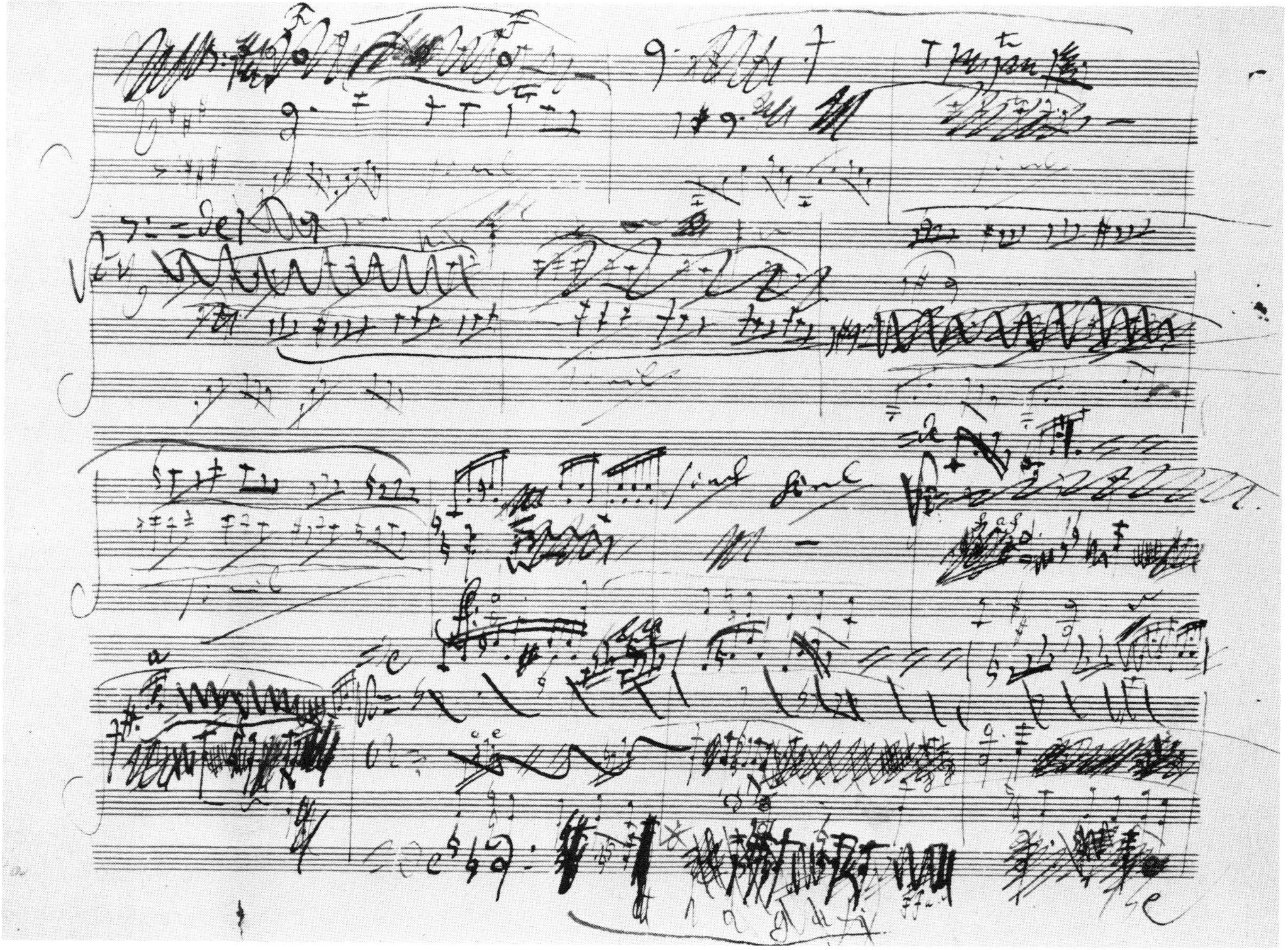

4 verso (bars 107–121)

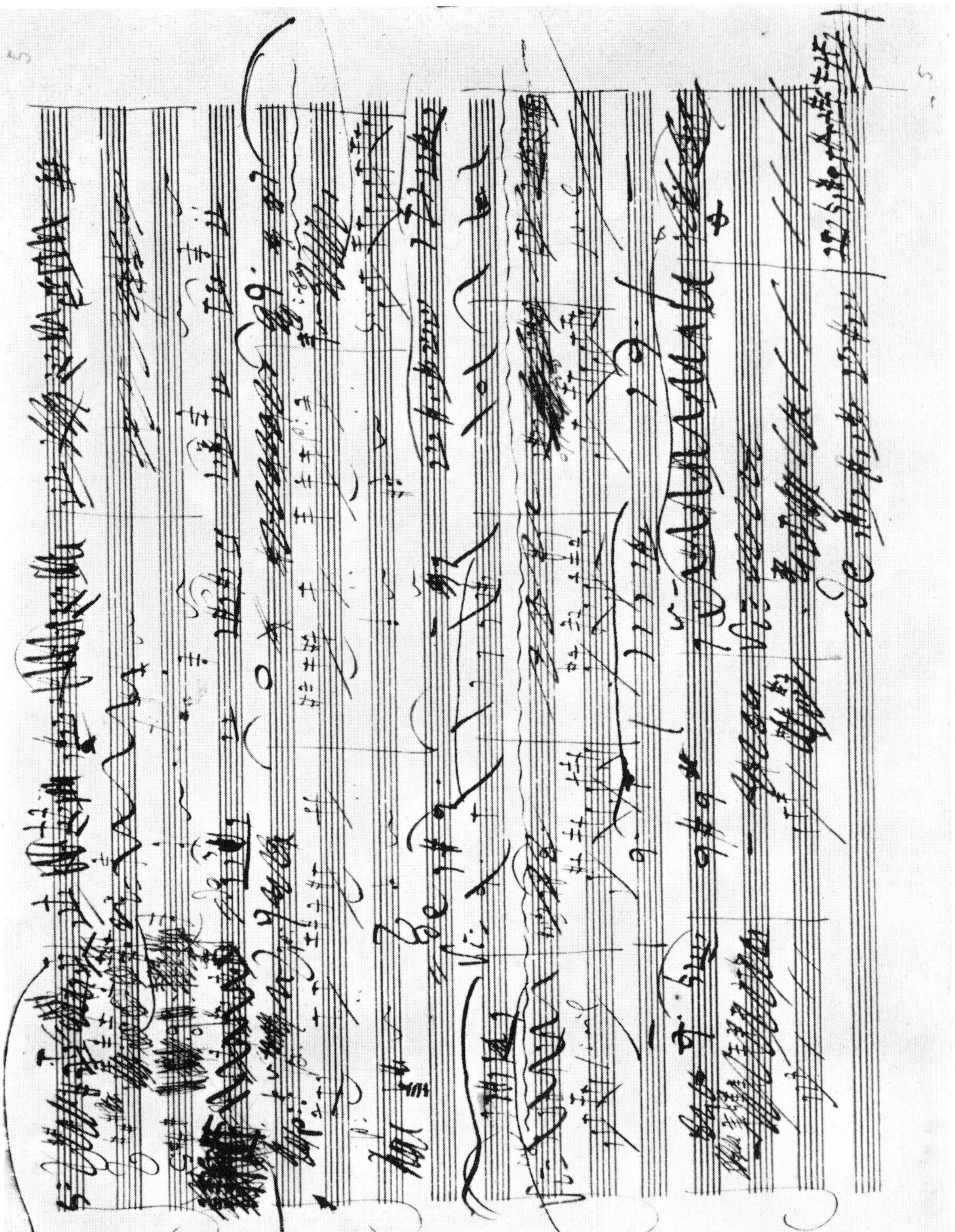

5 recto (bars 122–136)

5 verso (bars 137–160)

6 recto (bars 161–174)

6 verso (bars 175–189)

7 recto (bars 190–203)

7 verso (bars 204–216)

8 recto (bars 217–232)

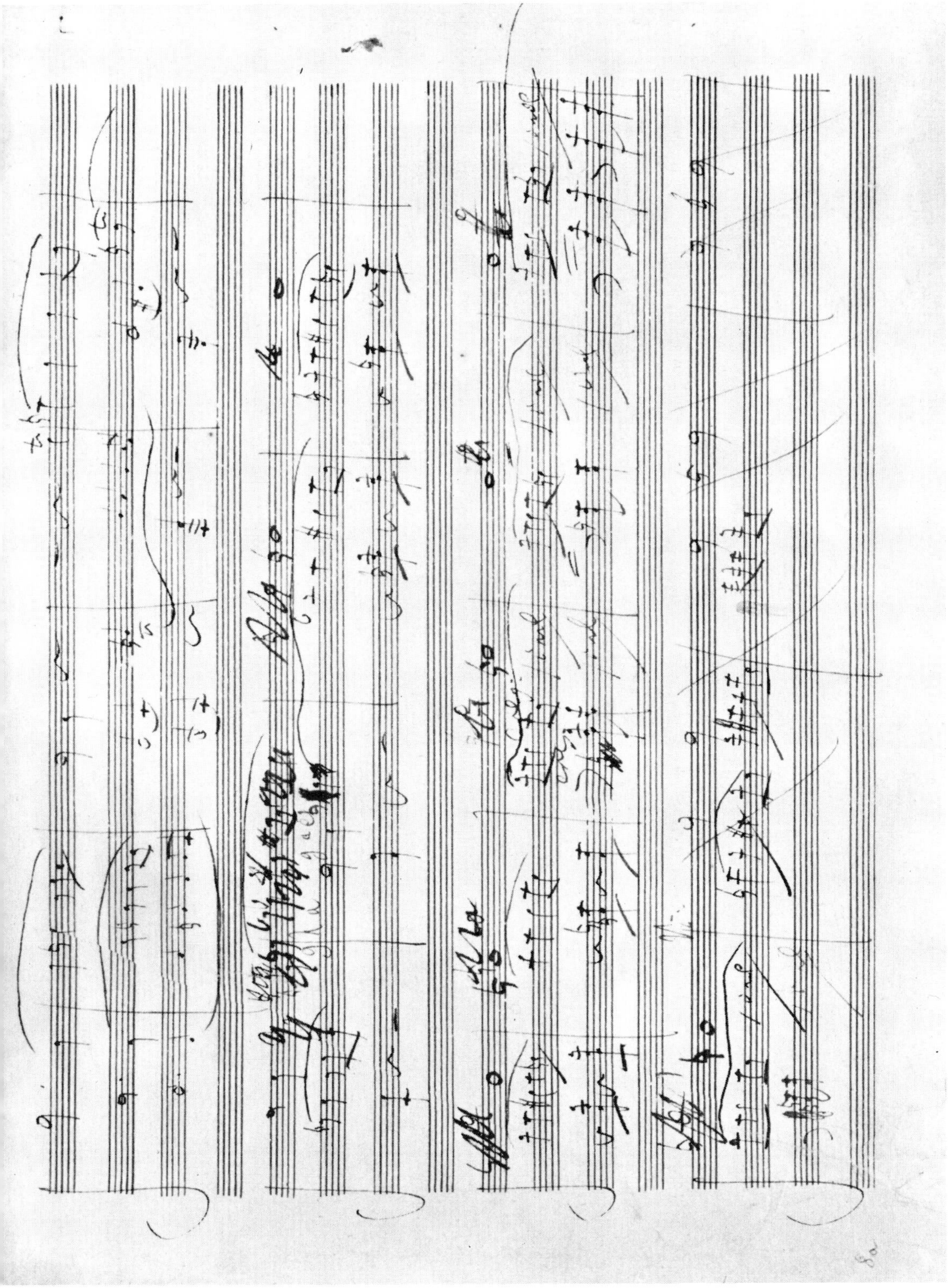

8 verso (bars 233–250; 248–250 canceled)

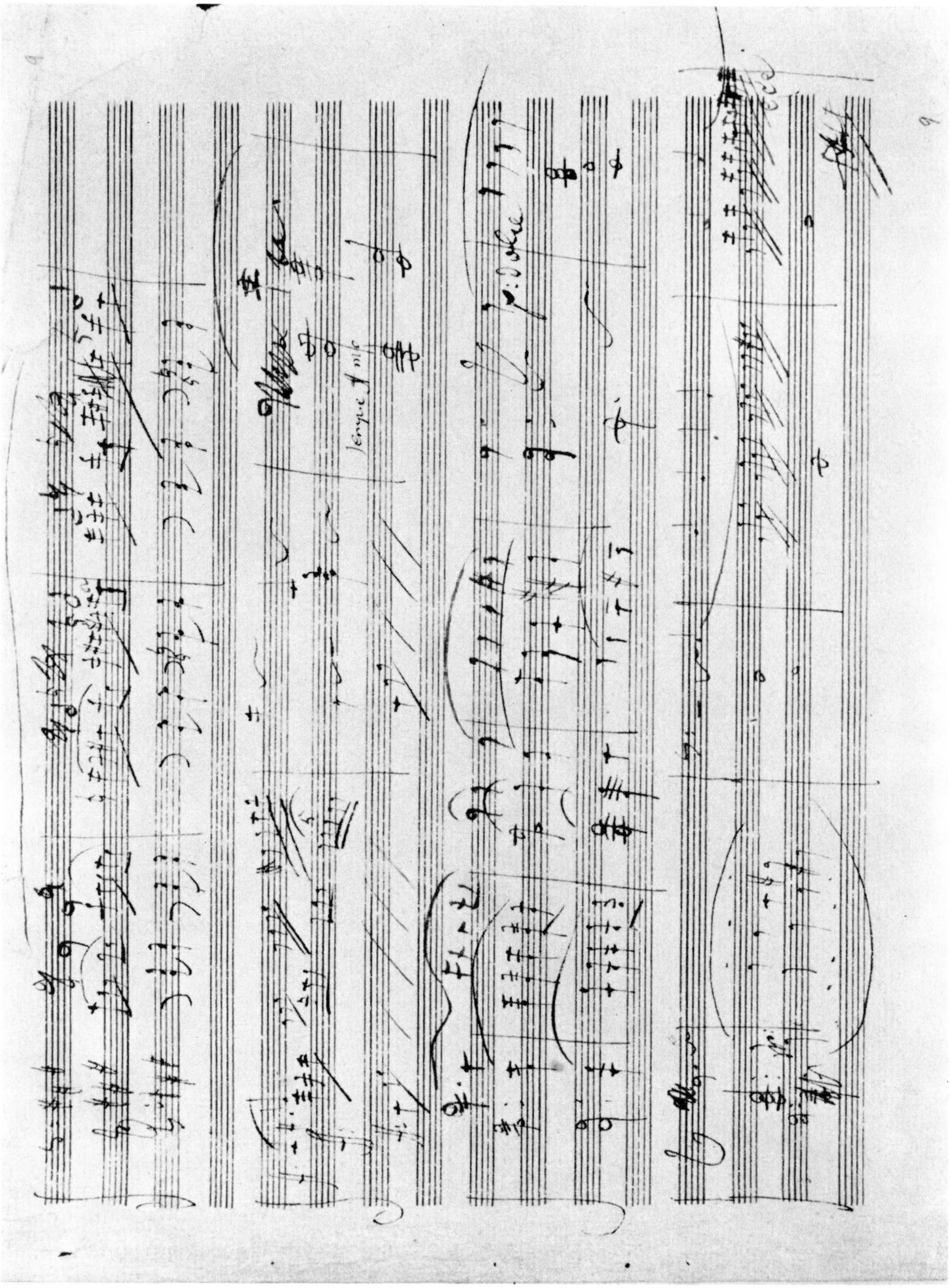

9 recto (bars 248–264)

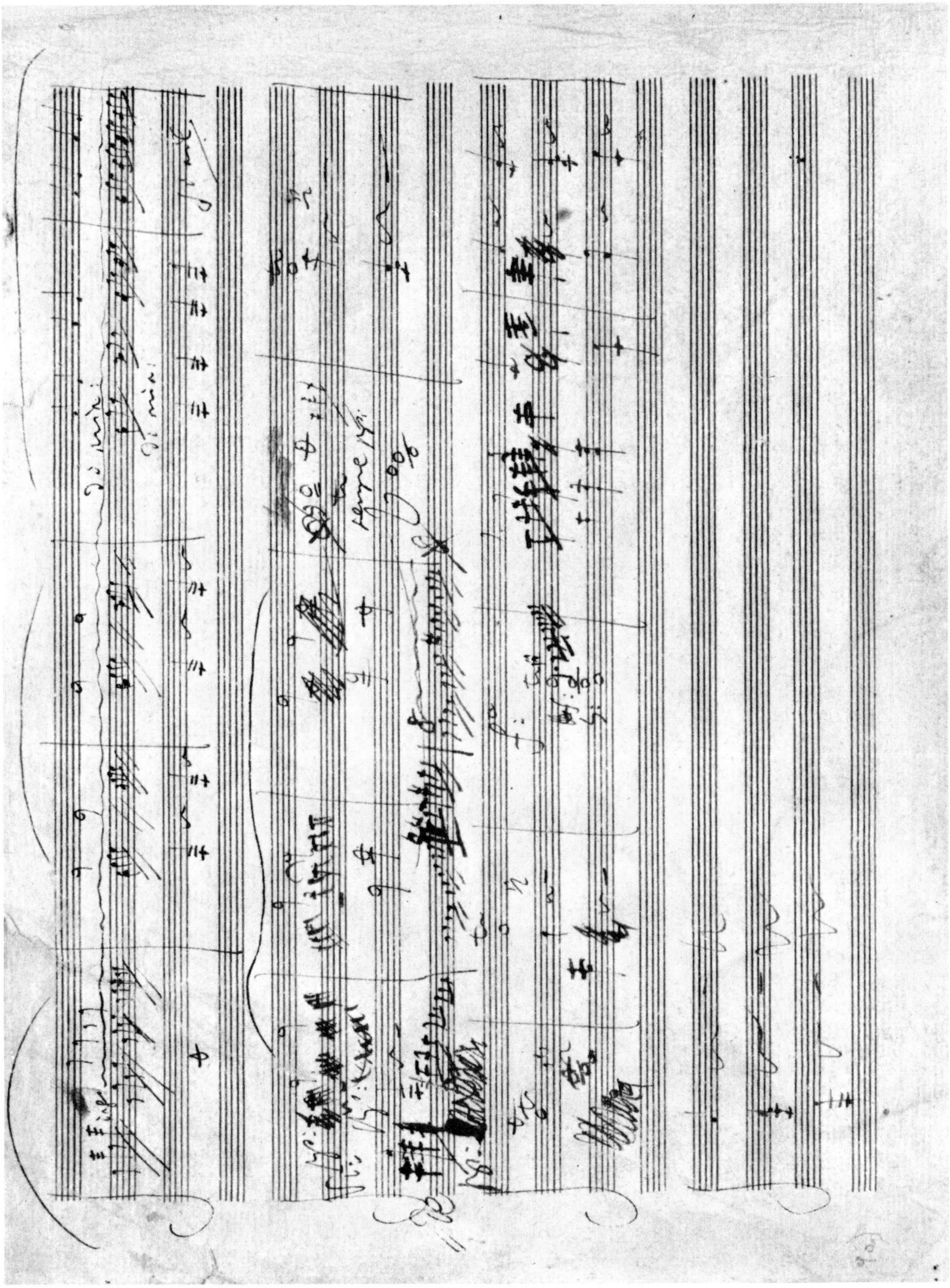

9 verso (bars 265–280)

corresponding autograph leaves for the Scherzo, Adagio, and Finale of the Sonata, nor is anything known of their present location.

The manuscript as it exists is a complete musical and physical unit. Unless the first movement could possibly have been set into score before the other movements were ready for that stage, this manuscript should have formed part of a larger unified manuscript containing the entire Sonata at about its own stage of development. But it shows no sign of separation. The entire first movement is fitted onto the nine leaves preserved here, with the last measures of the movement occupying most of the last available page (9v) and leaving only part of its last system vacant. In their physical features the leaves are wholly uniform, in contrast to some Beethoven autographs, and they are organized as two four-page gatherings with an additional leaf glued carefully to the last page of the second gathering to form folio 9r-v (see Appendix I for a tabulation of the physical characteristics of the manuscript). It is possible but not demonstrable that the added leaf at the end of the second gathering was originally the first member of another binary gathering, and that the putative folio 10 could have begun the Scherzo. All we can tell from the available evidence is that Beethoven worked here with one gathering at a time: first he filled out the first gathering in direct sequence, then continued directly on the second, then either cut folio 9 from an original bi-folio to finish the movement, or used the whole bi-folio and left it to pious posterity to cut the present folio 9 away.

In setting up the score of this composition on the page, Beethoven's choice of format was no doubt determined in part by obvious notational conventions, but in part too by the size and type of paper on which he was working. And the selection of paper, here and elsewhere, does not seem to have been entirely haphazard. Among the preserved autographs, oblong paper of the type used here is by far more common than tall, narrow paper, especially in chamber music.[9] Even with regard to choice of number of

[9] In addition to what is indicated for the piano sonatas, the following autographs also used oblong format: all the quartets from Op. 59 to 95; all the piano trios (except part of Op. 97); the Fourth to Eighth Symphonies (except part of the Eighth); the accompanied sonatas (including Op. 102, Nos. 1 and 2). The only exception seems to be the Violin Sonata, Op. 96, which has received a good deal of attention from American scholars because it is owned by the Morgan Library in New York; actually its format is highly exceptional among the chamber works. For facsimiles see E. Winternitz, *Musical Autographs from Monteverdi to Hindemith* (Princeton, Princeton University Press, 1955), Facs. Nos. 83–86.

staves, Beethoven's decisions in the autographs do not appear to have been as unsystematic as the legends and traditions would lead us to suppose. Our view of the situation may be somewhat colored by the unequal survival of sources from all periods: from the early years, when he was making his way as a composer and tended to publish from his own manuscripts, we have few complete autographs; from the middle and later periods, when he was a celebrated artist, we have a great many.

What we have shows some tendency to associate types of paper not merely with the spatial requirements of particular works but with categories. For piano compositions Beethoven evidently preferred oblong eight-staff autographs in which each page is entirely filled out by four two-staff systems of music, with no intervening staves left blank. The published facsimiles of Op. 26; 27, No. 2; 78; 109; 110; and 111 all show this arrangement, the use of which compelled him to extreme solutions when he found that he had to make corrections after all. But in the *Appassionata* autograph, on the other hand, he used the twelve-staff oblong format with intervening blank staves between systems, and the difference in relative clarity of the corrections is obvious at a glance. The oblong twelve- or sixteen-staff type is also the one favored strongly for the quartets, orchestral works, and compositions for pianoforte with single instrument, the latter requiring three-staff systems, as here. By choosing this type of paper for a three-staff score, Beethoven enabled himself to set up either three or four such systems on each page, thus assigning to each page-unit a substantial quantity of musical content that could be perceived as a single visual field, and also permitting him to leave a blank staff below each system throughout the manuscript. The blank staff not only helps to clarify the note-field by separating the systems, but provides useful and at times essential space for corrections to be made en route. The central folios of the Op. 69 autograph make the practical advantages of this format sufficiently clear.

Of the physical properties of the manuscript that are described in Appendix I, those relevant to particular aspects of the later parts of this commentary will be dealt with in due course. What is of primary concern at this point is a view of the defining features of the phase of composition represented by this manuscript, along with the problem of determining its destination and its relationship to other firsthand sources bearing on the genesis and final form of the work. Curiously, while it is quite obvious that this manuscript is very far from being a fair copy, determining the bearing of its various segments on the final form of the movement is more difficult than might appear. The first page of the manuscript looks deceptively like that of a final version in fair copy, with its bold and well-spaced strokes free of disfiguring erasures or cancellations. But as one progresses through the following pages of the exposition, the signs of recasting begin to spread and multiply. In the area of the development (folios 4r–5v), they become a dense tangle of changes and revisions involving compositional reconstruction on a massive scale; then in the recapitulation and coda they subside again to relative clarity.

While the later parts of this discussion will attempt to unravel the larger knots of the entangled middle pages, it might be observed here that the unequal relationship of the various sections of the manuscript to the final version in itself assists in undermining the simple conceptual distinction conveyed by the handy terms "sketch" and "autograph." While some parts of the score are sufficiently clear and final to imply that they could have been copied intact from an earlier source, others exhibit in full force the procedures of reconstruction typical of far less conclusive stages of composition.[10] In many passages two or more stages of decision are superimposed one upon another, so that these are at once the equivalent of one or more "sketches" plus, in some instances, a "final" version, all on the same page and even, at times, in the same measure. It may begin to appear, even in advance of the specific evidence to be considered, why "sketch" and "autograph" are broad generic categories at best, and that they cannot be stretched too far. Like many other terms in the professional vocabulary, their value is simply that of abbreviated designations by which we can reduce to manageable simplicity some of the more ramified complexities inherent in the continuum of evidence, evidence in this case of a process of composition and of reconceiving musical structure that must have been in some significant sense a continuous and unbroken line of development.

Despite these reservations, however, something fairly definite can still be

[10] Of the piano sonata autographs thus far published, only that of Op. 78 could reasonably be described as a true example of what we would call a fair copy. On the other hand, none of the others contains revisions as far-reaching as those of the middle folios of Op. 69; that is to say, all of them represent their material at a more nearly final stage of composition.

said, namely that the version represented by this manuscript can be described as "advanced" for the exposition and recapitulation (though these, too, are not entirely parallel) and "less advanced" for the development. But the central characteristic of this entire version is that it constitutes for the whole movement that phase of realization at which Beethoven felt himself ready to commit the work to paper in its entirety in a fully consecutive score and in all details, while doubtless also realizing as he was doing so that he would still have many vital changes to make. It is this characteristic that makes the manuscript the best approximation we have of what we usually mean by the "autograph," and which helps us to assign the manuscript its appropriate place among the sources that bear directly on the origins of the Sonata. Since these include not only musical manuscripts but early printed editions and even letters, it will be best to proceed by supplying here a brief catalogue of the known primary sources.

Manuscript Scores

Source A. The present manuscript (the autograph score of the first movement, to be referred to hereafter as the "Salzer autograph").[11]

Source B. A contemporary manuscript copy of the Sonata (now lost) reported to contain corrections, title, and dedication (to Baron von Gleichenstein) in Beethoven's hand, sometimes called the "Clauss copy."

This copy was apparently the printer's source for the first edition of the Sonata, and was given to Breitkopf and Härtel in 1808. Nottebohm in 1868 described the manuscript and listed it as being in the possession of Consul Otto Clauss of Leipzig.[12] But Kinsky–Halm reported no information about it beyond Nottebohm's reference,[13] and the Beethoven-Archiv in Bonn informs me that no trace of it can now be found. The loss of this copy is especially severe since it evidently represented the next stage of composition

[11] Kinsky–Halm, p. 164; a brief description by Max Unger in *Neues Beethoven Jahrbuch*, VII, 160–61.

[12] G. Nottebohm, *Thematisches Verzeichnis der im Druck erschienenen Werke von Ludwig van Beethoven* (Leipzig, Breitkopf and Härtel, 1868), p. 63. This is the same Consul Clauss who once owned the autograph of Bach's C-Major Organ Prelude and Fugue, BWV 545, and a Bach canon, BWV 1073.

[13] Kinsky–Halm, p. 164.

—presumably the only one—beyond the autograph but before the first edition, and may well have been made by Beethoven's copyist working directly from the Salzer autograph.

Related Manuscripts, Including Sketches

Source C. London, British Museum Add. 31766, folio 31v (see Plate I).

An isolated entry for Op. 69 in the large sketchbook devoted mainly to Op. 68 and Op. 70, Nos. 1 and 2, which has been published in transcription by Dagmar Weise.[14] The entry is for Op. 69, first movement, piano part only, bars 37–45 and 174–82 (beginning of "second group" in exposition and recapitulation), and it differs from all other manuscript entries listed in this section in several respects. It is an isolated portion of Op. 69 in a larger sketchbook devoted to other works; it is not a sketch but is really a part of the same phase of writing represented by the Salzer autograph, and is even in a sense beyond it; what is clear beyond doubt is that it relates to the Salzer autograph in the most direct way, as will be seen. It is written in the calligraphic hand normally used for fair copies, not in the rapid hand familiar from the sketches. Its connection to the autograph stage—though not to the Salzer autograph in its particulars—was first noticed by Nottebohm: "Doubtless these passages were written during the preparation of the fair copy."[15] For a preliminary view of the "fair copy" see the relevant passages on folios 2r and 6v of this autograph.

Source D. Vienna, Gesellschaft der Musikfreunde, Sketches for Op. 69, MS 59.

One leaf containing sketches for Op. 69, first movement, is described and published in part by Nottebohm.[16] He describes the Op. 69 sketch as forming part of a "set of sketches made up of four gatherings that belong together . . . 16 pages." He further describes its contents: one page of sketches for the Fifth Symphony, Scherzo (page 66); then twelve pages of

[14] Dagmar Weise, *Ein Skizzenbuch zur Pastoralsymphonie und zu den Trios Op. 70, 1 und 2* (2 vols.; Bonn, Beethoven-Haus, 1961), I, 14; see my review in *The Musical Quarterly*, LIII (January, 1967), 128–36. Plate I is reproduced by permission of the Trustees of the British Museum.

[15] G. Nottebohm, *Zweite Beethoveniana* (Leipzig, Rieter–Biedermann, 1887), p. 253.

[16] Nottebohm, *Beethoveniana* (Leipzig, Rieter–Biedermann, 1872), pp. 68–69.

sketches for the Leonore Overture, No. 1; then a sketch for Op. 69, first movement. He concludes: "From the order and character of the sketches mentioned and transcribed here, it appears that the Overture Op. 138 was begun when the C-Minor Symphony was fairly close to completion, and that when it was substantially finished in sketch form, the Sonata Op. 69 was still in an early stage of its conception." This remains to be verified by much further research.

Source E. Bonn, Beethoven-Archiv, MS Bodmer Mh 76.[17]

Three folios, oblong twelve-staff format, in ink throughout except page 5 (ink and pencil). Page 4 is blank. How much of the material in these pages is actually related to Op. 69 is open to question. Max Unger describes the contents briefly as follows: folios 1 and 2: Op. 69, first movement, and "Nur wer die Sehnsucht kennt" (second version); folio 3: Op. 69, second movement.[18]

But prior to Unger's description, an auction catalogue of K. Henrici had listed and described two of the same three folios. The correspondence of pages is as follows: Henrici, pages 1–2 = Bodmer Mh 76, folio 1r–v; Henrici, pages 3–4 = Bodmer Mh 76, folio 3r–v. The correspondence is clear not only from the written description but from a facsimile of "page 1" (Bodmer folio 1r) in the catalogue. It thus appears that the center folio (2r–v) was restored to the manuscript after 1928, presumably while it was part of the Bodmer collection. Henrici's catalogue had described the contents in this way: pages 1–2: sketches for string trio; page 3: blank; page 4: sketch for Op. 69, second movement (differs from published version).[19]

Although Unger's catalogue of the Bodmer collection is one of the most painstaking products of a great authority on Beethoven manuscripts, I find after close study and transcription of the opening leaves that I am more inclined to agree with the Henrici description than with Unger's. Although folios 1r and 2r are laid out in three-staff systems like those of a sonata for

[17] I am greatly indebted to Dr. Hans Schmidt of the Beethoven-Archiv, Bonn, for helping in obtaining photographs of this source and of others used for this study, as well as for much valuable information.

[18] Max Unger, *Eine Schweizer Beethovensammlung* (Zurich, Corona, 1939), p. 170.

[19] Firm of K. E. Henrici, Versteigerung CXLII (Auction of November 7, 1928 [Berlin, 1928]), p. 1, No. 3; p. 3 (facsimile).

piano and solo instrument, I am not able to associate any of their material directly with Op. 69, and agree that their linear content and figuration patterns suggest interpretation as a string trio sketch. Here is a provisional view of the contents: folios 1r, 1v, 2r: sketches for an unidentified string trio (?) in A major (almost all on three-staff systems, no clefs); folio 2v, staves 1–6: sketch for Op. 69, first movement; folio 2v, staff 7: entry for WoO 134, second version;[20] folio 3v, staves 1–7: sketch for Op. 69, second movement, with trio sketch wholly different from the final trio; folio 3v, staves 9–12: pencil sketches, almost illegible.

Source F. Bonn, Beethoven-Archiv, MS BSk 57.

One folio (2 pages), oblong twelve-staff format, ink. Folio 1r: sketches (mainly single staff) for Op. 69, first movement. Folio 1v: sketch entries, apparently for Op. 69, third movement (Adagio) at an early stage of composition. Other jottings on folio 1v perhaps for other works as yet unidentified.

Source G. Paris, Bibliothèque du Conservatoire (on deposit at the Bibliothèque Nationale), Beethoven MS 45.

Two folios, oblong sixteen-staff format, with all four pages containing sketches in ink. Folio 1r: sketches for Fifth Symphony Scherzo (mainly on single staff). Folios 1v–2v: composition sketch for Op. 69, first movement, mainly on three-staff systems, and largely following the outline of the entire exposition of the movement.[21]

Source H. Copenhagen, Library of the Royal Danish Conservatory of Music (no signature).

Two folios (four pp.), oblong twelve-staff format, ink. Folio 1r: no music; at lower right-hand corner is a note showing the presentation of the sketches by Niels W. Gade to the Danish composer J. P. E. Hartmann, with the date "14 Mai 1878." Folios 1v–2r: three-staff sketches containing material in the same format and closely related in content to the first pages (folios

[20] Nottebohm, *Zweite Beethoveniana*, pp. 531 f.

[21] Max Unger, "Die Beethovenhandschriften der Pariser Konservatoriumsbibliothek," *Neues Beethoven Jahrbuch*, VI (1935), 100 f. (brief description).

1r–2v) of the Bodmer Mh 76 sketches (source *E*). Quite possibly these Copenhagen pages originally belonged together with Bodmer Mh 76 as part of a larger gathering. Both sketches are interpretable as part of a string trio, using here some of the material finally developed in Op. 69, first movement. Folio 2v: abandons the three-staff systems of the preceding pages and contains single-staff sketch jottings relating to the opening motive of Op. 69, first movement.

Source I. Berlin, Deutsche Staatsbibliothek, MS Landsberg 10, pp. 47–51.

Five pages of sketches for Op. 69, Scherzo and Finale only, not the first movement. Partially described by Nottebohm.[22] This "sketchbook" is actually a mixture of originally separate pages and gatherings from different periods and originally different sources. Its contents range from c.1805 to c.1817, some pages having originally formed part of the sketchbook in the British Museum, Add. 31766 (see source *C*).

Earliest Editions

Source J. Grande Sonate / pour Pianoforte et Violoncelle / . . . Oeuv. 59 [sic] . . . Chez Breitkopf & Härtel / à Leipsic. Plate No. 1328.[23]

Source K. Grande Sonate / pour Pianoforte et Violoncelle / . . . Oeuv. 69 / Chez Breitkopf et Härtel / à Leipsic.[24]

Source L. Sonata / per il / Clavicembalo con Violoncello / . . . (Op. 59) [sic] a Vienna / presso Artaria e Comp / No. 2060 . . .[25]

22 Nottebohm, *Zweite Beethoveniana,* pp. 533–34; see also footnote 14.

23 Kinsky–Halm, pp. 164 f.: "April, 1809."

24 Kinsky–Halm, p. 165. Facsimile of title page in Robert Bory, *Ludwig van Beethoven, sein Leben und sein Werk in Bildern* (Zurich, Atlantis, 1960), p. 118. According to Kinsky–Halm, this printing contains the corrections submitted by Beethoven at the end of July, 1809. The copies I have seen contain no such corrections, or at most a tiny fraction of them and not necessarily made in 1809.

25 Kinsky–Halm, p. 165, where this printing is dated as early as the end of April, 1809.

Later editions listed by Kinsky–Halm include the following: Paris, Pleyel, n.d.; Hamburg, Böhme, 1828 (also as "Op. 59"); Frankfurt, Dunst (as part of "Oeuvres Complets de Piano," according to Kinsky–Halm the first edition in which the piano part contains the entire score); London, Monzani ("um 1815"), according to Kinsky–Halm no copy known.

To these can be added: Hamburg, Cranz, n.d.; Bonn, Simrock, n.d.; Mainz, Schott (all listed in Nottebohm, *Thematisches Verzeichnis*). Also: Offenbach, J. André (c. 1840), Publisher's No. 6464 (copy in New York Public Library).

Letters on the Text of Opus 69[26]

Source M. Letter to Breitkopf and Härtel of July 26, 1809 (Anderson No. 220).

For original text, see Appendix V.

Source N. Letter and Misprint list for Op. 69, sent to Breitkopf and Härtel c. August 1, 1809; received August 11 (Anderson No. 221). See facsimile published here as Plates II and III, and Appendix V.

Source O. Letter to Breitkopf and Härtel of August 3, 1809 (Anderson No. 223).

See Appendix V.

Although one of these sources, *A*, is incomplete and another, *B*, is missing, this list nevertheless includes the entire known body of primary sources for the Sonata. For an exhaustive study of the early history of the work, the whole network of materials would have to be taken into account, but for more limited aspects of study the significance of particular sources will vary a good deal. Thus, to establish a definitive controlled text for the Sonata (and strange as it may seem, no fully accurate edition has yet been published!), the sketches (sources *D* through *I*) are likely to be less essential than the other sources. While this commentary ought to contribute to establishing a final text for the work, it is not thought of as supplanting the detailed text-critical notes that will eventually have to accompany an authoritative edition, and not all textual problems are raised for discussion here. Rather, the primary focus of this study is upon the Salzer autograph itself, and what follows will attempt to determine something of its genetic and musical significance and to shed light on it from both earlier and later sources.

Perhaps the easiest way to sort the material initially is to divide it along categorical and apparent chronological lines, with sketches and isolated entries on one side, and manuscript scores and early editions on the other.

[26] Emily Anderson, ed. and tr., *The Letters of Beethoven* (3 vols.; London, Macmillan, 1961; New York, St. Martin's Press, 1961).

Whatever. shortcomings this classification may have, it offers the convenience of distinguishing the first fully consecutive score (the Salzer autograph) from earlier drafts (whether single-staff sketches or rudimentary scores) and from later and more nearly final versions. To simplify the discussion, the network of provisionally assumed connections among the sources is brought together in Appendix II.

Tacitly assumed in the left column of Appendix II is that the single-staff sketches *F* and *D* represent the earliest extant versions of the material, a view based more on their musical content than on consideration of their single-staff format, though both must be taken into account. Between these sketches and that of source *G*, I put sources *E* (or a part of it) and *H*, which are so closely connected in content that they may well have originally formed a single sheaf of sketches, and whose contents suggest an intermediate phase. That sketch *G* is a decidedly more advanced stage is evident not only from the internal character of its material but from its provision of a consecutive "composition sketch" for the whole of the exposition. Since the later sketches listed on the left side of the diagram either contain material for the Scherzo or Finale, or are not really interpretable as pre-autograph sketches, I infer a plausible line of derivation from *G* to *A*; in short, from a rudimentary three-staff score to the developed score that has reached what we instinctively call the "autograph" stage. The musical implications of this inferred connection will be taken up later.

In the right column of Appendix II, the consecutive ordering of sources and their implied derivations are more easily confirmed by external evidence. I assume that source *B*—the lost Clauss copy—was made for Beethoven by a professional copyist, presumably his long-time favorite, Schlemmer,[27] and that it could have been made directly from source *A*. Difficult as such a task may now seem, there is evidence from other autographs copied by Schlemmer that he could pick his way through apparently trackless passages in Beethoven's autographs with astonishing skill; the Fifth Symphony is a convincing case. The step from copy *B* to the first Breitkopf and Härtel edition, source *J*, is supported by inferences from the

[27] On Schlemmer as copyist see T. von Frimmel, "Beethovens Kopisten," *Beethoven-Studien* (Munich, Müller, 1906), II, 3–19; also G. Schünemann, preface to facsimile edition of the Fifth Symphony.

correspondence on Op. 69, and from *J* in turn to the later editions and to Beethoven's highly revealing letters and misprint list is once again a chain of inferences from fairly unambiguous evidence.

Perhaps more puzzling are the crossing lines of connection suggested in the table for these pairs: sources *A–C*, *C–B*, and *E* (folio 2v)–*B*. The special character of the single entry in *C* has been mentioned already and will be further developed; it supports not merely a link in material but chronological coincidence between them. As for *E*, I assume that only a portion of its contents coincides with the autograph phase represented by *A*, and this portion would appear to mesh with certain problems of reconstruction in the middle section of the movement at the autograph stage.

Of the period over which the preparatory sketches extend, little can be said in the current state of knowledge. Despite adventurous guesses, none of these sketches can really be dated with close precision, and the evidence of chronology based on other evidence is hardly conclusive. The account in Thayer–Deiters–Riemann, based on Nottebohm, included the assertion that the Sonata was sketched "years before its completion,"[28] and was taken up and finished quickly in 1808 as a means of compensating Beethoven's close friend, Ignaz von Gleichenstein, for the failure to dedicate the Fourth Piano Concerto to him, as Beethoven had originally intended to do.[29]

28 Alexander Wheelock Thayer, *Ludwig van Beethoven's Leben*, translated into German and edited by Herman Deiters; newly revised and completed by Hugo Riemann (5 vols.; Leipzig, Breitkopf and Härtel, 1901–11), III, 112.

29 The evidence connecting Gleichenstein with the Sonata convincingly explains its dedication to him as an intimate friend. But the general inference by biographers and earlier writers that it was intended for Gleichenstein in recognition of his ability as a cellist is not borne out by clear evidence. It is evident from Beethoven's letters to him that they were on close terms from at least 1804 (possibly earlier—see Frimmel, *Beethoven-Handbuch I* [Leipzig, Breitkopf and Härtel, 1926], art. "Gleichenstein") until 1812, and that Gleichenstein was one who Beethoven expected to take care of business and everyday tasks for him. That Beethoven originally intended to dedicate Op. 58 to him and later substituted Op. 69 is also clear enough from correspondence (see Anderson No. 172). But it is also evident that Gleichenstein was "no connoisseur," as Beethoven himself puts it in a recommendation written for him at just this time (see Anderson No. 173). It is much more interesting to realize that Beethoven himself, in 1809, suggested to Zmeskall that Op. 69, "which has not yet been performed well in public," be played by Baroness Ertmann and the famous cellist Nikolaus Kraft (son of Anton Kraft). Nikolaus apparently played the first performance of Op. 69 on March 5, 1809 (see *Thayer's Life of Beethoven*, revised and edited by Elliot Forbes [Princeton, Princeton University Press, 1964], p. 467; hereafter cited as Thayer–Forbes). The level of difficulty represented by the cello part surely demands a performer of more than average caliber, just as the cello part in the Triple Concerto had (first performed by Anton Kraft, according to Schindler). In this connection, note Beethoven's reference to [N.] Kraft in a

Minimally reasonable inference from the evidence permits us to say this much. The Sonata was probably nearly finished—perhaps entirely finished—when Beethoven offered it for the first time to Breitkopf and Härtel on June 8, 1808, along with Op. 67, 68 and 86 (Anderson No. 167). About four weeks later, Beethoven reaffirmed the offer and the negotiations culminated in a contract dated September 14, 1808 (Anderson, p. 1427), and in publication of the Sonata in April of 1809. But although there is no evidence to support Thayer's reference to sketches "years earlier," the physical association of the Op. 69 sketches with sketches for other works of 1807–08 makes it reasonable to assume that the Sonata took considerable time to germinate, and that the likely period of its composition is "middle of 1807 to the middle of 1808." Nottebohm, in an earlier essay, remarked in his usually cryptic manner that Op. 69 was finished by "January, 1808" but gave no reasons; yet, in his *Zweite Beethoveniana* essay on the "Pastoral Symphony" sketchbook, he simply dated the Sonata as "first half of 1808."[30] Of long-range importance is the association of work on Op. 69 with sketches for the Fifth and Sixth Symphonies, the Leonore Overture, No. 1, and the second setting of "Sehnsucht," WoO 134. But only when the long-awaited and urgently needed comprehensive publication of the sketches is considerably further advanced will we be able to clarify the apparent signs of cross-fertilization with the other major projects of 1807 and 1808.

As for the entire larger conception of this Sonata, it is worth reflecting on it from another point of view. That it occupies a principal and even central place in the literature of larger works for violoncello and piano—this is by now an established and familiar critical commonplace. What is less obvious is the absence of a clear-cut and relevant tradition of works for this combination which Beethoven could possibly have known or recollected—even to dismiss—in approaching the composition of this work. The definitive model provided by the Mozart violin sonatas had no contemporary

---

message to Zmeskall (who was also an "able cellist" by all accounts): "Kraft has offered to play with us today. It would be imperious not to accept his offer; and I myself do not deny, just as you will admit, that his playing affords us all the greatest pleasure." (Anderson No. 210, perhaps written April, 1809). Another performance of Op. 69, by Lincke and Czerny, is reported to have taken place in 1816 (Thayer–Forbes, p. 641).

[30] Nottebohm, *Beethoveniana*, p. 70; *Zweite Beethoveniana*, p. 254.

counterpart for the violoncello, and the older Italian tradition, culminating in Boccherini, scarcely seems relevant. The somewhat surprising fact is that Beethoven's own first sonatas—the two of 1796, Op. 5, Nos. 1 and 2, apparently written on the occasion of his trip to Berlin for performance by Jean Pierre Duport and himself—are actually the first sonatas for violoncello and piano by a first-rank composer of the period. And in the light of the preponderant importance of the piano in both these works, the solutions found in Op. 69 for the problems of range, relative sonority, and matching of importance of the two instruments in the entire texture, emerge as an achievement equal to that inherent in the originality and quality of its purely musical ideas. It should not be surprising in this sense to discover in the autograph that matters of range, register, and balance play a primary role throughout the complex revisions of its material, and it is not surprising either that these should dominate in a work in which the problem of establishing an adequate balance of function between these two instruments is faced for the first time by a major composer in a major work.

THE AUTOGRAPH AND FINAL TEXT

ALTHOUGH the primary focus of this study is on the autograph itself, some consideration of its bearing on the final text of the Sonata is not only appropriate but, in the actual state of that text in current editions, essential. Even a casual glance at the facsimile should dispel the fantasy that all one need do to establish a true reading is to "look at the autograph"; yet even when all the relevant evidence is considered, the problem of determining a fully authoritative text for the first movement will be extremely difficult. And in this instance the evidence is comprehensive enough to make the traditional and almost continuous mishandling of the text of the Sonata even less excusable than it is in more obscure cases.

As is well known, once Beethoven began to use a professional copyist for the preparation of his works it was his habit to make corrections in the copyist's version and submit it to the publisher for engraving. While this is not the place to do more than mention the intricacies of his relationships with his many publishers, the evidence at hand reinforces his profound concern over establishing the best possible versions of his works in print.

Repeatedly and emphatically, in his correspondence with Breitkopf and Härtel and with other publishers, he insisted that they exhibit the courtesy and common sense to send him a preliminary proof of a new piece together with their working manuscript, before making an entire press run, so that he could make needed corrections in time.[31] Despite the obvious advantages of this proposal, greed or laziness on the part of the publishers guaranteed that it should virtually never be carried out, with the consequence that much of Beethoven's correspondence with his publishers reflects his well-known and entirely justified exasperation over their incompetence.[32] More than once, on finally receiving first copies of newly printed works he set to work at once to proofread them with great care, and on several occasions sent the publisher a list of needed corrections to be entered in remaining copies or in subsequent runs.[33] At times he proposed to publish such lists separately for the benefit of the purchasing public, but in fact he never did. Since the publishers seem in general to have been no more attentive to the insertion of corrections than they had been to avoid errors in the first place, vivid blunders abounded in many earlier and later editions of his works[34] and a great many were uncritically taken over into the Breitkopf and Härtel Gesamtausgabe and later editions.

For Op. 69 it is safe to assume that the copy from which the engraver worked was the Clauss copy, with Beethoven's added corrections, and that

31 See for example these letters: Anderson Nos. 72, 79, 228, 230, 272, 278, 281, 294.

32 Letter to Breitkopf and Härtel of February 19, 1811 (Anderson No. 297): "At last you have adopted the sensible procedure of sending me the proofs of the Fantasia to correct, and you should always do so." But by no more than three months later he was incensed again by the publisher's actions; see Anderson No. 305 and especially No. 306: "Fehler—Fehler! Sie sind selbst ein einziger Fehler" (apropos of the Fifth Piano Concerto).

33 The most important lists or references to them, apart from the Op. 69 letters, are these: Anderson No. 5 (on WoO 40); Nos. 76–78 (on Op. 31); No. 199 (on Fifth and Sixth Symphonies); No. 218 (on Op. 70, No. 2); No. 228 (on Op. 70 and Fifth and Sixth Symphonies); No. 230 (on Op. 70, No. 2); No. 306 (Pfte arr. of Egmont Overture); No. 496 (on ariettas for George Thomson); No. 649 (on Op. 95); No. 675 (on Op. 92: "a list of all the mistakes will have to be printed"); No. 691 (corrections had *not* been made in Op. 95 copies, as promised); Nos. 938–39 (on Op. 104 and 106); No. 1053 (on Op. 108); No. 1060 (on Op. 109); No. 1061 (on Op. 109); No. 1187 (on Op. 120 and 111); Nos. 1190–1190a (on Op. 111); No. 1548 (on Op. 125 and 127).

34 Beethoven's own more general impression of the situation is shown in a letter to Simrock of Feb. 15, 1817: ". . . so many inaccurate editions of my works are prancing about in the world"; also in his draft proposal regarding a complete edition of his works (Anderson, III, 1450 f.): ". . . seeing that so many inaccurate and forged editions are wandering about . . ."

he delivered it to Breitkopf and Härtel's agent in Vienna for transmission to Leipzig not later than September of 1808, when the publication contract was signed. Letters of January, February, and March of 1809 indicate that the Sonata had not yet been published,[35] and after it did come out, in April, Beethoven seems not to have noticed the state of its text until three months later, when it was pointed out, he says, by a friend. Notable too is that in his first letter mentioning the text of Op. 69 (letter to Breitkopf and Härtel of July 26, 1809) he also mentions his deep disturbance over current conditions in Vienna, then under French siege: ". . . since May 4 I have managed to produce very little that is coherent, virtually only a fragment here and there. The whole course of events has affected me in body and spirit."

In this same letter (source *M* in my list) the relevant passage is as follows (see Appendix V for the original text):

Here is a goodly serving of printer's errors, which, since I never in my life trouble myself any longer about things I have already written, were pointed out to me by a good friend (they are in the violoncello sonata). I shall have this list copied or printed here and noted in the newspaper, so that all those who have bought the work already may obtain it. This again confirms what I have experienced before, that works published from my own manuscript are the most correctly engraved ones. Presumably there are many errors in the manuscript copy which you have, but in looking over the music the author actually overlooks the errors.

Although the misprint list he made was never published, it is preserved in the Beethoven-Haus in Bonn as part of the Bodmer collection.[36] Not only is it an important document for this work and evidence of Beethoven's capacities as a proofreader, but it seemed especially useful to include it here because of misreadings in the only available German text of the list,[37] and some discrepancies between various published readings of the text of the covering letter.[38] Appendix V provides the original text with translation, essentially following Emily Anderson's. The numbers in square brackets

[35] Anderson Nos. 192, 197, 199, 203, 204.

[36] With the kind permission of the Beethoven-Haus authorities it is published here in complete facsimile for the first time, along with the covering note that accompanied it to Breitkopf and Härtel in Leipzig.

[37] A. C. Kalischer, ed., *Beethoven's Sämtliche Briefe* (2d ed., newly revised by Frimmel; Berlin and Leipzig, Schuster and Loeffler, 1909–1911), No. 449.

[38] Especially those given by Donald W. MacArdle and Ludwig Misch, *New Beethoven Letters* (Norman, University of Oklahoma Press, 1957), No. 65, and by Emily Anderson.

indicate the misprints pointed out by Beethoven; of these there are twenty-three in all. I must add that the original letter and misprint list were also published by Max Unger in 1935 with an excellent commentary,[39] but the periodical in which Unger's study appeared is difficult to obtain, and I know of no evidence that his essay has resulted in any corrected editions since it appeared; nor is it faintly imaginable that more than a few of the most conscientious performers, who need it most, have had access to it.

A close comparison of the misprint list with the earliest editions sheds considerable light on Beethoven as proofreader. These documents leave no doubt about his capacity for painstaking care in producing the best possible readings of his work, and show something of his method. He proceeds by taking first the piano part and then the cello part, clearly because the earliest editions—and apparently most later ones up to about the 1840s—provided no score at all but only separate piano and cello parts with no cue staff in the piano part. Scrutiny of the earliest editions does turn up a few details—probable errors—which Beethoven did *not* include in his list, but these serve only to reinforce his explicit recognition of his own limits as an editorial consultant for his works. Since he must have been deeply engaged in far more significant problems, the task of correcting his publisher's mistakes some three months after the edition had appeared must have been even more distasteful than it would have been prior to publication. Now it was simply a matter of attempting valiantly to rid his work of needless errors and inconsistencies. That it really was futile is shown by the lack of evidence that Breitkopf and Härtel did anything at all about the errors he pointed out. Kinsky–Halm describe the second issue of the first edition (also 1809) as one which "contains the corrections which Beethoven sent them in late July 1809," but I know of no evidence to support this claim. Of the two complete copies of this edition I have seen, only one shows any handwritten corrections at all, and it covers only two of the twenty-three errors listed by Beethoven; the other has no corrections at all.[40]

[39] Unger, "Stichfehler und fragliche Stellen bei Beethoven," *Zeitschrift für Musik*, CII (1935), 635–42 and 744–50.

[40] In the Library of Congress copy these errors (numbered according to the misprint list in Appendix V and Anderson No. 221) are written in: Nos. 4 (the *ff*) and 11 only. The British Museum copy is entirely uncorrected, as is a copy of the piano part alone recently possessed by Scientific Library Service, New York. I have also compared the Vienna Nationalbibliothek copy of the first Vienna edition by Artaria and find it to contain all but three of the errors in Beethoven's list.

Relatively unambiguous are the errors he specifies in the misprint list that arise from incorrect notation of pitch (misprint list Nos. 1, 3, 5, 9, 13, 15, 16, 18, 21), or auxiliary signs (Nos. 2, 4, 10, 11, 14, 17, 19, 20, 22, 23), or duration (No. 12). But his discussion of the apparent dynamic for the opening of the Scherzo (and its subsequent returns) is so curious that it warrants special mention. Evidently sticking close to their original copy, Breitkopf and Härtel had placed a *p* on the upbeat to bar 1 and an *ff* on the third beat of bar 1, producing a remarkable reading (Example 1):

EXAMPLE I

Beethoven's first correction (misprint list Nos. 6, 7, 8) is to remove the *ff* at bar 1 and at the returns (bars 197, 393). The difference is obviously of drastic importance for the whole movement; but by the next day he had changed his mind once more. Now, he writes, the *ff* should be restored in all these places. Thus, so far as the evidence shows, his final stated intention was to have the piano's first phrase *ff* in all three of its statements, contrasting with *p* at the cello repetition nine bars. later—but every edition since the early ones has made the piano's passage *p*, as if they were following his first misprint list but did not know of the letter that followed two days later. However improbable the *ff* reading may seem, it represents his apparent last intention.[41]

[41] The right-hand reading *p—ff* in the upbeat to bar 1 and to bar 2 is found in at least these early editions: Breitkopf and Härtel, 2d ed. of 1809 ("Op. 69"); Artaria's first Vienna edition of 1809 ("Op. 59"); J. André, undated edition, evidently of the 1840s, Plate 6464; Breitkopf and Härtel ("Nouvelle Edition"), Plate 6870 of c.1843. In the GA and in editions of the later nineteenth century that followed it, puzzled editors evidently "solved" the apparent problem of this reading by converting the *p—ff* into an innocuous *p—sf*. This in turn was changed by Tovey in his Augener edition, with a reproving note: "The sforzando given in all editions (including the 'critical' Breitkopf and Härtel) at the second bar is an attempt to make sense of a bad misprint pointed out by Beethoven in the letter mentioned above."

The "letter mentioned above" is the misprint list alone, and by following it Tovey makes the passage simply *p* in the piano part each time it appears. The situation illustrates what can happen when one has only a part of the source material: if Tovey had had Beethoven's letter of August 3, 1809, as well (my source *O*), he would have been compelled to let the *ff* stand, and most modern performances would consequently differ drastically in this important detail.

Finally, a word on the possible role of the Salzer autograph in the first-movement misprints listed by Beethoven. In his first letter to Breitkopf and Härtel he observed that "the copy you have" may contain errors, thus readily admitting that the errors might have been made by the copyist and overlooked by him, not made by the printer. But it is interesting to see that of the ten first-movement mistakes he discovered in the piano and cello, *only one* can be traced to his own autograph reading: No. 3, in which the autograph also lacks the natural on the a in the piano cadenza. For Nos. 1 and 2 the autograph clearly agrees with his correct readings in the misprint list, while in No. 4 the copyist might have missed the *ff* at bar 115, though it is hard to see how; as for No. 5, the autograph version has a different figuration, hence the origin of the error is post-autograph. And none of the cello part errors in the first edition is traceable to the autograph. A few inconsistencies that are *not* mentioned by Beethoven have also plagued later editions and performers, and at least one to be discussed later (concerning bars 36 and 173) remains unsolved. But despite the maze of cancellations and revisions that cover the autograph and despite the troubled later history of the text of this work, the autograph contains remarkably little that is really uncertain or imprecise. It presents an essentially pure text.

REVISIONS AND LAYERS OF CORRECTION

TO FACILITATE reference to the facsimile from here on, the following methods of abbreviation will be used: folio number/staff/bar number will be indicated in that order—for example, 4v/3/5 means folio 4 verso/staff 3/bar 5; reference to bar numbers alone indicates the bar numbering of the entire first movement, with the convention that the first and second endings have the same number; I count the whole movement as having 280 bars.

The chain of errors is extended by the modern Peters edition (C. F. Peters, No. 748), Walter Schulz, ed. Schulz is the only editor I know of who gives the "last corrected reading"—the opening *ff*—but he follows it with an undocumented *sff* and then writes in a note: "In the manuscript, the reading of which was also taken over by the Gesamtausgabe, the reading is *p* and *sf*." While Schulz knows the letter of August 3, 1809, I doubt that he really knows the "Manuskript" of the Scherzo; for no one since Beethoven's lifetime has ever reported its existence or whereabouts. Almost certainly Schultz is working from the confusions of the early prints, as all other editors have also been forced to do.

References to internal subdivisions of measures are given in terms of quarter-note units, e.g., bar 38/3 means bar 38, third quarter. Hereafter, Pfte = pianoforte; Vcl = violoncello.

Methods of Correction

To sum up, the Salzer autograph is perhaps the most essential link in the chain of sources leading from early sketches to the finished version of the movement, but it is also a score in a mixed stage of development. In part it is a developed score close to the finished product, in part a "composing score" representing more than one layer of elaboration within itself. The reader interested primarily or exclusively in the analytical side of the manuscript will find that even to perceive its content he will have to thread his way through the labyrinth of corrections and puzzling entries that bear on the content; while the student who may be mainly interested in the autograph as a genetic document will discover that to piece its material together requires a consistent view of the musical structure of the movement. And both need a firm base in perceiving its methods of graphic procedure.

A close look at the manuscript as a whole reveals three types of corrections: consecutive, local, and vertical. By "consecutive" I mean the replacement of one passage (at least a full measure in length) by another which is set down directly after it on the same staff or staves. Considering the unsettled appearance of many of its pages, it is surprising to find only one such correction in the entire manuscript: in the coda, bars 248–250 (8v/13–15/2–4). Here Beethoven first wrote the Vcl part out to the very end of the page, then went back to fill in the last system of the Pfte but inadvertently omitted a measure (the equivalent of bar 248). Discovering the lapse after a measure and a half, he crossed out the last three measures on the page, marked a "Vi–" to show the beginning of an omission, and rewrote the passage correctly at the top of the next page. The change was so immediate and obvious that he did not even bother with the "–de" at the top of folio 9r that would have completed the word "Vi–de."

This consecutive correction depended, of course, on immediate recognition of his own lapse of attention in a sequential passage. It was easily made. But the majority of the corrections need not have been immediate, did not result from a direct evaluation of an original version as being plainly and mechanically "wrong," and arose not from lapses in writing but from studied reformulation of the material. They are revisions at the compositional level, and if there is anything anomalous about them it is only that they should have been packed so densely into a single score.[42]

By "local" corrections I mean those which rectify a local passage by cancellation and insertion of a new version next to the old (within the same measure) or by overlaying the new reading on top of the old *on the same staff*. Looking carefully through the manuscript one sees that this is the primary method used for minor changes in the exposition, for instance for the last Vcl triplet in bar 26 (1v/9/2), where two versions of the triplet were in turn canceled and a third inserted in the remaining space. Similarly, many of the changes in register that abound in the movement, especially in the Vcl, were handled in this way (e.g., 1v/13/4 and 2r/1/1–3). It was used again to replace triplets with pizzicato quarters at bars 65–70 (3r/staves 1 and 5) despite the difficult appearance that resulted. Corrections by overlaying or close adjacency were the most rapid and most obvious methods used by Beethoven, presumably while working at considerable speed. He resorted to vertical corrections involving extra staves and "Vi–de" signs only when compelled to do so because the original staves were filled in beyond even his ambitious hope of legible addition.

"Vertical" corrections, as I am using the term, are those using the intervening staves originally left blank, with "Vi–de" to mark the connections to the main staves. There seem to be two ways in which he used the extra staff for new material: first, to indicate an alternative to what he had written on the main staff; second, to put down a replacement for it. The

[42] Perhaps distantly relevant to this aspect of the score is a much later reference by Beethoven to his own procedure of writing, in a letter to A. M. Schlesinger (Anderson No. 1060) of November 13 (1821). Beethoven explains that to send both his own MS and a copy of a work would be too risky, for they might be lost. "This is what happened the last time when on account of my ailing condition I had written down the draft more fully than usual. But now that my health appears to be better, I merely jot down certain ideas as I used to do, and when I have completed the whole in my head everything is written down, but *only once*" (my italics at the end). The German text was published for the first time in *Music and Letters*, XX (1939), 236–38: ". . . das Vorigemal geschah es, indem ich, meiner kränklichen Umstände wegen, mein *Concept* weitläufiger aufgeschrieben als gewöhnlich, jezt aber wo wie es scheint meine Gesundheit besser ist, zeige ich wie sonst auch nur gewisse Ideen an, u. bin ich mit dem Ganzen fertig im Kopf (?), so wird alles nur einmal aufgeschrieben" (question mark by the editors, B. Schofield and D. Wilson).

difference is simply determined: when Beethoven wrote in an alternative reading on the extra staff he left the earlier version intact; when he wrote in a replacement he crossed out the original. Apart from possible lapses, I take the latter to represent more decisive revisions, while the former represent a less settled stage at which more than one reading could still be considered; in short, they resemble the functions of the sketches. Examples of the two procedures are not difficult to find, and I have tried to list them all in Appendix III, which shows all uses of intervening staves within the manuscript with an indication of what they alter or replace, and which sort of reading they represent. Again they center on the development, and by following the indications in the table the reader ought to be able to thread his way through the central part of the manuscript and should be able to associate the facsimile pages with each of the transcriptions given here.

One other method of correction remains to be mentioned which is distinguished not by spatial assignment but by writing implement. While the bulk of the manuscript is written in brownish ink with revisions in a darker ink, there is some use of red pencil for further corrections, *but only in the first few pages of the manuscript* (folios 1v–3v). The use of the red pencil seems to represent a separate pass through the manuscript by Beethoven, a pass which he did not carry all the way but only through the exposition, presumably because the development pages were already too well populated by inked-in changes; perhaps also because he may have expected he could depend on his very able copyist, Schlemmer, to carry red changes in the exposition over into parallel passages in the recapitulation. The red pencil was useful for correcting notes or accidentals, to reinforce certain passages (e.g., 3r/2/1) or to cancel (e.g., 2r/11/2). Most revealing of all is his use of it for the wavy horizontal lines on 2r, between staves 6–7 and 7–8. These turn out to have a special meaning—to indicate to the copyist that another version of these measures (bars 38–45) was to be found not in the autograph itself but on a separate page elsewhere. As mentioned earlier, this interpretation receives the most positive confirmation when we find precisely these measures for the Pfte written into a blank page in the sketchbook Beethoven was then using, listed here as source *C*. It is only by examining the autograph that this entry becomes truly meaningful, and we need to recognize it not as a "sketch" but as an external component of the autograph itself.

Exposition and Recapitulation

Initial clues to the underlying musical importance of the Salzer autograph are furnished by study of certain passages in the exposition and recapitulation, even though the equivalence of content in the two sections is limited at the stage of writing represented by the autograph. Not all passages that were to be parallel in the final version of the movement are parallel here in all details, and not all are corrected in the same way. Some of the differences shed further light on the processes inherent in the writing of the movement, and to give a precise account of these it will be necessary to relate their readings not only to one another but to the final text of the movement. At the same time it should be kept in mind that for certain discrepancies we are faced with an insoluble dilemma. When we find disagreements between apparently parallel passages in exposition and recapitulation it is sometimes difficult to decide if these are intentional and calculated subtleties, or if they are due to lapses in inserting corrections intended for both sections but actually inserted only in one—or simply to undue haste in writing, especially in sections of the recapitulation that may have been conceived as mechanical repetitions of their counterparts in the exposition, but into which errors infiltrated during the process of writing.

Bars 25–26 and 164–165. At bars 25–26 radical changes are made in both Pfte and Vcl. In the first version the Pfte had octaves in the left hand, with triplets in the Vcl (see Example 2a). Before abandoning this version entirely, Beethoven took the trouble to touch up the voice leading at the end of bar 26 in the Vcl, twice revising the final triplet as shown in Example 2a. He then overlaid a second reading upon both measures (Example 2b) which reorganizes the registral layout of the lower voices, makes the Vcl the bass to the Pfte, transfers the triplets to the Pfte and to a different register, and clarifies the sonority by removing the triplets from the Vcl at low register. The second version agrees with the final one, and it is doubly instructive that at bars 164–165, the parallel passage in the recapitulation, *only the second version* is present, with no trace of revision and without the further revision in the Vcl that Beethoven would later insert (probably by altering the Clauss copy). From this example two possible hypotheses flow: 1) Beethoven could have reconceived bars 25–26 as he was writing a new

EXAMPLE 2a

Bars 25-26, stage 1

*Last triplet replaces two canceled readings:  and  .

EXAMPLE 2b

Bars 25-26, stage 2

version of the material at bars 164–165, and then decided to go back and revise bars 25–26 in the light of the version desired for the recapitulation; or 2) he may have revised bars 25–26 at once, or while working on the exposition, before writing down bars 164–165 and perhaps before he was entirely sure in just what details the recapitulation would differ. In cases of this sort, where second choices in the exposition appear as first choices in the recapitulation, the recapitulation represents a later stage in more than the obvious sense.

Bars 33/1, 34/1 and 170/1, 171/1. In the exposition the first triplet in each measure is  ; in the recapitulation it is 

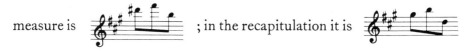

Whether the variant is intended or not is left undetermined by the context, since either version offers plausible local voice leading. The earliest printed editions maintain the two readings, as does the GA, and in the absence of other evidence the problem remains open.[43]

Bars 35–36 and 172–173. The problem here is similar to the one preceding, but more conspicuous and more vital to the structure of the movement. Contrasting with the previous problem is that here the disagreement is between autograph and printed editions.

In the autograph, bars 35 and 36 are *not* identical to one another in pitch-content, and the distinction is clear from positive notational evidence, not merely inferred from elliptical or imprecise use of signs. At bar 35 the Pfte triplets bring c♮ and a♯ as neighbor notes to b; in bar 36, as the Vcl picks up the figure, Beethoven changes the c♮ to a bold and clear c♯ on the first triplet of the measure. The reading in the autograph not only lets the change in linear contour reinforce and coincide with the change in sonority, but it effects a transition from the implied E-minor $\left(\begin{smallmatrix}6-5\\4-3\\V\end{smallmatrix}\right)$ preparation of the preceding measures to the culminating tonicization of E major at bar 37, anticipating the E-major resolution by means of the c♯ at bar 36.

Exactly parallel is the autograph reading at bars 172–173. Bar 172 has f♮ and d♯; bar 173 alters to f♯ and d♯.[44] Neither passage shows erasures or cancellations.

The first edition and almost all subsequent editions I have seen, including the GA, give c♮ at both bar 35 and 36, but f♮ at bar 172 followed by f♯ at bar 173.[45] On this reading the exposition and recapitulation are *not* parallel, and generations of players must have noticed the distinction without being able to determine what the evidence shows. If they did notice the problem, they were more astute than the editors of the many editions

43 On comparable problems regarding parallel passages see Unverricht, pp. 67–70 and Mies, p. 14 (on Op. 96), p. 51 (on Op. 27, No. 2).

44 Noteworthy too is that the Pfte at bar 172 is an octave higher than in the final version, in which the parallel passages agree in register.

45 The modern C. F. Peters edition differs in giving c♮ at bars 35–36 and f♮ at both bars 172 and 173, without notice of any kind. Exactly the same arrangement then appears in the International Music Co. edition (Leonard Rose, ed.), which is identical in every typographical detail with that of Peters. This compound error seems to have begun with the G. Schirmer edition by Leo Schulz, copyright 1905, which is still being issued in unrevised form.

showing the discrepancy, since none ever alluded to it before Tovey in his edition of the sonatas. Of the two obvious interpretations, one is imperiously offered by Tovey in a footnote.[46] At bar 173 Tovey puts the f♮ on the staff but adds a "♯?" above it, and writes: "It is quite characteristic of Beethoven, as of Haydn and Mozart, to produce an intentional change here, and the passage is not referred to in his own list of misprints. But the question must remain open." A look at the autograph might have punctured Tovey's grand confidence in his knowledge of what was "quite characteristic" in Beethoven's handling of such details, at least at the autograph stage. Again, the loss of the Clauss copy makes it impossible to judge whether the autograph readings at bars 36 and 173 were later intentionally changed as Beethoven reconsidered the details of the movement. As for the misprint list, there is no doubt of its value for the final text of the Sonata, but it will also be seen that Beethoven himself acknowledged his limitations as a proofreader in connection with it. While we cannot doubt the validity of those points that are explicitly brought up in his correspondence, there is plenty of room for doubt about those left unmentioned, and it contributes nothing to assume that because Beethoven was careful he must have been infallible. Tovey, then, is right—the question must remain open. But the Salzer autograph brings positive and convincing evidence that at a late stage of composition of the movement, the two passages in exposition and recapitulation did match, and did have the chromatic, nonrepetitive reading, not the simple repetition found in the editions. In the present state of the evidence, this reading is the best available, and only contrary evidence from the Clauss copy, if that were to turn up, could challenge it.

Bars 37–45 and 174–182. This passage has been cited earlier for its special method of correction and its link to the Pastoral Symphony sketchbook (source *C*). Now to the corrections themselves.

An important assumption in the version of this passage given in the autograph is that the Vcl part at bars 37–45 and 174–182 is by this time

[46] Augener edition, No. 7660. Despite its shortcomings this is still the best edition yet available, since it represents at least an honest attempt to grasp the text-critical nettles. Of all the recorded performances I know of, however, only that made by Emanuel Feuermann and Myra Hess appears to be based on this edition; perhaps because it was made in England?

fixed in form, and in all but one detail represents the final version. This is of interest both with regard to the strategic location of the entire passage (as the beginning of the "second group" in the exposition at the moment of the first decisive motion to the dominant) and also with regard to the nature of the material devised to articulate this motion; in the Vcl an ascending scale pattern expanding through almost three octaves coinciding with a descending harmonic prolongation of the E-major triad through a nearly comparable range in the Pfte. The whole is organized into two four-bar complementary phrases moving I–V and V–I. It was only at the late stage of correction represented by red pencil that Beethoven changed a single detail of the Vcl: he altered the repetitive b♯ in bar 44 to d♯.[47] With this stroke he abandoned the parallel with bar 40 but achieved a local linear crest for the phrase and also a reading of considerably greater motivic significance for the movement (compare bars 44–45 with 89–90, 91–92 and their recapitulation complements).

To the established Vcl material, he apparently began by adding the octave upbeat figure in the Pfte shown in Example 3a, but abandoned this after only a measure. The notation of bar 37 in the Pfte makes it difficult to be certain of priorities, since neither version is amply spaced within the measure. But I assume that Example 3a constitutes an earlier idea for the Pfte entrance at this point, reinforcing the tonicized e at bar 38/1 and suggesting a descending arpeggiation by means of the renewed attack at bar 38/3. This idea is lightly sketched again at bar 42 (2r/10/4), where two d♯'s, in the rhythm ♩ 𝄽 ♩ 𝄽 are faintly visible in the right hand in a tiny hand, as if this possibility lingered as an afterthought.

The second stage suppressed this in favor of the arpeggiated descending triad of Example 3b. This version of the Pfte material, in simultaneous octaves, is simpler in articulation than the final imitative version that was to supplant it, but it may be said of this second version that it explicitly effects an exact rhythmic correspondence between Pfte bars 38–40 and Vcl bars 1–3, in short, between the principal subject of the entire movement and this significant thematic landmark in the course of its subsequent unfolding. The correspondence is made less obvious in the final version of bars 38–40,

47 Notably he did not take the trouble to make the parallel change at bar 181. But again one must either assume that the copyist did so or that Beethoven corrected the copy before the first printing.

EXAMPLE 3a

Bars 37-45, stage 1 (Pfte only)

EXAMPLE 3b

Bars 37-45, stage 2 (Pfte only)

not only through the more complex articulations of Pfte bar 39 that arise from the imitation, but through the suppression of the eighth-notes at Pfte bar 40/4. It should be noted too that the descending version in simultaneous octaves was entered into both the exposition and recapitulation before further changes were made in it.

The process of elaboration becomes perfectly clear, however, when the next step is closely examined. Evidently having decided to convert the descending arpeggiation in octaves to a one-measure imitation, in both first and second phrases, Beethoven must have found that there was no clear way in which he could change the autograph to show precisely what he wanted to keep and what to delete. So he crossed out everything in the Pfte from bars 38 to 45 and from bars 175 to 182 in ink, leaving only the parallel bars 41 and 45 and 178 and 182 intact—as if to hold them temporarily open—and then turned to the red pencil for clarifying marks. He crossed out the alternate arpeggiation (from stage 1) at bar 40 in red pencil, reinforced the cancellation at bar 44, and then added the long horizontal wavy lines above and below the Pfte from bars 38 to 45. In effect, these wavy lines are a direction to the copyist—they tell him to consult another version of these measures, for the Pfte only, in another source. And this turns out to be the blank page in the sketchbook—the principal sketchbook Beethoven was then using—on which he entered precisely the equivalent of what is crossed out on this page, and precisely what is covered by the wavy lines: only the Pfte, bars 38–45 and then bars 174–182 (where the wavy lines are in ink but mean exactly the same thing, since Beethoven used no red pencil in this manuscript after folio 3v, for some reason).

Plate I shows folio 31v of the sketchbook (our source *C*), with its two entries for these measures, and it will be obvious that they exactly fit the corresponding pages in the autograph. Writing for a professional eye, Beethoven put down only what was necessary, and as mentioned earlier he wrote in the hand normally reserved for fair copies intended for the eyes of others, not the rapid sketchbook hand intended for himself.[48]

Bars 65–70, 71–76 and 202–207, 208–213. In the later exposition, this is the first larger segment to undergo considerably more than partial or local correction. To clarify the web of corrections visible in folios 3r and 7r-v, I shall center discussion on the exposition transcriptions given as Examples 4a, 4b, and 4c, with the expectation that on the basis of these the reader will

[48] On the distinctions between these methods of writing, see Max Unger, *Beethovens Handschrift* (Bonn, Beethoven-Haus, 1926), pp. 22 f. Some relevant comments of his own appear in later letters, e.g., Anderson No. 1019 (of 1820) and No. 1402 (of 1825): ". . . tell him [the copyist Rampel] that I write quite differently now, much more legibly than during my illness."

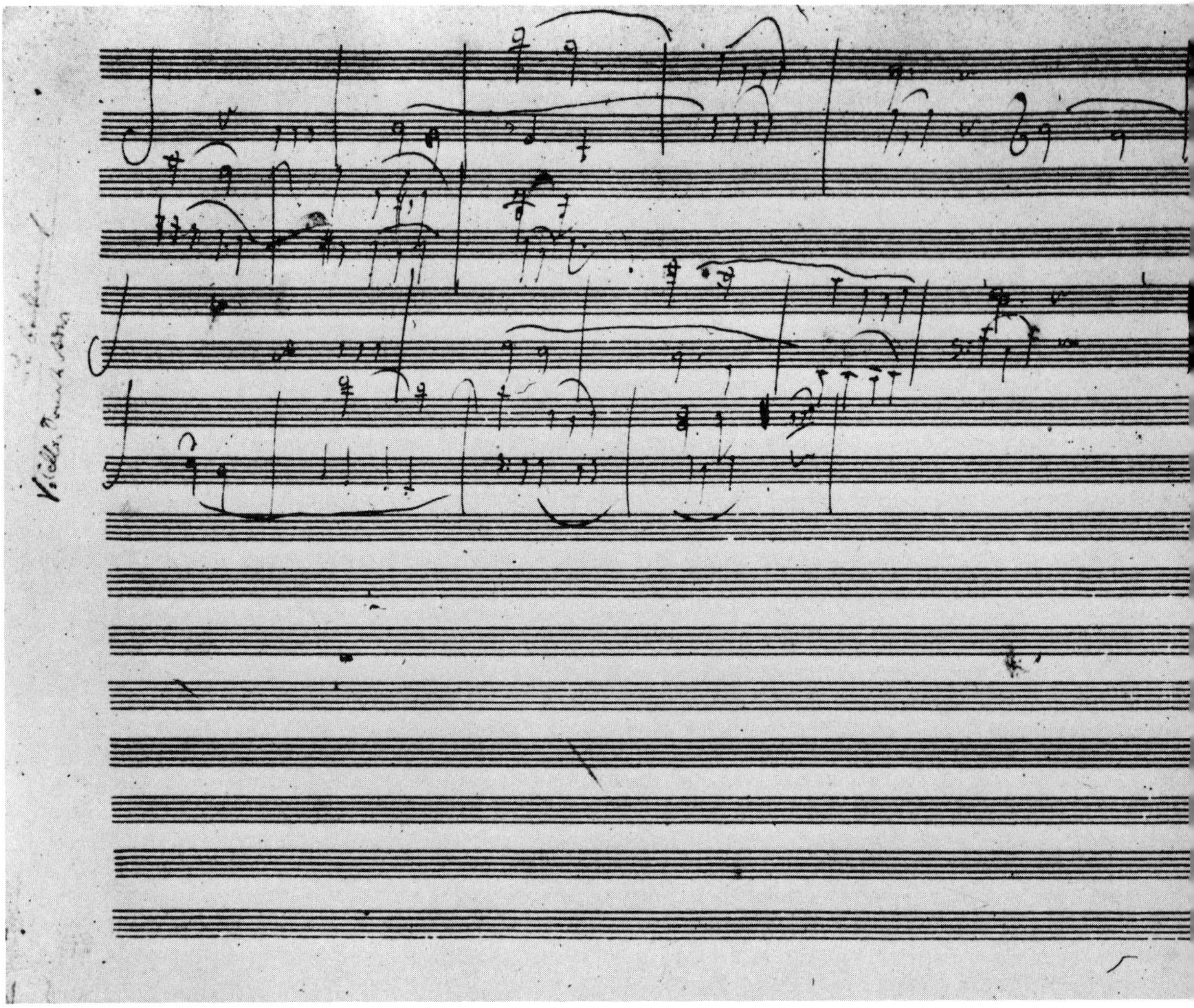

PLATE I. FOLIO 31V OF SKETCHBOOK (SOURCE C)

be able to make his own comparable observations about the recapitulatory details on folio 7r-v, where the revisions are simpler and clearer. The three examples are also offered as paradigms for later examples in which two or more layers of composition are derived from a composite transcription. The transcriptions in Examples 4b and 4c are meant to follow from 4a in this way: Example 4a is a complete diplomatic transcription of bars 65–76, giving all possible detail; Example 4b extracts from 4a what I take to be its first stage of composition; Example 4c represents a similarly extracted second stage.

Even a first glance at these revisions suggests both distant and nearby connections and associations. From the main course of events in the exposition in its final version, it is obvious that bars 65–70 represent a well-defined, emphatically articulated phrase-segment that begins a new area of the exposition after its first large-scale tonicization of the dominant; further, that the stage of motivic development reached at bars 65–70 is reconfirmed at bars 71–76 by means of the instrumentally interchanged repetition that has also been used for every previous larger phrase-segment in the movement. Of the uses of interchange in the movement more will be said later; it suffices now to emphasize in the final version the intensification of the first statement (bars 65–70) at bars 71–76 by change of sonority, expansion of register, and the progression from triplet to sixteenth-note figuration. In this entire movement, as in other Beethoven works of this period, a primary means of foreground sectional contrast is through the identification of successive segments with successive prevailing rhythmic units, taking these at times in graduated diminution, and with the area of maximum diminution coinciding with maximum metrical accentuation and with a rise to a higher dynamic level.

With the final effect of bars 65–70 and 71–76 in view, it becomes doubly instructive to see that, at an earlier but still autograph stage, the rhythmic organization of the two passages was essentially identical, with both in triplets, and that even the revisions for bars 71–76 introduced sixteenths only partially and in local alternation with the prevailing triplets. Still more surprising is the recapitulation: at bars 208–215 there is as yet no sign of sixteenths at all, and only the first layer of composition is represented!

More distantly associated with bars 65–70 is the earlier transition passage at bars 25–26 already described in this section. In both passages the first conception of the material included low-register triplets in the Vcl in a strongly articulated forte context, with supporting left-hand octaves in the Pfte. In both, the basic exchange of functions is between Vcl and Pfte left hand, with considerations of sonority and spacing apparently combining to influence the redistribution. At the same time an important difference distinguishes the first-stage Vcl triplets: at bars 25–26 they embody the relatively simple functions of repeated rising arpeggiated triads in the familiar 2-plus-1 phrasing that insures each one a down-bow attack; but at bars 65–70 they are expanded to include differentiated types of diminution: triadic arpeggiation in both directions (bar 65); chromatic neighbor-note figures (bars 65/3, 66/1), and the rising figure with detached repeated note () at bars 68–70. That the last was still experimental, though, is shown by bars 205–207 (see facsimile, folio 7v/1/2 and 7v/4/1–2) where it has two forms, the one in Example 3b being the second, corrected, version.

Close comparison of Examples 4a, 4b, and 4c with one another, with the final version, and with the facsimile (folio 3r) should yield some insight into the problems of interpretation offered by the most difficult passages in the Salzer autograph. For all that Example 4a strives to reproduce the present state of the page in all its ramified detail, it will inevitably fall short of representing the material in its true completeness, since many of the subtle nuances and visual cues of the original handwriting are lost in transcription.[49] The chain of rapid cancellation strokes leaves the contents clear enough at staves 1, 3, 5, and 7; but in staves 9, 11, and the very end of 14 it covers the writing so densely as to make decoding difficult even after close study of the original. Intact even though partly obscured are the words used on folio 3:

a. 3r/1/3: "pizz" (determined not only by the final version and the context but by comparison with the appearance of the term in other

[49] See my remarks in *The Musical Quarterly*, LII (January, 1967), 133 f.

scores).[50] At 3r / between 8 and 9 / 3, the swirling flourish may stand for "arco," which would fit bar 71.

b. 3r/11/1: under the arabesque of cancellations lurks the word "bleibt," referring to an earlier stage at which Beethoven had first canceled the left hand, then decided to let it remain, then canceled it once more.

c. 3r/14/right margin: again the word "bleibt" is canceled.[51]

Another sample of notational detail that can only be understood by reference to the original writing is the hint of successive stages of decision regarding the Vcl at bars 65–68, after the triplets had been transferred to the Pfte left hand. In bar 66, a half note, e, is canceled and replaced by the quarter notes e, b; but in bar 67–68 three successive half-note heads are partially filled in to convert them to quarters. The half-note pattern was doubtless the first step in replacing the triplets; in turn it was displaced by the quarter-note pattern. Did the idea for a unique change of Vcl sonority to pizzicato to intensify the articulation coincide with the quarter-note stage?

For bars 65–70 the interrelation of Examples 4b and 4c seems clear enough. To what has been said already, it need only be added now that we can attach importance to the change in register in the Vcl as well as the change in durations, i.e., the replacement of the low Vcl e and d♯ (bars 65–68) by pizzicato an octave higher, presumably with a view to reserving the lowest register until its effective arco attack at bar 71.

For bars 71–76 the situation is much more complicated. Stages 1 and 2 show two readings for the Vcl, changing its octave (I assume from low to middle register) while the Pfte problems include both the handling of the triplet-to-sixteenth-note progression and the function of the left hand throughout. In the first stage Beethoven worked out triplet patterns (staff 10/3) resembling those of the Vcl at stage 1 (bars 65–70) and planned to bring both hands in octaves from bar 71 onwards—thus the writing out of the left hand at bars 71–72, with the intention of continuing "in 8" as

[50] Compare the following indications of "pizz" in published facsimiles: Fifth Symphony autograph, p. 22, bar 2; p. 87, bar 1; p. 91, bar 1; p. 95, bars 1–2; p. 99, bar 2; p. 107, bar 2; p. 119, bar 1; p. 184, bar 6; and others. Also in the sketchbook Add. 31766: fol. 47v/3/2; 45r/3/ right margin; 45r/6–7/ 3–4; 42v/10; 43r/ above st. 4: "Violoncello pizzicato."

[51] Compare the autograph of Op. 57, 14v/1/1, where the sequence of indications is "bleibt——in 8va——loco."

marked at the end of bar 72, left hand (3/11/4). At a later stage Beethoven considered strengthening the bass register, presumably to bring out the new position of what had formerly been an upper line (bars 65 ff.). To do so he marked "Vi–" for the left hand at bar 71 and added the "left hand" interpolation visible on staff 12 just below the triplets. This second possibility lasted a little longer, as expressed in the verbal direction below bars 73–74: "col Violoncell in 8"—but eventually it too gave way to a return to the idea of restricting the Pfte to the upper register only, in octaves, with the Vcl as sole bass support. I assume that at this stage of events the sixteenth-note "Vide" entered the right hand at bars 71–72, with the first version spelled out above at staff 8—and that to this last autograph stage alone belongs the direction at bar 73: "16^{tel} in 8^{en}." "Sixteenths in octaves" does indeed represent the final decision for the Pfte at this climactic passage in the exposition, but it is apparently the product of a process of shuttling back and forth among possible and seemingly plausible stages of decision, the remnants of which can still be exhumed from the maze of cancellations across the page.

Finally, it is worth speculating as to how the final version of bars 71–76 (and 208–213) was put down and clarified. While the last stage of bars 65–70 and 202–207 in the autograph are virtually the same as the final reading, even the last versions visible for bars 71–76 and 208–213 are not. The sixteenths of the final version are partially added for bars 71–78, though they are not fully worked out on the page; but for bars 208–213, as we saw, there are no sixteenths stipulated at all. We are left to assume either that Beethoven made extensive alterations in the passage in the lost Clauss copy, or else that he may have worked out the details for the copyist on sketch-sheets that have not been preserved.

Bars 77–83 and 214–220. Further discrepancies between exposition and recapitulation appear in these measures, the last revised passages to be dealt with here apart from those in Appendix IV. The Pfte figures at the *ff* bars 77–78 do not at first appear to be revised from an earlier stage. But they are. Originally both hands were to be in triplets throughout these two transitional measures, and the four sixteenths entered at the beginning of bars 77 and 78 were actually triplets continuing the first-stage triplets of

EXAMPLE 4a

Bars 65-76 (complete); folio 3r-v

EXAMPLE 4a (*continued*)

EXAMPLE 4b

Bars 65-76, stage 1, folio 3r-v

*Alternate reading of final triplets in bar 65 is agreeing with bar 66.

EXAMPLE 4b (*continued*)

EXAMPLE 4C

Bars 65-76, stage 2, folio 3r-v

EXAMPLE 4C (*continued*)

*I interpret the l.h. at bars 73–76 as follows: "col Violoncell in 8" represents an intermediate stage continuing what I allocate to "stage 2" in bars 71–72; "16tel in 8en" represents a later decision to transfer the written-out triplets to sixteenths, continuing the r.h. at bars 71–72 but extending the sixteenths to both hands.

bars 71–76. The conversion to sixteenths simply necessitated the adding of a fourth member at the end of each group—but only in the exposition was the addition carried out.[52] Again Beethoven failed to take the trouble to change the parallel passage in the recapitulation, either because he was working rapidly, or knew that he could rely on the good sense of his copyist. Whatever the reason, bars 214–215 (7v/14–15/2–3) remain in unmodified triplets.

Similarly curious is the revision of the Vcl at bars 80 and 82, along with their later counterparts. On the original conception of bars 71–78, the *pp* interchange beginning at bar 79 had furnished a continuation of the previously established triplet figuration. But with the introduction of sixteenths in bars 71–78, the decrescendo from *ff* to *pp* with continued sixteenths brings a slightly more palpable contrast at bar 79, a more effective sense of a new departure, than the triplet transition could have done. Thanks to the change in figuration at bar 79, any sensitive pianist recognizes the need for an expressive extension of the first note of the measure, not only to heighten the significance of the descent through two octaves by a slight delay in its initial downward motion, but also to sharpen the distinction between the sixteenths of bar 78 and the renewed triplets at bar 79.

As for the Vcl at bar 80, it contains no fewer than three versions of its answering pattern within the same measure, and a fourth sketched lightly below in a tiny hand (3v/8/1).[53] The first idea was to begin the ascending Vcl triplets on b (the triplet is visible in the left center of the measure), but after one triplet this was canceled in favor of a version starting on d♯ and rising directly to the fixed goal, g♯. Yet the preferred voice leading remained that of beginning the Vcl ascent on the pitch just being reached by the descending Pfte; thus the new trial on b once more, curving chromatically through a♯ to c♯ and down to the g♯. Then the final idea for the Vcl contour

[52] For an example of the opposite procedure, altering groups of four sixteenths to triplets, see Nottebohm, *Zweite Beethoveniana*, p. 279 (on Op. 95).

[53] For a similar addition on an intervening staff in the Op. 96 autograph, see E. Winternitz, Plate 85, which also exhibits the significant words "klein geschrieben" as an indication to the copyist, as is pointed out by Winternitz, I, 84. See also the Fifth Symphony autograph, pp. 173–77 (trio of the Scherzo), bottom of each page. Valuable here is the letter to N. Simrock of April 23, 1820 (Anderson No. 1019), in which he himself remarks on the problems a copyist encountered who was unfamiliar with his hand: "which frequently produces only very sketchy [notes] [B. gives sample note-shapes], etc., and these might hardly be described even as *little notes*."

is sketched below, with its grace-note turn suggesting a long-range connection with the turn in the Vcl cadenza at bar 24, which produces a similar change of direction after an ascending six-note scale pattern. The d♯ version at bar 80 paralleled the first stage at bar 82, beginning now on g♯, and the change to a version a third lower, with letters added for clarity, needs no transcription. Worth noting, however, is that in the final version the Pfte remained fixed in register at bars 79–82, but the Vcl was transferred up an octave once more, again showing that registral adjustments in this Sonata were matters of continuing concern down to stages of revision extending considerably beyond the autograph.

The Development

Bars 95–151. In what has been seen so far, the passages revised—however varied in length, function, and type of revision—have formed delimited units that can be readily distinguished in a context that is basically clear in content and direction. The corrections in the middle section, on the other hand, form a long and continuous chain of problems that extend across this entire area of the movement. With the close of the exposition at bar 94, the beginning of the middle section at bars 95–101 unfolds from the second ending in a form that is essentially the final one for this phrase, free of major changes. But, starting in the next measure, bar 101–102 (4r/9–11/3–4), the entire section up to bar 152 displays alterations in every measure, and these reveal nothing less than the total recasting of the roles of Vcl and Pfte throughout the section.

Even in advance of the details, one wider conclusion can be anticipated. In the exposition, the revisions affected smaller units within a scheme essentially established in all major respects. But in the development, the revisions represent a wholesale conversion of this entire area of the movement from one means of instrumental realization to another. What is remarkable in these revisions is not simply their close relevance to the considerations of balance, sonority, register, and instrumental functions that arose in the exposition as small-scale problems, but also that such massive reconstruction with regard to these parameters could be accomplished by Beethoven in an autograph without his finding it necessary to radically recast the material itself.

Once this principle of revision is seen, however, the rest is comparatively easy, and even the most formidable corrections begin to fit together. It thus becomes possible to distinguish two major phases of composition in the section, phases I have sought to represent as Examples 5a and 5b, and 6a and 6b, as follows:

Stage 1 of bars 101–114	Example 5a
Stage 2 of bars 101–114	Example 5b
Stage 1 of bars 115–151	Example 6a
Stage 2 of bars 115–151	Example 6b

But before proceeding to consideration of the transcriptions, a close look at the facsimile of folios 4 through 5v is needed to obtain a clear view of the physical features of the notation of this section and of the character of its corrections. These corrections, even more than those of other parts of the manuscript, make it possible to reconstruct Beethoven's procedures over extensive musical terrain and in illuminating detail.

The first clear hints are offered by the corrections that begin at bar 102 (4r/9–11/4). From here, through the entire last system of folio 4, Beethoven first wrote out in all detail both the Pfte and Vcl (as in Example 5a), then turned back to the beginning of this phrase and began the process of interchange and revision that led to stage 2. While the Pfte is clear enough in the last system of folio 4, the Vcl is crowded with cancellations of stage 1 and the insertion of stage 2 in overlay upon it. Having used the intervening staff 12 for a left-hand change of register at bar 102, Beethoven was forced to make purely local corrections in the Vcl throughout bars 103–106. This point deserves very close attention, for it is a good deal more revealing than might appear at first, owing to the means of continuation. At the top of folio 4v, Beethoven continued the procedure of systematically canceling stage 1 and fitting in stage 2, taking advantage of originally blank measures (e.g., the Pfte 4v/2–3/1–2) for maximum clarity, but using "Vi–de" vertical corrections when it became necessary.

Most revealing is folio 4v. In the first system (staves 1–3) all corrections are local.[54] In the second system (staves 5–7) the first "Vi–" appears, for

[54] Above bars 1 and 2 at the top of 4v is the letter "F" to clarify the Vcl reading.

the Vcl, with its replacement "–de" directly above on staff 4 (4v/4/1–3). But at the third system, the "Vi–de" replacement for the Vcl that had been on staff 4 is continued not on an extra staff but as *uncorrected material on the main Vcl staff* (staff 9). That is to say, the Vcl from bar 101 to 113 shows two complete stages—an original and a total revision; but beginning at bar 114 *the previous revision line becomes the main text for the Vcl part.* This implies that all the corrections from bar 101 to bar 113 must have been made before bar 114 was written, and that the process of correction and reversal of the instrumental roles was not wholly a later decision but one that emerged in the course of working out this section in the autograph. Then, in what follows, new interchanges of material between instruments necessitate new vertical corrections that go even further afield. Yet the reason for dividing the transcriptions of the middle section into two units of unequal length (bars 101–114 and 115–151) should now be clear.

A glance at Examples 5a and 5b suggests strongly that stage 2 followed quickly upon stage 1, and that its main features of correction superseded the earlier readings even before a few details of stage 1 had been entered in full. Indicative of incompleteness in Example 5a is the handling of bars 105–106: I read the half-note succession in the Vcl as representing stage 1, a reading then transferred to the right hand in stage 2. This leaves the right hand blank in stage 1 (apart from the remote possibility of an intended doubling in octaves in stage 1), with no rests discernible. The obvious result in stage 1 is a breakdown in rhythmic activity at bars 105–106 that could scarcely have been allowed to stand even if the interchange of instruments and consequent rewriting had not enlivened it; the solution is the connecting Vcl phrase in quarters which begins at bar 104/4. Curious also in the two versions of Example 5 is the change in register at bars 104–105, as a result of the instrumental interchange; also the double-stops in the Vcl that are lightly sketched in at bars 111/4 and 112/3 in stage 2 (Example 5b)—unidiomatic for the instrument even as rolled arpeggios, and sensibly suppressed at a later stage. Worthy of mention too is an unsettled detail in pitch reading: at bar 114 where both Pfte and Vcl seem in both versions to converge on the triplet succession that leads to the firm tonicization of E minor at bar 115/1, the pitch readings in the two instruments do not agree. The Pfte has an explicit g♯ at the third beat of bar 114, while the Vcl has

EXAMPLE 5a

Bars 101-114, stage 1, folio 4r-v

EXAMPLE 5a (*continued*)

no sharp but does imply it owing to the natural at bar 114/4. In the final version, Beethoven deleted the Pfte doubling in bar 114 altogether, and left the preparation wholly to the Vcl—but the first edition and the GA have a natural at bar 114/3. While this reading anticipates the tonicization of E minor as resolution of the second half of bar 114, it lacks the interesting ambiguity of a major–minor approach to a minor tonicization, which might have formed a subtle parallel to the problem at bars 35–36 described earlier at a similarly decisive move into the tonicization of E major.

Comparable means of interchange between stage 1 and stage 2 are visible in Examples 6a and 6b, which present the entire remainder of the development section, and can be read as the direct continuation of their counterparts in Examples 5a and 5b. Among many suggestive details several points of interest claim priority.

EXAMPLE 5b

Bars 101-114, stage 2, folio 4r-v

*NB curve in slur over r.h., to bring it under cancellations in Vcl; this helps to show that the latter were already present when the slur was entered.

EXAMPLE 5b (*continued*)

† R.h. as in stage 1: did Beethoven forget to cancel here? Later editions have whole rest in r.h.

First to be considered is the treatment of diminution at bars 115–116, at which the firm tonicization of E minor coincides with the reintroduction of sixteenth-note motion in *ff*, the highest dynamic level yet reached in the movement. Within stage 1 the first substage of bar 115 must clearly have consisted in the assigning of sixteenths to the Pfte right hand (bars 115/2 through 116/1) with the clarifying letters "g e g e" over bar 115/2 and oblique repetition marks in the right hand at bars 115/3–4 and 116/1. But these Pfte sixteenths were then canceled in favor of the arpeggiated Vcl sixteenths, and although I include both Vcl and Pfte sixteenths as part of

EXAMPLE 6a

Bars 115-151, stage 1. folios 4v-5v

EXAMPLE 6a (*continued*)

EXAMPLE 6a (*continued*)

*Assume this barline added at stage 2. †Grace notes unclear.

EXAMPLE 6a (*continued*)

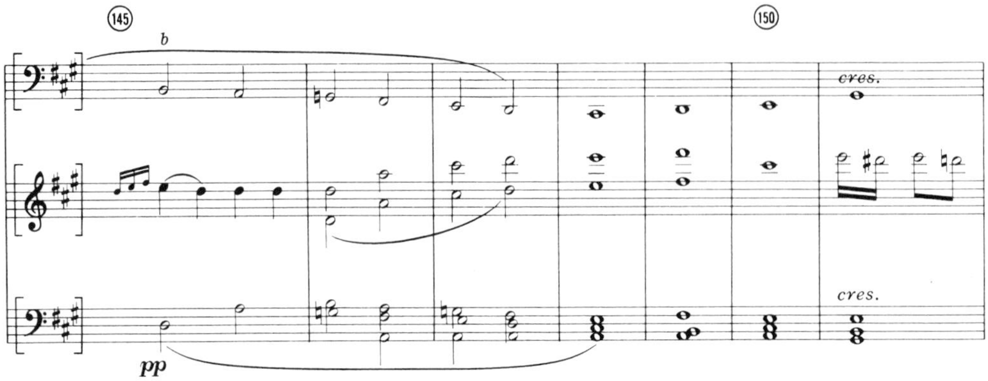

stage 1, the Vcl figuration must have been entered after that of the Pfte, since the Vcl sixteenths are crowded in on the left and right sides of the clarifying letters over the right-hand sixteenths at bar 115/2; the Pfte sixteenths must already have been present. Important for stage 1 in both its substages is the cessation of the sixteenth activity: in the version of bars 115–116 in which the Pfte did have arpeggios, these continued as a primary representation of the upper voices all the way to bar 122, while the Vcl was to abandon its sixteenths for the new developmental figure derived at long range from the thematic unit that dominates the entire movement, here used in imitative alternation with the left hand. In other words, in stage 1 the Vcl and Pfte were to exchange sixteenths at bars 115–117 ff., and the evidence that Beethoven considered this possibility beyond a moment's thought is provided by the clarifying letters at bars 115, 117, and 119, which would hardly have been needed for a version at once suppressed.

In stage 2 the alternation plan is significantly abandoned in favor of the consistent relegation of independent developmental processes to each instrument. The Vcl is now definitely assigned the function of supplying bass and mid-register harmony in intensified rhythmic activity by means of its sixteenth-note arpeggios throughout the segment—the only extended sixteenths in the entire Vcl part; while the Pfte develops the sequential imitation of the basic quarter-note figure in both hands, balancing both in octaves. Stage 2 (bars 115–122) is eminently clear in purpose and

EXAMPLE 6b

Bars 115-151, stage 2, folios 4v-5v

*The two oblique repetition signs are visible just below the Vcl staff.

†This octave crossed out because of poor spacing(?)

‡Material on cue staff seems to correct both stage 1 (sixteenths) and stage 2 (several versions) in this measure only; next measure = stage 2, then transferred to r.h. staff.

EXAMPLE 6b (*continued*)

EXAMPLE 6b (*continued*)

EXAMPLE 6b (*continued*)

*Renewal of bass clef not visible but to be assumed.

EXAMPLE 6b (*continued*)

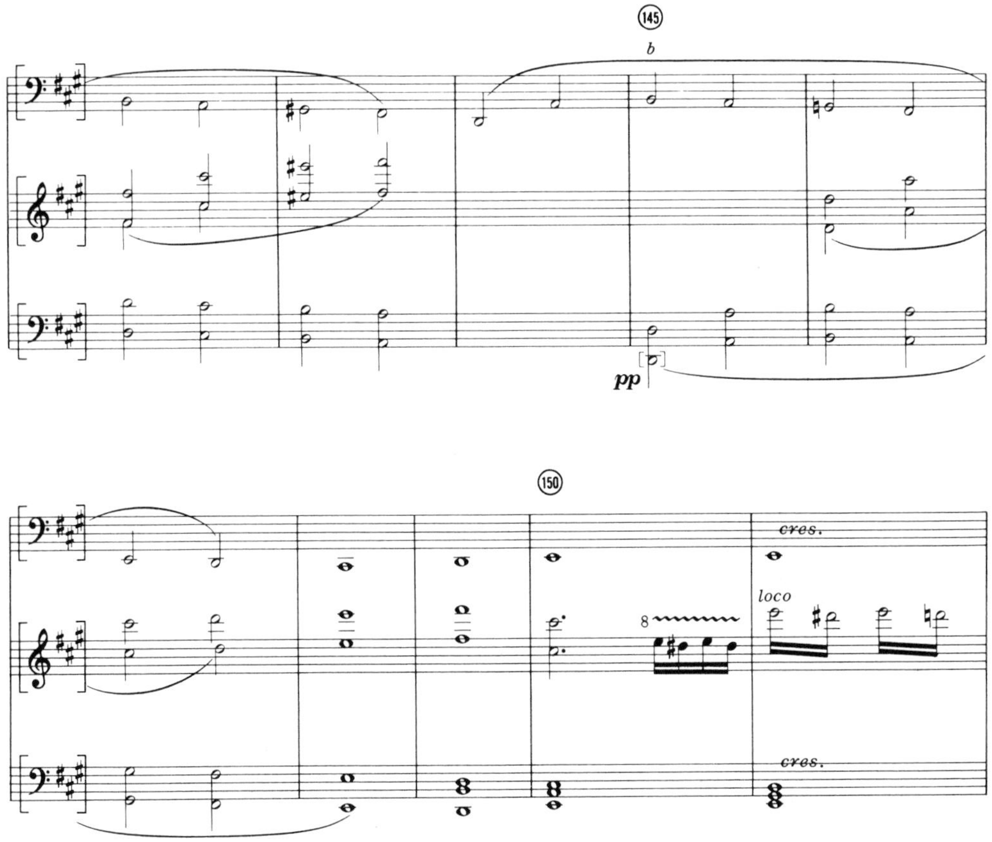

realization, and the contrasting motivic and rhythmic functions of the two instruments are admirably matched to their contrasting registers and sonorities.

Especially curious is a sidelight on Beethoven's procedures at bars 117–122 that is provided by one of the extant sketch-pages for the movement (our source *E*). On folio 2v of this set of pages we find an isolated entry (Example 7). Typically for Beethoven's monolinear sketches of the most rapidly written type, it lacks clefs and clarifying marks of articulation

EXAMPLE 7

Source E, folio 2v, staff 6

altogether. But we can supply these without too fertile speculation, and when we do, the result is as shown in Example 8.

The sketch represents, in linear compression, bars 117–122, showing the chain of transpositions of the primary motivic figure in both Pfte and Vcl and incorporating elements of what I am calling stages 1 and 2. In all probability this fragmentary entry represents a rapid jotting made while the work on this part of the autograph was in process, indeed when it had run into trouble. Once again one sees the use of a sketch-page as a clarifying addition to a problem that had already reached the autograph stage—and once again one sees how an apparent sketch is really supplementary to a concurrent autograph rather than being a simple predecessor of the autograph stage.

Although many significant aspects of revision are discernible in the remainder of the development section, I shall restrict what follows to discussion of four principal points. These will once again focus mainly on stages 1 and 2 of the autograph as represented in Examples 6a and 6b.

The first concerns the striking effects of revision on Beethoven's treatment of register in this part of the movement. Beginning at bar 117, the essential change from stage 1 to stage 2 involves the exchange between Vcl and Pfte right hand, and their interchange effects important modifications in the registral location of comparable material. Thus at bar 117, the sixteenth-note arpeggios that had been the uppermost voices in stage 1 become bass and mid-register support in stage 2, while the Vcl line of stage 1 (bars 117–122) is transferred from an interior role to the prominence of

EXAMPLE 8

The same sketch with clefs interpolated

the right hand in high register, where it is doubled in octaves. Registral considerations are even more in evidence at later points in the development, and the post-autograph changes that resulted in the final version clearly reflect Beethoven's special pains with this aspect of the setting: bars 123–126 and 129, compared in stage 1, stage 2, and the final reading, will supply an adequate initiation to these subtleties.

On the rhythmic side this portion of the autograph contributes further insight into the genesis of the final version in ways that supplement what we have seen in the exposition. The treatment of triplets and sixteenths in the later part of the exposition (especially bars 65–79) is the background to the revisions in the development. Especially prominent is the rising sequential transition figure at bars 123–126, which prepares the decisive and significant tonicization of C♯ minor at bar 127. From all the evidence at hand, it appears that from his first advanced conception of this part of the development, Beethoven sought to clarify the larger phrase-segmentation of the section on a rhythmic basis, and that the sequence of phrase-segments forms a series in which the choice of predominant rhythmic units permits a steady path of elaboration within the movement, and also permits the association of segments separated from one another by considerable intervening terrain (e.g., bars 107–114 and 127–136, which form a crucial parallel).

The climactic effect of the Vcl sixteenths at bars 115–125 is the decisive contribution of stage 2. In stage 1 the Pfte sixteenths had simply and abruptly shifted to triplets in the Vcl at bar 123, perhaps too crudely breaking the continuity developed at maximum diminution (sixteenths) in the preceding passage. In the stage 2 version, the Vcl sixteenths proceed all the way to bar 125, and at bar 123 the Pfte joins its triplets against the Vcl sixteenths to heighten the activity leading to the cadence at bar 127. But at a still later stage Beethoven must have considered the sixteenth-plus-triplets combination insufficiently developed for his purposes, and, as part of his final conception of the whole passage from bars 115 to 127, he converts every available unit to sixteenths: the Pfte right hand at bars 117–122 is transformed from its relatively relaxed and cantabile right-hand statement (Example 9) to the octave diminution of this figure in sixteenths that is used

EXAMPLE 9

in the final version. Comparably, the sequence at bars 123–126 is converted from triplets to sixteenths, thus also articulating the return to triplets at bar 127 and supplying a clearer association of the long-range poles of the development section, bars 107 and 127.

Finally, an element unique to the autograph version deserves mention. It appears in stage 1 only, at bars 140–141: a brief linear segment in the right hand, as a trailing-off continuation of bar 139 (Example 10). This

EXAMPLE 10

short segment is introduced here for the first time in the movement, and its evident function is to effect a transition from the dotted even eighth-notes of bars 137–139 to the sustained augmentation in even half-notes at bars 140–147. Nor was it merely to have a local transitional use: in the coda, near the very end of the movement at bars 270–271 (9v/6/1–2), Beethoven found a similar use for it in a passage reintroducing half notes after quarter-and-triplet combination, but he suppressed it at bar 270 once he had determined to do so at bars 140–141. Its removal at bars 140–141 only enhances the care with which the process of gradual augmentation of rhythmic values unfolds toward the end of the development section, and the care with which the segmentation of larger phrases is associated with specific units of rhythmic activity at every step of the entire section.

THE GENESIS OF THE FIRST PHRASE

IN DEALING here primarily with the opening phrase of the movement, I have tried to single out the element that seems most obviously to exert a far-reaching influence on the larger design of this remarkably subtle movement, while at the same time I must explicitly dissociate these remarks from what would be expected of a thoroughgoing analysis of the comprehensive flow of events in the entire movement. The requirements of such an analysis should go far beyond what is possible in this commentary on the autograph, and should deal at length with matters that can only be hinted at here, including the larger linear and contrapuntal structure of the movement, its means of harmonic articulation, and its phrase-structure. It should also, of course, encompass the entire Sonata, not merely the first movement, in the context of Beethoven's other major works of this period, one of the most productive of his career. The extraordinary and even now too little-known analyses of major Beethoven works by Heinrich Schenker are not only the most exhaustive published works of their type,[55] but—despite their diversity and whether or not the Schenkerian approach is taken—stand as models of a consistent and powerful attack on a broad range of musical problems, problems that for the vast majority of Beethoven's works have yet to be publicly adumbrated, let alone adequately discussed.

[55] The extended published analyses, representing different periods of Schenker's work, include the monograph on the Ninth Symphony (Vienna, Universal-Edition, 1912); that on the Fifth Symphony in *Der Tonwille* (1921 and 1923) and also published separately; also the *Erläuterungsausgaben* of Op. 101, 109, 110, and 111; and the exhaustive analysis of the Eroica Symphony in *Das Meisterwerk in der Musik*, Vol. III (Munich, Drei Masken, 1930). In addition to other essays on piano sonatas (Op. 2, No. 1; Op. 49, No. 2; and Op. 57) important material is also presented in the analyses in *Neue Musikalische Theorien und Phantasien*. Vol. III: *Der Freie Satz* (Vienna, Universal-Edition; 2d ed., revised and edited by Oswald Jonas, 1956). The further development of the Schenkerian approach in Felix Salzer's *Structural Hearing: Tonal Coherence in Music* (2d ed.; New York, Dover, 1962) will need no introduction to readers of this book.

Within the boundaries of this commentary, then, I would suggest as an essential point of departure for this movement the restriction of its opening six-measure phrase to the Vcl alone, with the subsequent engrafting of a complementary six-measure phrase in the Pfte (bars 6–12). With one stroke this opening phrase (bars 1–12) establishes certain conditions that bear significantly on the remainder of the movement: it presents the primary motivic material for the movement as components of a self-contained linear segment first associated with the Vcl alone in low register; and it immediately establishes a balanced, complementary relationship between the two instruments for which even a crude outline shows a symmetrical partitioning of the first twenty-four measures, divided into two larger phrases:

1. Vcl solo (bars 1–6) — Pfte/Vcl (bars 7–11) — Pfte cadenza (bar 12) to 𝄐
2. Pfte solo (bars 13–17) — Pfte/Vcl (bars 17–23) — Vcl cadenza (bar 24) to 𝄐

While the entrance of the Pfte at the upbeat to bar 7 divides the first twelve measures into six plus six, the complementary entrance of the Vcl at the upbeat to bar 17 avoids what might have been considered too square-cut a symmetry within the larger division of phrases. Significant in this connection is the sketching-in of the Vcl doubling in the autograph during the entire first part of the second larger phrase (bars 13–16) (1r/13/1–4) and its eventual exclusion from these measures. Reserving the Vcl instead for a reinforcing entry at bar 16 not only contributes to the larger symmetry of bars 1–24 but assists in the exploration of range which is the other major aspect of organization at the opening of the movement.

Although the structural and expressive quality of the opening phrase has hardly escaped Beethoven commentators, I know of no discussion of it beyond the most perfunctory. Yet even a fairly close look at the movement, long prior to a more intensive analysis of it, yields some observations on the phrase that seem to me as inevitable as they are obvious. The first is that its establishment of the tonic within its first four measures is not at all a simple expression of the tonic triad but one in which the tonic-defining opening interval is immediately and strongly colored by its continuation implying

VI (bar 2), articulating the progression I–VI en route to V as early as possible. Second, the entire first phrase (bars 1–6) forms an intervallic and motivic sequence whose components and derivations from them will have a pervasive importance for the course of the movement. Third, the internal formulation of the phrase exhibits a high degree of sequential differentiation, in such a way that no two of its measures or subphrases are identical in their rhythm, just as no two subphrases are identical in length, shape, or even point of attack within the measure. Nor do all statements of the motive, as expressly grouped in the autograph, show exactly the same phrasing. At the four main statements of the opening phrase (bars 1, 13, 152, 254), the articulation varies not only from one to another but even between Vcl and Pfte, though this may not have held fast in the later version of the copy; and both curious and suggestive is the appearance of the phrasing  only *after* its exploration in the development.

One consequence of such subtlety of articulation in the opening phrase is the sense it conveys of the slow unfolding of connected motives within the linear stream, an impression enhanced by the continuity of the Vcl sonority, the entirely nonpercussive legato of its phrasing, the dynamics *p* and *dolce*, the emphatic *ma non tanto* after the tempo marking, and even the time-honored performance practice, familiar to every cellist, by which the first four measures are fingered entirely on the Vcl G-string rather than crossing from G- to D-string on the rising fifth (a–e)—a procedure parallel to the G-string opening of the first movement of Op. 59, No. 1, bars 1–2.

As for the genesis of the opening phrase, the full details of its development will have to await the full presentation of the sketches; but two of them are nevertheless sufficiently clear and sufficiently important to warrant discussion here. These are the sketches listed earlier as sources *F* and *G*. Although I regard them as representing a stage well beyond the earliest jottings for the movement, their versions of the opening clearly predate and anticipate that of the autograph in an enlightening degree. And in considering them, it ought to be kept strongly in mind that the opening phrase of this movement is, by the time of the autograph, firmly fixed in its rhythmic and linear form, in comparison to many of its derivations and many other elements of the movement.

EXAMPLE 11

Source F, folio 1r, staves 1-2

*Words after NB are difficult to decipher, and I am indebted to Dr. Hans Schmidt of the Beethoven-Archiv in Bonn for the following suggested interpretation: "NB im 3ten aus S 1."

EXAMPLE 12

Source F, folio 1r, staff 4 (excerpt)

Source *F* (folio 1r) presents a fairly clear consecutive single-staff sketch for the exposition, of which the opening is shown in Example 11. Further down on the same page we find a transformation closer to the final version, which preserves the syncopation of bar 4 but suppresses the internal symmetry of bar 3 (Example 12). From these it is a further step to source *G*, which offers a three-staff composition sketch for the whole of the exposition, and of which the opening up to bar 24 is given in Example 13.

Despite the apparent omission in bar 2, which is evidently due only to Beethoven's working at top speed at the very beginning, the final form of the first phrase is reached. What follows then supplies the basic outline of events to be elaborated in the autograph: the quarter notes at bars 7–9 continue the prevailing units of the opening without the significant diminution that is to be supplied in the left hand; and the cadenza in bar 12 is given only as a flourish of the pen. But the fundamental material and the basic procedures of the opening, including the instrumental exchange and the expansion of its range, are all but fully presented, although the finer details have yet to be worked out. In connection with the first sketch given here, from source *F*, it might be noted that its resolution to e at bar 6 explicitly provides a resolution in the same register as the d in bar 3, which in the final version remains undisplaced in its own octave. The source *F* version anticipates therefore the registral rearrangement which was outlined by Schenker in his analysis of this phrase,[56] an analysis laden with implied subtleties that cannot be taken up here beyond noting a few details. The inferred a♯ and consequent vi$^{\sharp 3}$ of bar 2 in Schenker's analysis clearly results from the explicit presence of this harmony at the corresponding place in the recapitulation, bar 154. While this helps to strengthen his further reduction of this analysis through two more levels, it nevertheless obscures a distinction critical to the foreground of the movement, in which the difference between the totally linear i–vi of the first phrase and the triplet-accompanied and accordingly harmonized i–vi$^{\sharp 3}$ of the recapitulation is more than a mere detail. Indeed, it could be argued that the combination of Vcl theme and Pfte triplets at bar 152 ff. not only reinforces the structural functions of the opening of the recapitulation, but that the whole course of events in the movement from bar 1 to bar 152 forms a process of development from a first expression of the basic thematic material to a more complex expression of it—from purely linear to linear-contrapuntal, from partial harmonic ambiguity (bars 1–3) to resolution of ambiguity (bars 152–154).

[56] Schenker, *Der Freie Satz,* Fig. 109e2.

EXAMPLE 13

Source G, folio 1v, staves 1-9 (bars 1-24)

*E and d perhaps present as faint traces in Vcl, bar 3/1–2.
†Lowest note of l.h. written a step lower.

EXAMPLE 13 (*continued*)

To scrutinize the exposition in the light of its opening phrase and with an eye for connections is to see a significant influence of that phrase on the contour or rhythmic form of every primary motivic idea introduced en route at important structural junctures. Without quoting elaborately, which should not be necessary, such connections ought to be visible enough at the following points: bar 25, Pfte right hand (the brief tonicization of A minor on the way to the preparation of the dominant area of the exposition), where the relationship is obviously one of contour; bars 38–45, Pfte, the arpeggiated portion of the "second group," whose final version reveals, as mentioned earlier, a virtually complete rhythmic identity with the opening phrase; also bar 89, Vcl, in which the characteristically compressed "closing theme" is given close motivic associations with the opening of the first phrase, expanding its opening interval to a minor sixth but maintaining the element of rhythmic association.

In the development, new treatment of the initial motivic material results, as Schenker observed,[57] in new formulations that are open to elaborative possibilities of a new kind. The principal figures are shown in Example 14.

EXAMPLE 14

Figure a is the primary unit of articulation throughout the development, significant especially as the element linking the two parallel passages, in f♯ minor and c♯ minor (bars 107–114 and 127–136), that furnish the main balancing areas in the whole section. Figure b appears in this form at bars 140–143 and 144–147 as the last new figure in the development and in effect the last new motivic unit in the movement. Its associations are complex: in rhythm and partial contour it connects with bars 95–98 at the inception of the development, while it associates through contour alone with bars 25–26, the A-minor area of the exposition. The special effect of bars 140–144 seems to derive from the simultaneous coordination of several factors: the progressive augmentation of prevailing metrical subdivisions in the second half of the development (note, for example, sixteenths at bars 115–126; return of triplets at bars 127–136; eighths at bars 137–139; half notes at bars 140–147, and at last the whole-note augmentation at bars 148–151 just prior to the return); the elaboration of the initial rising fifth of the movement through unison and octave imitation in which its bar 1 combines with bar 2 when used in this form, taking advantage of the contrapuntal possibility that is carefully worked out in sketches and in the autograph itself (Example 15).

57 Schenker, *Der Freie Satz,* Anhang, No. 128, 5a; text-volume, p. 169, Section No. 273.

EXAMPLE 15

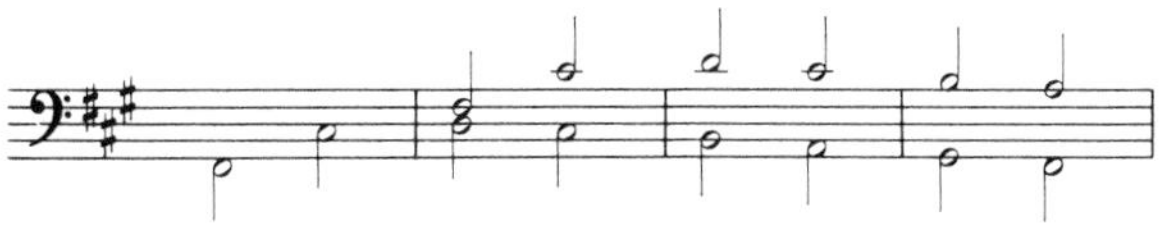

Of this, a later consequence is the Vcl augmentation at bars 240–243 and again that at bars 244–251; also the final imitation of this type (Vcl and Pfte left hand) at bars 270–272, elaborating this combination for the last time in the movement.

The last aspect to be considered is that which capitalizes on use of range. Here, too, a few words must stand for a great deal, and it should not be surprising that the same points of major structural articulation appear once again. The initial feature of greatest importance here is the expansion of range which follows upon the specific restriction of the opening phrase to the Vcl in low register. In the course of bars 1–24, the first large segment of the whole exposition, two expansions of range occur: 1) in bars 1–12, the Vcl contour woven around the single octave E–e builds to the four octaves separating the Vcl E from the Pfte high point first reached at bar 10. Crucial to this procedure is the persistence of the Vcl E in bars 6–12 as bass to the Pfte, and corroboration of its importance is provided by the complete linear exploration of that range, once established, via the four-octave descent of the Pfte in the cadenza at bar 12; 2) at bars 13–24, the opening material is restated in the three lower octaves of the total span, then, as the Vcl joins it, it expands to the same four-octave span once again at bar 24.

Of the innumerable ways in which such a movement capitalizes on links and associations of register, I can only allude to a few, especially those that form prominent parallels to the procedure established in bars 1–12, with its direct expansion of range, from a limited sector to the whole spectrum, as part of a single larger phrase. This sort of range-expansion links the opening with the "second subject" at bars 38–45, the Vcl rising in linear scale-steps through two and a half octaves while the Pfte descends simultaneously through three; the rapid exchange of rising and falling scale-patterns (in triplet diminution) at bars 79–82; the range-expansion from two to four octaves within four measures at bars 95–98; and, most important of all, the parallel upward expansion (in *pp*) at bars 140–143 and 144–147 —now moving up from low point to high point through four octaves again within four measures, and now bringing each successively articulated octave in each new measure, owing to the imitation.

With this much seen of this mode of association throughout the movement, we can turn back at last to the autograph, the main subject of this discussion. At the beginning I alluded to the clear and uncanceled state of the first page (bars 1–17), the serenity of which assures us firmly that it had reached a definite and virtually final state. From what we have seen of the first phrase it could be argued that not only its general character but its motivic construction is suggested by the broad physical spacing of bars 1–5 across the first system, which forms an example of what Paul Mies has called Beethoven's "hörmässige Schreibart"[58]—his "auditory method of writing." What Mies is referring to is visible in many aspects of Beethoven's musical handwriting, which can be seen as a means of notation whose graphic properties mirror the spatial and organizational properties of their musical contents and even suggest something of their appropriate style of performance. Similarly impressive is the immense space accorded the descending Pfte cadenza in the third system of folio 1r, which occupies as much space in its system as four measures do in the preceding systems. Spatial too is the grouping of triplets in the transition to the dominant in the exposition: one observes on folio 2r in the second system the relatively close crowding of the Pfte triplets at bar 35 and the expanded space accorded the Vcl repetition (*with its change of mode*) at bar 36, as if to imply a slight broadening-out as the dominant of E is prolonged prior to resolution at bar 38; if this seems doubtful, consult folio 6r for a precisely similar spacing in the corresponding measures in the recapitulation. Beams and slurs play equally prominent roles, as Schenker insisted long ago; witness the long arching slur over the entire Pfte phrase at bars 51–54 (2v/system 2) and slurs at later passages, including bars 140–148 (both instruments), 175–182 (Vcl), 188–195 (Pfte), and in the coda throughout the last two pages.

[58] Mies, p. 51.

Brief and scattered as these examples may be, they nevertheless reinforce what ought by now to be a widely acknowledged truism, namely that in musical masterpieces the means of organization of content and the means of expressing that organization in graphic form are bound up with one another in the closest possible way. While the very publication of this manuscript ought ideally to give rise to intensive study of both aspects of this work, one may also hope that it will stimulate the publication of many more comparable primary sources of works of this caliber, whose preservation could not be better served than by this means of renewal.

APPENDIX I

Some Physical Features of the Autograph Manuscript of Beethoven's Opus 69, First Movement

Paper. Nine leaves, uniform size and type. Oblong format, average size of page, 21.5 × 31.5 cm. Sixteen staves per page. Gatherings: folios 1–4; 5–8; 9 attached to second gathering. Watermark: letters (cut off at upper edge) with fleur-de-lis surmounting shield with oblique band (left to right). Apparently identical to the watermark described by Dagmar Weise as belonging to the paper used for the "Pastoral Symphony" sketchbook (source *C*). This further corroborates the musical connection between the autograph and this sketchbook described earlier.

Writing and Implements. With the trivial exception of the penciled folio numberings, all the writing in the MS appears to be in Beethoven's own hand, to judge from comparative evidence and from special studies such as M. Unger, *Beethoven's Handschrift.* The two folio numberings are in pencil, one in the upper right-hand corner (recto only), the other in both lower left- and right-hand corners ("1" and "1a" for recto and verso). The main musical content is written throughout in brownish ink with occasional use of a darker black ink to make complex corrections more prominent. Folios 1v, 2r–v, and 3r–v also show the use of red pencil (Emily Anderson called it "Beethoven's famous red pencil, of monstrous size"), partly to add new notational elements as corrections and partly to write over certain elements either crossed out or preserved and made more prominent. The special meaning of the red-penciled wavy lines on folio 2r is discussed on p. 49. It should be mentioned that the corresponding wavy lines on folio 6v are in brown ink, not red pencil. On his use of the red pencil, see A. Tyson, "The Text of Beethoven's Op. 61," *Music and Letters*, XLIII (1962), and Beethoven's note to his publisher Haslinger (1818?), Anderson No. 925: "You are requested to send red pencils for marking . . ."

Heading of the MS. The heading on folio 1r is all in ink, with no over-writing visible. In dark ink: 1) "ma non tanto" in large letters, canceled; 2) "Violoncello" and "piano" at left of Vcl staff. All other words in the heading are in lighter ink of fairly uniform quality. I interpret the mixture of words and cancellations in the heading as follows: Beethoven apparently began by writing "Son" (for "Sonata") at the upper left, but realized almost at once that he would leave himself no room to insert the tempo marking in its usual place at the upper left-hand corner. So he canceled "Son" and wrote

"All°." Later he must have decided to change "Allegro" to "Allegro ma non tanto" and so added these three additional words in bold strokes and dark ink. At a still later stage he may have been disturbed by the discrepancy in appearance between "Allegro" and the remainder, so he canceled the bold strokes and squeezed in the same words in smaller writing above them. With the tempo markings and cancellations occupying the upper left-hand area, the upper middle and right-hand side is now the place for the title of the work and his signature in German script: "Sonate für Piano und Violonzell von LvBthwn." (On his signature see Unger, *Beethoven's Handschrift*, p. 15 f.; and Anderson, I, 20, who notes that in early letters he "frequently signs his name in abbreviated forms of this type.") Compare his signature in the right-hand margin of folio 6r.

Words and Letters Inserted in the Autograph (excluding dynamic and expression markings). As previously, each reference is in terms of folio/staff/bar number.

1v/5–6/1: "in 8va"
1v/5/2: "loco"
2v/9/3: "h"
3r/1–2/3: "pizz"
3r/ bet. 8 and 9: "arco" [?]
3r/12/ below 3: "l.h." [*linke Hand*]
3r/14–15/1: "16tel/ in 8en"/"col Violoncell in 8 [a]"
3v/5/3: "e f g a h c d e f g a h"
3v/6/2: "d e g"
3v/14/1: "8——loco"
4v/1/1 and 2: "F"; "F"
4v/3/2,4; 4v/7/2: "siml"
4v/9/3; 4v/11/1: "siml"
4v/below 16/2–3: "c h a g a fis" followed by "f f a a"; at end of st. 16: "e"
4v/10/2: "g e g e" (canceled)
4v/10/4: "f a f"
4v/13/1: "a"
4v/14/2: "e e"
5r/5–6/3: "in 8~~~~~~"
5r/9–10/1–5: "in 8~~~~~~"
5r/10/1,5: "siml"
5r/13–14/1: "loco" (canceled)
5v/10/1: "loco"
6r/6/ r. margin: "e"
6r/7/ r. margin: signature "LvBthwn"
6r/below 8/4: letter "F" superimposed upon letter "h"
6r/11/3: "in 8en"
7r/7/2: "g"
7r/7/3: "h g a"
7v/below 8/3: "l.h. col Vcllo in 8va"
7v/11/1: "in 8ven"
8r/1/1: "a h c d e f g a h"
8r/9–10/1: "in 8——loco"
8v/below 5/1–2: "g h a g a e"
8v/10, 11, 14, 15: "siml"
9r/1–2/2: "a"

On the use of the letters "Vi–de" throughout the MS, see pp. 40–42 of this commentary and Unger, *Beethoven's Handschrift*, p. 17.

APPENDIX II

Relationship of Sources for Opus 69: A Provisional Stemma

Note: a dotted line indicates possible chronological order; a continuous line indicates definite chronological order and possible derivation.

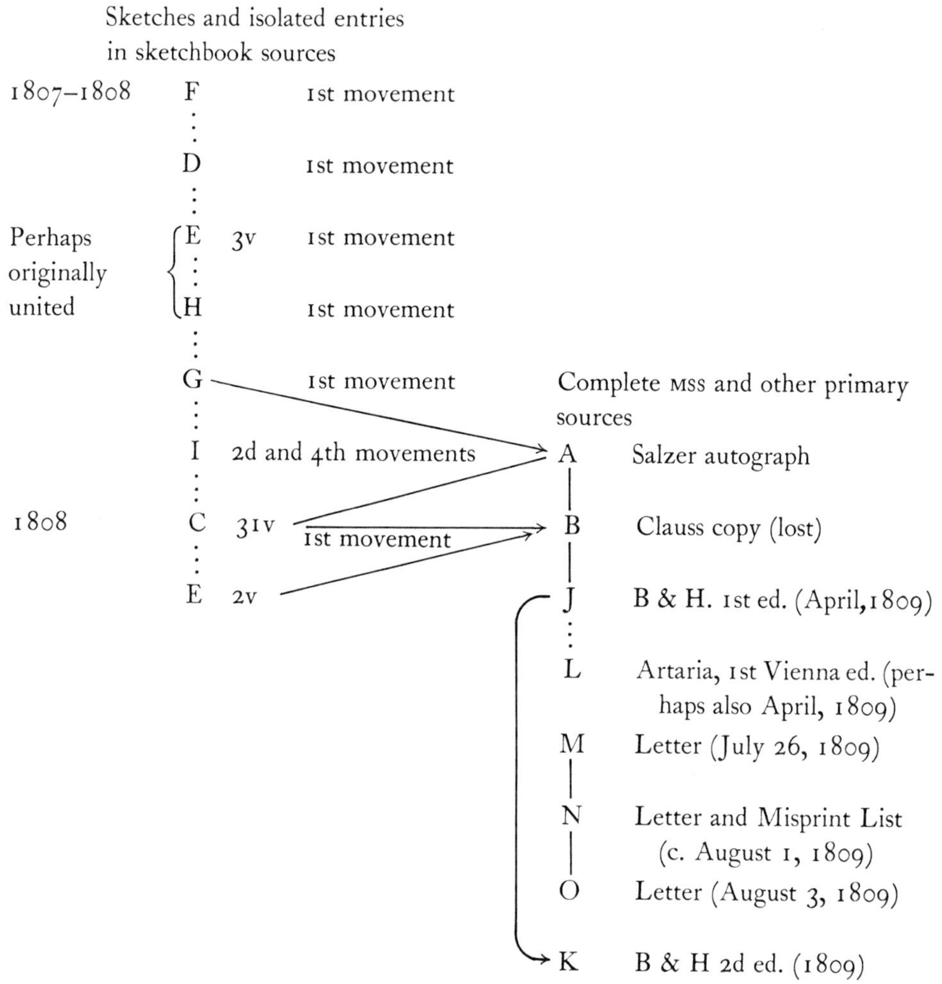

APPENDIX III

Use of Additional Staves in the Autograph

Note: *A* means used as alternative; *R* means as replacement. See pages 42–43.

1r: None.
1v: None.
2r: None (at 2r red pencil and ink corrections go into extra staff below; there is evidently no concern here to save space).
2v: None.
3r/8: St. 8 as Vide *A* for Pfte r.h. in st. 10.
3r/12: St. 12 as Vide *A* for Pfte l.h.; marked "l.h." to clarify.
3r/16: St. 16 as Vide *R* at bar 2 for clarification of Pfte l.h. on st. 15; and again at bar 4 to replace Pfte r.h. on st. 14.
3v/8: St. 8 used for bar 1 to sketch in later version of Vcl figure.
3v/12: St. 12 used to sketch in later version of Pfte l.h. on st. 11, bar 1 (Vide *A*); and again in the same way at st. 11, bar 3.
4r/12: St. 12 as Vide *R* for Pfte l.h. on st. 11, for change of octave only.
4v/4: St. 4 as Vide *R* for Vcl on st. 5/1–3; also revises within st. 4.
4v/8: St. 8 as Vide *R* for Vcl on st. 9/4.
4v/12: St. 12 as Vide *R* for Vcl on st. 13/2–4.
4v/16: St. 16 as Vide *R* for Pfte r.h. on st. 14/2–4, and revises heavily within st. 16.
5r/4: Vide *R* for Pfte r.h. on st. 2/1–3.
5r/8: Vide *R* for Vcl on st. 9/2–5.
5r/12: Vide *R* for Pfte r.h. on st. 10/1–5.
5r/16: Vide *R* for Pfte r.h. on st. 14/3–4.
5v/4: Vide *R* for Pfte r.h. on st. 2/1–4 *and also* for sketch for Pfte l.h. on st. 3/5–7.
5v/12: Vide *R* for Pfte r.h. on st. 10/5.
6r: None.
6v: None.
7r/12: St. 12 as replacement for Vcl figuration on st. 13/2–3.
7v/8: St. 8 as alternative to Pfte r.h. at st. 6/3.
7v/12: St. 12, continuing st. 8; alternative for Pfte r.h. at st. 10/1 (cf. fol. 3r/st. 8–12).
7v/16: Clarification of Pfte r.h. at st. 14/1.
8r: None.
8v: None.
9r/16: Clarification of Pfte r.h. at st. 14/5.
9v/8: New version of Pfte r.h. at st. 6/1–3.

APPENDIX IV

A Provisional List of Variants in the Autograph of Opus 69 (excluding variants discussed in text)

Note: Aut = autograph; GA = Gesamtausgabe.

Bar	
1	Time signature "C" in all staves (GA has "¢"); early editions are inconsistent.
12	Pfte: cadenza has no ♮ before a in descent (see Beethoven's own misprint list in Appendix V).
13–16	Vcl: in octaves with Pfte in Aut (sketch handwriting).
18	Vcl: an octave too high in Aut even with treble clef implying pitch an octave lower, as it does throughout the MS.
19	Vcl: "dolce" in Aut.
21	Pfte l.h., third quarter: three-note chord (from bottom, c♯–e–a) in Aut.
23–24	Vcl: below its notes has "in 8va . . . . ." with "loco" at bar 24. The Vcl notation at bars 18–22 had been treble clef implying pitch an octave lower; in bar 24, if not changed, it would involve too many ledger lines in cadenza; accordingly, bar 23 is clarified for the sake of the "loco" in bar 24.
24	Aut has neither "ad libitum" as in GA nor any other verbal additions. Note too that "6" appears only over the second group of sixteenths in the Vcl cadenza.
27/1–3	Pfte: lower octave A crossed out.
28/1	Pfte: lower octave A crossed out.
29/1–2	Pfte: lower octave B's crossed out in favor of low B only.
30/4	Pfte, r.h.: repetition sign for fourth quarter note omitted from Aut; phrasing for l.h. not in GA.
31–34	Vcl: two stages in Aut, first an octave lower than second, in bars 31–32/3 and 33/2–34/3.
45/4–46/1	Pfte: I interpret the l.h. as simply a quarter rest crossed out by a swirling motion—not as a string of notes.
47/4	Vcl: apparent erasure below last eighth-note in measure is simply rubbing of red pencil from facing page.

Bar

47/4 Pfte: last f♯ in measure correctly notated with natural plus sharp, to cancel previous double-sharp in measure; but in the apparently identical preceding measure Beethoven had forgotten to cancel the double-sharp; or is it possible that the two measures are not identical?

48/1 Vcl: erroneous repetition of d♯ canceled.

49 Pfte: heavily inked c♯ evidently added later.

51 Vcl: no slur in Aut.

53 Pfte: double sharp written over what appears to be f♯ eighth-note followed by canceled g♯ eighth-note.

54 Pfte, l.h.: has rhythm of half note followed by quarter note, not dot.

55–56 Pfte: both hands in octaves in Aut.

56 Vcl: correction made to bring Vcl into conformity with Pfte at bar 43.

58–59/1 Vcl: neither reading in Aut contains connecting eighth-notes for Vcl at end of bar 58.

62 Vcl: first note in Aut is quarter, not eighth-note; eighth rest and sharp crossed out on beats immediately following first note.

63 Pfte, r.h.: overlaid with red pencil for emphasis.

77 Pfte: marking below l.h. in bar 1 is *ff*.

81 Pfte: triplet gone over heavily and note-names written in below: "d e g."

94b Pfte: second ending has only octave e's in Aut.

152 Pfte and Vcl: *fp* is written over *p* in both parts. Only Vcl has "dolce," corresponding to bar 1.

155 Pfte: has "vi–de" correction of first two triplets.

155/4–156 Pfte, l.h.: rests until bar 156/4; in GA supports Vcl an octave higher.

157–163 Pfte, l.h.: repeats E octaves (parallel to bars 19 ff.); in GA has triplets with r.h. throughout.

161/4 Vcl: has two eighth-notes instead of dotted eighth and sixteenth (c.f. bars 10, 22).

163 Vcl: no verbal indications over cadenza (as at bar 24).

167/4 Pfte: complex set of changes, of which the last visible reading produces the explicit "e" in the r.h. against the explicit "f" (changed from "h") in l.h.; both of these are confirmed by the letters written in. To this Beethoven adds his signature in the r. margin as an indication to the copyist that the dissonant reading is his true intention.

168–169 Vcl: dynamic in bar 168 was originally *f* with "cresc" written in over it. The same is found in the Pfte part at bar 168.

169/4–170/1 Pfte l.h.: doubles r.h. an octave lower (see GA reading).

Bar

171/4–172/1 Vcl: f-triplet instead of GA reading (c–b–a–e).

183–184 Pfte: originally in l.h. reading was $\substack{a\\d}$ moving to $\substack{a\\a}$; changed to d–a an octave higher. Originally an initial eighth rest in r.h. in each measure.

186/3 Pfte: f♯ added later (cf. bar 49).

190 Pfte: last four eighth-notes in l.h. are b♯–c♯–e–c♯ (e canceled and replaced by a); GA has earlier reading!

191 Vcl: low e changed to quarter notes rising an octave; put entirely in upper octave in GA reading.

192 Erased scale in Vcl was apparently the result of momentary lapse, immediately corrected.

196–197 Vcl: group of three eighth-notes leading to each first beat is added later to each measure.

218 Pfte, l.h.: triplet was originally c♯–e–a, changed to g♮–a–c♯.

224–225 Pfte: no dynamic markings on trills.

230–231 Vcl: a slur over each measure, not over both.

238–239 Vcl: revision results from double change of octave, pitch sequence remaining in each case the same.

238–250 Pfte, l.h.: in Aut not yet elaborated into final continuous eighth-note figures.

240–250 Vcl: first reading an octave higher than final reading as given in GA.

253 Vcl: originally had  .

257 Vcl: earlier reading appears to have been written a step too low, then clarified by thickening of note heads up to correct pitches. The problem of notes apparently written a step too low is rampant throughout many of the sketchbooks.

270 Pfte: original reading brought back in r.h. the motive earlier introduced at bars 140–141 and subsequently suppressed there. See text, pp. 80–81.

278 Pfte, r.h.: originally had four quarter notes: a–f♯–e–$\substack{g\sharp\\d\\b}$.

APPENDIX V

Beethoven's Correspondence on the Text of Opus 69

Source *M.* Letter to Breitkopf and Härtel of July 26, 1809 (Anderson No. 220). German text from E. Kastner, *Briefe*, No. 222 (translation given in text, p. 36). This excerpt begins the second paragraph of the letter.

Hier eine gute Portion Druckfehler, auf die ich, da ich mich mein Leben nicht mehr bekümmere um das, was ich schon geschrieben habe, durch einen guten Freund von mir aufmerksam gemacht wurde (nämlich in der Violoncellsonate). Ich lasse hier dieses Verzeichnis schreiben oder drucken und in der Zeitung ankündigen, dass alle diejenigen, welche sie schon gekauft, dieses holen können. Dieses bringt mich wieder auf die Bestätigung der von mir gemachten Erfahrung, dass nach meinen von meiner eigenen Handschrift geschriebenen Sachen am richtigsten gestochen wird. Vermutlich dürften sich auch in der Abschrift, die Sie haben, manche Fehler finden; aber bei dem Übersehen übersieht wirklich der Verfasser die Fehler.

Source *N.* Letter and misprint list (undated; Anderson dates both items "Vienna, August 1, 1809," on the basis of internal evidence). See Plates II and III.[59]

Letter

Here are the misprints in the violoncello sonata. Czerny [Traeg?][60] has corrected them in the copies which he still possessed. By the next post I will send the song I promised you and perhaps a few more songs as well. You can do what you like with them.

In haste
Beethoven

59 Earlier publication of letter or list, or both: Frimmel, *Beethoven-Handbuch*, II, 187 (wrongly dated "11 August"); Kalischer, No. 449 (misprint list only, wrongly assigned to the year 1815, which in turn was followed by Tovey in the Augener edition); Fritz Prelinger, ed., *Sämtliche Briefe und Aufzeichnungen* (Vienna and Leipzig, Stern, 1907–1911), No. 1252 (letter only); Emerich Kastner, ed., *Sämtliche Briefe* (Leipzig, Hesse, 1910), No. 228 (letter only); Emerich Kastner, ed., *Sämtliche Briefe* (new edition by Julius Kapp; Leipzig, Hesse and Becker, 1923), No. 204 (letter only); MacArdle–Misch, *New Beethoven Letters*, No. 65 (letter only); Anderson No. 221 (letter and misprint list); Unger, *Zeitschrift fur Musik*, CII (1935), 635–42, 744–50 (second part quotes all correspondence on Op. 69 in full and lists errors; except that Unger did not have access at this time to the earliest editions, his commentary is the most complete to date).

60 All earlier editors of this letter read this name as "Czerny," but Anderson reads it as "Traeg."

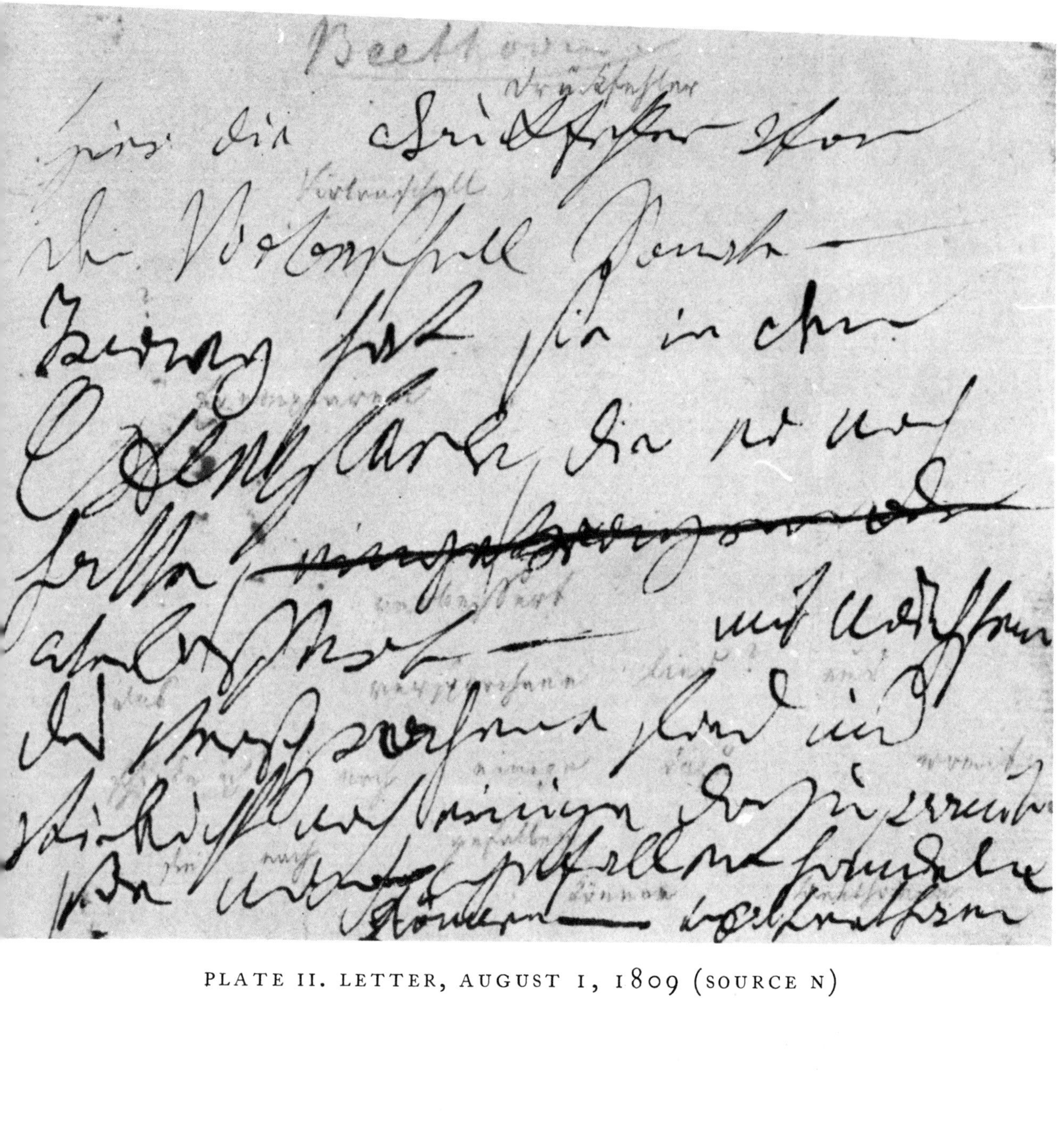

PLATE II. LETTER, AUGUST 1, 1809 (SOURCE N)

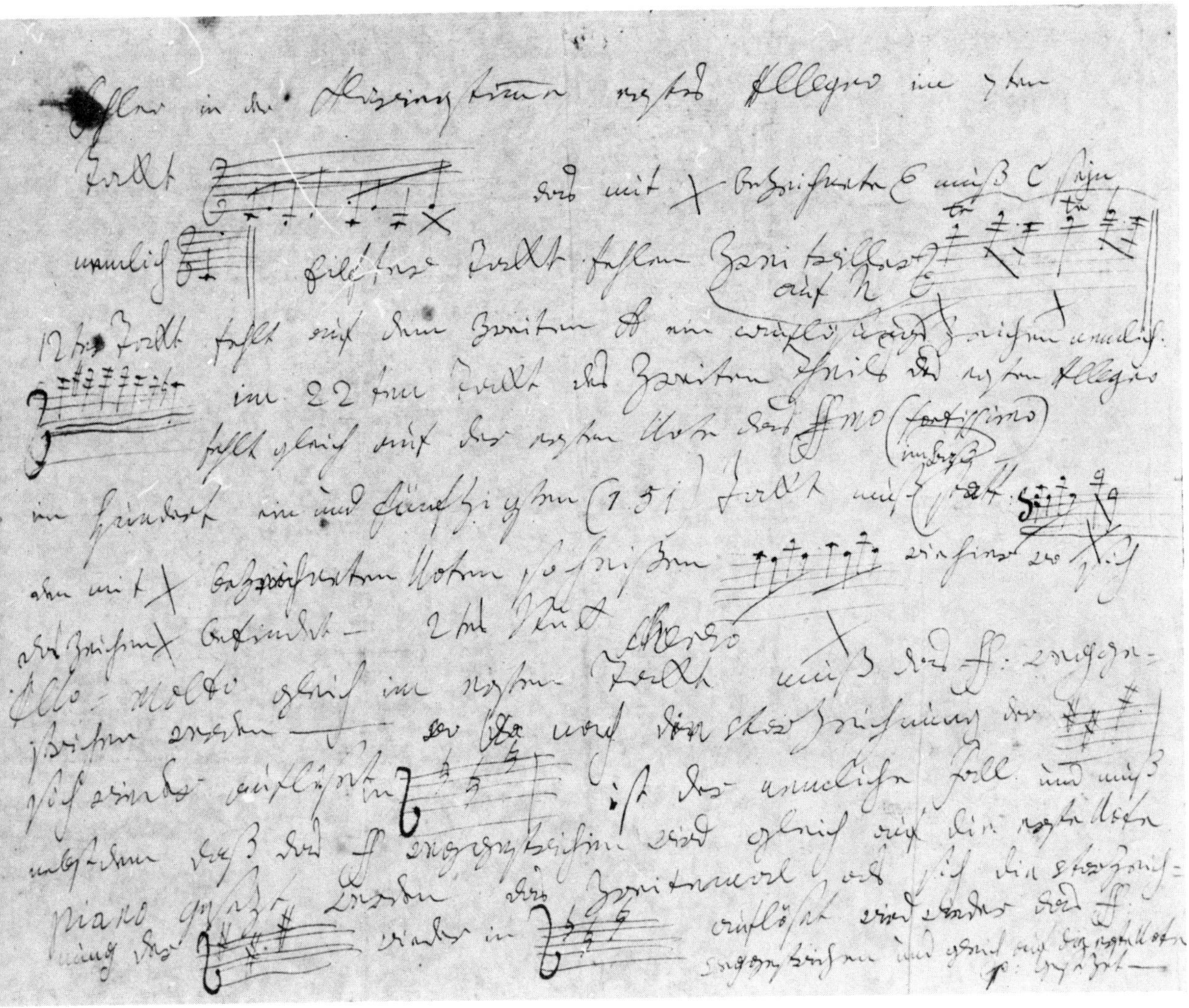

PLATE III. MISPRINT LIST (SOURCE N)

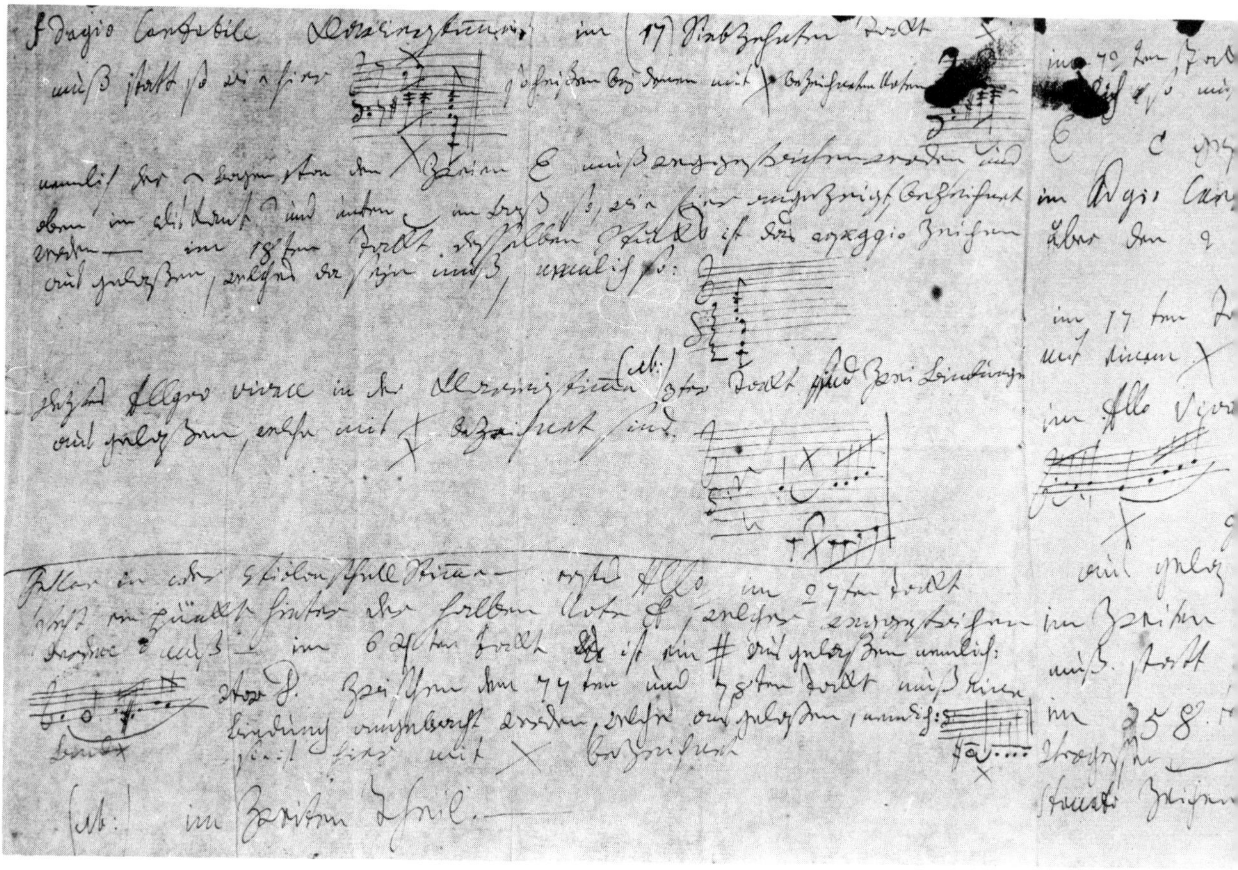

PLATE III (*continued*)

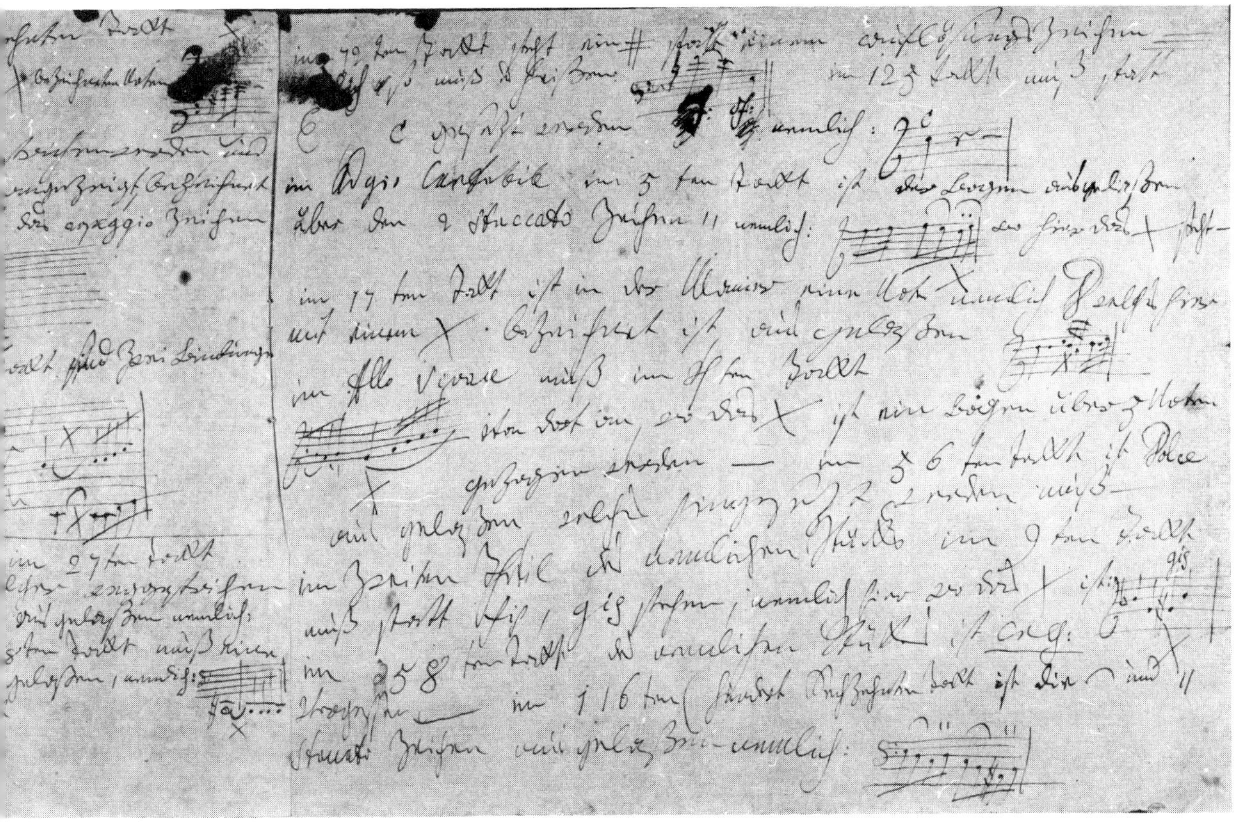

PLATE III (*continued*)

Misprint List

["Ex." in brackets indicates a musical example. The examples are given in the translation which follows.]

Fehler in der Klavierstimme.

[1] Erstes Allegro im 7ten Takt [Ex.] das mit x bezeichnete E muss c sejn, nemlich [Ex.].

[2] Eilfter Takt fehlen zwei triller auf h [Ex.].

[3] 12ter Takt fehlt auf dem zweiten A ein Auflösungszeichen, nemlich [Ex.].

[4] Im 22ten Takt des zweiten Theils des ersten Allegro fehlt gleich auf der ersten Note das ffmo (fortissimo).

[5] Im Hundert ein und fünfzigsten (151) Takt muss (im Bass) statt [Ex.] der mit x bezeichneten Noten so heissen [Ex.] wie hier, wo sich das Zeichen x befindet.

2tes Stück. Scherzo Allo molto.

[6] Gleich im ersten Takt muss das ff weggestrichen werden.

[7] Wo da nach die Vorzeichnung der [Ex.] sich wieder auflöset [Ex.] ist der nemliche Fall und muss nebst dem dass das ff weggestrichen wird gleich auf die erste Note piano gesezt werde.

[8] das zweitemal als sich die Vorzeichnung der [Ex.] wieder in [Ex.] auflöset, wird wieder das ff weggestrichen und gleich auf die erste Note p gesezet.

Adagio Cantabile. Klavierstimme.

[9] Im (17) Siebzehnten Takt muss statt so wie hier [Ex.] so heissen bej denen mit x bezeichneten Noten [Ex.] nemlich der ⌒ Bogen von den zwene E muss weggestrichen werden und oben im Diskant ⌒ und unten ‿ im Bass so, wie hier angezeigt, bezeichnet werden.

[10] Im 18ten Takt desselben Stücks ist das arpeggio Zeichen ausgelassen, welches da sejn muss, nemlich so [Ex.].

Letztes Allegro vivace in der Klavierstimme.

[11] (NB) 3ter Takt sind zwei Bindungen [Ex.] ausgelassen, welche mit $\frac{x}{x}$ bezeichnet sind.

Fehler in der Violonschell Stimme.

[12] Erstes Allegro im 27ten Takt steht ein Punkt hinter der halben Note A, welcher weggestrichen werden muss.

[13] Im 64ten Takt ist ein ♯ ausgelassen nemlich [Ex.] vor D.

[14] Zwischen dem 77ten und 78ten Takt muss eine Bindung angebracht werden, welche ausgelassen, nemlich: [Ex.] sie ist hier mit x bezeichnet.

[15] (NB) im zweiten Theil, im 72ten Takt steht ein ♯ statt einem Auflösungszeichen—nemlich so muss es heissen [Ex.].

[16] Im 125 Takt muss statt E c gesetzt werden nemlich [Ex.].

[17] Im Adagio Cantabile im 5ten Takt ist der Bogen ausgelassen über den 2 Staccato Zeichen ꞌ ꞌ nemlich [Ex.].

[18] Wo hier das x steht, im 17ten Takt ist in der Manier eine Note nemlich D, welches hier mit einem x bezeichnet ist, ausgelassen [Ex.].

[19] Im Allo Vivace muss im 4ten Takt [Ex.] von dort an, wo das x ist ein Bogen über 5 Noten getzogen worden.

[20] Im 56 Takt ist Dolce ausgelassen, welches hingesetzt werden muss.

[21] Im zweiten Theil des nemlichen Stücks im 9ten Takt muss statt fis, gis stehen, nemlich hier, wo das x ist [Ex.].

[22] Im 58ten Takt des nemlichen Stückes ist *c r s* vergessen.

[23] Im 116ten (hundert Sechzehnten Takt) ist die ⌒ und ꞌ ꞌ Staccato Zeichen ausgelassen nemlich: [Ex.].

Mistakes in the pianoforte part.

[1] In the 7th measure of the first Allegro,

the E marked with x should be C, namely:

[2] In the 11th measure, two trills over B are missing, namely:

[3] In the 12th measure, a natural on the second A is missing, namely:

[4] In the 22d measure of the second part of the first Allegro [bar 115], the *ffmo* (fortissimo) is missing on the very first note.

[5] In the 151st measure (151) in the bass [bar 244], instead of the notes marked with x

there should be

exactly as it is here where the x has been placed.

Second movement. Scherzo Allegro Molto.

[6] In the very first measure, the *ff* should be removed.

[7] Afterwards, when the key signature

is again altered to

the *ff* should again be removed and *p* should be inserted for the very first note

[8] and similarly the second time that the key signature changes, the *ff* should be removed and *p* should be inserted for the very first note.

Adagio Cantabile. Pianoforte part.

[9] In the 17th measure instead of the passage

there should be this passage for the notes marked with x, i.e., the ⌢ slur over the two notes E must be removed and marked above in the treble ⌢ and below in the bass ‿, as has been indicated here.

[10] In the 18th measure of the same movement, the arpeggio mark has been omitted. It should be inserted, i.e., in the following way:

The final movement. Allegro Vivace.

[11] The pianoforte part, NB: in the 3d measure, two ties have been omitted which have been marked with x.

Mistakes in the violoncello part.

[12] In the 27th measure of the first Allegro, there is a dot after the minim A which must be deleted.

[13] In the 64th measure a ♯ before D has been omitted, i.e.,

[14] A tie which has been omitted should be inserted between the 77th and 78th measure, i.e., This has been marked here with x.

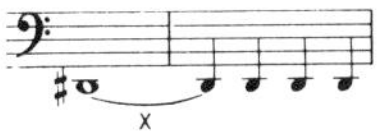

[15] In the 72d measure (NB, in the second half of the movement) [bar 165], there is a ♯ instead of a natural, i.e., it should be thus:

[16] In the 125th measure [bar 218] instead of an E, there should be a C, i.e.,

[17] In the 5th measure of the Adagio Cantabile, the slur has been omitted over the two staccato marks, i.e., where the x is

[18] In the 17th measure, a note, i.e., D, has been omitted in the grace notes. It is marked with an x.

[19] In the Allegro Vivace in the 4th measure from the point where the x has been put, the slur should be drawn over 5 notes.

[20] In the 56th measure, Dolce has been omitted. It should be added.

[21] In the second half of the same movement, in the 9th measure, there should be G sharp instead of F sharp, i.e., where the x has been put.

[22] In the 58th measure of the same movement, Cresc has been forgotten.

[23] In the 116th (one hundred and sixteenth) measure, the ⁀ and staccato marks have been omitted, i.e.,

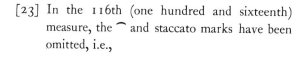

Source *O*. Letter to Breitkopf and Härtel of August 3, 1809.

Lachen Sie über meine autormässige Ängstlichkeit. Stellen Sie sich vor, ich finde gestern, dass ich im Verbessern der Fehler von der Violoncellsonate selbst wieder neue Fehler gemacht habe. Also im Scherzo allegro molto bleibt dieses ff * gleich anfangs wie es angezeigt war und auch die übrigen Male, nur muss im neunten Takt vor die erste Note *piano* gesetzt werden und ebenfalls die beiden anderen Male, beim neunten Takt, wo die ♯ ♯ ♯ sich in ♮ ♮ ♮ auflösen. So ist die Sache. Sie mögen hieraus sehen, dass ich in einem wirklichen solchen Zustande bin, wo es heisst: "Herr, in deine Hände befehle ich meinen Geist!"

* Nämlich wie es anfangs gestanden hat, so ist es recht.

Laugh at my author's anxiety. Imagine, I find that yesterday, in correcting the errors in the violoncello sonata, I myself made new errors. Thus, in the Scherzo allegro molto let this *ff* * remain at the very beginning just as it was indicated, and also the other times—only in the ninth measure should the first note have *piano*, and similarly the other times, at the ninth measure, where the signature ♯ ♯ ♯ resolves to ♮ ♮ ♮. This is the way it should be. You may see from this that I really am in a situation about which one could say, "Lord into Thy hands I deliver my soul!"

* That is, the way it stood in the first place is correct.

Mathematical Aspects of Music

DAVID LOEB

THE ROLE of mathematics in music has expanded rapidly in the past half-century. A system of composition based on numerological procedures is one of the current "mainstream" styles; several theoretical systems have attempted to formulate music mathematically from different viewpoints; the use of statistics is changing musicology. But beyond such applications of mathematics lies a fundamental question: is the basic nature of music mathematical?

The answer depends very much on what one considers music to be. To consider music as ideas expressed in sound and unfolded in time is hardly precise (although generally accepted). Yet even this vague a definition is too restrictive for some people.[1] A comprehensive view of the different styles throughout the history of music might regard them as a succession of linguistic systems, each with its own range of vocabulary and syntax, but this is more useful in consideration of the structure than the nature of music. Ultimately one may settle upon such words as "meaningful" and "coherent" to specify further the types of sounds and ideas to be classified as musical. As each of these terms is worked into a definition, one more segment of the musical world departs in disagreement. The ultimately refined definition will satisfy only its author.

One must also consider what is meant by mathematical. Preciseness of detail or orderly arrangement in sequence does not necessarily constitute use of mathematical procedure. Characteristics such as symmetry or logical simplicity are not necessarily mathematical properties. In a formal structure

[1] *If* one is willing to accept rearranging of park benches or the immersion of a cellophane-wrapped cellist as music, then traditional definitions of music as "organized successions of sounds" or even "well-ordered sets of aural events" are no longer all-inclusive. As one's concepts of music embrace more varied presentations the definition becomes more vague.

such as rondo or A–B–A, the characteristics of symmetry and logical simplicity aid in creating coherence and possibly pleasing sensations of design, but do not make these forms mathematical, any more than the use of visual symmetry and perspective in painting necessarily constitute applications of projective geometry. If such characteristics are exhibited in a complex manner, then one tends to regard them as mathematical properties. It is almost superfluous to point out the impossibility of specifying the degree of complexity at which such characteristics become mathematical.

In addition to subjective definitions, there is also the problem of perception. Aural perception is probably not the sole basis for meaningfulness of mathematical usages or properties in music, but it is the most usable criterion, especially if "inductive" perception is included. The famous "untrained listener" may not consciously perceive the complex mathematical or quasi-mathematical systems that underly musical compositions, but may perceive them intuitively. This is as applicable to *Kunst der Fuge* as it is to Babbitt's *Composition for Four Instruments* or Schoenberg's *Moses und Aaron.* In practice, this intuitive perception seems more frequent with Bach. This may be due to greater aural coherence in the music of Bach or to greater familiarity with the stylistic elements of Bach on the part of listeners. Although the latter possibility cannot be disproved, it seems fair to say that both factors probably operate to some extent. In any case, this intuitive perception gives the listener a sense of form or coherence without his necessarily being able to explain its basis.

Even if sonata form, primary row, or tonal structure goes unnoticed, the listener is not thereby deprived of enjoyment,[2] perhaps not even deprived of comprehension. If such structural features are not perceived on first hearing, the listener may be induced to try again until repeated observation enables the perception to be refined.

The importance of technical elements is frequently unrelated to ease of perception. An example of a relatively unimportant element which is quite prominent occurs in Richard Strauss's *Vier letzte Lieder.*[3] Four solo violins

[2] Enjoyment, or pleasure, is another problematic term. The intellectual pleasure derived from ascertaining technical information mingles in the mind with general esthetic pleasure. The relatedness (or integration) of these two types of pleasure varies with the listener.

[3] "September" (Boosey and Hawkes), pp. 21–24.

are heard quite distinctly and significantly, but actually only duplicate the prevailing harmonies. They do not provide any motivic material, nor does the texture reappear. On the other hand there are such cases as the first four measures of Beethoven's Op. 110, in which the figuration in the last half-measure recapitulates the melody stated in the first three-and-a-half measures, an important element frequently overlooked (see Example 1).

EXAMPLE I

Concealing important elements is an old game, pleasurable within limits, but the game loses its point if even the clues are imperceptible. When this process becomes an attempt to exceed the limits of perception, it does not necessarily endow a composition with musical value. It may, as an attempt to extend our perception, be a useful psycho-acoustic exercise.

MUSIC AS A SEMANTIC SYSTEM

ANY MUSICAL composition contains many elements or aspects which exhibit a fascinating combination of autonomy and interdependence. Melody, harmony, rhythm, sonority, articulation—all have principles of their own; all conform to an inclusive mixture of variety and repetition. The art of organization frequently becomes an element itself. These aspects of a composition have quite different degrees of mathematical property. The components of rhythm are additive, as is also the large-scale organization of rhythmic patterns. Yet for the composer, the effective organization of rhythm is as much a question of understanding the listener as anything else. What else can determine when a particular pattern has been used enough or too much? Construction of melodic ideas seems the least mathematical of all (it includes many of the other elements in constantly varying degrees), although manipulation of these ideas frequently takes the form of mathematical operations. Harmony might be said to have two mathematical aspects, one concerned with acoustical interval ratios and their influence on harmony, the other with attempts to mathematize the succession of harmonic events within a piece. The problems of mathematical aspects of form have already been indicated.

Complexity is not sufficient reason to label music a mathematical system. Nor can one say that music is a mathematical language because numerical or quasi-numerical systems are used in notation. These systems utilize symbols of a mathematical character as a convenience; the use of such symbols does not automatically endow such a system with a mathematical character, nor does it make such a system susceptible to mathematical methods of analysis. Once again, if simple numerical relationships are present (such as doubling, tripling, or halving a tempo at the beginning of a new idea), they do not have to be defined as being mathematical in character. In more complex cases, the question arises whether such relationships are audible as precise *quantifications* (a change from ♩ = 80 to ♩ = 104 will be heard as becoming considerably faster, not as an increase of tempo in the ratio 10:13).

This is not intended to deny that music is put together in an essentially logical fashion (often with psychologically derived premises). The semantic character of music is more realistically described as a metalinguistic system than as a mathematical system. Any style reveals several "vocabularies" operating simultaneously (characteristic patterns of melody, harmony, rhythm, etc., germane to the style under consideration), each with its own syntax (the "rules" for each aspect, associated with the particular style), combined in an intertwining pattern (any of the forms associated with that style) analogous to the various literary genres.[4] Analysis of music on the basis of this approach is subject to the limitations of any kind of semantic

[4] Perhaps even this is an oversimplification. A strong case could be made for a separate system for each composition, or for each composer.

analysis. The chief limitation is that the "meaning" of any single element is to some extent dependent on context (probably much more the case with music than with other semantic systems) as well as place in history. In mathematical terms, it becomes impossible to preassign fixed values to many of the elements. Until and unless mathematics finds methods of dealing with multivalued and often deliberately ambiguous elements, mathematical analysis must be confined to relatively trivial examples, although results even in such simple cases must be considered highly suspect.

Some of these obstacles are most clearly evident in the tonal system. One immediate difficulty would be assigning values of relative importance to chords (for convenience, assume a homophonic piece). In many situations a roughly workable scale might be constructed. It would be far more difficult to index structural importance on a larger scale, considering chordal relations to more remote chords as well as to adjacent chords. Example 2, from the slow movement of Sibelius' Second Symphony,[5] is relatively simple at first glance. However, what level of importance should be attached to the III-chord in the 2/4 measure? It is not only a III-chord, it is also a substitution for a prolonged I-chord (compare with the beginning of the passage). Despite its limited importance, it is easily the most striking harmonic feature of the passage. Another problem is the occurrence of the I-chord as a $\text{I}_{\natural 3}^{4}$ of the final bar. Such problems cannot be ignored; details of this type are an important factor in making compositions beautiful. Psychological expectation and its inverse (unexpected factors) undoubtedly are involved in reactions of this type.

One of the most precious assets of the tonal system is one that is least susceptible to mathematical analysis; this is the ability of an element to project beyond itself, to firmly imply another element (which may or may not actually appear). Single notes can imply a complete harmony; a chord can suggest a chord other than itself.[6] Neither of these phenomena is a rarity. Substitution and implication, used as means of obtaining variety, have helped keep the tonal system alive for more than half a millennium.

One can safely say that non-Western and early Western music are not generally susceptible to mathematical analysis, even though they appear to

[5] Breitkopf and Härtel edition, p. 45.

[6] See Brahms's A-Minor String Quartet, Op. 51, No. 2, 3d movement, bars 9–12, and bar 78.

EXAMPLE 2

be considerably less complex than most later Western music. Post-tonal systems might be susceptible to mathematical analysis given the fact that many of them rely heavily on mathematical construction. For example, if one defines serialism as the totality of the mathematical procedures involved, then not only is such analysis possible, it is relatively easy. If there is more to serial music than the procedures, then the question of analytic susceptibility rests on whatever additional elements there may be.

The foregoing suggests the disadvantages of considering music as a mathematical system. However, the existence of a perceptible rationale behind much, if not all, music, even if only an intuitive rationale, suggests that music can be subjected to some form of logical analysis.[7] The possibilities of a comprehensive semantic analytic system for music have not yet been explored. In addition to practical problems in such analysis, there is the reluctance on the part of most musicians to analyze such intuitive things; appreciation frequently seems more important than analysis.

MATHEMATICS IN THE STUDY OF MUSIC

THE EARLIEST use of mathematics in the study of music was the determination of frequency ratios of intervals; this dates back to Greek searches for expression of numerological perfection in nature. During the Renaissance intonation theory became quite complicated. Elaborate tuning systems were devised; many were adopted for practical use. With the universal adoption of the equal-tempered system,[8] intonation theory ceased to be an active area of inquiry. Interest in interval ratios continued, however, and played an important role in Rameau's theories. His idea of the fundamental bass is clearly inseparable from the concept of deriving the triad from ratios and the overtone series. In most other eighteenth-century theory, the triad (whether meticulously derived or taken for granted) is of *established* importance; it was recognized as one of the essential elements of composition for at least two centuries preceding its own time.

In the nineteenth century, interest turned to philosophic systems, which led to the proliferation of mathematical formulations in the twentieth century. Within such systems, compositions have been analyzed as transformations or extensions of basic structural patterns. Not all such systems are mathematical; Schenker's is not, despite its high degree of organization and complexity. Beyond this, mathematics has been used to devise myriad systems of composition, and more recently to study the communicative aspect of music.

[7] The intuitive mental apparatus that guides one to the proper deductive steps may operate similarly in the understanding of music. The similarity of thought processes seems to explain the frequent occurrence of persons with talents in both fields.

[8] The *theory* of equal temperament developed in the seventeenth and eighteenth centuries, but it is almost certain that some type of equal-tuning must have been in use earlier. Much of the chromatic music from around 1600 could hardly have been performed otherwise.

The idea of defining basic musical entities in mathematical terms is not objectionable, although no one has yet succeeded in creating any really workable "translations."[9] Translation problems arise when relationships between these entities have to be included in the system. Contemporary theory avoids this problem by treating individual elements as independent. This restricts the studies to twentieth-century music in which entities seem to exhibit this type of independence. As the complexity of theoretical systems increases, the models chosen become simpler and more restricted, losing their value as analytic illustrations. Frequently the systems themselves, rather than the compositions they supposedly describe, become the subjects of analysis.

Another large problem concerns "redundancy," which in its scientific sense means some amount of information already presented (and therefore superfluous from the communication viewpoint). In music, "redundancy" is not only desirable, but absolutely necessary in considerable amounts. A piece without it would require a listener to extract every bit of information from each sound in order to comprehend the composition. It is very difficult to quantify precisely the ideal amount for a piece. Composers vary considerably in the amounts of redundancy used. Evaluation can be problematic when one is dealing with an exact repetition of a phrase, section, or movement. This provides considerable vital information concerning the form, but no new information concerning any other aspect of the piece. Quantification is partly subjective, since some people find certain repetitions tedious and others find them interesting.

It is highly unfortunate that whatever useful work exists often gets buried in an avalanche of inferior work containing inaccuracies, misconceptions, and errors of reasoning and calculation, to say nothing of pure sham.[10] But even if these writings are accepted as the growing pains of a new branch of study, how *relevant* are these studies? More specifically, as one reads through them, the level of concentration is one of great detail of things which

[9] This is one of the major problems confronting the application of information theory to musical analysis.

[10] See John Backus' article "*Die Reihe*: A Scientific Evaluation," *Perspectives of New Music*, Vol. I, No. 1 (1962). In commendable manner this article exposes the ludicrous excesses of the first five issues of *Die Reihe* the "Bible" of the avant-garde during the late 1950s and early 1960s. Since the publication of Backus' article, many more writings have appeared in dire need of similar chastisement.

in themselves are details; one somehow never emerges with the feeling that any new insight concerning *music* has been brought forward. Many articles are so laden with linguistic involutions and mathematical apparatus that they seem to cry out for a computer in order that they might be unraveled and made comprehensible to readers without extensive mathematical backgrounds.

It would seem that the basic purpose of music theory, even mathematically oriented theory, is, or should be, the explanation and codification of the principles of musical composition and the nature of musical structure, based on analysis of the existing literature. It is perhaps natural to conjecture how music *could* be conceived and constructed according to predetermined principles, although speculative theory of this type has limited value. As contemporary theory moves closer to systemic perfection and consequently farther from consideration of actual pieces it becomes less relevant. It is not enough to analyze primitive mathematical representations of compositions. In this manner certain contemporary analysts slip into the practice of analyzing systems rather than pieces.

It takes but little imagination to visualize musicians of the twenty-first century looking back on twentieth-century theory as a hopeless tangle of attempts to reduce to mathematics something quite irreducible (and perfectly workable as is), ending up with a dehumanized set of principles and analytic methods having very little to do with the material at hand. Such an evaluation would be the logical successor to our own view of nineteenth-century theory: a condescending and patronizing glance at the massive overdose of Hegelian reasoning before dismissing it as unusable.

Theory must concern itself with the music of all periods. Unlike science, in which most earlier work is superseded if not actually discarded, musical works of earlier times remain important as long as people still appreciate their vitality and derive a sense of meaning from listening to them. If certain compositions or groups of compositions do not fit into a system, then one has to discard the system, or at least acknowledge its limitations; this is far more realistic than disregarding large numbers of compositions.

MATHEMATICS IN MUSICOLOGY

ONE of the more important tasks of musicology is to discern stylistic traits in music of different periods. Once hypotheses have been formulated, they can be verified by mathematics. Assertions of the form "in such a case, this or that normally occurs" result from observations of the relevant literature and are based on informal statistical confirmation. Causal observations ("in such a case, this or that occurs because of thus and such") follow the same principle of repeated confirmation. Systemization nearly always arises from such experiences, applied more or less rigorously to the needs at hand. The only advantage offered by more precise use of statistics is greater accuracy; the results can only be as meaningful as the premises and as accurate as the data supplied.

Thus if a musicologist considered the works of one fourteenth-century composer more chromatic than those of another, this might be statistically confirmed by the more frequent occurrence of accidentals in the works of the first composer. However, the result might be dismissed (shortly after publication) by a second musicologist who discovered that the relative absence of accidentals in the works of the second composer resulted from using a B♭ key signature in most of the pieces (thus implying that many of the accidentals found in the works of the first composer would vanish if a key signature were introduced).

More serious problems are raised when one asks how meaningful are percentages of chord occurrences in chorale settings? The importance of a chord of a particular degree is far more likely to be determined by function than by number of occurrences. The principle applies with equal strength to various scale degrees within a melody. The statistically most predominant tone is most likely to be the third or fifth degree of the scale rather than the tonic.

In using statistical analysis one must also be careful that the implications concerning the exceptions to the given principle are examined carefully. If one were to find that 98 percent of the compositions of the eighteenth century began on some form of a tonic chord, one has still learned very little about the other 2 percent. Any conclusions concerning the tonality of the 2 percent would require additional information.

One limitation to the use of statistics in musicology concerns the number of objects under consideration. Statistical studies consider small representative portions of very large numbers of objects which are treated as being uniform for the purpose at hand. (This too can cause trouble on occasion—

seemingly irrelevant factors can invalidate an entire sampling.) The extent of such conditions in musical literature is not vast. Even within aggregates of supposedly similar compositions by a single composer (e.g., the Haydn symphonies, or the fugues of the *Well-Tempered Clavier*), the realm of similarities shrinks to very small proportion upon close examination.

There is another limitation to the application of statistics. The scientist, in studying large numbers of objects (millions and billions for the most part, rather than hundreds), is concerned with percentages and probabilities; the behavior of a single element is usually irrelevant and unpredictable beyond the limit of assigning a probability. But the study of music is very much concerned with the individual elements and their unique aspects. The unique features of a piece are far more likely to influence the "greatness" of a work than the features found in many other pieces. It is just these qualities that fall outside the statistics.

MATHEMATICS IN THE COMPOSITIONAL PROCESS

MATHEMATICAL and quasi-mathematical techniques have been used by composers for over a millennium. For the most part these techniques have been applied to rhythm and meter and to manipulations of melodic ideas. This century has seen application of mathematical techniques to virtually every aspect of composition.

One of the earliest applications of mathematics to rhythm was the use of the rhythmic modes in the thirteenth century. The free and supple chant rhythms were replaced by continuous repetitions of rhythmic cells of two, three, or four notes. Eventually larger shapes were superimposed; the cells were grouped in units of two, three, or four. This very likely was a detail of the evolution of the current system of musical meter. The impulse towards regularity was strengthened further by still larger organizations of units into periods.

All of this operated on an intuitive level, based on additive accumulation reinforced by the innate human sense of even pulse. Actual utilization of techniques that might be considered mathematical involved higher levels of complexity. The most significant examples of this type were the multiple prolation works of composers like Ockeghem and Pierre de la Rue around

1500. Although this school died out fairly quickly, it had the effect of freeing rhythm. Even motoric Baroque rhythms have a definite amount of flexibility and variety within their well-defined basic shapes.

At this time there was also a tendency toward far greater freedom. The Baroque and Classical toccatas and fantasias subdued the regularity of metric flow by use of improvisatory style. The trend continued in the nineteenth century with interruptions of metric flow (Schumann), currents of displaced impulses (Brahms), and near-amorphous tempo variation (Chopin). Yet none of these developments was mathematically conceived.

In the twentieth century the situation changed. Freedom within an elastic structure gave way to freedom from structure. The problem of the twelfth century reappeared: how to organize sounds in time? Once again mathematical solutions were sought. Consciously or unconsciously, new composers used historical solutions. Serialization of rhythmic values is similar to the rhythmic modes in limiting the number of rhythmic possibilities. Complex cross-rhythms and simultaneous differences in tempo and meter (whether resulting from a high degree of organization or from improvisatory or random processes) descend directly from the prolation complexities. The rigidity of such systems may at some future time seem as arbitrary as the rhythmic modes now seem to us, although perhaps this rigidity will lead to a new freedom if we develop the ability to comprehend.

The mathematical techniques involved in melodic treatment have been in use for a very long time. These operations include transposition, inversion, retrogradation, augmentation, diminution, changes of mode, changes of intervals, and fragmentation (mathematics concerns itself with the nature of operations as well as with their use). All of these techniques are still used today except that nontonal composers obviously do not change modes, and do not resort to interval modification as a means of achieving variety. This last is precluded by their styles, which rarely permit any one interval the prominence required to ensure recognition after modification.

Counterpoint could be considered a mathematical art, especially after inspection of various numerical systems designed to teach students safe and easy ways of constructing invertible counterpoint. Historically, contrapuntal technique has been the judicious and artistic selection of intervallic and rhythmic relations between two or more parts consistent with a particular style and with the language of the piece in which counterpoint is employed. These considerations arise out of general musical concepts which were presented above as being semantic rather than specifically mathematical. This is not affected by the fact that mathematical methods have been used to achieve similar results. The dissimilarities arise from the inability of the mathematical methods to provide any assurance of esthetic quality.

In the twentieth century, serial composition has used mathematical technique extensively. The twelve-tone (or dodecaphonic) system designates the twelve notes of the chromatic scale with the numbers 0 to 11. Intervals are determined by subtraction (modulo 12). It is then possible to treat the numbers as a set. A particular set is constructed for a desired composition. Various mathematical operations are performed on the set. The transformations of the set are decoded back into pitches, yielding transformed versions of the original sequence of tones. However, *mere enumeration of pitches does not automatically endow them with numerical properties.*[11] This endowment is taken for granted by serial composers; they assume that tones may be used as isolated entities with relationships determined at the will of the composer, and somehow automatically communicated to the listener. The validity of this depends on whether or not the acoustical properties of intervals assert themselves in such contexts. If they do, then a set (or any more sophisticated algebraic system) is not an accurate representation of pitches, since it would not be able to account for the implications of stability or instability (expressed in "tendencies" toward other intervals) of melodic intervals. This would not rule out the possibility of an accurate mathematical representation, but such a device does not seem to exist at present. Since association undoubtedly plays some part in associations with intervals, no definite conclusions seem possible one way or the other.

[11] Ordinal (designative) numbers rarely have the properties of cardinal (quantitative) numbers. One can, for example, add and subtract intervals, but it means very little. A charming misapplication of ordinal numbers would be to claim that 5th Ave. − 2d Ave. = 3d Ave; however, it would make sense to use the numerical relationship to assume that there are three blocks separating 2d and 5th Aves. Casual experience with New York City soon reveals that even this is not a safe assumption.

Serial technique proceeds from the twelve-tone technique to application of the set operations to elements other than pitch. Choices of possible durations, dynamics, articulations, etc., are assigned numerical values and arranged in series. The series is again transformed, and the permutations are again decoded back into transformed versions of sequences of durations, dynamics, etc. These elements seem not to function in such a way that two versions of a sequence of dynamics or of articulations are likely to be heard in relation to one another. Accomplishing this would require listeners to become as acutely aware of specific values of these elements as they are of intervals or form. The context of relative uniformity that prevails in serial music (despite the use of special effects and extreme registers) is a further obstacle to the development of such perception.

The ultimate value of serial music, however, does not depend on properly or improperly applied mathematics. The tonal system has produced both masterworks and trash; the serial system may yet do the same. Much depends on the ingenuity with which the composer designs the basic set (it can even be constructed so that segments will be transformations of one another), but this alone will not suffice to break the hypnotic effect of sheer technique. Composers seem unwilling to alter lines or rhythms for fear of losing the relation to the set. The changes of intervals or of modes (or the use of ornamental prolongation) have no analogue in serial technique because they rely in part on an environment of previous knowledge on the listener's part. The sense of pleasure that the listener might derive from the use of an operation is more likely to be enhanced than lessened by slight distortions. Without reducing the feeling of identity a new element is added (an important principle of the variations form).

In the two Bach subjects from the Gigue from Partita VI in E Minor (Example 3a), and the C-Major Fugue from the *Well-Tempered Clavier*, Book I (3b), subtle changes add interest. In the Gigue the last four notes of the inversion were placed a third lower than exact application of inversion technique would have placed them, which helps to maintain a solid harmonic framework. The points of harmonic change in the two versions do not coincide, which adds further variety. Absolute purity in the use of operations is neither a virtue nor a defect in itself, but when modified usage

EXAMPLE 3

a)

Subject

Inversion

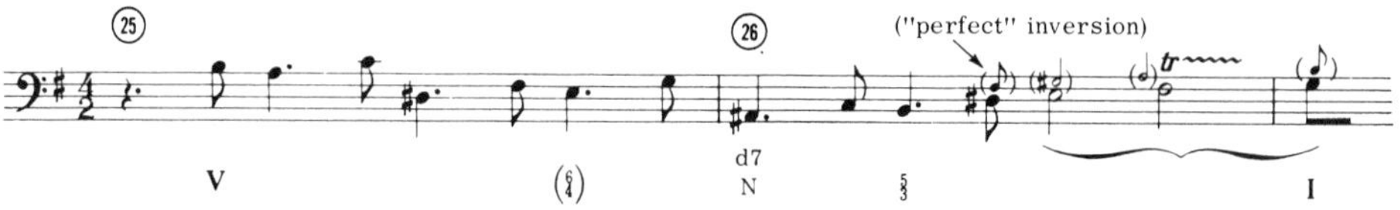

b)

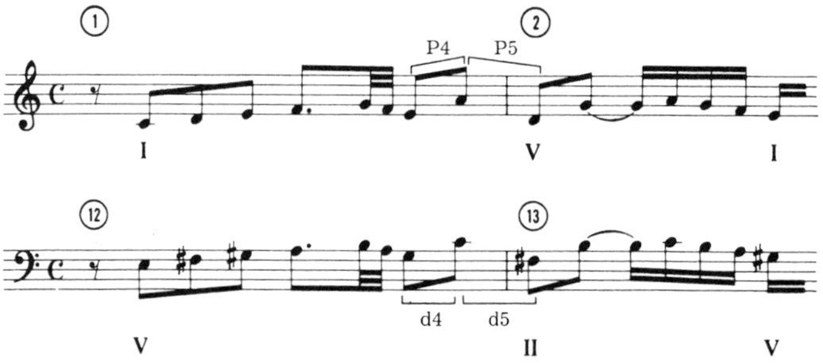

is sacrificed, a significant flexibility disappears.[12] In the Fugue subject, an alteration enables it to be used in the relative minor. A new element is added by the introduction of the diminished fourth and diminished fifth, creating different harmonic implication. All great works in the tonal system have frequent instances of small but telling changes that add inestimable value to the music; serialism and post-serial styles have yet to develop a replacement for this subtlety.

Some of these post-serial styles make extensive use of mathematics. Composers of electronic music perhaps come closest to the purest sense of

[12] Inversions may be symmetric rather than tonal. Tonal inversions are generally preferred for harmonic reasons (increased variety and solidity). Alterations of this sort do not seem possible in serial or post-serial music. A particularly interesting case of symmetric inversion is found in J. S. Bach's *Clavierübung*, Teil 3, Duetto II, bars 69–78. Bars 74–78 contain the symmetric inversions of *both* lines of bars 69–73, each in the part opposite to that in which the first version appears. In other words, one finds two different symmetric inversions simultaneously, in invertible counterpoint.

"sounds organized in time." Durations of sounds, as well as their frequency (pitch), distribution of partials (timbre), and intensity (volume), can all be calculated precisely before transferral to tape for performance. Electronic music employs a continuum of values for each aspect as opposed to the set of discrete values of units, as one finds in traditional music, although the mathematics involved is more time-consuming than abstruse (this is true of other post-serial styles).[13] The medium is still largely unexplored (although certain areas have been overly exploited); composers have at their disposal electronically generated sounds as well as recorded traditional sounds, and the infinite possibilities of combination and manipulation of these two categories. The chief problem (familiar by now) is the control and organization of this wealth of resources. Thus far electronic composers have avoided burdening themselves with excessively constricting rules.

Perhaps one should include within the domain of electronic music the compositions that have been written for the RCA Synthesizer. The mathematical processes are much the same, although the manner of realization (the complex process of transferring the composer's ideas from sketch-graph to a final tape, which requires technological knowledge as well as compositional skill) is quite different.

The composers who have availed themselves of aleatory (random) processes use mathematics only if the choice of determinant utilizes a mathematical process (usually a random number sequence). Even in this case, the use of mathematics is confined to compositions based in whole or in large part on aleatory processes. More limited use of this technique is nearly always accomplished by one of a large number of possible specifications for partial or complete improvisation, which does not include mathematics.

In all these systems, mathematical processes are used to aid the composer in making decisions. As the mathematical processes become rigorously and widely applied, they cease to function merely as an aid in making decisions; the decisions become determined by the mathematics (predetermined). In the

[13] Mathematics employed in music rarely, if ever, goes beyond material covered in a one-year undergraduate survey course in mathematics and in a course on computer programming. This is unlikely to change very much in the immediate future, since few musicians have even this much mathematical training.

case of completely aleatory music the composer carries this concept to the extreme of abdicating all decisions (except for his original abdication).

COMPUTERS AND MUSIC

THE COMPUTER is very possibly the most thoroughly misunderstood creature of this terrifying century. It is alternately worshiped and recommended for instant destruction. It is salvation or an enslaver.

The hysteria might be allayed if we would consider that the word "computer" merely means a device or person who calculates, which is not very ominous. A computer does not think or create; it carries out precise arithmetic operations according to precise instructions (programming). The computer does not provide any answers that are not *theoretically* obtainable by human beings; by operating at high speed it is able to carry out certain operations which might have been *impractical* previously.[14] And so it is with the computer in music. It will not explain why composers of a certain period avoided a certain practice. It could survey enough pieces in which such a practice might have been used to find out what else was generally substituted, enabling a human being to discover the explanation. As the nature of the work done becomes more conceptual and analytic, the use of the computer is harder to apply. As mentioned before, there exists the difficulty of "translating" music into a mathematical notation which would enable a computer to "answer questions." It is unfortunate that some people working with computers have yet to learn of these limitations.

The use of computers in composition works the same way. The computer is fed information (rules, materials to be used, instrumental limitations, etc.) which it operates on as directed. This may in one sense yield new flexibility to composers, yet it also limits the possibilities of any computer composition to a finite range of predictable alternatives.

It is important to remember that a computer will reason, but that it is not "reasonable." *All* logically possible responses will be considered (other

[14] For example, research being done by Allen Forte, "Context and Continuity in an Atonal Work: A Set-Theoretic Approach," *Perspectives of New Music* Vol. I, No. 2 (1963), p. 72, attempting to demonstrate correlations between different segments of Schoenberg's atonal piano on the basis of interval content requires a computer for the vast amount of statistical data needed before any definitive statements concerning motives or form will be possible.

than those specifically excluded by the programmer), not just those which mortals consider "plausible." If a composer wishes to have a string quartet worked out on a computer, he must specify very precisely what double-stops and harmonics are impractical (or impossible), and under what conditions will others (normally possible) be unreasonably difficult. The basic decision-making process is still in the composer's hands. The elements are arranged by the computer according to the program he has worked out; the control over the end-product is about the same as that possessed by the serialist.

MATHEMATICS AND THE FUTURE OF MUSIC

IT IS very likely that the use of mathematics in music will increase in both importance and diversity. New applications will be formulated for theory and musicology, and resourceful composers will unearth new possibilities for mathematical operations in the compositional process. It is also likely that the mathematics employed will be more advanced and more sophisticated than current usage.

As these developments occur, musicians will hopefully come to realize the function of mathematics as a tool rather than as an end in itself. Many possible investigations of various facets of music, not merely those cited earlier, stand in danger of considerable vitiation if the current trend of mathematical rigor persists. This awareness must include an understanding of which areas of music can be profitably studied with mathematical means, and which are best left to other approaches.

Composers would do well to reconsider their own preoccupation with mathematical rigor. It is quite possible and very much desirable to make use of mathematical operations in contemporary styles as flexible rather than rigorous procedures. This would offer some hope that the combination of identity and variety, so essential to traditional styles, might yet become an equally important aspect of contemporary music. Example 4, from the Fourth String Quartet of Béla Bartók (bars 55–63 of the third movement),[15] illustrates flexibility in canonic treatment. The canon between 1st violin and cello lasts eight measures. Half of the canon is in inversion, then it reverts to

[15] Reproduced with permission of Boosey and Hawkes.

EXAMPLE 4

rectus. Corresponding melodic intervals are occasionally of different size. In each phrase the violin begins two beats after the cello, and then approaches to a distance of only one beat by shortening the first long note.[16] Melodic seconds sometimes progress in the "wrong" direction in order to change vertical intervals. Yet when one listens to the music, these devices do not disturb; they do not disrupt one's impression of canonic treatment. Bartók accomplishes this by not tampering with the most prominent elements: the perfect intervals are always answered by perfect intervals (they are quite prominent in a texture of clusters), and the rhythmic patterns employing various dotted figurations are given exact rhythmic answers. The altered elements are those least likely to be heard precisely: the precise duration of long tones and the direction of stepwise motion at one given point will not make a strong impression, if remembered at all.

It cannot be denied that today's compositional styles suffer from the absence of a common referent. Against this backdrop of chaos new compositions seem small and lost, to the detriment of the communicative aspect of music. This will not disappear through the invention of new systems or procedural refinement of present systems; such remedies would shortly lead back to the original dilemma. If systems are to participate in a restoration of meaningfulness, they must be made flexible. The fear of the past must also be done away with. If the primacy of *musical* values can reassert itself, then the long estrangement between composers and the world might subside, and music might once again become a force in the world.

[16] The first two notes of the cello entry are considered to be an augmentation—to allow smoother transition from the previous section.

"Varied" imitation, in which either the vertical *or* horizontal intervals are altered can occasionally be found in unexpected places, e.g., Brahms's Op. 119, No. 1; Borodin's Second String Quartet, Nocturne, bars 111–130; Haydn's Symphony No. 44, Minuet.

Landini's Treatment of Consonance and Dissonance

A STUDY IN FOURTEENTH-CENTURY COUNTERPOINT

CARL SCHACHTER

ANY investigation of the constructive principles of fourteenth-century counterpoint might well begin with the problem of consonance and dissonance.[1] In dealing with polyphony of the fifteenth century and later, we can at least assume a consensus regarding the identity of the consonant intervals. No such consensus exists with respect to the fourteenth-century repertory. Neither Medieval theorists nor modern scholars agree about the classification of the third and the sixth; the perfect fourth, to a lesser degree, presents a similar problem. The analysis of later music can deduce specific instances of behavior from general principles; the analysis of the music of Landini and his contemporaries must first induce many of these principles from a careful examination of behavior.

CONSONANCES IN TWO-PART COUNTERPOINT

MARCHETTUS OF PADUA, in his *Lucidarium*, classified thirds and sixths among the dissonances. He specifies, however, that the ear tolerates these intervals—unlike the other dissonances—if they proceed by contrary motion to one of the consonances. Marchettus considers the perfect fourth

[1] The sections of this article dealing with Landini's two-part compositions originally formed part of my master's paper. I want to take this opportunity to thank my adviser, Professor Gustave Reese, for his invaluable advice and help.

a consonance.[2] Prosdocimus de Beldemandis, writing about fifteen years after Landini's death, accepted thirds and sixths as consonances albeit imperfect ones; the perfect fourth he regarded as dissonant.[3] Most modern writers accept the consonant classification of thirds and sixths for fourteenth-century music; virtually all label the perfect fourth a dissonance. Leonard Ellinwood, however, has regarded thirds and sixths as dissonances.[4]

The consonant or dissonant classification of these intervals is of more than nominal importance. If we fail accurately to recognize and classify significant similarities on the most elementary level, it may well prove impossible for us to deal adequately with the more complex problems of voice leading and dissonance treatment.

A logical first step is to determine how Landini treats the unequivocal consonances—the unison, the fifth, and the octave—in contrast to the undoubted dissonances—the second and the seventh. If we discover any consistent patterns of treatment, we shall have established a standard by which to judge the doubtful intervals. We shall then be in a position to determine, for example, whether thirds and sixths belong definitely to either the consonant or dissonant group or whether they might properly form an intermediary category of their own.

Examination of Landini's two-voice compositions yields the following observations:

1. Unisons, octaves, and fifths occur in long as well as short rhythmic values. Seconds and sevenths occur only as short notes, almost never exceeding a value of two minims.[5]

[2] Marchettus of Padua, *Lucidarium musicae planae*, in Gerbert, *Scriptores ecclesiastici de musica sacra potissimum* . . . (Typis San-Blasianis, 1784; photographic reproduction of the 1784 ed.: Hildesheim, Olms, 1963), III, 80.

[3] Prosdocimus de Beldemandis, *Tractatus de contrapuncto*, in Coussemaker, *Scriptorum de musica medii aevi nova series* . . . (Paris, Durand, 1864–76; photographic reproduction of that ed.: Hildesheim, Olms, 1963), III, 195.

[4] Leonard Ellinwood, ed., *The Works of Francesco Landini* (Cambridge, The Mediaeval Academy of America, 1939), p. xxxiii. Ellinwood does not discuss this problem in his more recent chapter, "The Fourteenth Century in Italy," in Anselm Hughes and Gerald Abraham, eds., *New Oxford History of Music* (London, Oxford University Press, 1960), III, 31–81.

[5] The relation of rhythm to dissonance treatment forms an extremely important aspect of Landini's contrapuntal style. The subject is too complex for elaboration at this point; see the section on dissonance treatment for a detailed exposition.

2. The perfect intervals occur frequently in note-against-note texture. Dissonances rarely appear as note-against-note intervals, even in the smaller rhythmic values.[6]

3. As a corollary of point 2, the consonances appear frequently in parallel motion both in note-against-note and figurated texture. The use of parallel fifths, octaves, and unisons represents a continuation of earlier contrapuntal procedures.[7] Parallel seconds and sevenths occur only in figurated texture; in this case, the parallel motion occurs between ornamental rather than essential tones.

4. Unisons, fifths, and octaves usually occur at points of articulation. Landini always employs the unison or octave to end a composition or a large section. The perfect fifth is the most frequently employed interval at the beginning of a piece; out of 100 two-voice compositions, 60 begin with a fifth, 32 with an octave, 7 with a unison, and 1 with a twelfth. Interior articulation—beginnings and endings of phrases—employs all these intervals. Landini never uses a dissonance (second or seventh) at any of these points.

Let us now consider Landini's treatment of thirds and sixths with respect to the above-mentioned four points.

1. Thirds and sixths frequently occur in note values as large as perfect breves and longs. In this their behavior resembles that of the perfect consonances.

2. Thirds and sixths appear freely in note-against-note texture. Here, too, the similarity with the undoubted consonances is obvious. Example 1 serves as illustration for both points.[8]

[6] This observation as well as the preceding tends to confirm the explanation of Prosdocimus that dissonances occur "in cantu fractibili" rather than "in contrapuncto." Coussemaker, III, 197.

[7] In an interesting and valuable attempt at establishing the criteria for a chronology of Landini's works, Kurt von Fischer cites the extensive use of parallel consonances as evidence for an early date of composition. See Kurt von Fischer, "Ein Versuch zur Chronologie von Landinis Werken," *Musica Disciplina*, XX (1966), 40.

[8] N.B. throughout the music examples indicates the specific point under discussion.

Music examples in this paper are reproduced by permission from Leo Schrade, ed., *Polyphonic Music of the Fourteenth Century:* Vol. IV. *The Works of Francesco Landini* (Monaco, L'Oiseau-Lyre, 1958) and appear in the Schrade edition as follows: Ex. 1, p. 22; Ex. 2, p. 25; Ex. 3, p. 199; Ex. 4, p. 89; Ex. 5, p. 64; Ex. 6, p. 135; Ex. 8, p. 129; Ex. 9, p. 130; Ex. 10, p. 119; Ex. 11, p. 150; Ex. 12, p. 152; Ex. 13, p. 172; Ex. 14, pp. 138–39; Ex. 15, p. 134; Ex. 16, p. 55; Ex. 17, p. 19; Ex. 18, p. 29; Ex. 19, p. 42; Ex. 20, p. 23; Ex. 21, p. 207; Ex. 22, p. 55; Ex. 23, p. 207; Ex. 24, p. 132; Ex. 25, p. 220; Ex. 26,

EXAMPLE I *Ballata: S'i' ti son stato*

3. Thirds and sixths appear quite frequently in parallel motion involving note-against-note texture (see Example 2).

EXAMPLE 2 *Ballata: Va pure, amore*

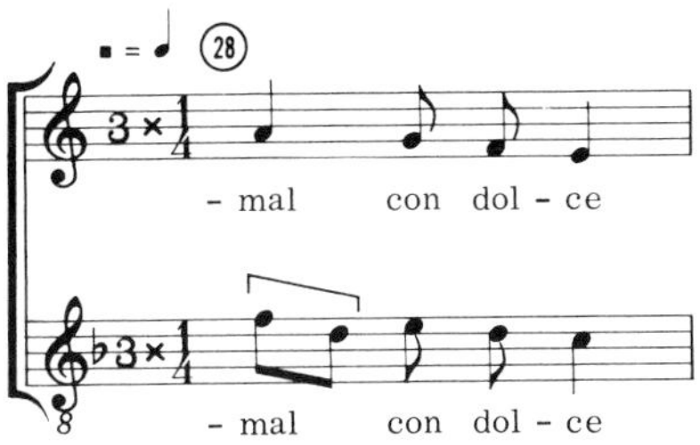

4. Thirds and sixths rarely appear at points of sectional articulation. They never end a composition or large section (neither do fifths); they never begin a composition. Very occasionally, however, these intervals occur at the beginning of the second section of a composition. Of the 91 two-part

---

p. 193; Ex. 27, p. 31; Ex. 28, p. 156; Ex. 29, p. 50; Ex. 30, p. 29; Ex. 31, p. 160; Ex. 32, p. 2; Ex. 33, p. 6; Ex. 34, p. 29; Ex. 35, p. 17; Ex. 36, p. 116; Ex. 37, p. 97; Ex. 38, p. 99; Ex. 39, p. 206; Ex. 40, p. 186; Ex. 41, p. 209; Ex. 42, p. 176; Ex. 43, p. 140; Ex. 44, p. 184; Ex. 45, p. 67; Ex. 46, p. 19; Ex. 47, p. 18; Ex. 48, p. 203; Ex. 49, p. 81; Ex. 50, p. 197; Ex. 51, p. 24; Ex. 52, p. 35; Ex. 53, p. 168; Ex. 54, p. 192; Ex. 55, p. 8; Ex. 56, p. 148; Ex. 57, p. 89; Ex. 58, p. 101; Ex. 59, p. 203; Ex. 60, p. 4; Ex. 61, p. 176; Ex. 62, p. 2; Ex. 63, p. 148; Ex. 64, p. 60; Ex. 65, p. 21; Ex. 66, p. 166; Ex. 67, p. 30; Ex. 68, p. 12; Ex. 69, p. 206; Ex. 70, p. 76; Ex. 71, p. 91; Ex.,72, p. 103; Ex. 73, p. 139; Ex. 74, p. 11. See Schrade, pp. 58, 148, and 183, for music of examples 75, 76, and 77 respectively. Example 77 can also be found in A. T. Davison and W. Apel, *Historical Anthology of Music* (Cambridge, Harvard University Press, rev. ed., 1950), I, 56 f.

ballate, 7 employ one of these intervals at the beginning of the *secunda pars.*[9]

These same intervals occur rather frequently at points of interior articulation. Many phrases begin or end with thirds or sixths, although, of course, fifths, octaves, and unisons are far more commonly used. In Example 3, a phrase begins on a tenth; in Example 4, a phrase ends with a major sixth.

EXAMPLE 3 *Madrigal: Non a Narcisso*

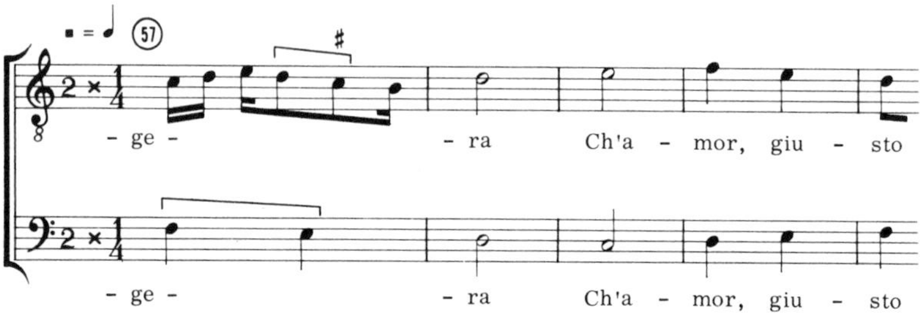

EXAMPLE 4 *Ballata: L'onesta tuo biltà*

On the basis of our observations, the consonant classification is definitely to be preferred. To be sure, Landini uses the perfect consonances at points where maximum stability is needed; not one of his two-voice compositions begins with a third or sixth. Furthermore, a series of parallel thirds or sixths will almost surely lead to a unison, fifth, or octave. To confuse such a motion with the resolution of a dissonance, however, is to misunderstand Landini's contrapuntal style. The genuine dissonances—seconds and

[9] In Schrade, the ballate are Nos. 6, 33, 38, 39, 42, 76, and 84.

sevenths—never proceed in a series of parallel intervals before resolving. Indeed, it is often to thirds and sixths that the dissonant intervals resolve. We shall retain the term "imperfect consonance" for these intervals; it serves to distinguish them from the more stable perfect consonances without drawing too sharp a boundary.

If we apply our four criteria to the perfect fourth, we soon discover that this interval belongs to the dissonant group as far as two-part writing is concerned. (The fourth, as we shall see, acts as a consonance between the upper parts of a three-voice texture.) The fourth seldom occurs in note values longer than two minims; it is never sustained as long as the sixth of Example 1. This interval occurs quite rarely in note-against-note texture; parallel fourths are quite infrequent in two-part counterpoint. The fourth does not appear at points of articulation.

Exceptions to the norms of dissonance treatment, however, occur more frequently with the fourth than with seconds or sevenths. In Example 5 the coincidence of a leap in the tenor with a passing tone in the superius produces a note-against-note fourth. (Even this sort of sonority occurs infrequently in note-against-note texture. The second eighth note of the same measure shows a more typical neighboring fourth against a sustained tenor tone.)

EXAMPLE 5 *Ballata: Se la vista soave*

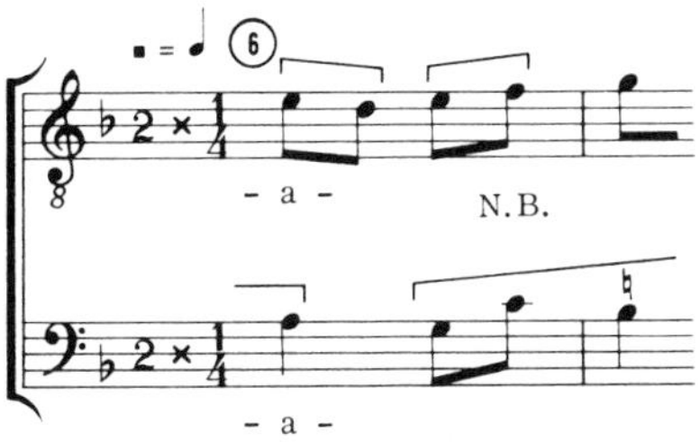

We shall have occasion to point out other instances in which the fourth seems to assume some of the privileges of consonance. These, however, are not frequent enough to challenge the dissonant classification of the fourth. Here again, Landini's practice finds a sympathetic echo in the *Tractatus de*

contrapuncto of Prosdocimus, who asserts that the fourth is less dissonant than the other dissonances and that it holds, as it were, an intermediary position between consonance and dissonance.[10]

The exclusion of the perfect fourth enables us to complete our list of consonances. Landini's consonant intervals are those of later polyphony. Their behavior, however, shows significant differences as well as similarities. Two differences are of particular importance:

1. There is no evidence to suggest that Landini considered thirds more stable than sixths. They behave in much the same fashion.

2. The maximum stability of the perfect consonances seems to exact few if any restrictions. Even the unison, subject to strict control in later polyphony, occurs quite freely. To be sure, unisons (and octaves) in values longer than the breve usually occur at beginnings or ends of phrases; sometimes, however, they appear in the middle of a phrase.[11]

CONSONANCES IN THREE-PART COUNTERPOINT

IN examining Landini's two-part compositions we discovered that the consonant intervals occur in long rhythmic values, in note-against-note texture, in parallel motion, and at points of articulation. Let us now study the three-part music in the light of these categories of behavior.

1. In three parts, as in two, the dissonant intervals occur in short rhythmic values. In general the maximum duration is the imperfect semibreve of two minims; this is the same as in the two-part music. Occasionally, in perfect prolation, the perfect semibreve (equal to three minims) is dissonant. Example 6 shows a passing seventh that occupies a perfect semibreve.

Values longer than three minims are always filled by the following sonorities (in present-day terminology): the triad, the $^6_3$, and the consonant intervals with one tone, usually the lower, doubled. These form the equivalents, in three-part texture, of the consonant intervals of the two-part compositions. These sonorities are consonant as a whole and not merely in relation to the tenor. Therefore a combination of sixth and fifth above the tenor and of fifths above and below the tenor will appear only in the short values of figurated counterpoint.

[10] Coussemaker, III, 195.

[11] See the ballata "Tante belleçe in questa donna," bar 32, in Schrade, IV, 67.

EXAMPLE 6 *Ballata: Gientil aspetto*

EXAMPLE 7

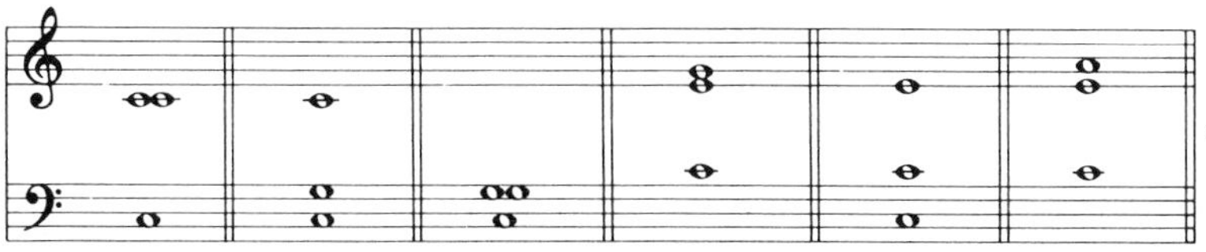

EXAMPLE 8 *Ballata: Gram piant' agli ochi*

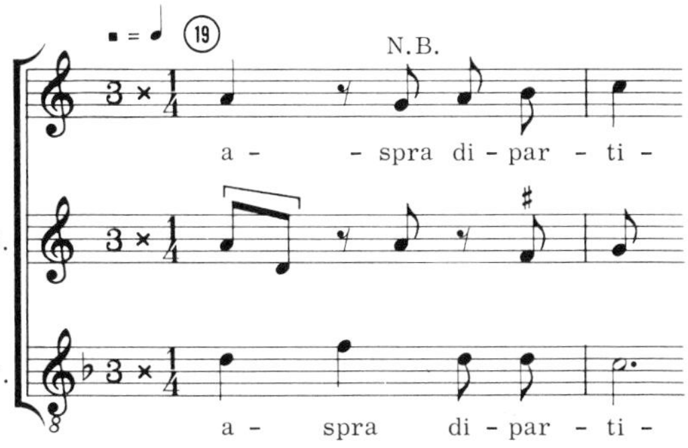

In two of Landini's consonant chords, the $^{6}_{3}$ and the $^{8}_{5}$, fourths can appear between the upper voices. As in later polyphony, these fourths function as consonances. A fourth with respect to the lowest voice, as in later music, is dissonant. Example 7 shows some of the typical consonant combinations of Landini's three-part pieces and includes illustrations of the fourth between upper parts.

2. Note-against-note dissonances, in quick time values, occur more often in three parts than in two. The dissonance of Example 8 results from the

coincidence in a texture punctuated by rests of a consonant leap in the contra with a neighbor in the superius.

3. When rapid figuration occurs in two voices at the same time, parallel dissonances occasionally arise. As in Example 9, parallel dissonances are

EXAMPLE 9 *Ballata: Quanto più caro fay*

EXAMPLE 10 *Ballata: Po' che partir convien*

limited to two consecutive intervals. Compare Example 9 with Example 10, which contains five consecutive thirds between the tenor and the contra. In addition, the note values are longer, perfect semibreves as against minims.

Example 11 shows five parallel fourths between the two upper parts. Landini occasionally writes a series of fourths between the superius and the contra against a sustained tone (or several sustained tones) in the tenor. Such consecutive fourths never appear in the two-part compositions, nor do they occur with respect to the lowest voice in a texture of three parts. We may conclude, therefore, that the fourth functions as a consonance when it occurs between the upper parts of a three-part texture, and that it does so even when it is not part of a $^6_3$ or an $^8_5$ sonority.

EXAMPLE 11 *Ballata: Conviens' a fede*

EXAMPLE 12 *Ballata: Donna, i' prego*

Landini rarely leads all three voices in parallel motion, and he never does so for more than a few chords. Example 12 illustrates two consecutive triads with all the voices moving in the same direction.

EXAMPLE 13 *Ballata: Divennon gli ochi*

Graph 13a

Graph 13b

Graph 13c

A series of parallel triads or $^6_3$ chords frequently underlies a figurated passage. Triads form the consonant foundation for the melismatic top voice of Example 13. The main tones of the superius run parallel to the tenor and the contra, but the underlying parallel motion is disguised by the figuration.

4. At most important points of articulation, Landini uses sonorities composed of the perfect consonances. The $^8_5$ is the preferred opening chord and the almost invariable closing chord for a three-part piece (a few pieces end on a tripled unison). In almost 20 percent of the three-part ballate,

however, the *secunda pars* begins with a sonority containing a third or sixth; the *verto* cadence of a repeated section occasionally ends on a triad. As in the two-part music, phrases sometimes begin or end on chords containing an imperfect consonance.

On the basis of the preceding observations, we can conclude that the triad, the $^{6}_{3}$, and the sixth and third with doubling are to be classified as consonant sonorities. Their behavior is analogous to that of the imperfect consonant intervals of two-part texture. Sonorities composed of seconds, sevenths, and fourths with respect to the lowest part are dissonant: these are never sustained for a long time; they do not occur in extended parallel motion; they never appear at points of articulation.

In general the tenor takes the lowest tone of a chord, the contra takes the middle tone, and the superius takes the top. Because spacing is usually close this means that the contra is normally assigned the third of a triad or $^{6}_{3}$ and the fifth of an $^{8}_{5}$; the superius, then, will take the fifth, sixth, or octave. Owing to the frequent crossing of the voices this normal pattern is not rigidly adhered to. Example 14 suggests the variety of distribution achieved through voice crossing.

EXAMPLE 14 *Ballata: Lasso! di donna*

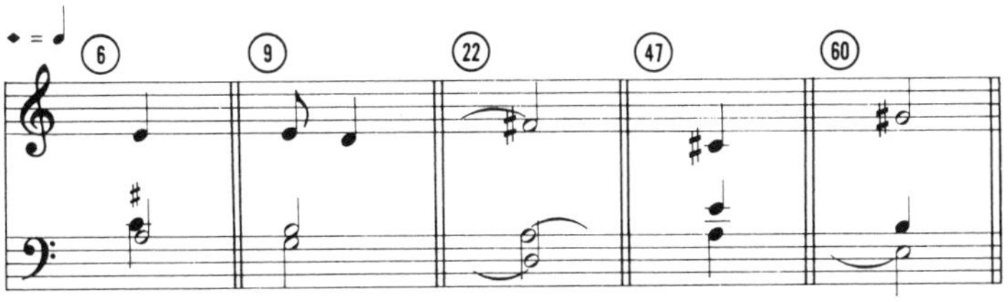

Even when the voices cross, Landini rarely allows the tenor to take the lower tone of a consonant, supported fourth. For example, in the chords E–G–C or C–G–C the tenor will not sound the G even if the contra supports the fourth with the lower E or C. Perhaps this curious avoidance results in part from an additive procedure of composition. For during the process of composition the fourth would appear between the tenor and the superius without the support of the contra, the last-written part. This explanation, although it accords with frequently held views about fourteenth-century composition, cannot be the full answer. For it fails to take into account the possibility either of prior planning or of subsequent adjustment.

One result of this restriction is that most of the three-voice compositions are performable in two voices through the omission of the contra; this would not be the case if the tenor were allowed to participate in the sounding of the fourth. It is at least conceivable that some of the three-voice compositions were purposefully written so as to make musical sense in a two-voice performance. (The caccia "Chosi pensoso" contains three "abnormal" fourths, in which the tenor has the lower tone; they are supported by a lower fifth in the contra. In a caccia, of course, a two-voice performance would destroy the meaning of the composition. The canonic madrigal "De! dinmi tu," in which a two-voice performance is also excluded, does not contain such fourths, but in this madrigal the lower parts do not cross.)

In listing the consonant sonorities found in Landini's three-part music I have used the term "triad" and some of the symbols of thorough bass. I have done so purely for reasons of convenience; I certainly do not wish to suggest that the function of these sonorities is the same as in later music. In eighteenth-century polyphony, for example, the $^{8}_{5}$ bears the meaning of an incomplete triad. In Landini's music the $^{8}_{5}$ is a complete and self-sufficient chord. Indeed, most of the larger structural relationships are governed by chords built of the perfect intervals; the $^{8}_{5}$ is the most important of these. The triad and the $^{6}_{3}$ function within contexts determined, to a large extent, by the $^{8}_{5}$. Within these contexts they enrich the sound and enliven the contrapuntal movement. Example 15 deals with a larger context; the voices move through a tonal space defined by the $^{8}_{5}$ chord, c–g–c^1; this chord is prolonged by a second $^{8}_{5}$, g–d^1–g^1. Although the perfect consonances supply the structural framework, the connective tissue is, for the most part, formed of imperfect intervals. The many sixths, in particular, give the contrapuntal setting its fluid character. The v in parentheses, here as elsewhere in this article, serves to identify chords without necessarily implying harmonic function. Nevertheless, the analyst

EXAMPLE 15 *Ballata: Gientil aspetto*

Graph 15a

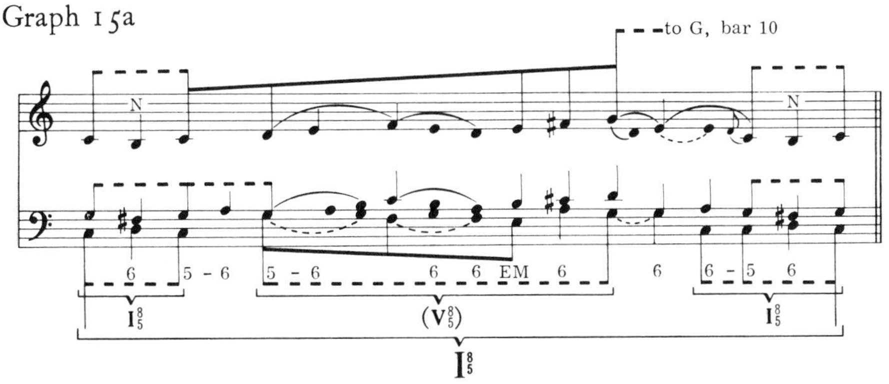

of Landini's music cannot fail to notice how frequently sonorities pitched a fifth apart are associated. Whether or not this association adumbrates the tonic–dominant relationship must await further investigation.

DISSONANCE TREATMENT

Rhythmic Considerations

In investigating Landini's dissonance treatment, the analyst can expect little help from Medieval theory. As Claude Palisca remarks,[12] the fourteenth-century theorists deal mainly with note-against-note relationships and do not describe specific modes of dissonance treatment. I have already touched upon the rhythmic aspect of Landini's dissonance treatment. Before we can explore the subject in greater detail, it will be necessary to clarify a troublesome point of terminology. The majority of Landini's compositions come down to us in a notation that is substantially that of the French Ars nova. Only a comparatively small number of compositions employ the Italian notation. The rhythmic structure of most of Landini's music, however, reflects the characteristic patterns of the Italian *divisiones*. For most pieces the original notation was probably Italian; the surviving sources in French notation represent later transcriptions, often with the long replacing the breve as the unit of measure. The breve, of course, represented the measure in all the *divisiones* of Italian notation. Transcription of the most complicated of these *divisiones*—*octonaria* and *duodenaria*—requires the substitution of the long for the breve so that the three levels of rhythmic subdivision can be represented.[13]

In referring to specific tones, I shall quote the note values that actually appear in the surviving source, rather than in any (perhaps hypothetical) original. I shall, however, employ the terminology of the Italian *divisiones* in referring to the mensuration of a piece, even if the piece in question shows French notation. Thus, we might refer to a piece in *octonaria* as

[12] Claude V. Palisca, "Kontrapunkt," in *Die Musik in Geschichte und Gegenwart* (hereafter cited as *MGG*; Kassel, Bärenreiter, 1958), Vol. VII, col. 1531.

[13] For an explanation of the Italian system of *divisiones*, see Willi Apel, *The Notation of Polyphonic Music*, 900–1600 (Cambridge, The Mediaeval Academy of America, 1953), pp. 370–74. For an explanation of the transcription into French notation, see Schrade, commentary, IV, 28.

containing two breves per measure; this will indicate that the composition displays the rhythmic structure of *octonaria*, but is notated in the French manner and with long replacing breve as the unit of measure. (The subdivided breves of *trecento* music create the impression of "measures"; I shall, therefore, use the modern term.) This method, although inconsistent, has certain advantages. It makes possible accurate specific references as well as valid generalizations. If each piece were to be referred to on the basis of its individual notation, all general statements would have to occur in terms of both French and Italian notation; this duplication would prove unnecessarily cumbersome.

Perhaps the most striking aspect of Landini's dissonance treatment is the consistency with which he adheres to a maximum rhythmic value for dissonant tones. In the two-voice compositions, the duration of a dissonance is almost never prolonged beyond two minims (in French notation, an imperfect semibreve). This maximum value remains constant regardless of *divisio*; even in *senaria imperfecta* and *novenaria* (seldom used in the two-voice compositions), the perfect semibreve (equal to three minims) is regularly consonant. In the three-voice music, the maximum length of two minims remains in force for most of the *divisiones*. However, the perfect semibreve is occasionally dissonant in *senaria imperfecta* and *novenaria*; these *divisiones* occur with greater relative frequency in the three-voice than in the two-voice compositions.[14] Examples 16 through 21 illustrate the maximum value for dissonance in all six *divisiones* (see Example 6 for a dissonant perfect semibreve in three-part texture).

The reader will note that the dissonant tone assumes the value of a quarter note in Examples 16 through 19, whereas Examples 20 and 21 contain eighth-note dissonances only. This discrepancy results from the exigencies of transcription into modern notation and does not exist in the manuscript sources. Leo Schrade has transcribed pieces written in French notation with *modus* by reducing the breve to a quarter note. (Compositions employing the *modus* level seem to be transcriptions of the Italian *octonaria*

[14] In the article referred to in footnote 7, Kurt von Fischer remarks upon the relatively greater frequency of the *senaria imperfecta* (or *senaria gallica*) in the three-part music than in the two-part. He interprets this as the result of French influence and, consequently, as evidence for the generally later composition of the three-part music. See Fischer, p. 35.

EXAMPLE 16 *Ballata: Chi più le vuol sapere*

Dissonance in *quaternaria*

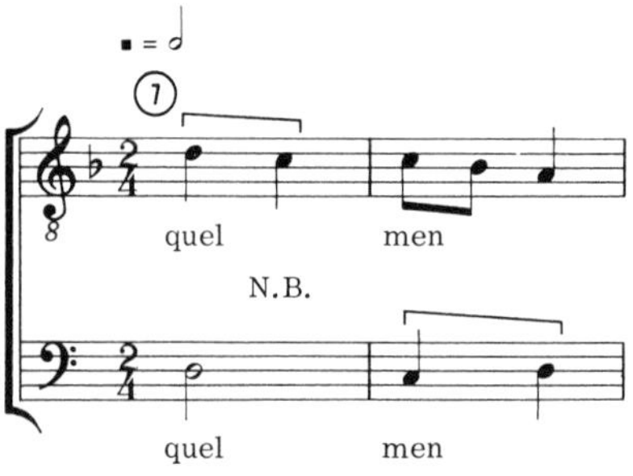

EXAMPLE 17 *Ballata: Sia maladetta*

Dissonance in *senaria perfecta*

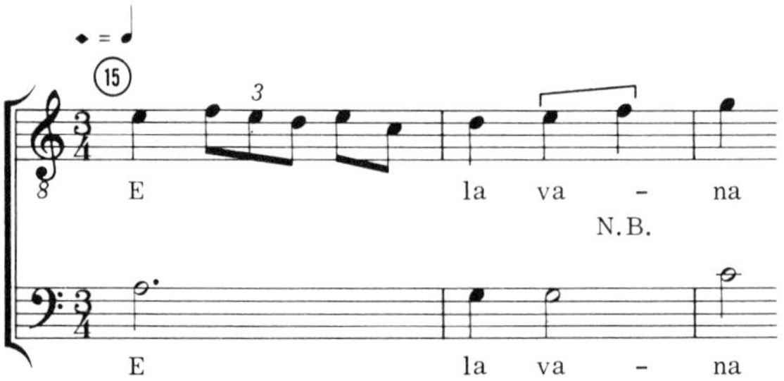

EXAMPLE 18 *Ballata: Vaga fanciulla*

Dissonance in *senaria imperfecta*

EXAMPLE 19 *Ballata: Perchè virtù*

Dissonance in *novenaria*

EXAMPLE 20 *Ballata: Or' è ttal l'alma*

Dissonance in *octonaria*

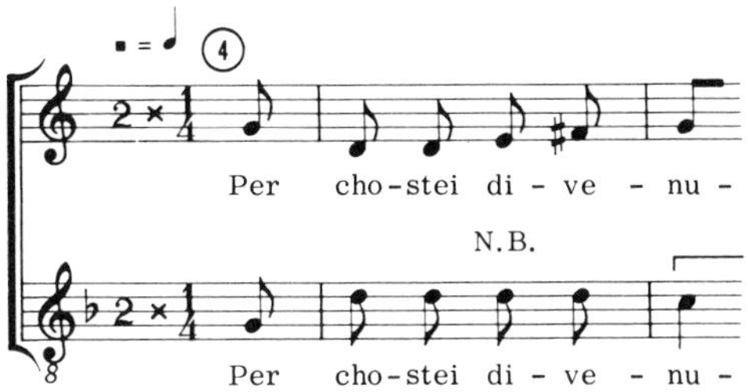

EXAMPLE 21 *Madrigal: Somma felicità*

Dissonance in *duodenaria*

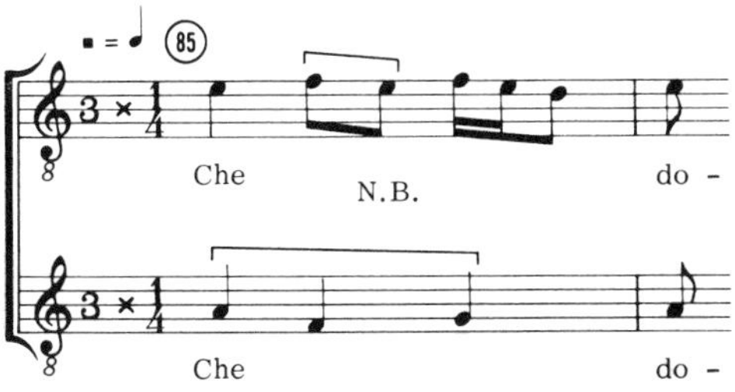

for *modus imperfectus* and *duodenaria* for *modus perfectus.*) In compositions without the *modus* Schrade has represented the semibreve by the quarter note.

As we shall see, dissonances are often produced by the rapid melismatic figuration characteristic of *trecento* music. Such dissonances regularly assume minim rather than semibreve value. An important idiom often found in melismatic passages is the changing-note figure, a four-tone group composed of main tone, upper neighbor, lower neighbor, and main tone. This ornament sometimes occurs in note values longer than the minim; when it does so the longer notes are so counterpointed as to make them consonant (see p. 172). This indicates—though it does not prove—that the restrictions on the length of dissonant tones stem from conscious control. Later in this article I shall have occasion to discuss some exceptions to Landini's usual procedures. Reference to Schrade's edition will reveal how seldom such exceptions occur.

The rhythmic aspect of dissonance treatment includes position within the temporal flow as well as duration. Examples 16 to 21 were chosen partly to indicate the variety of metrical position open to dissonance in Landini's style. It would be incorrect to assume, however, that a purely random behavior is evident. Landini tends to avoid the dissonance of maximum length at the beginning of the measure; he quite frequently writes dissonances of a minim's value or less at this point. The avoidance of the two-minim dissonance at the outset of the measure is noticeable in all *divisiones*;

EXAMPLE 22 *Ballata: Chi più le vuol sapere*

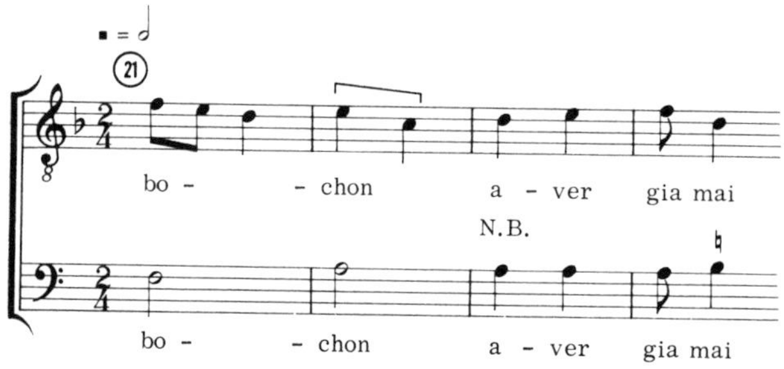

exceptions, however, occur with comparative frequency in all but two. In *quaternaria* and *senaria perfecta*, such exceptions are scarcely ever encountered. It is perhaps significant that it is only in these *divisiones* that the maximum length for dissonance takes up a full beat. Example 22 shows a rare exception to this principle; the reader will note that the dissonance is the relatively mild perfect fourth. Thus the exposed effect of a long dissonance on the first beat of a *quaternaria* measure is somewhat softened. I shall return to consideration of rhythmic problems as they affect specific types of dissonance treatment in the sections devoted to those specific types.

Textural Considerations

I have remarked that dissonance rarely occurs in note-against-note texture. In Landini's practice, repeated short tones are equivalent to a single long tone; indeed, variants of a given composition in several manuscripts frequently contain a long tone in one source and repeated short tones in another. In Example 20, therefore, the dissonance on the third semibreve must not be considered a violation of the rule; instances of this sort, as a matter of fact, are extremely frequent. Whether the dissonance sounds against a single long tone or several repeated short tones, it is a transient event moving against a more stable background. Exceptions to this rule occur infrequently in two-part counterpoint. In Example 5 we saw a note-against-note fourth; Example 23 shows a seventh. Here the dissonance results from the rhythmic displacement in the tenor; the premature arrival of the tone a (the first note of the ligature), prevents the normal resolution of this seventh to a sixth.

As we have seen, note-against-note dissonances are encountered more frequently in three-voice writing. They occur in short rhythmic values (a minim or less) and generally between the superius and the contra. In Example 24 the dissonance arises out of the coincidence of a leap to a consonance in the contra and an anticipation in the superius. Occasionally a rhythmically active tenor will participate in a note-against-note dissonance. In Examples 24 and 25, a reduction of the dissonant figuration reveals the underlying voice leading. Within the framework of that voice leading, the dissonant tones fulfill logical functions. We shall investigate these specific functions later in the article.

EXAMPLE 23 *Madrigal: Somma felicità*

EXAMPLE 24 *Ballata: La mente mi riprende*

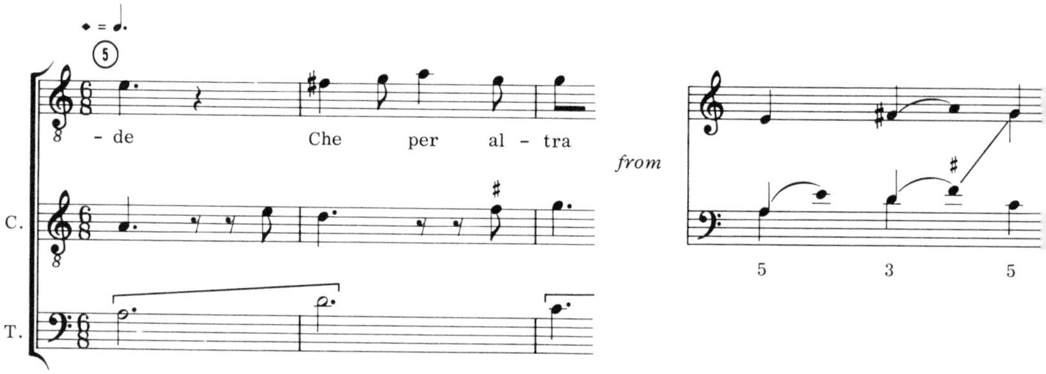

EXAMPLE 25 *Caccia: Chosi pensoso*

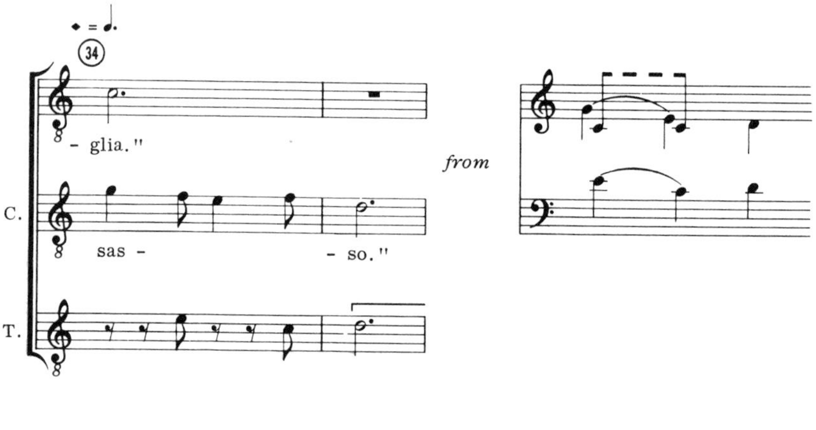

Most exceptions to the rule prohibiting note-against-note dissonance involve diminished and augmented intervals (and chords in the three-part music). Ellinwood, who considers all triads in Landini to be dissonant chords, states that the diminished and augmented forms occur as freely as the major and minor.[15] This view does not seem tenable; the majority of triads are major or minor. However, it is difficult to frame an accurate generalization owing to the divergent use of accidentals in the various sources and the complicating factor of musica ficta.

Melodic Considerations

The dissonant tone can occur in any part of the texture. Because of its more florid character, the superius will generally contain more dissonance than the tenor; in the three-part music the contra sometimes resembles the superius, sometimes the tenor. Except for the greater frequency of occurrence in the superius (and sometimes the contra) there seems to be no differentiation of treatment between the voices. (The reader will bear in mind that I am discussing vertical dissonance only.)

Landini's melodic lines show a marked preponderance of conjunct motion, particularly in the superius. Therefore it is not easy to determine whether the stepwise introduction or quitting of a dissonant tone is purposeful or fortuitous. In this connection, examination of dissonances in tenor parts proves helpful. Here, where disjunct motion is considerably more common, stepwise treatment of dissonant tones is again the usual procedure. Landini employs dissonant types (like the passing tone and neighbor) in which the dissonance is in stepwise connection with both preceding and following tones. He also makes frequent use of types like the échappée and appoggiatura, where only one stepwise connection occurs.[16]

Dissonant tones approached and quitted by leaps are quite rare in Landini's works. Later we shall investigate idioms in which the interval of a third seems to serve as substitute for (or extension of) the more usual stepwise progression. Dissonant tones are almost never both approached and followed by a melodic interval larger than the third. Example 26

[15] Ellinwood, p. xxxv.

[16] The twofold stepwise connection became the norm only in the fifteenth century. See Carl Dahlhaus, "Konsonanz-Dissonanz," *MGG*, Vol. VII, col. 1508.

presents an interesting exception. Here the dissonant ninth is irregular not only because of the framing melodic leaps but also because of the unusually long duration. Indeed, this passage differs so markedly from Landini's characteristic manner that one is tempted to question the authenticity of the repeated a^1 (but the piece survives in two manuscripts, and they agree). Examination of the madrigal as a whole, however, reveals considerable motivic use of the fifth d^1–a^1, as well as repeated appearance of a^1 as a melodic peak. An emendation (substituting g^1 for a^1, for example) seems inadvisable.[17]

The Passing Tone. This dissonance occurs in all note values from the quickest to the normal maximum of two minims. In a binary mensuration the passing tone occurs on both odd and even numbered pulses; similar freedom obtains in triple mensuration. The passing tone, however, seldom occurs at the beginning of the measure, particularly in longer rhythmic values. As Example 22 indicates, however, exceptions are occasionally found. The passing tone, like all the types of dissonance, occurs more frequently in the superius than in the tenor.

Often, particularly in melismatic passages, passing tones are preceded by rests. These rests do not function as true articulations; they represent surface discontinuity within a single phrase rather than a demarcation between two distinct phrases or sections. Passing tones preceded by rests are usually short; the minim is the typical note value for this idiom. Examples 27 and 28 illustrate this usage in imperfect and perfect prolation. In imperfect prolation, the rest seems to function as a variant of the *punctus additionis*. Indeed, the quasi-equivalence of dot and rest is borne out by the fact that the same piece, preserved in several sources, often survives with the rest in one source and the dot in another.[18]

The Neighboring Tone. Like the passing tone, the neighboring tone can occur in all rhythmic values appropriate to dissonance; it can appear in any

[17] Such an emendation, together with a rhythmically incorrect reading, appears in Johannes Wolf, ed., *Der Squarcialupi-Codex* (Lippstadt, Kistner and Siegel, 1955), p. 200.

[18] See, for example, Schrade, commentary, IV, 151, note about the madrigal "Non a Narcisso," bar 70.

EXAMPLE 26 *Madrigal: Fa metter bando*

EXAMPLE 27 *Ballata: Dè! volgi gli occhi*

EXAMPLE 28 *Ballata: Posto che dall' aspetto*

metrical position available to the passing tone. As a rule, both upper and lower neighbors can be used; the choice depends on the melodic contour desired. If the reader will refer back to Examples 19 and 21, he will find an upper neighbor in relatively accented position and a lower neighbor in unaccented position.

In triple prolation, however, a three-minim group will usually contain the lower neighbor. Properly speaking this restriction results from melodic procedure rather than dissonance treatment as such; Landini tends to establish stringent control over the melodic contour of quickly moving figuration, independently of the dissonance or consonance produced. Example 29 shows the lower neighbor; Example 30 presents a more unusual configuration with the upper neighbor. Rests can occur in conjunction with the neighboring dissonance just as with the passing tone (Example 31).

The Appoggiatura. We shall restrict the use of the term *appoggiatura* to relatively emphasized tones preceded by a melodic leap. In other words, we shall distinguish between appoggiature and other emphatic dissonance types such as first-beat passing tones, restruck suspensions, etc. This dissonance, if so restricted in definition, is bound by stepwise connection only to the following tone.

The appoggiatura can assume any time value up to and often including the maximum of two minims. It occurs within the measure (frequently following a rest) as well as at the beginning. Unlike the passing tone and neighbor, this dissonance shows a marked tendency toward downward resolution, particularly at the beginning of the measure. In most instances, the melodic leap before the appoggiatura is a third or fourth; one seldom encounters a larger interval. Where the leap is greater than a fourth, the appoggiatura usually reiterates a prominent tone heard shortly before. In Example 32 the dotted line points up this quasi-preparation of the dissonant tone. Example 32 contains a second highly characteristic feature of the style: the initiation of a passage in syncopation by an appoggiatura.

Example 33 shows the appoggiatura at the beginning of the measure. Here too the dissonance receives preparation from the consonant statement of the same tone in the preceding measure. Note the density of dissonance

EXAMPLE 29 *Ballata: Ma' non s'andra*

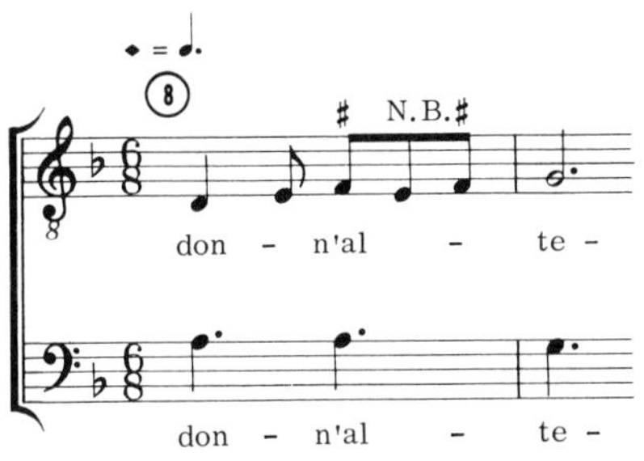

EXAMPLE 30 *Ballata: Vaga fanciulla*

EXAMPLE 31 *Ballata: Donna, per farmi guerra*

EXAMPLE 32 *Ballata: Già perch'i' penso*

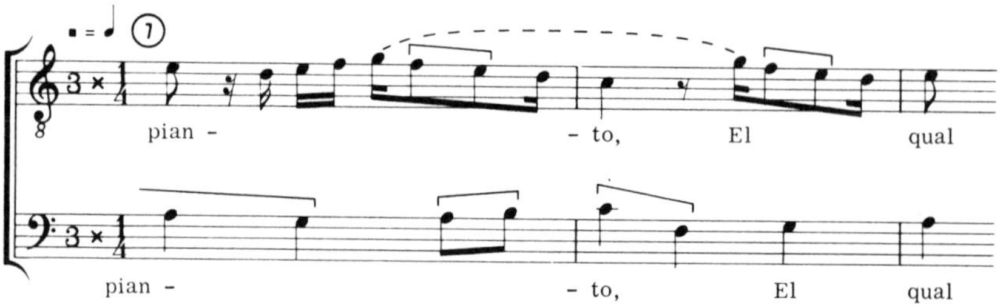

EXAMPLE 33 *Ballata: Non creder, donna*

EXAMPLE 34 *Ballata: Vaga fanciulla*

in bar 18 (third bar of example). Of the six triplet minims of the descending scale, four are dissonant; three of the four sound in immediate succession. Consecutive dissonances are not at all uncommon in the smaller time values —particularly at cadences.

Finally, let us study Example 34. Here the melodic leap preceding the dissonance (bar 41, fifth bar of example) is only a third. We include the four preceding measures to show the preparation of the appoggiatura through the prominence of d^1 in bar 38 as well as by the sequential pattern of the superius. The dissonance of bar 38 is a rather emphatic neighbor; that of bar 41 is an appoggiatura.

To an even greater degree than other types of dissonance, the appoggiatura is generally restricted to the superius. Occasionally it occurs in the tenor or contra, especially if they are more than usually figurated.[19]

The Échappée. The échappée (or escape tone) is best understood as an unresolved neighbor. It appears with great frequency in Landini's work. This dissonance appears only in a weak metrical position (in duple mensuration as an even-numbered minim or semibreve; in triple mensuration, as a minim other than the first of a group of three). The échappée can assume any durational value appropriate to dissonance. Example 35 shows both consonant and dissonant échappées; the consonant échappée occurs with great frequency as a cadential elaboration (in the under-third, or "Landini," cadence). Usually the échappée is approached from below, as in Example 35. At cadences, however, and occasionally elsewhere, the reverse direction occurs (Example 36).

In general, a leap of a third follows the échappée. Sometimes the leap is larger; fourths and fifths are not uncommon. Example 37 is unusual in that a sixth follows the dissonance. (The melodic descending sixth as such is not foreign to the style.) This example shows the échappée in perfect prolation. There are two instances of the dissonance; in the second, the échappée is continued by the normal leap of a third.

The Ornamental Melodic Third. The échappée consists of a leap (usually a third) following the dissonant tone. It is also possible to introduce the

[19] See, for example, the madrigal, "O pianta vaga," bar 38. Schrade, IV, 196.

EXAMPLE 35 *Ballata: Per allegreçça*

EXAMPLE 36 *Ballata: Questa fanciull' amor*

EXAMPLE 37 *Ballata: Già d'amore sperança*

dissonance by a leap and follow it by a step. In this case the leap is virtually always a third. Landini employs this latter type of figuration much less frequently than the échappée. It occurs often enough, however, to be considered an integral part of his style.[20]

In Example 38, the dissonance attains semibreve value. Note the rest between the fifth and seventh. The dissonance is interpolated between a fundamental tone and a first-beat neighbor. Example 39 is more unusual. Here the dissonance is quitted as well as approached by a leap; it forms a sort of disjunct neighbor.

A second type of ornamental melodic third sometimes occurs. In this type the dissonance appears in an emphasized metrical position and is followed by a melodic progression of a descending third. The effect of this dissonance is that of an irregular appoggiatura "resolving" by a third instead of a second. The idiom always involves the vertical intervals of seventh and fifth; I shall refer to it as the 7–5 appoggiatura. In Example 40 the seventh arises through the reiteration of a consonant tone belonging to the previous group.

Example 41 shows a particularly beautiful use of the 7–5 appoggiatura. Here the imitation of a melodic motion engenders the dissonance. This motive permeates the entire ritornello of the madrigal.

Sometimes a dissonance approached by a leap of a third represents a manipulated passing tone. In Example 42, the leap into the dissonant second results from the use of a single passing tone—rather than the usual two—within the space of a fourth. Such "skipped passing tones" are not uncommon—especially in the three-part works. In Example 43 the dissonance occupies only a minim's value; it follows a rest.

We may not exclude the possibility that some dissonances preceded or followed by the leap of a third may result from mistakes in the sources. In Example 44 the dissonant c^1 of the superius shows no clear melodic function and is not in keeping with Landini's usual treatment. I would suggest an emendation (the piece survives only in one source—Squarcialupi).

20 This type of ornamentation sometimes receives the name *cambiata*. It is, however, quite different from the familiar Renaissance idiom called *cambiata* by Fux. The Renaissance cambiata group is not characteristic of Landini.

EXAMPLE 38 *Ballata: Per la beleçça*

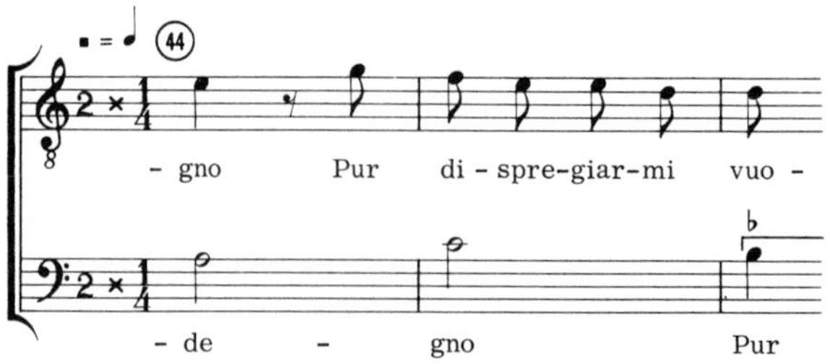

EXAMPLE 39 *Madrigal: Somma felicità*

EXAMPLE 40 *Ballata: Debba l'anim' altero*

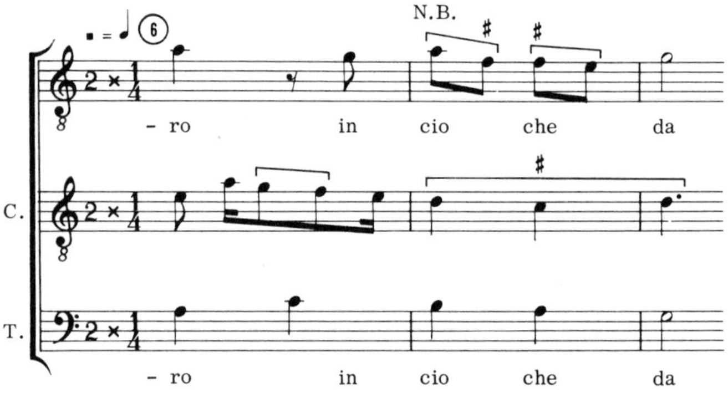

Graph 40a

EXAMPLE 41 *Madrigal: Una colonba candida*

EXAMPLE 42 *Ballata: Amar sì gli alti*

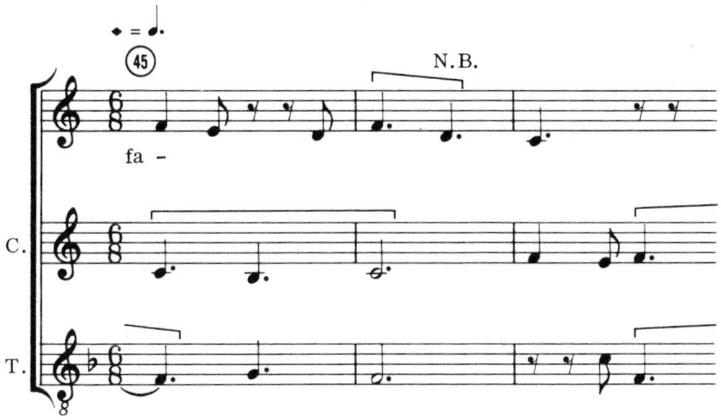

Graph 42a

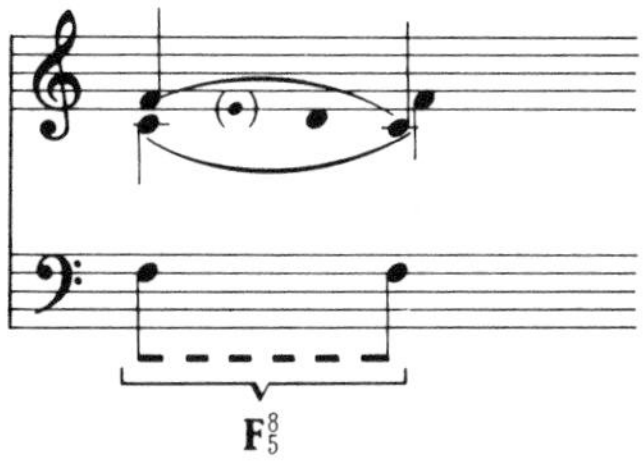

EXAMPLE 43 *Ballata: S'i' fossi certo*

EXAMPLE 44 *Ballata: Orsù(n), gentili spiriti*

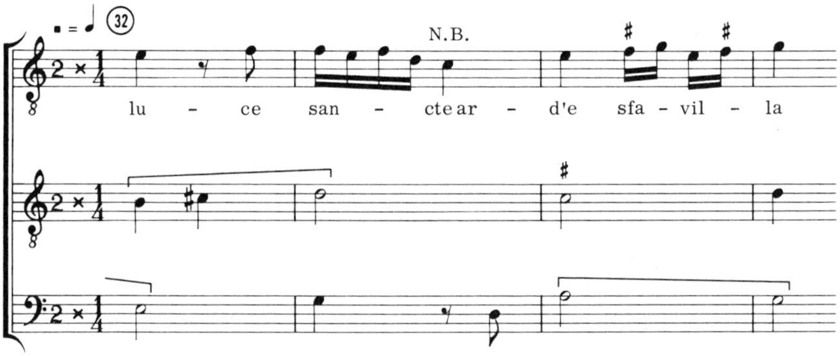

EXAMPLE 44a

Suggested emendation

Suspensions and Anticipations (Dissonance through Repeated Tones and Rhythmic Displacement). The repetition of a single pitch forms a highly characteristic feature of *trecento* style; in short note values it creates a declamatory, *parlando* effect. Often, particularly in the tenor part, the process of repetition does not in itself cause dissonance; in Example 20 the dissonance arises through the passing tone of the superius rather than the reiterated d^1 of the tenor. In many instances, however, tonal repetition directly produces dissonance. It is this situation that we shall investigate here.

In Example 16 the dissonance assumes the form of an anticipation. (Anticipations occur rather infrequently in values as long as the semibreve; the minim is the typical length of this dissonance. In this example the anticipation, abnormally, is longer than the tone it anticipates.) In Example 45 there are two dissonances. Here the dissonance repeats a note previously heard as a consonance; such dissonances are often termed restruck suspensions. (The two-minim value is slightly more characteristic of the suspension than of the anticipation.)

Landini's compositions contain many examples of suspensions, both single and in chains: 7–6 progressions like those of Example 45 occur with great frequency, as do 4–3 and 9–8 progressions. Suspensions, like the other dissonances, appear with comparative infrequency in the tenor part; 2–3 and 4–5 progressions, however, will occasionally occur. Chains of repeated tones, whether or not they produce suspensions, almost invariably descend. Consequently, restruck suspensions resolve downward.

The preparation for a suspension need not always be a consonance. Quite often a dissonant passing or neighboring tone is reiterated on the next pulse before being resolved. In Example 46 a passing seventh is restruck as a 4–3 suspension.

In Landini's style the suspension is almost as unobtrusive and fleeting a dissonance as the passing tone. The suspension carries with it none of the tensions associated with it in later periods, in which it often represents the delay of an expected event. The characteristic chains of repeated tones produce anticipations as well as suspensions; there seems to be no preference for one type of dissonance rather than the other. Indeed, a single passage will often contain examples of both suspensions and anticipations. These

EXAMPLE 45 *Ballata: Tante belleçe in questa donna*

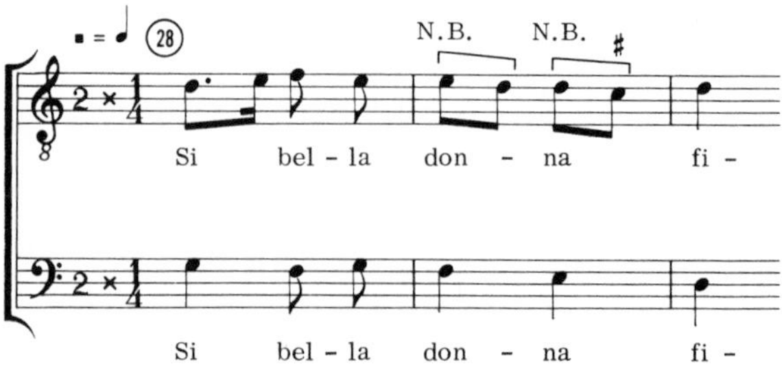

EXAMPLE 46 *Ballata: Sia maladetta*

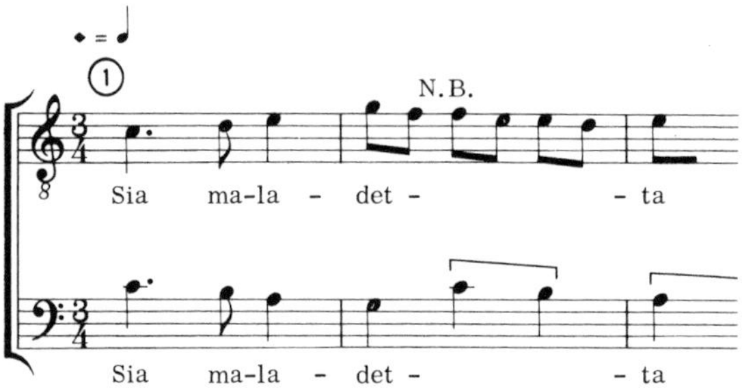

EXAMPLE 47 *Ballata: La bionda treçça*

EXAMPLE 47a

dissonances, like the other types, result from the interaction of the melodic lines; the desire for a specific dissonance at a particular point seems never to assume a primary role in Landini's compositional style.

The analysis of passages of repeated tones can prove difficult. These passages often contain appoggiature and échappées as well as suspensions and anticipations. Example 47 shows two short chains of minims. In the first, dissonance occurs on the second and third groups; in the second chain, the initial tones contain the dissonance.

We have called attention to the fact that repeated and sustained tones often substitute for each other in variant readings of Landini's compositions. If, in the first measure of Example 47, we were to substitute semibreves for the repeated minims, we should produce a rhythm of minim, semibreve, semibreve, minim in the superius part. The relation of dissonance to consonance would remain unchanged despite the rhythmic alteration (See Example 47a).

In modern terminology the rhythm of Example 47a is syncopated. In the fourteenth century, however, "syncopation" merely denoted the division of a tone into parts and the separation of those parts by the interpolation of other tones. Fourteenth-century theory, moreover, discusses (and defines) syncopation mainly in terms of perfect mensuration. Furthermore, it is doubtful whether syncopation was understood as a shift of accent.[21]

For our purposes it seems most convenient to use the term "syncopation" in its modern sense, applying it to binary as well as ternary mensuration. Whatever the accentual differences between passages like Example 47a and later instances of syncopation, a significant contrapuntal similarity remains. Normal vertical relationships are shifted or displaced; dissonance often ensues as a consequence of this displacement.[22]

Example 48 demonstrates a relatively obvious application of displacement technique. The underlying vertical relationships involve the characteristic alternation of octaves and fifths. The dissonances arise through the delay

[21] See Carl Dahlhaus, "Zur Geschichte der Syncope," *Die Musikforschung*, XII (1959), 385.

[22] For an analysis of displacement technique in the music of Machaut, see Gilbert Reaney, "Fourteenth Century Harmony and the Ballades, Rondeaux, and Virelais of Guillaume de Machaut," *Musica Disciplina*, VII (1953), 143.

EXAMPLE 48 *Madrigal: Per la 'nfluença*

EXAMPLE 49 *Ballata: Da poi che vedi'l mie fedel*

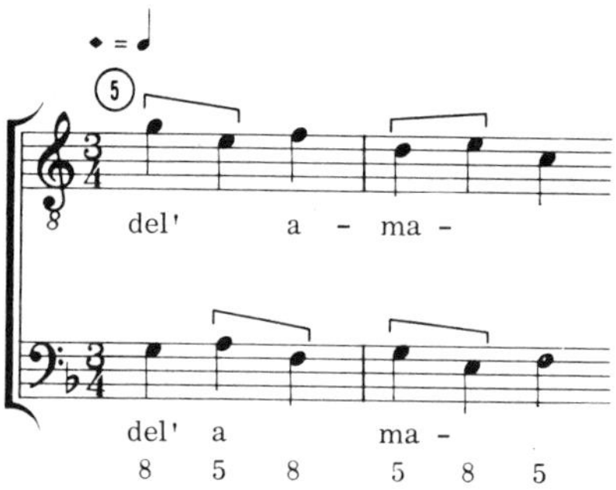

EXAMPLE 50 *Madrigal: O pianta vaga*

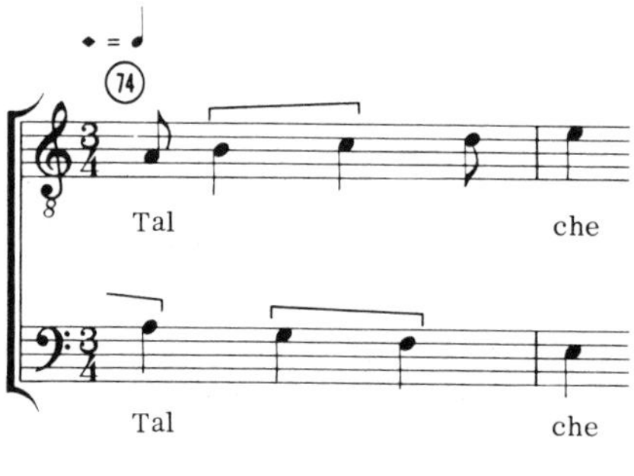

EXAMPLE 50a

of the essential intervals; the causal factor is the syncopation in the superius. Example 49 shows the octave–fifth alternation without syncopation.[23]

In Example 50 the dissonances result from anticipation, rather than delay. Here the underlying relationships are slightly more difficult to uncover than in the preceding example with its obvious sequential treatment. Example 50a shows the progression in contrary motion (passing from a unison to an octave) without the rhythmic displacement.

Syncopated dissonance occurs with comparative frequency in the tenor part—especially at cadential points. The reader is referred back to Example 23, which presents a characteristic instance of tenor syncopation. (The untypical aspect of this example is, of course, the note-against-note seventh. Even in syncopated passages, note-against-note dissonances occur quite infrequently.)

Thus far our examples of syncopation have included instances of ascending as well as descending melodic progression. Ascending passages syncopated against the macrorhythm occur fairly often. Nevertheless, descending direction is far more typical of syncopation in Landini's style. The familiar 7–6, 4–3, and 9–8 suspensions, as well as anticipating dissonance, arise frequently from descending passages in syncopation. From the point of view of dissonance treatment, however, these passages offer no new difficulty; they are exactly like the chains of repeated tones described earlier in this section.

Quite often, syncopation in one voice (almost always the superius) sounds against a sustained tone (or several repeated tones) in the other (see Example 3). Generally, the syncopated tones are semibreves; sometimes, however, breves will occur. In these instances, dissonance will occasionally assume breve value. Indeed, this configuration presents the greatest number of exceptions to the rule that dissonant tones will last no longer than a semibreve. Example 51 shows a passing tone of breve value. Here the dissonance is the perfect fourth.

In Example 52 the still more unstable seventh occurs; the tenor tone is repeated rather than sustained. Again, the dissonance is a passing tone.

[23] Example 49 is cited by Ellinwood, p. xxxii. Ellinwood calls attention to the importance of this interval progression as a basis for compositional (or improvisational) elaboration.

EXAMPLE 51 *Ballata: Anna, donna*

EXAMPLE 52 *Ballata: L'alma leggiadra*

EXAMPLE 53 *Ballata: Nè'n ciascun mie pensiero*

Except for the occasional breve dissonance (and this occurs with the greatest infrequency), syncopation against a sustained or repeated tone offers no difficulties of interpretation.

In the three-voice compositions, syncopation occurs most frequently in the superius. However, the contra and tenor parts sometimes contain syncopated passages. In Example 53 a fleeting displacement occurs at the same time in both of the lower voices.

The virelai "Adiu, adiu, dous dame," in keeping with its French text, shows an unusual amount of syncopation. Example 54 presents a particularly challenging passage. It is not at all easy to determine the underlying voice leading that is displaced by the shift in the rhythm of the contra. Example 54a suggests a possible solution. A consequence of this solution is

EXAMPLE 54 *Virelai: Adiu, adiu, dous dame*

EXAMPLE 54a

the elimination of the ficta b♭ supplied by Leo Schrade; b functions as an essential tone, not as the neighbor of a.

Melismatic Figuration. Rapid, melismatic figuration, particularly in the superius, forms one of the most characteristic features of *trecento* style. This figuration usually involves minims; semiminims and minim triplets also occur. Melismatic passages often contain types of dissonance already discussed (passing tones, appoggiature, neighbors, etc.). In addition a number of idiomatic ornaments occur. It is these that I shall discuss here.

Before describing specific types of ornamental dissonance, let us point out a few general characteristics:

1. Most ornaments possess a preferred melodic direction. Either ascending or descending motion is associated with a given ornament; melodic inversion of the ornaments seldom occurs. (I have called attention to the fact that neighboring-note figures in triple prolation generally employ the lower neighbor.)

2. Ornamental groups occupy fixed positions within the temporal framework. An idiom of four minims, for example, will begin only on the first, fifth, or ninth minim in *duodenaria.*

3. Ornamental groups are short, consisting of either three or four minims (depending, of course, on the prolation). Long melismatic passages will contain several of these groups, interspersed, perhaps, with scale figures, etc.

4. Some ornamental groups occasionally occur in note values larger than the usual minims. As a rule dissonances will not occur in the larger rhythmic values.

Perhaps the most commonly used ornament is the changing-note group, a four-note figure consisting of main tone, upper neighbor, lower neighbor, and main tone.

This idiom represents the embellishment of a stationary tone. Example 56 shows the superius of Landini's three-part ballata, "L'alma mie piange," bar 15. The first version (after Squarcialupi, Paris, and Florence) is without ornamentation; the second (after London) contains the ornament. Variant readings of this sort are rather common; they indicate that the fourteenth century regarded this ornament in much the same fashion as did later periods.

EXAMPLE 55 *Ballata: Per servar umiltà*

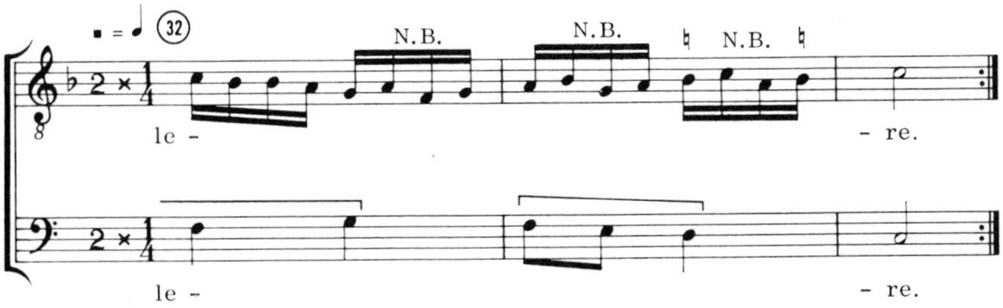

EXAMPLE 56 *Ballata: L'alma mie piange*

EXAMPLE 56a

EXAMPLE 57 *Ballata: L'onesta tuo biltà*

EXAMPLE 57a

In Landini's style the upper neighbor almost always precedes the lower; we have been unable to find more than a few instances of the reverse direction.[24] Example 57 seems to present such an instance; Schrade's grouping, however, is probably responsible. We have notated the example in an alternative fashion in which the idiom disappears completely.

Let us digress briefly from the consideration of purely melismatic writing to observe instances of the changing-note figure with increased rhythmic value. Almost invariably Landini counterpoints the figure in such a manner that the second and third tones are no longer dissonant. In Example 58 the idiom appears in the tenor; the counterpoint is based on the familiar octave–fifth alternation.

Example 59 presents a different rhythmic configuration. Here the first two notes of the figure (it now occurs in the superius) are lengthened to semibreves; the last two are the typical minims. The only dissonant tone (the third note of the figure) retains the normal minim value.

In examples 60 and 61, the dissonant tone is a semibreve. Instances like this are so infrequent as to be of negligible importance in a general evaluation of Landini's style. What is indeed significant is the consistency with which Landini adheres to the minim value when the decorating tones are dissonant.

If the reader will refer to the last few examples, he will note that dissonance can occur on the second or third tone of the changing-note group (or, as in Example 55, first measure, second beat, on both interior tones). The main note represents a consonance; if the other voice is stationary, the first and fourth tones will both remain consonant. If figuration occurs in the other voice, the main tone will possibly be involved in a dissonant relationship (see Example 55, second measure, first beat). The fourth tone is generally followed by a stepwise progression upward; exceptions like Example 60 are not uncommon.

A second melismatic idiom—not quite so frequently found as the changing-note group—consists of a repeated, two-note figure (Example 62). This figure almost always appears in ascending direction and conjunct

[24] See, for example, the ballata "L'antica fiamma," bars 14 and 19, Schrade, IV, 12–13.

EXAMPLE 58 *Ballata: Se la nimica mie*

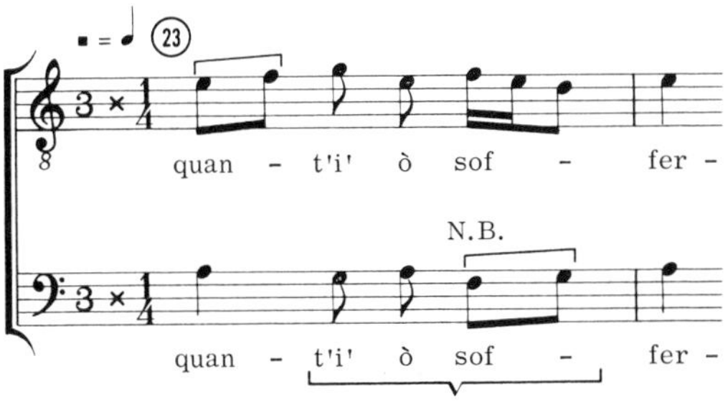

EXAMPLE 59 *Madrigal: Per la 'nfluença*

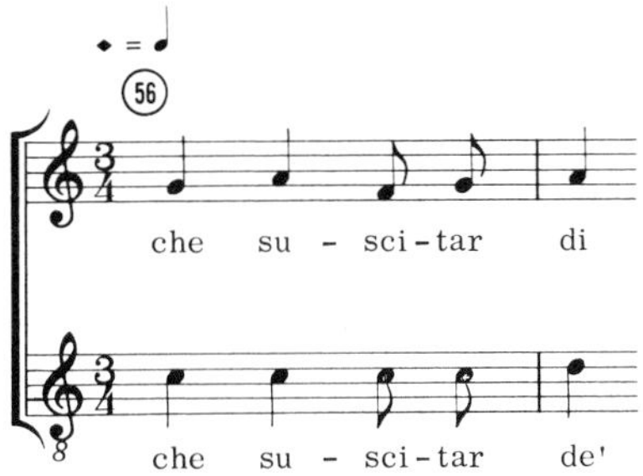

EXAMPLE 60 *Ballata: Dè! pon quest' amor*

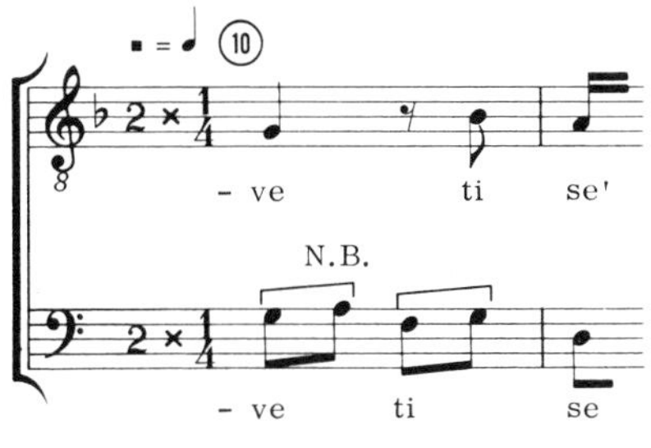

EXAMPLE 61 *Ballata: Amar sì gli alti*

EXAMPLE 62 *Ballata: Già perch'i' penso*

EXAMPLE 63 *Ballata: L'alma mie piange*

Florence, Paris, and Squarcialupi

EXAMPLE 63a

London version

EXAMPLE 64 *Ballata: Ochi dolenti mie*

EXAMPLE 65 *Ballata: Donna, se'l cor*

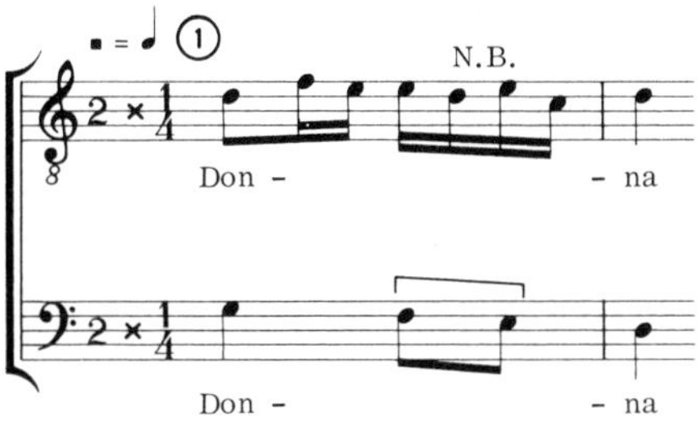

EXAMPLE 65a

EXAMPLE 66 *Ballata: A le' s'andrà lo spirto*

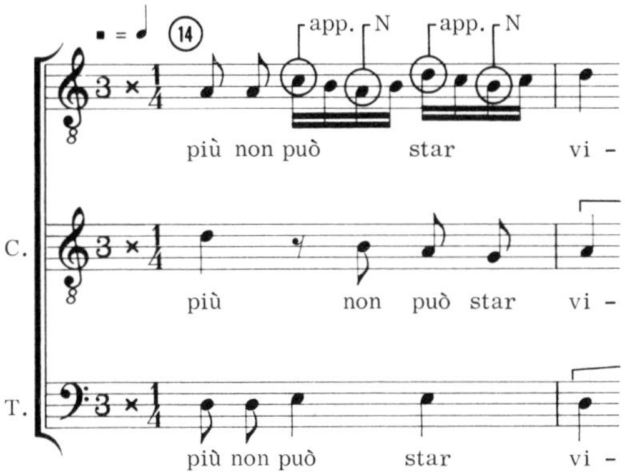

EXAMPLE 66a

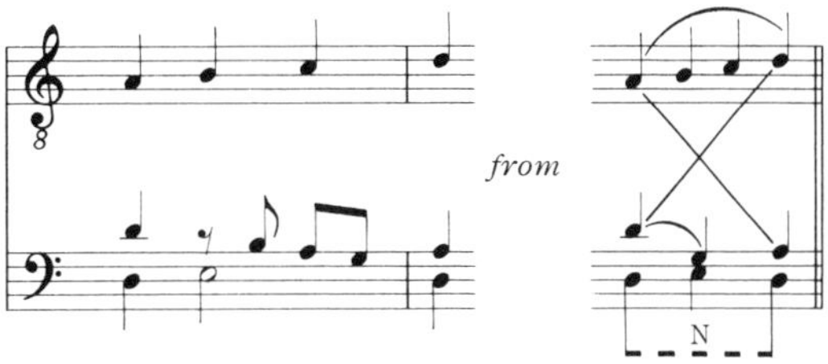

EXAMPLE 67 *Ballata: Chi pregio vuol*

motion.[25] One of the two component tones will be consonant with the other part; the consonant tone need not be the first of the two. Like the changing-note idiom, the repeated duplet represents the elaboration of a simpler melodic event; here, the underlying figure proves to be a two-note, ascending, stepwise semibreve group. Variant readings provide confirmation in this case too. Example 63 derives from the same three-part ballata as does Example 56. Here, too, the London manuscript provides the more complex variant; Florence, Paris, and Squarcialupi adhere to the simpler reading.

Example 64 presents a third characteristic idiom. In this figure the first and third tones are the same; the second tone is a major or minor second lower; the final tone is a third lower. Here the second tone is dissonant; it could be considered a neighbor but would be better analyzed as a passing tone separated from its resolution by the third, consonant tone. The idiom, however, can occur with dissonance on any of the four tones except the last one. Example 65 contains a group similar in melodic contour to, but different in contrapuntal meaning from, the one in Example 64. Here the first tone is dissonant; it is best analyzed as a restruck suspension. If we eliminate the ornamental tones, the analytic reduction shows the underlying intervallic structure to be 5–6–6–6–8.

It is not our intention to list here all the types of ornamental figuration. As in Example 66, most of them are easily understood as combinations of types of dissonance already familiar. Example 67 is important chiefly as a curiosity; it represents one of the exceedingly few instances of a figure resembling the Renaissance cambiata group.[26]

Diminished and Augmented Intervals; Musica Ficta

Here, of course, we shall concern ourselves only with vertical intervals. Landini's surviving sources contain a large number of accidentals. Furthermore, we are not lacking in evidence concerning musica ficta from contemporary theory—notably the writings of Ugolino d'Orvieto.[27] Nevertheless,

[25] A rare instance of the repeated duplet in descending direction occurs in "Oyme! el core," bar 6. Schrade, IV, 71.

[26] A similar figure occurs in the ballata, "I'vegio ch'a natura," bar 6. Schrade, IV, 63.

[27] Ugolino's views on musica ficta appear in *Ugolini Urbevetanis Declaratio musicae disciplinae*, Albert Seay, ed. (Rome, American Institute of Musicology, 1959–62), II, 44–53. For a summary of the relevant passages, see Gustave Reese, *Music in the Middle Ages* (New York, Norton, 1940), p. 381.

the modern editor and performer must proceed in a largely empirical manner, judging each case individually. In making judgments a knowledge of Landini's usual procedures regarding length of dissonance, note-against-note treatment, etc., can prove helpful.

Ugolino requires fifths and octaves to be perfect. Our sources for Landini contain a plentiful number of ostensible violations of his rule. The octave (and unison) will be augmented or diminished when an accidental occurs in only one voice or, on occasion, when only one part is supplied with a signature. In both instances the diminished or augmented interval should be corrected.

Dissonant fifths can occur in a great variety of situations. Sometimes they arise because no accidental appears in the source; sometimes they are produced by an accidental in one or more of the surviving sources. We shall examine instances of both types. Example 68 shows a diminished fifth in note-against-note texture; an accidental is required to correct this fifth. The reader will note that Leo Schrade supplies the editorial accidental. The sharp is almost certainly correct; the approaching cadence on g as well as the note-against-note texture point to the use of f♯.

Example 69 is more problematic. The second measure contains a suspension from a tritone to a fifth. Schrade's editorial e♭ removes the tritone from the suspension. It does so, however, at the cost of having the resulting perfect fourth "resolve" on a diminished fifth. Furthermore, the e♭ weakens the eventual melodic progression to f^1. (See the voice-leading graph.) All in all, it seems best to avoid any application of musica ficta here. (The use of b♮ in the tenor would be unconvincing melodically.)

In Landini's works diminished and augmented fifths often occur in cadential passages; these dissonances are often situated in a rather exposed or stressed position. In Example 62 an augmented fifth occurs in two of the five surviving sources; it is eminently logical in terms of melodic progression.

Almost identical voice leading occurs in the ballata "Fior di dolceça" (Example 70). Here the extant sources lack the accidental. Schrade's application of musica ficta seems open to question. The changing note idiom—particularly in minim values—represents the embellishment of a single tone. The sharp should almost certainly be applied to the first tone of the group.

EXAMPLE 68 *Ballata: L'antica fiamma*

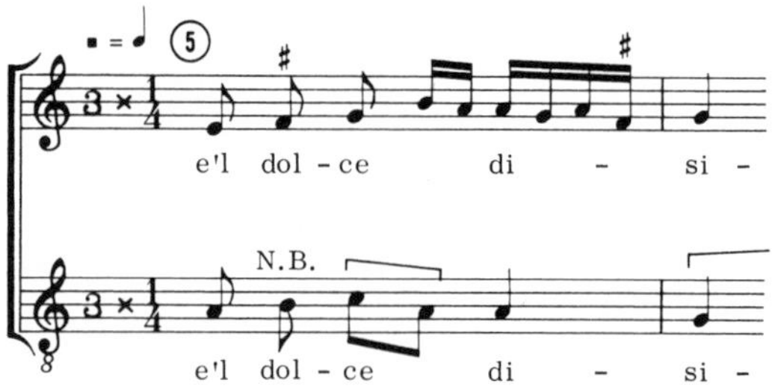

EXAMPLE 69 *Madrigal: Somma felicità*

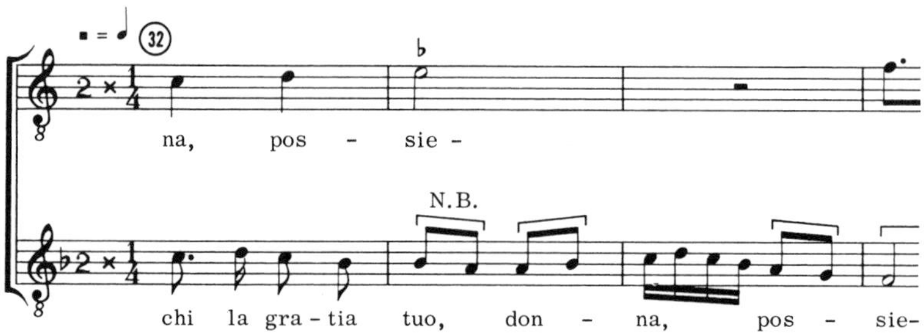

Graph 69a

EXAMPLE 70 *Ballata: Fior di dolceça*

Augmented fifths arise through the use of accidentals in the source; diminished fifths occur when "corrective" accidentals are lacking. In many instances the diminished intervals—like the augmented ones—accompany logical and idiomatic melodic progression. It would seem that such dissonances should be retained even if they occur in somewhat exposed positions. This problem quite frequently arises when the tenor moves up stepwise from the fifth tone of the scale to the final, while the superius moves down, also by step, from fifth to final. In these cases Schrade's application of musica ficta seems rather inconsistent. Examples 71 and 72 present similar passages; note the presence of an editorial sharp in only one of these examples. In my opinion, it should occur in neither. The dissonance lasts but a fraction of a beat; the sharp contradicts the descending, cadential impulse of the superius.

Sometimes diminished and augmented intervals occur in note-against-note texture. In Example 73 the g♯ of the contra produces a diminished

EXAMPLE 71 *Ballata: Altera luce*

EXAMPLE 72 *Ballata: In somm' alteça*

EXAMPLE 73 *Ballata: Lasso! di donna*

EXAMPLE 74 *Ballata: D'amor mi biasmo*

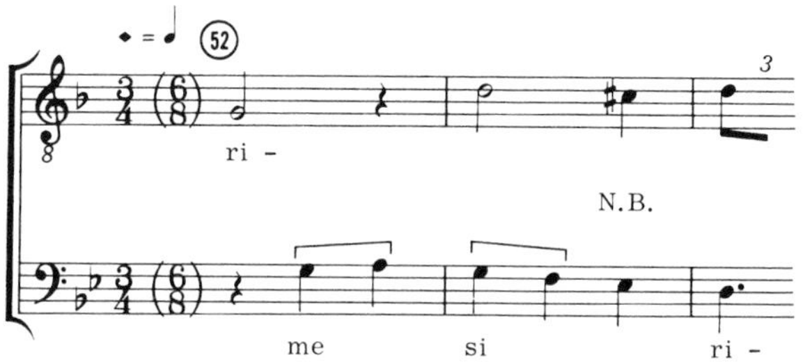

triad. The dissonance is justified by the neighboring function of the g; the sharp, however, occurs in only one of the three surviving sources.

The ballata "D'amor mi biasmo" presents us with a highly unusual note-against-note augmented sixth. The interval occurs twice (bars 48 and 53); it arises out of the simultaneous presence of e♭ in the tenor signature and c♯ as a temporary accidental in the superius. The accidental occurs in two of the three surviving sources. The omission of the sharp or the temporary use of e♮ would produce a conventional major sixth. I am of the opinion, however, that the augmented interval ought to be retained. It results from convincing melodic motion in both parts; it occurs in a composition rather individual in other respects as well. This ballata contains the only use of a♭ in Landini's works; the signature of two flats is also quite unusual.[28] Example 74 shows the second occurrence of the augmented sixth.

LANDINI'S COUNTERPOINT

THE MUSIC of Landini (and of the *trecento* in general) creates an impression of clarity, euphony, and gracefulness. This impression arises from a number of causes. Landini's rhythms, though supple, are never so complex as to baffle or confuse the listener. Textures are thin; rapid figuration usually occurs in only one voice at a time—generally the superius. There is none of the density of the French Ars nova repertory in which several highly figurated parts often move simultaneously.

Perhaps the most important of these causes, however, is the treatment of consonance and dissonance. The perfect consonances form the matrix out of which Landini's tonal fabric grows. But the imperfect consonances begin to play an exceedingly important role. The sixth, in particular, assumes an importance far beyond that accorded it in the music of Machaut and helps to give Landini's textures their characteristic fluidity and lightness. Landini's dissonance treatment is neither rigidly uniform nor random and haphazard. The logic of melodic syntax, the avoidance of note-against-note impact, and the comparative brevity of the dissonance contribute to the clarity of Landini's counterpoint. The variety of metrical position helps to avoid a mechanically uniform alternation of dissonance and consonance. This happy balance is in part responsible for the freshness and spontaneity of Landini's music.

In investigating Landini's use of consonance and dissonance we have had to concern ourselves, for the most part, with details of voice leading. A real understanding of this wonderful music, however, will arise only when these details are viewed in relation to the broader context and, ultimately, to the whole composition. We shall conclude this article, therefore, with analytic graphs of three of Landini's ballate.

Example 75 presents the graph of a short and simple two-voice composition. Reference to it will indicate some points of general relevance. Note that

[28] Schrade, although he accounts for it in his *Revisionsbericht*, does not include the a♭ (bar 27, tenor), in his edition. It is found in Ellinwood, p. 58. In Ellinwood's transcription it occurs in bar 28.

EXAMPLE 75 *Ballata: Ecco la primavera*

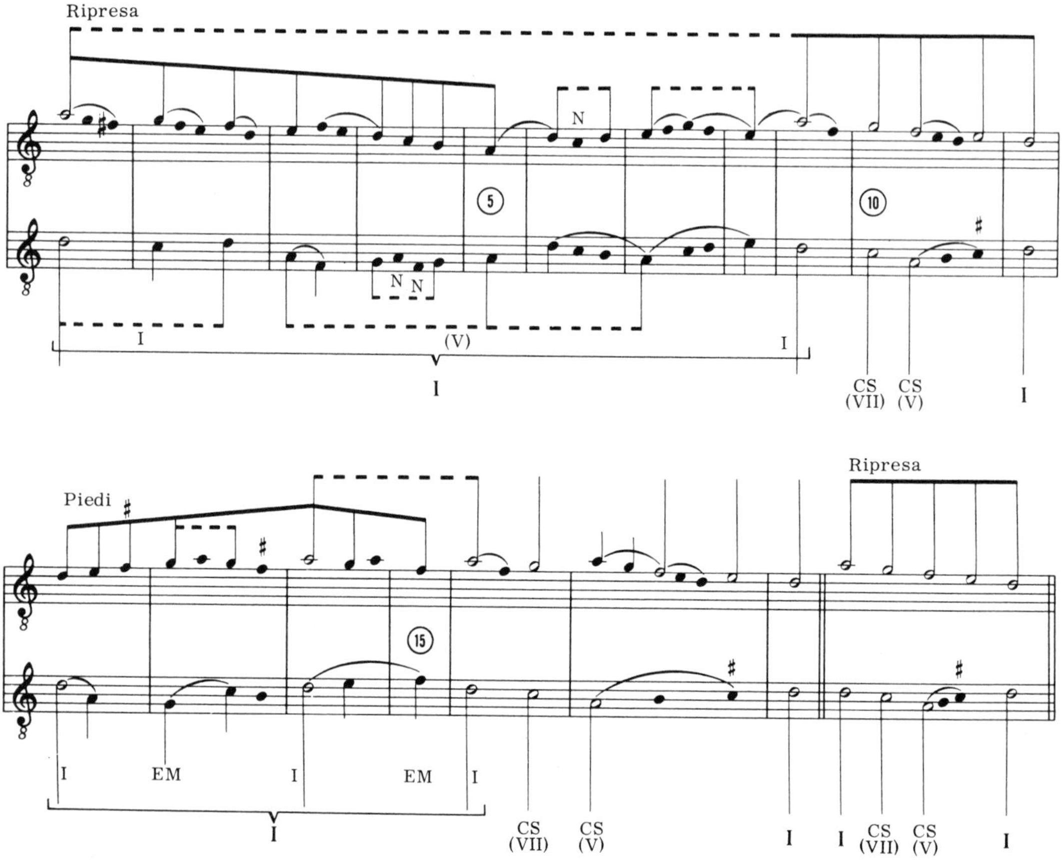

stepwise continuity characterizes the melodic motions of the superius. The structural line is a descending fifth; it is presented twice, in the *ripresa* and in the *piedi*. This stepwise progression serves as the source for ancillary motions; many of these are also stepwise. Note in particular the descending octave of bars 1–5, the ascending fifth of bars 12–14, and the descending third (a preliminary descent) of bars 14–15. The organization of the tenor is not so bound by stepwise progression; the structural points can be separated by intervals larger than a second. However, stepwise passing motions often connect these structural points. The basic structure of top voice and tenor is the same in the two sections; the *secunda pars* is a quasi-variation of the *prima pars*.

Example 76 shows the *ripresa* of a longer and more complex three-part ballata. Again, the fundamental structure of the superius fills a descending fifth. The initial tone of this descent, a^1, marks the culmination of a twofold melodic ascent from the initial d^1. The a^1 is first reached in bar 9, but its structural significance becomes clear in bar 23, after the second ascent. Note the use of e^1 as upper neighbor to the d^1 that begins both ascending motions. The second e^1 occurs in the contra as well as in the superius; in bars 12–15 the contra temporarily becomes the top voice. In the graph, the tones of the contra are connected by dashes.

EXAMPLE 76 *Ballata: L'alma mie piange*

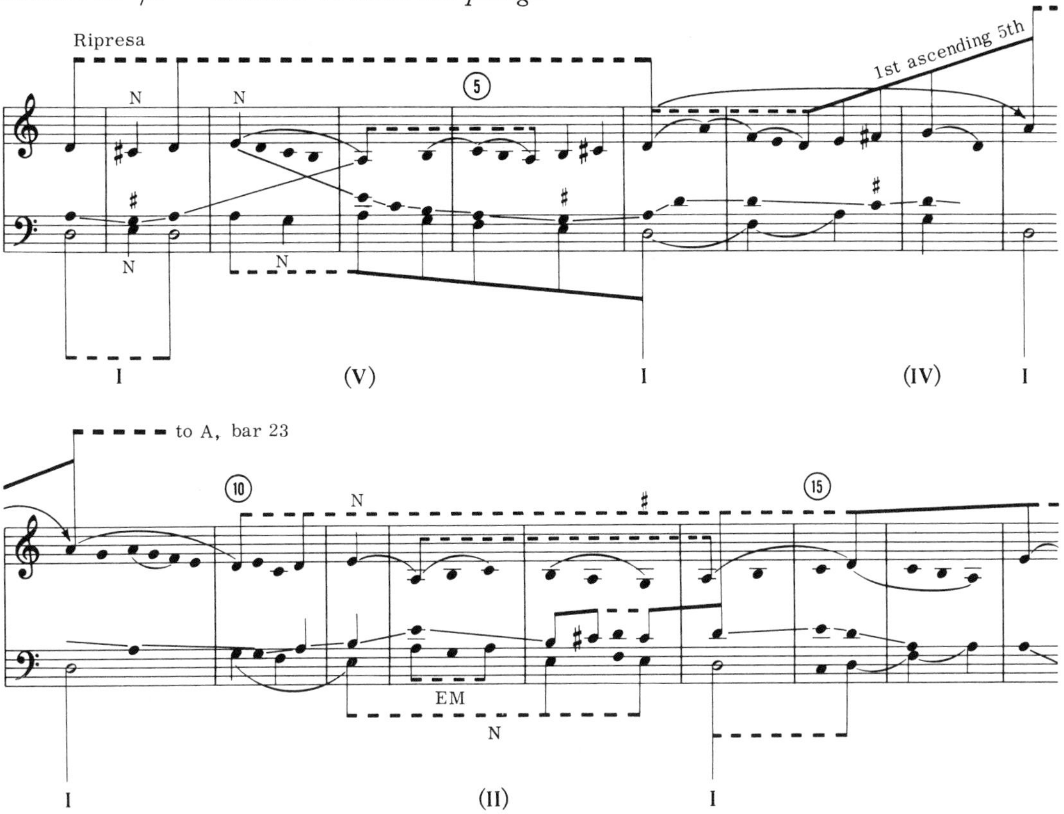

EXAMPLE 76 (*continued*)

Our final example requires little comment. Example 77 shows a more finely differentiated and integrated melodic design than does Example 76. Of particular interest is the structural similarity between the first six bars of this composition and "L'alma mie piange" (Example 76). The broad outlines of the tenor and superius parts are almost identical, although the differences in rhythm and texture disguise the similarity. The reader is advised to compare the two graphs.

EXAMPLE 77 *Ballata: Amor c'al tuo sugetto*

EXAMPLE 77 *(continued)*

Fusion of Design and Tonal Order in Mass and Motet
JOSQUIN DESPREZ AND HEINRICH ISAAC

SAUL NOVACK

THERE are many facets to the study of the history and development of musical form, some of which already have received a fair amount of attention. Perhaps the most characteristic and obvious one concerns the simple division of a composition into several parts, the division being caused by one of several factors. In Gregorian chant one is drawn to the elements of form created by textual repetitions which are fused with musical repetitions, e.g., the simple threefold statement of the *Kyrie* sections. More complex are those involving purely musical repetitions to different texts, as in the case of sequences.

The secular *formes fixes* that evolved during the Middle Ages and were adopted by composers of polyphonic music are clear-cut in their formal divisions and are essentially word-born. These large-scale divisions, such as the two parts of a virelai, represent the "outer form" of the composition. The significant breakthrough in musical thought comes in the permeation of these outer forms with inner life. Basically, it comes from two sources: first, the disposition of thematic design; second, the structure of the tonal relationships. Most significantly, it is the fusion of design and tonal structure that provides us with the diversity and richness of compositional order in the history of tonal music. On the one hand, it is not too difficult to trace the various manipulations of thematic repetitions, whether in the patternistic manners of the Notre Dame composers or in the sometimes complex isorhythm of the fourteenth century. On the other hand, the emergence of tonal clarity appears most obvious via the rhythmic trenchancy of the dance, or in the frottola and the villancico.[1] The cadence, singled out as the strongest ingredient of tonality, appears in these genres in its most incisive manner, to which the verticalized texture created through the monorhythmic movement of all voices gives added emphasis.

Important as these popular forms are, the extended Masses and motets offer greater richness in tracing the varied ways in which composers created inner life and outer form simultaneously. In the Masses and motets of the fifteenth century, dependency upon outer sources for unity and coherence is very strong. A *cantus prius factus*, whether liturgical or secular, became the modus operandi. An entire Mass could be given its overall unity by the employment of a single melody, e.g., "L'Homme Armé," which was reiterated in any number of ways in the various movements of the Mass. This outer source, superimposed upon the work, provided the composer with a sufficient apparatus for viewing his composition as a unity of large dimensional character. Within even this rigid relationship, fluidity was achieved, and the creative instinct of a Dufay, Ockeghem, or Obrecht, among others, added much that unified and solidified their works. The turning point in the evolution of musical order on a large scale occurred through freedom from dependency upon these "authoritarian," self-determining sources. Unity of thematic design is created through repetition, both exact and inexact. But mere repetition is not sufficient, for it may indicate perhaps nothing more than a mosaic or manneristic viewpoint, e.g., Dufay's *Gloria ad modum tubae*, which, although completely held together by the short ostinato figure, is unified procedurally rather than conceptually. Josquin Desprez's *Missa Hercules* is a tour de force; yet, while it has very admirable qualities, the presence of the *soggetto cavato* in its varied forms creates unity only in the most obvious way. The composer proceeds from one point to another without extricating himself from the almost omnipresent design.

The sense of unity through an extension of tonal order is a primary matter. The whole question, "modality vs. tonality," is an unfortunate barrier to a clear understanding of that statement. In whatever mode a composition may be, the basic question is: does a specific tone establish

[1] See the detailed discussion by Edward Lowinsky in *Tonality and Atonality in Sixteenth-Century Music* (Berkeley, University of California Press, 1961), ch. 1.

itself as a center to which all other tones, by direction and function on various hierarchies, become subservient? For example, the fact that a composition is in the Phrygian mode is a matter of importance, but it is secondary to the matter of key if one is concerned about the structural unity of the composition. Thus, from this viewpoint, one can speak of the key of any tone, in the Phrygian mode, or in the Dorian mode, or in the Ionian mode, etc. In the following study, modality and tonality are not considered appositional in any way. Yet, while one is mindful of the different conditions offered by each mode for achieving tonality, and the relative degrees of intensity and success of each, the entire question is tangential, and is not pursued at this time, though its importance deserves extensive investigation.

The study of design is in itself a problem in this music. A considerable amount of the texture in the Mass and the motet at the end of the fifteenth century is very linear, particularly achieving the so-called polyphonic style through the abundant use of interphonic repetition, i.e., imitation. It is incorrect to assume that all the voices are equal. It is true that they may be equal in their roles as agents of thematic ideas, especially in interphonic repetition. The top line, however, assumes a structural role which, through its direction, has primary meaning in the achievement of tonal unity. But one cannot find "direction" in the middle parts. One cannot analyze these voices in the same way one treats the uppermost line. They are different. They carry thematic material, but they bend to the exigencies of the structure. Frequently a middle voice becomes a temporary outer voice, and suddenly it assumes a greater importance. The bass, always the solid foundation upon which the tonal order and coherence are secured, moves with greater freedom not dictated solely by linear or thematic considerations, and its freer intervallic motion is prompted by its new responsibilities in the utilization of relationships for emphasizing and clarifying the tonal order.

The interplay of design and tonal organization achieved status by the end of the fifteenth century, in effect becoming a reality in which the infinite possibilities of their fusion gave birth to the spirit of inner form, the essence of continuity and integration. Nowhere is this seen more significantly than in the Mass and the motet.

The following works will be discussed—some briefly, some in detail:

Compère's *Missa Alles Regretz*, Josquin's motets "Sancti Dei omnes" and "In illo tempore assumpsit Jesus duodecim discipulos," the "Osanna" from Josquin's *Missa Mater Patris*, his *Missa Pange Lingua*, Heinrich Isaac's *Missa Carminum*, and Josquin's motet "Miserere mei, Deus." Each of the compositions selected is different in concept and approach. In each, an attempt is made to understand a particular achievement of large-scale order not realized solely through the imposition of an outer source. In some of the works discussed the outer source is there, but it only serves as a springboard for creative musical thought which reveals a new and unique way of realizing an extension of musical space based upon unifying principles that emanate from a higher order of design and tonal organization.[2]

COMPÈRE: MISSA ALLES REGRETZ

THE OUTWARD appearance of integration is frequently created through the intensive reiteration and manipulation of thematic design. When this procedure is not fused with tonal organization, however, "inner form" is lacking. While such a work may possess the excitement of thematic unity, it nevertheless may be quite static in its tonal structure. In compositions such as Josquin's *Missa Hercules* or *Missa La sol fa re mi*, the ostinato technique, because of its constant reiterative character, offers a basis for stability of tonal centrality, particularly when it lies in the lowest voice. One must conclude, however, that the procedure basically is mosaic.

Compère's *Missa Alles Regretz* offers an excellent example of dynamic thematicism. The resultant tonal order is stable and clear, yet structurally the work is static. The Mass, based on the chanson by Ghizighem,[3] combines the techniques of partial "parody" (*imitatio*) and cantus firmus. It is cyclic, and each of the movements commences with the opening of the

[2] Three of the compositions are extended, large works. It is suggested that a copy of each be available for constant reference when they are discussed. They have been published in other than scholarly editions and, therefore, are readily accessible. The *Missa Carminum* of Isaac and the *Missa Pange Lingua* of Josquin have been printed in *Das Chorwerk* editions: Isaac, *Missa Carminum*, Reinhold Heyden, ed., *Das Chorwerk, No. 7* (Berlin, Kallmeyer, 1930); Josquin, *Missa Pange Lingua*, Friedrich Blume, ed., *Das Chorwerk, No. 1* (Berlin, Kallmeyer, 1929). Josquin's Psalm motet, *Miserere mei, Deus*, has also been issued in a performance edition (Berlin, Merseburger, 1956), Gottfried Grote, ed. All Josquin works are available in Josquin des Prés, *Complete Works*, A. Smijers, ed. (Amsterdam, Alsbach, 1921–).

[3] In *Harmonice Musices Odhecaton A* (hereafter cited as *Odhecaton*), Helen Hewitt, ed.; literary texts, Isabel Pope, ed. (Cambridge, The Mediaeval Academy of America, 1942), pp. 341 f. (No. 57). Also available in Josquin, *Complete Works: Missen*, IV, 83 f. (No. 20).

chanson, but never in the same way. The superius and the contratenor of the chanson, the portions immediately relevant to the present analysis, begin as shown in Example 1. The shapes of these two fragments are strongly

EXAMPLE 1 *Ghizighem chanson*

tonal-defining. The superius can be heard either as a motion within the F-major triad or as an outline of the C-major triad before moving to the A, the third of the F-major triad. The contratenor outlines in descending motion the F-major triad.

Although there are examples of repetition of thematic design at various places in the Mass, it is in the *Benedictus* that stronger repetition of thematic design begins, and this serves to set the stage for the *Agnus Dei*, in which the intensification of reiteration unquestionably becomes a technique for attaining climax. In *Agnus Dei I*, the tenor states the contratenor of the chanson in its entirety with, however, the rhythmic flexibility demanded by other factors in the polyphony. The altus and bassus also share in portions of the opening phrase of the superius, which now appears in the superius of the *Agnus Dei*, in diminution (of the chanson), and becomes an ostinato motive. The beginning of *Agnus Dei I* is shown in Example 2.[4] A reduction of the opening seven measures follows (graph 2a).

It is almost a patchwork procedure. Each fragment of the chanson melody severely limits the conditions for the ostinato. The remaining voices, therefore, must work within this restricted framework. Aside from bar 2, in which the prolongation of the v stems from the chanson itself, it is only at bar 6 that another dominant prolongation is possible. Bars 4–5 indicate the extension of the A-triad and the motion within it. At bar 7 the B♭-triad is prolonged. For the remainder of *Agnus Dei I* no other v extension appears. The bass, taken by itself, appears most interesting, but leaps that sometimes seem to suggest possible harmonic implications have in effect other functions

[4] Reprinted by permission of the publisher. The entire Mass is reprinted in Loyset Compère, *Opera Omnia*, Ludwig Finscher, ed. (Rome, The American Institute of Musicology, 1958), Vol. I; also, by the same editor, in *Das Chorwerk, No. 55* (Berlin, Möseler, 1956), pp. 26–50.

EXAMPLE 2 *Missa Alles Regretz: Agnus Dei I* Compère

EXAMPLE 2 (*continued*)

Graph 2a

*Leap as motion to tones of consonance.

somewhat akin to the old voice-crossing contratenor of which earlier composers were so fond. The leaps (e.g., at the asterisk in bar 3 of the reduction) serve primarily as motions to tones of consonance, which meet the requirements set by the combination of the ostinato figure and the cantus firmus. As such, they might be regarded as nonlinear counterpointing tones. Nevertheless, it is apparent that Compère utilizes the bass voice for definition of prolongation in many cases, as though he were struggling to articulate special unities as, e.g., the effective attainment of the tonic at the beginning of bar 7, at which point the text, "Agnus Dei," terminates in the lowest voice, and "qui tollis" commences. There is no consistency, however, to this spatial association of structure and word.

The reader who has access to an edition of the complete Mass will find in *Agnus Dei II* and *III* further evidence of thematic repetition and tonal clarity. *Agnus Dei II* has more fortuitous circumstances for control of thematic fragments of structure, since the chanson melody in the tenor is in long extended tones, and the motivic melody, derived from the chanson, is even more economically triadic (Example 3). This superius figure, even

EXAMPLE 3

more forceful in its tonal definition in its descending form, is not only tied interphonically to the altus and bassus, but is also combined with the ascending figure used in the *Agnus Dei I.* Nevertheless, in both of these two final movements, the constraint imposed by the cantus firmus is much too strong to free the voices sufficiently to permit them to achieve an overall unity that is based on other than static, mosaic extensions. The *Agnus Dei* as a whole, contrasting strongly with most of the preceding movements of the Mass, is an unquestionable climax to the entire Mass, winning this effect through the intensified repetitions and combinations of the triadic motives and the chanson melody. But with all its power and intensity, it remains static and formless, except for the shape created by the beginning of the chanson melody and its end (mid-point and final), supported by the close on the tonic. The primary guiding principle seems to be the exacting of every advantage from the reiteration of a motive within the contrapuntal requirements dictated by the chanson melody. The choice of motive itself, through its shape and varied use, intensifies the fragments of prolongations.

JOSQUIN: TWO MOTETS AND THE OSANNA FROM MISSA MATER PATRIS

BEFORE PROCEEDING to the exposition of a composition which reveals a high order of fusion of thematic design and tonal structure, the *Missa Pange Lingua*, the reader's attention is invited to two motets of Josquin Desprez to illustrate partial success in this regard. Since the structures of these compositions are not consisdered *in extenso*, the music is not quoted in detail. The interested reader who wishes to study these motets will find them available in the Complete Works edition. It has already been shown in Examples 1 to 3 that the repetition of thematic design is in itself insufficient to establish large-scale order.

The first of these two motets, "Sancti Dei omnes,"[5] emphasizes the point that the consideration of repetition alone can only lead to a description of "outer" form in a very limited and unrewarding manner. The opening line, "Sancti Dei omnes, orate pro nobis," acts as a refrain. In the long text it is brought back four times (!) after the opening, with intervening sections. Thus, in its reiteration, it acts as an integrative large-unit repetition to the extent that one might regard it as an incipient example of the rondo. Furthermore, the repetitions are almost exact, except that the first and final statements are more extended, the latter even containing an extension which functions as a coda. The tonal clarity of the theme, which one can designate properly as a refrain, is apparent: in each statement of the refrain, the contrapuntal and harmonic factors are unequivocal in the delineation of the tonic. The uppermost voice descends clearly from the third of the triad to its root, and then regains the third. Further, in each of the refrains succeeding the opening statement, the general harmonic structure is I–IV^{6}–V–I. This is particularly emphasized in the "coda" of the last statement.

Thus far the conditions are highly favorable to this "rondo." The reiteration of a textual refrain is given esthetic intensification through its

[5] Josquin, *Complete Works: Motetten*, V, 27 (No. 74).

fusion with musical identity. The intervening sections are thematically different, though the contrast is not very great because of the restrictive ambitus of the uppermost voice. The differences lie principally in the emphasis on different textures, e.g., paired voices, interphonic repetitions, or rhythmically emphasized declamation. There is, however, one very strongly unifying quality evident in each of the sections: each one commences clearly in the tonic and terminates with a V–I cadence. These extensions are clear-cut and make ample use of the V–I relationship. Subdivisions are created purely through design change. The subdivisions within these sections are interesting in the correlation of thematic design and text grouping, particularly where words are related through the same case endings. Thus the subdivisions are created solely through the disposition of the thematic material, the tonal structure being, in effect, a succession of units each of which terminates on I and is self-contained. While this lacks organic dynamism, it is not to be dismissed lightly, for it reveals the conscious association of text and music to create a series of units. The arrangement of the text to utilize the principle of the refrain is deliberately conceived. The composition, however, does not measure up to others which achieve a more significant fusion of design and structure.

The second motet, Josquin's "In illo tempore assumpsit Jesus duodecim discipulos,"[6] does not depend primarily on the reiteration of a thematic unit but rather upon a motive. Constant reiteration of one thematic motive, as in the case of ostinato pieces, is in itself a pervasive unifying force, but it is a self-limiting device, not only bound by the almost rigid necessity of almost continuous restatement (although ingenuity may be revealed through the variety of statements among single and combined voices), but also made static by the limits of tonality imposed by the brief motive, even when stated in long sustained tones. In this composition, however, the motive is an intervallic one, and although its use is almost procedural rather than conceptual, its prevalence throughout the entire composition in both augmentation and diminution merits attention. It is dominated by the interval of the third.

Each textual section commences with a new theme, which most frequent-

[6] Discussed by Helmuth Osthoff in *Josquin Desprez* (Tutzing, Schneider, 1962–65), II, 103, in which the opening of the motet is given. Complete motet in Josquin, *Complete Works: Motetten*, V, 85 (No. 79).

ly moves among all four voices in free imitation that sometimes is intensive and in tight stretto. The opening fifteen measures, projecting with rhythmic declamation the first three words, are fugal in texture, the second and third entries at the fifth, an added entry in the tenor correspondingly closing the section. Only a few of the themes in the motet are quoted here to point out the degree of intervallic similarity which prevails. The bracket, ⌐¬, has been used to indicate the various manifestations, both large and small, of the interval of the third. The opening theme, for example, not only commences immediately with the third (falling), but also outlines the same tones in its own frame, i.e., from its beginning to its end (Example 4). Were this the sole basis for unity, it would be sufficiently interesting to merit attention. The text is drawn from the Gospel According to St. Matthew, and the thematic material reveals, in its unified construction based upon the third, the same quality of homogeneity that prevails in the recitation of the Gospel. Through his tonal structure, the composer has given us a clear realization of the importance of the third. The motet is divided into a number of successive sections based on the text organization. In each of these sections one can see that the direction is determined by the interval of the third. It is true that the bass joins equally with the other voices in the imitative activity, yet it is handled subtly in such fashion as to achieve its goals in the structure at the same time. An outline of the structure-defining motion of the bass for the entire motet is given in graph 4a.

The opening section illustrates the control of the bass, for not only does the bass share in the thematic statement with the motivic third when it enters in bar 9, it also beautifully supports the last added statement in the tenor with a concluding augmented reiteration of the third at the very end. The plan of the bass-motion points out clearly the constant smaller motions of thirds. In some of these motions the bass is carrying thematic motivic material in the imitative scheme as, for example, in the section between bar 62 and bar 75. But at other times it follows pathways dictated by tonal functions, i.e., in prolongations of a chord moving from its root to its third, as in the opening section, or in triadic horizontalization, as in the section immediately preceding bar 53. Most interesting are the spatially augmented versions of the third, i.e., the large-scale motions that frequently mark the beginning and the end of a section. For example, the second section of the motet begins at bar 16 on C and terminates on A. The framework of the

EXAMPLE 4 *In illo tempore* Josquin

third is in the section from bar 39 to bar 46, and, from this point to bar 61, the large motion is C–A–F. At bar 62 the section starts on F and ends on A; the next section ends on C (bar 105). Harmonic motions are the exception and occur both internally and only three times as sectional cadences, this paucity despite the fact that the motet is in the Ionian mode, in which opportunities for harmonic movement are greater than in any of the other modes. Josquin chooses instead paths that are dictated by other factors, achieved with a consistency that implies a purposive viewpoint. The third lends itself admirably to close-knit stretto possibilities, and one can find many similar examples of this stretto technique in the music of Josquin. But in this case the motivic content is given spatial significance and function. The final section (immediately following bar 111) illustrates the technique of climax of which Josquin is so very fond, now adapted to the motivic life of the motet: the fall in thirds, C–A–F, a momentary interruption, then again, C–A–F–D to C, to complete the octave. While this C is sustained in

Graph 4a

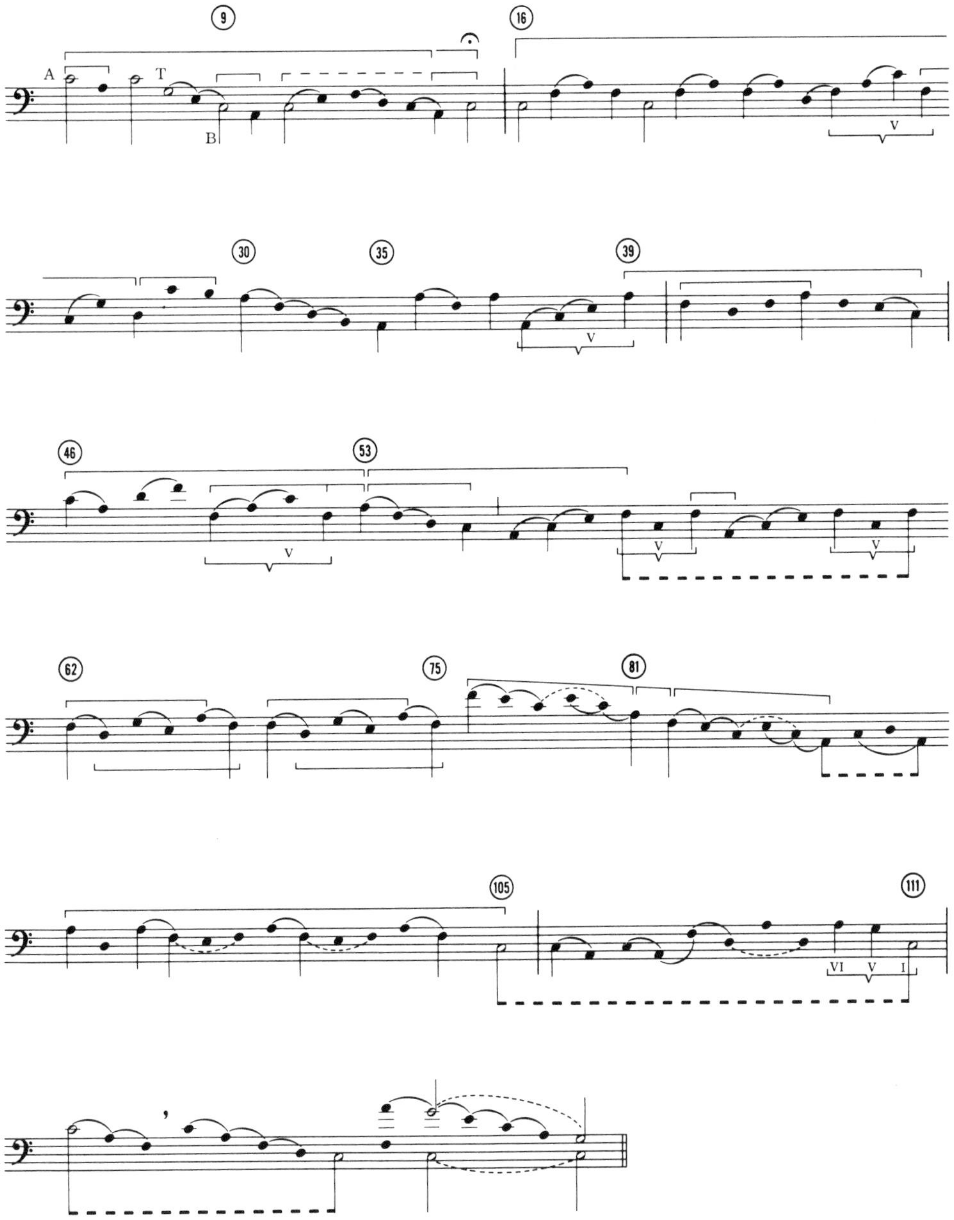

the bass, an upper voice also moves through the octave in descending thirds plus a second!

Example 5, the "Osanna" from Josquin's *Missa Mater Patris*,[7] will illustrate the more dynamic collaboration of design and tonal organization. The repetition of text is a simple one, for, in this unit of the *missa ordinarium*, there are only three words. Although the underlaying of the text is not complete, and therefore subject to question, the repetition of a refrain (designated by the letter R) of only two measures duration, projected by four voices moving in rhythmically unified fashion, contrasted by intervening sections involving only two voices of different texture, suggests the following possible interpretation:

R_1	A	R_2	B_1	R_3	B_2	R_4	C
Osanna	in excelsis	Osanna	in excelsis	Osanna	in excelsis	Osanna	in excelsis.
bars 1–15	16–18	19–23	24–27	28–32	33–36	37–41	42–48

The manner of stating this brief theme is not schematic as it is in the fugal procedure. Yet the two active voices, bassus and altus, that act as the protagonists, share the role generally assumed by four or more voices in a fugal presentation of a theme. It is stated first by the bassus, beginning on G, its shape made of lower and upper neighboring tones, immediately followed in the altus on G, and reiterated in the bassus on G. At bar 7 the theme is stated in the altus on D, in bar 9 in the bassus on A, and in bar 11 in the altus on A. This is the preparatory stage, i.e., the initial statement of the thematic material by two voices only, which, in following the course of ascending fifths, G–D–A, realize a fugal technique used by Josquin and Obrecht for three or more voices in other compositions. It is at bar 13 that the four voices come together in reiteration of the same theme, which, in its immediate relationship to the previous statement, is to be found in the altus, supported by the other voices of which the superius supplies a sonorous addition of a parallel third above the theme. The bassus and altus, having provided the introduction, now carry the first episode that constitutes the first departure from the theme. From this point on, the theme returns only

[7] Josquin, *Complete Works: Missen*, III, 1; reproduced with permission of the publisher. A discussion of the Mass as a whole is given by Osthoff, I, 151 ff.; also in Edgar Sparks, *Cantus Firmus in Mass and Motet, 1420–1520* (Berkeley and Los Angeles, University of California Press, 1963), pp. 360 ff.

EXAMPLE 5 *Missa Mater Patris: Osanna* Josquin

EXAMPLE 5 (*continued*)

EXAMPLE 5 *(continued)*

EXAMPLE 5 (*continued*)

in statement by the four voices. In the concluding section the sonority attains a new climax through the change in register, moving up an octave, and achieving a touch of thematic finality through the use of Josquin's personal signature, the last descending third, in the tenor. An analysis of the entire movement is given in graphs 5a and 5b.

The dotted line in graph 5a indicates the course of the theme at the outset. As mentioned above, the reiteration of the initial statement on different degrees embodies one of the principles found in the fugue. While the bassus and altus carry the responsibility of the entries at first, it is the subsequent reiteration on different degrees that realizes one of the important through-compositional principles of thematic articulation. If this were the only basis upon which the procedure were to rest, we still would have a more sophisticated piece than the "Sancti Dei omnes." More than that, however, is the unique way in which the tonal order is achieved in cooperation with these design repetitions. The upper voice is the altus and must so be considered from the structural viewpoint, the superius being added at the appropriate moments for intensifying sonority, remaining always subservient to the altus. The initial statement of the theme three times on G, then D, and finally twice on A, completes the quasi-fugal procedure, the section then being clearly defined by the four-voiced statement (bar 13). The first episode at bar 16 returns to D at bar 19 to complete the extension of the D triad, and the refrain then recurs. The following episode, a close stretto at the unison, has moved directly to the B♭-major chord, which is prolonged until bar 28, the next statement of the refrain. Immediately afterwards a similar unison stretto of the same material attains the tonic G triad, and this, too, is affirmed at bar 37 by the four-voice refrain. Thus far the motion of the bassus, as indicated in graph 5b, has been G–D–B♭–G, successively outlining in descent the G-minor (or Dorian) triad, and each triadic tone intensified by a statement of the refrain. Thus the tonality has been defined through the spatial disposition of the triad. Now comes the concluding section, in which the harmonic structure definitively and climactically asserts the tonal order of the movement. While the first large-scale prolongation projects the G-minor triad through its horizontalization, the overall structure achieves it harmonically. The direction of the upper voice unfolds parallelisms: the rapid rise of the fifth at the beginning, and the descent of the fifth at the completion of the prolongation at bar 37; and the reiteration of the descending fifth (D falling to G, but now stepwise) in the final section. This interval plays an important role in the episodes as well, as indicated in graph 5a, by the various diminutions that take place, both in ascending and descending form.

It is obvious that the recurrence of the theme, conditioned in itself by esthetic principles, is not left to chance. The points chosen seem so purposeful. How magnificent is the reiteration of the falling fifth and its strong harmonic support by I–V–I–IV–V–I as an achievement of climax! This is a jewel of unified musical logic, sensitively reflecting a totality of order.

Graph 5a

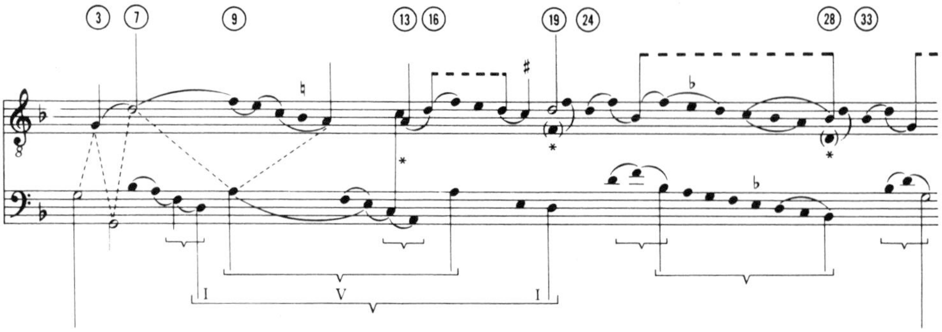

Graph 5b

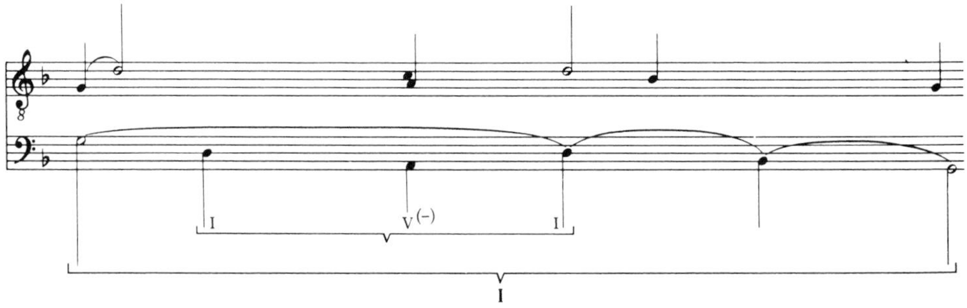

*Sonority statement of main theme, i.e., the refrain, after the initial section.

JOSQUIN: MISSA PANGE LINGUA

JOSQUIN's *Missa Pange Lingua* (Examples 6 through 24) is a paraphrase Mass based on the Feast of Corpus Christi hymn.[8] It is permeated by a flexible and fluid imitative texture of extremely clear character, yielding to declamatory representation at a few telling points. Its adherence to a *cantus prius factus* is traditional, and the settings of two sections of the *Agnus Dei* approach the old-fashioned cantus firmus technique; in the final section

[8] A detailed discussion is given in Osthoff, I, 193 ff.; also in Sparks, pp. 372 ff.

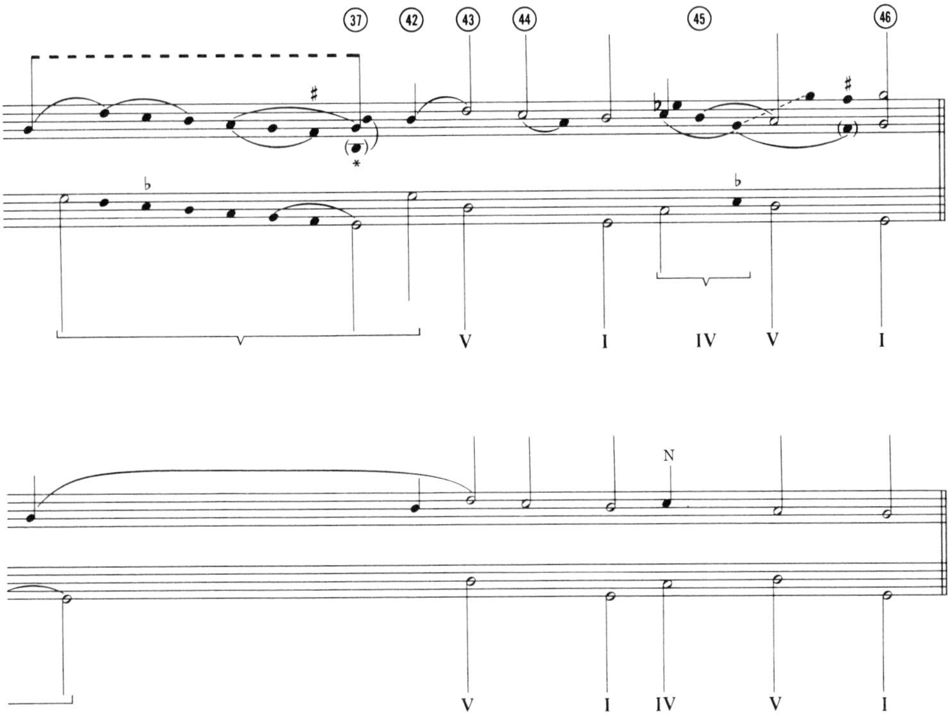

sustained tones are used. It is therefore the relationship to the chant melody that provides a structural support for this work. The clarity of the relationships of the movements to the hymn source is obvious in the use of incipits of the hymn, and one can trace the path taken by the composer in paralleling the melodic course of the Gregorian melody. But marking these tones (see Sparks) only provides a skeletal guide that is sometimes difficult to follow. At other times the parallelism breaks down or becomes too obscure to be of any importance for purposes other than of reference. But there is so much that is new in this Mass, that provides integration and creates unity, that one realizes this is a composition which reveals both the traditional concept and a new vision. Certainly the genius of Josquin in this work is that of the traditionalist who knows how to bend his material to serve his own esthetic ends. Thus, the old and the new are unfolded simultaneously, the former yielding to the latter.

EXAMPLE 6 *Missa Pange Lingua: Kyrie I*

Graph 6a

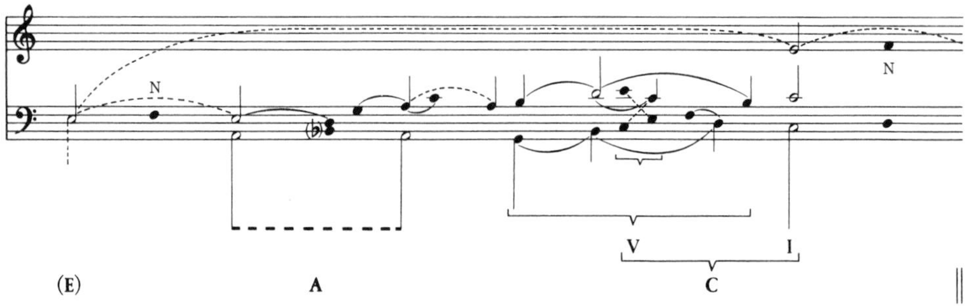

The chant melody is Phrygian, and Josquin remains faithful to it. This mode, however, when used in polyphony, presents certain limitations if the composer is to remain true to it. Musica ficta cannot be applied readily without threatening to contradict the mode's most characteristic features. The half-step between the first and second degrees precludes the use of the leading tone, since the diminished third or augmented sixth cannot be admitted. The use of a v, i.e., a triad based on the fifth degree, is impossible as well, because of the presence of the diminished fifth. Therefore, tonality, if it is to be used as an underlying, unifying principle, must rely upon other devices. In this case the composer finds these other ways, and while the total viewpoint is not systematic, the procedure adopted reveals a consistency which compellingly signals a unique approach to large-scale order.

The setting to the opening of *Kyrie I* (Example 6) will serve as the point

Josquin

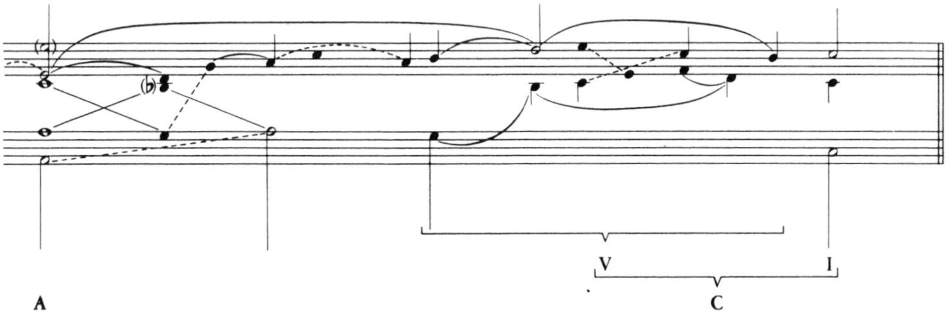

of departure. The rise of the opening of the chant melody from E to C is tightly paraphrased by the top voice, but this is only the beginning, for, the direction having been set by this path, the motion is continued to complete the large phrase, the ending of which is marked by the entry of the paired lower voices (graph 6a). The first eight tones of the chant melody are stated at the outset. Tone A of the chant is followed immediately by tone C in bar 3. The immediately succeeding second C of the chant is attained only at the end of the phrase in bar 5, thus having the chant phrase as a whole paralleled by the polyphonic phrase. Between these two C's, however, a motion is unfolded that gives the opening a specific and important character. These tones are not equal in importance. The first one is absorbed in the prolongation of the A in bar 3, which moves directly to the important B. This latter tone, now prolonged until it reaches the definitive, phrase-ending C, is supported by the G-chord, the dominant of C. Thus the chant

EXAMPLE 7 *Gloria: Et in terra*

Graph 7a

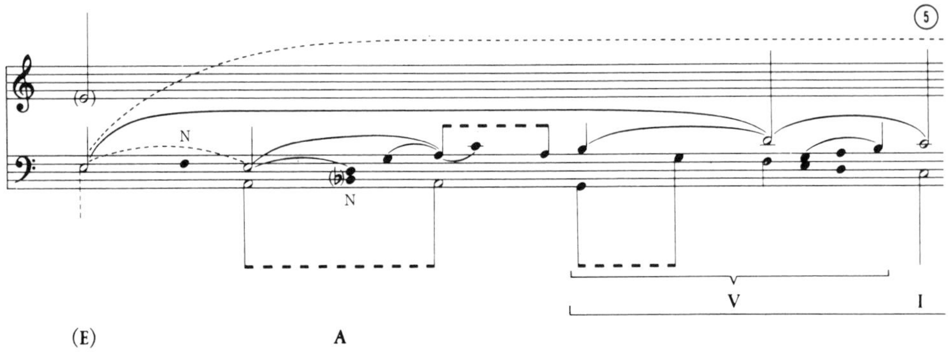

material has been spatially controlled to permit this technique, which becomes basic to other parts of the Mass, as will be shown. The motion to the C-chord is a deliberate choice. It is far more dynamic than the other possibilities, i.e., supporting the C with either A or E. It allows the use of the V–I to the C, which is thus not only attained with strength but also articulated as a spatial division of primary importance.

Thus the first point of stability, generally described as "cadence," is attained at the C-major triad, a process which is immediately repeated (with an overlapping beginning) by the paired upper voices. The opening imitation at the fifth below is a parallel to the fifth relationship in the motion from G to C. This twofold descending fifth relationship provides the essential basis for the opening of a number of succeeding sections. They are not necessarily the same. The opening of the *Gloria*, while choosing the same basic route, elaborates the dominant and tonic of C in a different fashion (Example 7).

The importance of C as an initial goal of motion is confirmed by its

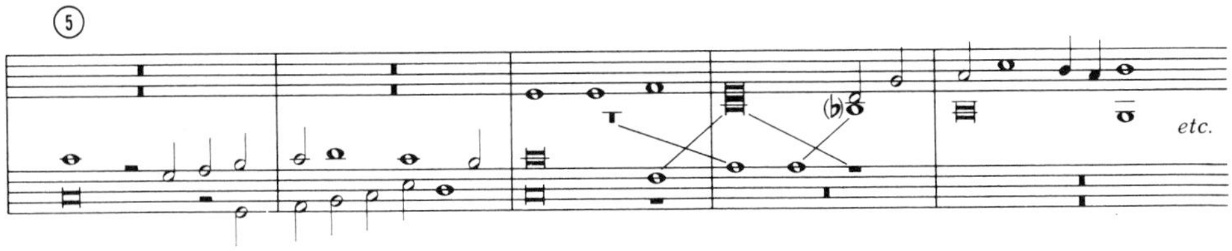

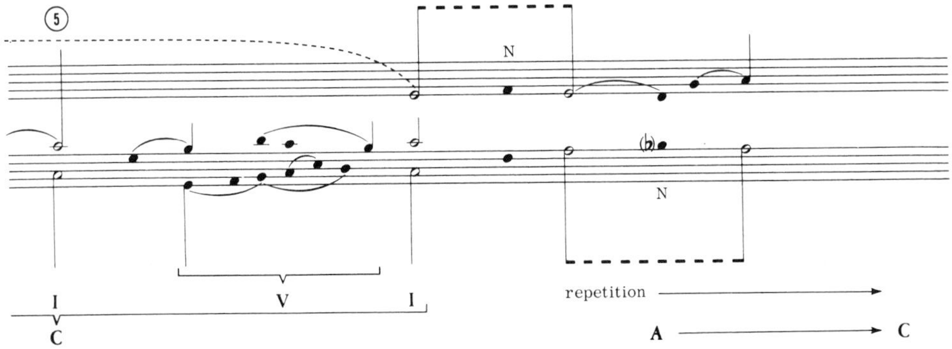

similar position in the openings of the *Credo* (and "Crucifixus"), *Sanctus*, and *Agnus Dei I*. In each of them, as will be shown subsequently, the treatment is different, yet the goal remains the same. It is in the *Agnus Dei III* that the composer reveals his consistency of goal, for there the involvement with a cantus firmus of long, extended tones creates a completely different environment no longer conditioned by the immediate implications of the paraphrase route. Nevertheless, C is attained unequivocally, as will be shown later. The importance of the C as a goal, however, must be considered in the light of the subsequent events, and in each of the settings it is different.

An analysis of the opening of the *Credo* ("Patrem omnipotentem") now follows (Example 8). The dominant and tonic are expanded considerably. Again the upper voices in paired fashion successively restate the substance of the paired lower voices in the opening. When this repetition is concluded, on C, of course, the next textual phrase, beginning on "visibilium" (bar 30), is completely prolonged within C. An interesting point is the definitely indicated B♭ that appears in bar 5, and again in bar 20, further support for

EXAMPLE 8 *Credo: Patrem omnipotentem*

Graph 8a

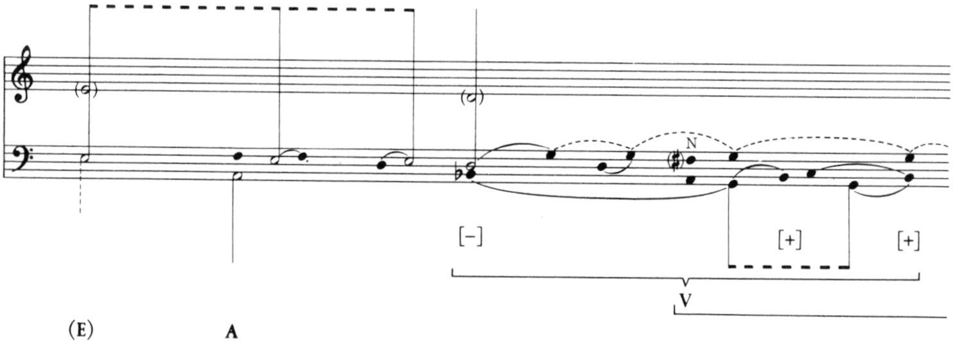

interpreting through musica ficta all similar openings in the Mass, to effect exact repetitions or "real" imitation.

As stated above, *Agnus Dei III* (Example 9) affirms the consistency of structure in its adaptation to the cantus firmus. Obviously the extended tones commencing at bar 7 preclude the use of paired voices as in the opening statements of *Agnus Dei I* and *II.* The cantus firmus superius is preceded by a four-voiced interphonic statement at the unison and octave, a paraphrase of the initial tones of the hymn, a simple extension of the opening E on which the cantus firmus enters. By avoiding this time the imitation at the fifth and a premature motion to A, the preparatory character of the opening is ensured. It is only after the superius enters that the motion begins (graph 9a).

The *Credo* is textually the longest unit in the Ordinary, thus accounting for the beginning of the paraphrase again at "Crucifixus." Yet in this case the treatment is somewhat different, although the paraphrase thread in the upper voice remains the same (Example 10). Its chief differences lie in the

function of the lower voice, now commencing on E instead of A. While this modification may be dismissed as a simple variation in imitative technique, i.e., imitation at the eighth instead of at the fifth, it is conditioned by other factors. Since this occurs in the middle of the *Credo*, it reveals its continuous relationship to the previous section, "Et incarnatus est," which concludes on C, strongly unified in several ways (Example 11). Primarily, the reiteration of the beginning of the "Pange Lingua" paraphrase creates a stable framework for the possible extension within the C Ionian (C major), the paraphrase occurring on the longer extended tones, as shown. The tonal center, C, is established with strong harmonic intensification. It is partly affirmed through the clear-cut direction of the uppermost voice which, drawn from the paraphrase, moves within the C-triad. Further, the paraphrased melody itself has been given such strong emphasis through the careful disposition of its triadically outlining melody, i.e., the occurrence of these tones at the moments of long extension. The conclusion of this section therefore clearly flows into the beginning of the "Crucifixus." Now it

EXAMPLE 9 *Agnus Dei III*

Graph 9a

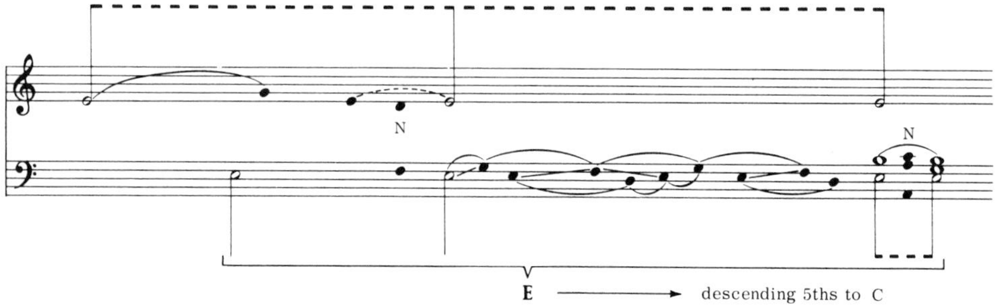

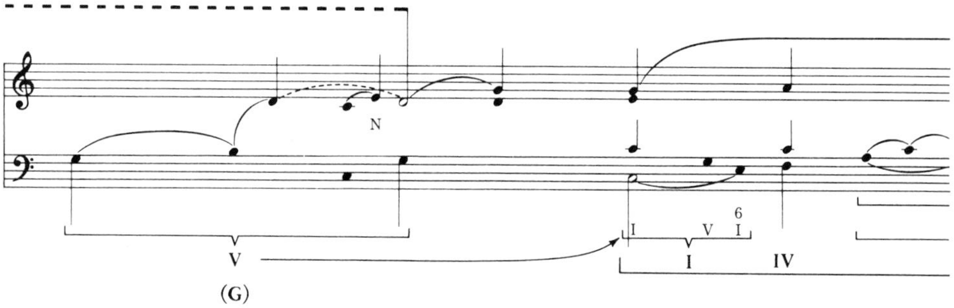

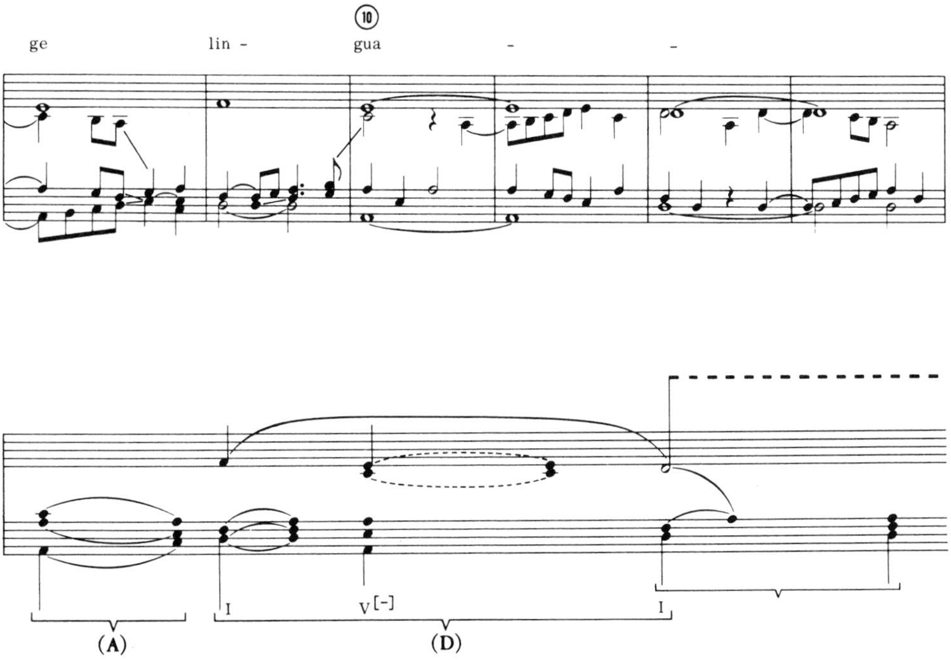
10
ge
lin -
gua
-
-
I
V[-]
I
(A)
(D)

20
- si) 25
Qui tollis
N
V[-]
I
[-]
6
V
I
(II)
V
I
C

EXAMPLE 10 *Credo: Crucifixus*

Graph 10a

*End of preceding section, "Et incarnatus est."

becomes obvious that its beginning must become subservient to the central role of C, hence the deviation from the previous implications of the paraphrased incipit.

The *Sanctus* beginning is similar to the other openings, fulfilling the motion from A to Ç, but varies somewhat in the extension of C. It also uses the paired-voices technique, and, due to the brevity of the movement, ends appropriately in C. *Agnus Dei I* projects again immediately the prolonged C which, consistent with the ultimate destination achieved in the other openings, arrives at the E (Phrygian) tonality, but not until the very end of the section, hence reflecting, in a sense, the compromise that obviously is being made with tradition. The clarity of the opening with C as its center is quite strong, achieved primarily through the use of imitation at the eighth, as was the case in the "Crucifixus," though in different fashion. Paired voices are not used this time, primarily because the tenor and superius are given the role of paraphrase, in canon, in its closest relationship to the chant melody.

The consistent use of the fifth relationship in the bass gives the Mass a strong quality of harmonic stability, i.e., the achievement of tonality not only through directed contrapuntal means, but also through the fifth relationship. In a sense this achievement cannot be won at the final cadences to each large movement since the Phrygian mode excludes the V–I relationship. As has been demonstrated, the very outset of the paraphrase, as treated by Josquin, sets the stage for the fifth relationship, i.e., the motion to the C of the end of the first phrase being realized through G. First, it acts as a strong connecting link between some sections of the Mass's movements (though there are exceptions); instances can be found in Example 12. Second, it acts as a strong factor for continuity within some of the sections, most interestingly in the manner in which it groups its motion from one point to the next in fusion with the thematic material.

In the *Gloria*, it is not the fifths alone that divide the sections into smaller units; each unit is also conditioned by the text. The outset of the *Gloria* begins on A and moves to C, as shown before. This motion is repeated through the paired-voices technique. The new text unit now starts at "Laudamus te," followed by "benedicimus te, adoramus te, glorificamus te." This obvious textual unity is fused with parallel musical treatment through an interphonic technique involving a repetitive design fragment (Example 13, superius). At the same time the bass and tenor share the theme in a different form (Example 13, bassus). Now, as the text changes, the motion is to G, which is prolonged (with neighbor-note motions to C) until the text reaches "Domine Fili," at which point C is regained, with repeated thematic design for the semi-rhyme "unigenite, Jesu Christe." For the concluding portion of the section, the basic motion to the final E is through the fifth relationship. This first large section, from "Et in terra pax" to "Filius Patris," may be represented as in Example 14.

The section which follows is fascinating in its use of the technique of descending or ascending fifths in association with imitation.[9] The opening to "Qui tollis" is so important that it is quoted (Example 15) to point out the obvious use of musica ficta at the entrance of the bass to articulate the already clearly defined exact imitation. The motion in descending perfect fifths proceeds then from the opening B through E, A, and to D. The bass then falls to A, at which point a chordal setting of "miserere" occurs. A

[9] The technique of successive fifths, either ascending or descending, was used by Obrecht and Josquin, among others. See Josquin's chansons "Fortuna d'un gran tempo," and "Cela sans plus," both printed in the *Odhecaton* (pp. 375 f. [No. 74] and pp. 349 f. [No. 61], respectively, the former with different signatures for each of the three parts, immediately related to the real imitation of the entering voices.

EXAMPLE 11 *Credo: Et incarnatus est*

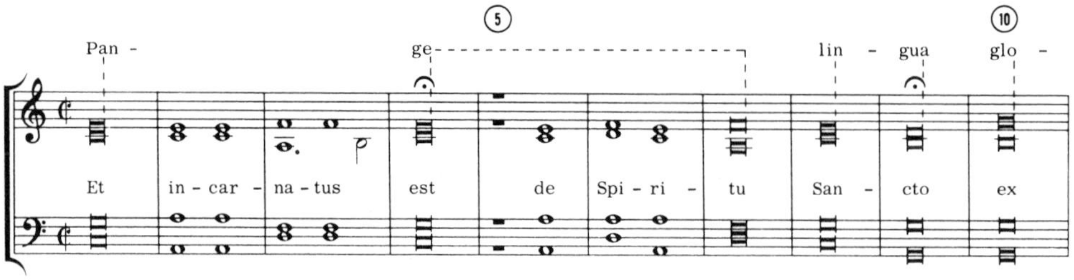

Graph 11a

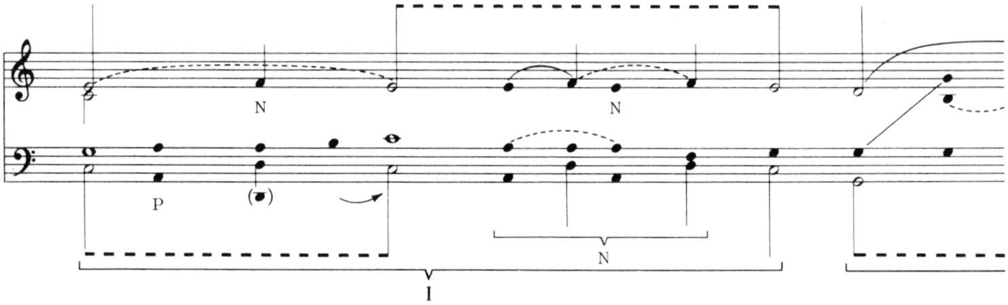

representation of the bass motion from the beginning of "Qui tollis" to the end of the entire *Gloria* is given in Example 16. The tonal divisions are accented through the relationships as indicated, fused as they are with the changes in the text. In addition, the changes in musical texture further articulate subdivisions. This is particularly so in the succession of the chordal "miserere" and the two-line imitation on "Qui tollis." "Suscipe" now follows in chordal texture, and breaks up in a flowing ending to the phrase. Particularly noteworthy is the disposition of the fifths among the alternating paired voices at "Quoniam," the continuation of the fifths succession, and alternating voices applied to the "Tu solus" and again on "Cum Sancto Spiritu."

The *Credo*, because of its great textual length, offers more difficulties than other movements of the Mass. The text, however, subdivides into various sections, offering the possibilities of design contrast. In this setting Josquin has varied the thematic material, though the paraphrased incipit still retains a primary position. Not only is it used at the outset of the move-

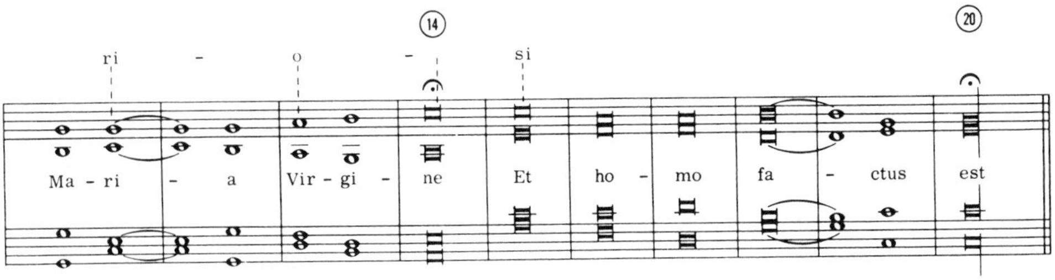

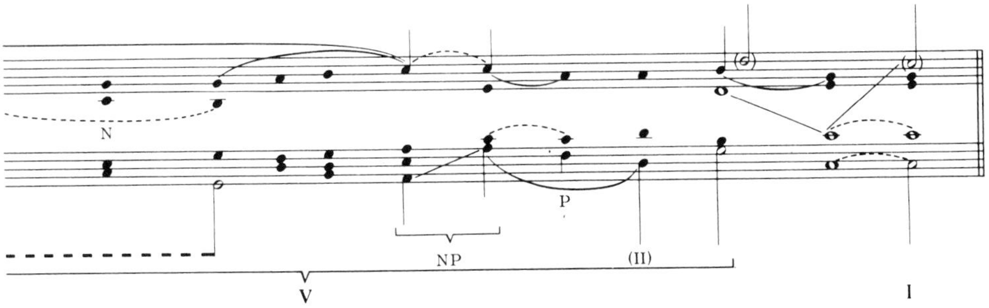

ment, but it also is brought in, as shown previously, at "Et incarnatus est," which symbolically stands at the center of the *Credo*, and also at the beginning of the "Crucifixus" section. The various subdivisions remain internally unified by prevailing design repetitions that are sometimes interphonic and at other times declamatory. A figure approximating an extended motive occurs in the "Crucifixus" section, i.e., the repeated tone motive which appears first at "sub Pontio Pilato" and which is used with much frequency, reaching its climax in "Confiteor," and continues almost without pause until "Amen."

Yet, even though the thematic design is primarily mosaic, the unity of the movement is achieved through the order of the tonal motion. The fifth-degree relationship is not only consistently maintained but is also closely allied with textual units and subunits, as indicated in the outline of the bass motion (Example 17). C Ionian assumes a central position in the *Credo*, attained quickly at its beginning, and prolonged essentially throughout until the final motion at the approach to the "Amen" section. In its long

EXAMPLE 12

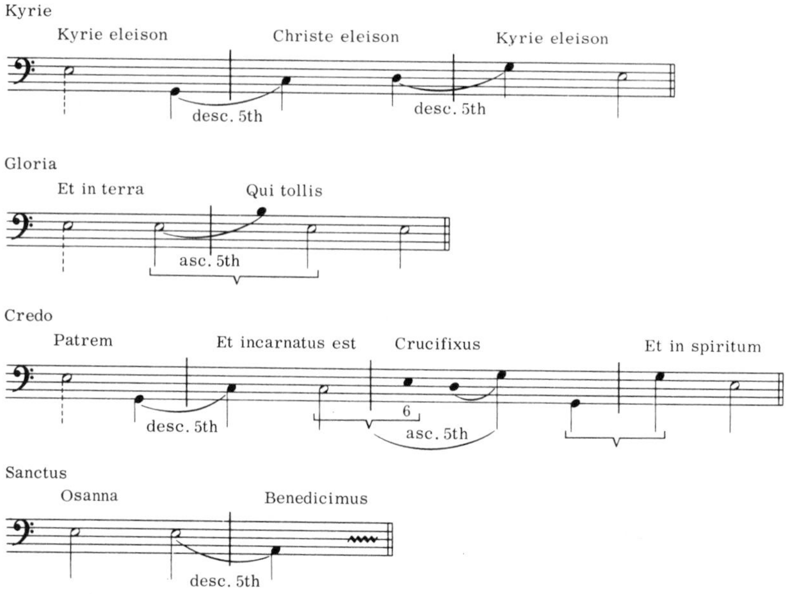

EXAMPLE 13 *Gloria: Laudamus te*

extension, C Ionian is in itself divided, the larger and main textual subdivisions either terminating on C or on G, in effect achieving a fundamental tonal organization in the full sense of tonic–dominant relationships. The subdivisions therefore fulfill the union of tonal motion and design manipulation. The subdivisions themselves are tonally not static, and, within these units as well, the employment of the relationship of the fifth provides the

EXAMPLE 14 *Gloria: Et in terra*

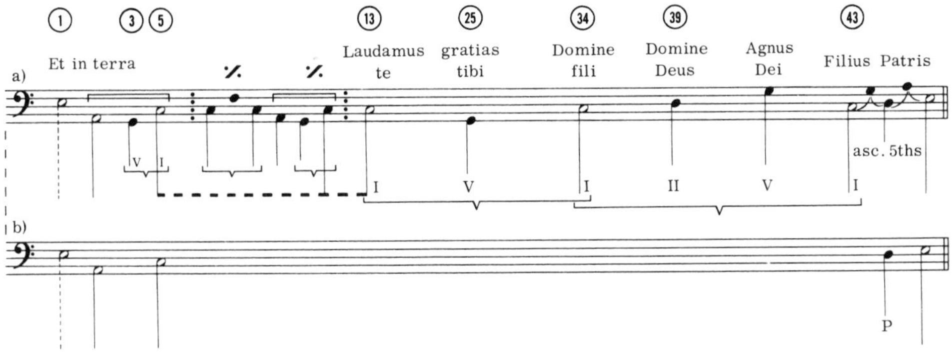

EXAMPLE 15 *Gloria: Qui tollis*

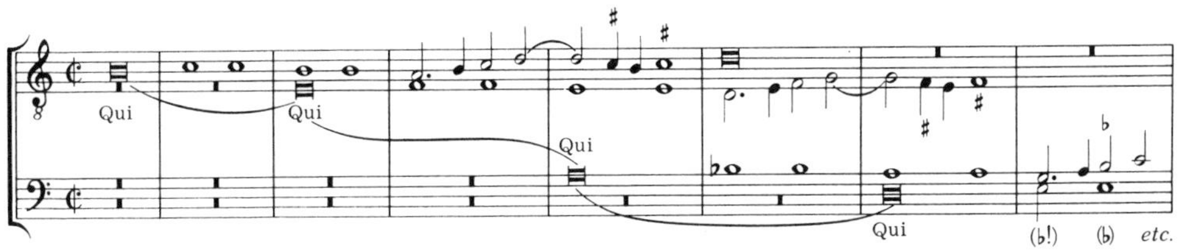

impetus of motion. It is only at the end of the *Credo* that a final motion to A, to coincide with a sectional completion, is made through its dominant, and in this case through the unequivocally indicated use of the leading tone with the dominant. The consistency of the Phrygian setting is realized at the very end by the subservience of the A-chord to the E-triad. Although one might point to the ambiguity of the E as a tonal center, the significance of the E is unquestionable as an affirmation of the entire Mass's structure. Further, consideration must be given to the top voice's role in the tonal organization, and, as will be shown later, its nature confirms the primacy of E to which, as in this movement, the A is functionally subservient.

The opening section of the *Sanctus* moves from A to C in a fashion parallel to the other incipits. The prolongation of the C Ionian completes the *Sanctus*, the bass plan of which is given in bars 1 through 20 (Example 18). Is it not possible to view these two prolongations in terms of harmonic structure, i.e., each organized by a basic harmonic progression as indicated?

EXAMPLE 16 *Gloria: Qui tollis*

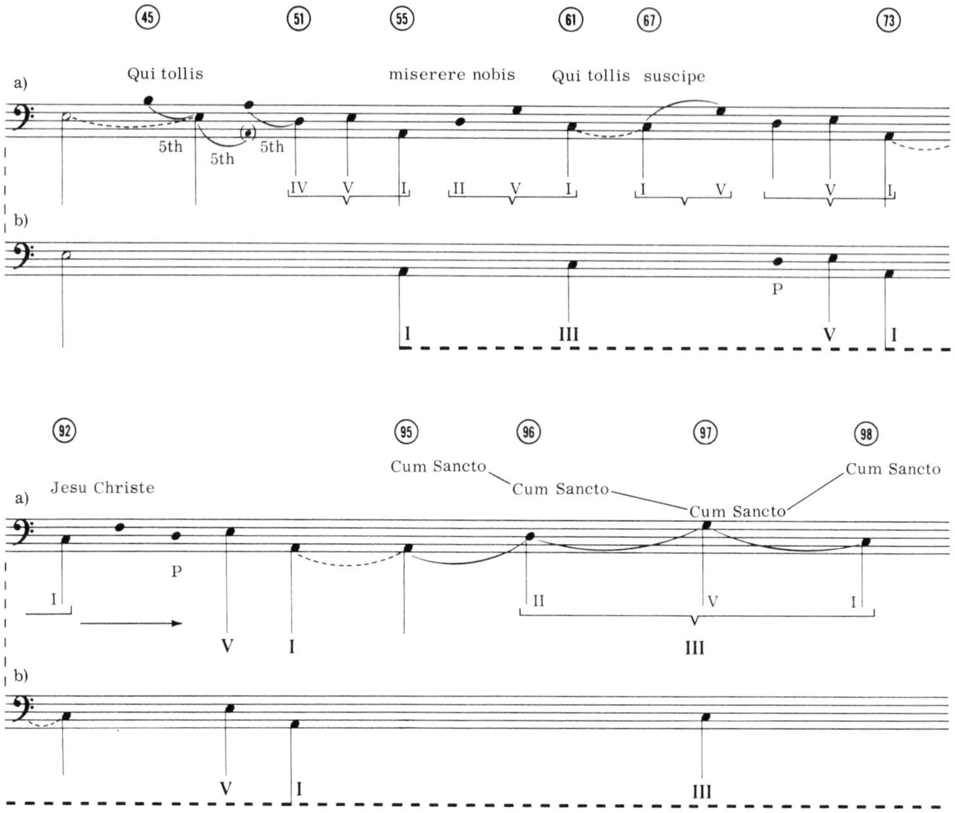

Can we dismiss such pieces as "modal" and "contrapuntal"? In the example, starting at bar 21, it can be seen that "Pleni sunt coeli," for two voices only, begins on E. Proceeding in changing canonic fragments up to the last section (the change to imperfectum), the sense of E is projected, and the techniques of tonal divisions are sharply related to the textual–thematic units. The importance of C as a spatial divider is affirmed by its occurrence at the point of textual change, just as it is in the other units.

While the section lacks an harmonic structure, the use of fifths is still applied to prolongations of subunits, e.g., the beginning of the "gloria tua" closing section. The final intensification of E lies in the repetition of the mode in scale form in the lower voice and the octave leap at the end, a

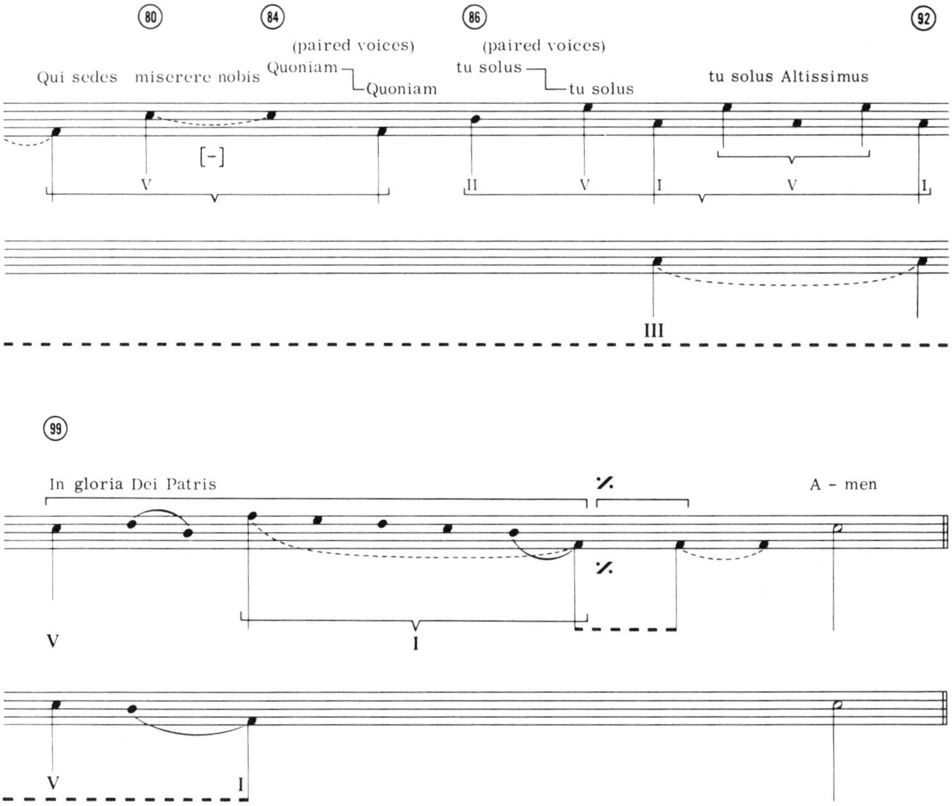

typical terminal climax unique to Josquin. Now the entire example, from the beginning of the *Sanctus* through "gloria tua" can be seen as a continuous whole. Not only are they intimately bound together, but an interesting spatial symmetry (in retrograde) is achieved, as seen in Example 18b.

Another point of particular interest is the twofold setting to the word "Sanctus" at the beginning, wherein the paired upper voices overlap the entry of the succeeding two lower voices, also imitatively paired, in such a way as to achieve a v, effecting thereby a return to the I for the repetition of the design corresponding to the second statement of the word "Sanctus." This is very similar in concept to a first and second ending, a true *overt* and

EXAMPLE 17 *Credo*

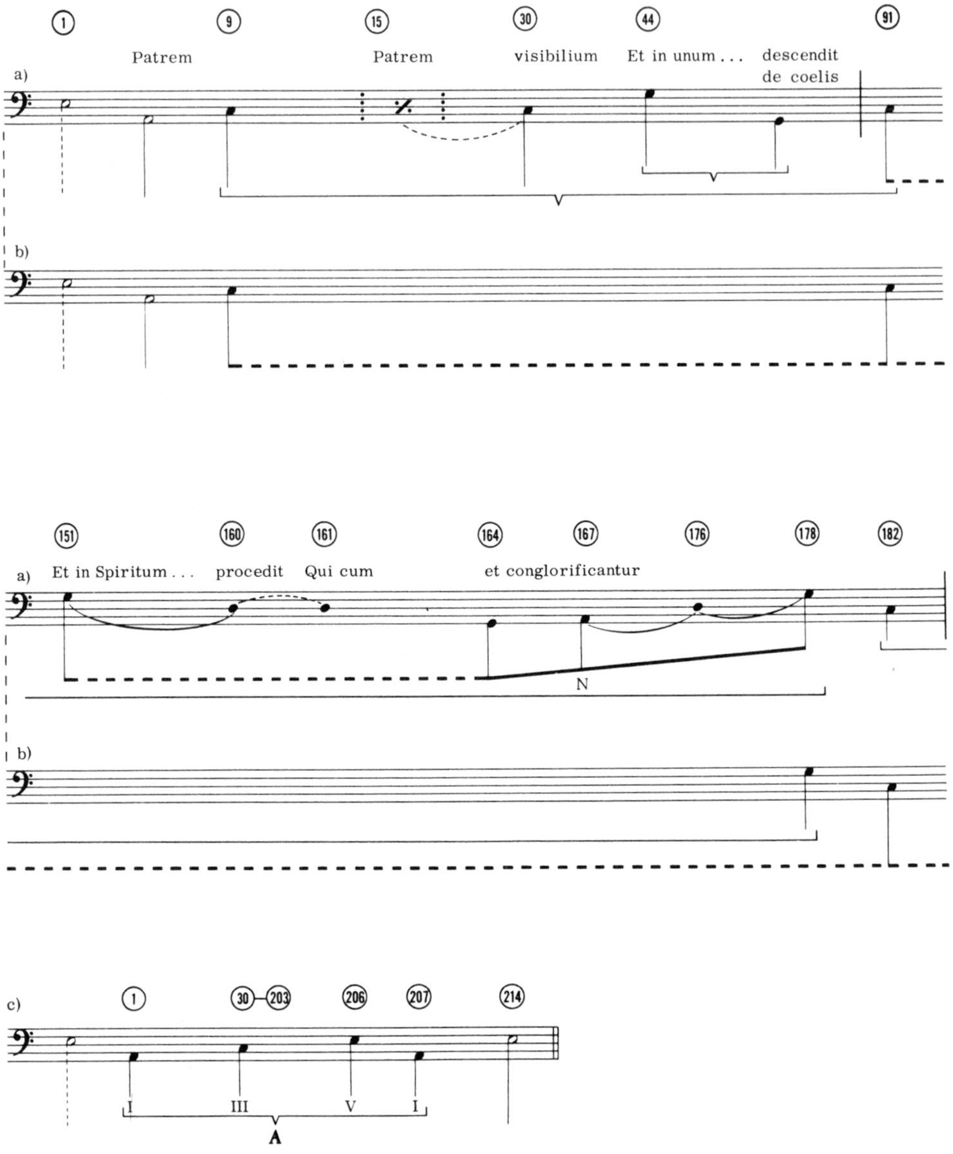

91
Et incarnatus est . . .
111
Crucifixus
121
136
. . . et iterum venturus est
6
I
V
I
II
V
I
V
182
183
Confiteor
200
et vitam venturi
207
214
Amen
I
V
I
II
V
I
P
P
V
I

EXAMPLE 18 *Sanctus*

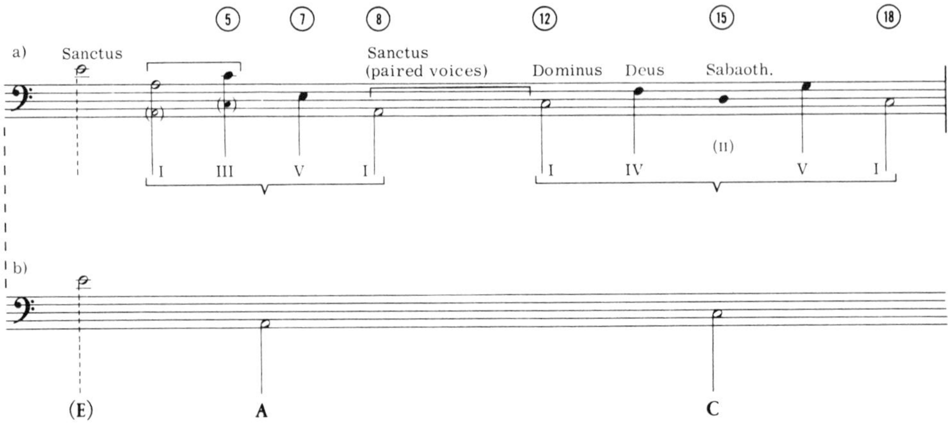

clos, fused with tonal structure and, in basic principle, not unlike the frequent use of large-scale I–III–V–I progressions with corresponding repetitions of thematic material in music of later periods.

The consistency of the fusion of harmonic motion and thematic design is focused sharply and brilliantly in the "Osanna." Now the motions are controlled not only by the subdivisions of text, but also by sonority–space contrasts, i.e., the use of paired voices. The ending of the preceding section is on E, on which structural tone the "Osanna" begins. The first phrase is stated three times by alternating paired voices. An outline of the movement is given in Example 19. It is obvious that C is the goal of motion in descending fifths from the starting E. The paired voices profile the motion to each succeeding point, and at the moment the C is attained, a new section, textually, texturally, and rhythmically, begins. Again, through the fifths, now in ascending form, but without the added clarity of the previously used technique, the motion is completed to the A, at which, falling to the final E, the section is completed. A beautiful symmetry is achieved: descending fifths from E to C; ascending fifths from C back to E. The similarity to the overall structure of "Pleni sunt coeli" is striking, i.e., E–C–A–E.

The fascinating parallelism of the chant in the utilization of the paired-voices repetitions, as well as the repetitions of the neighboring tone motive

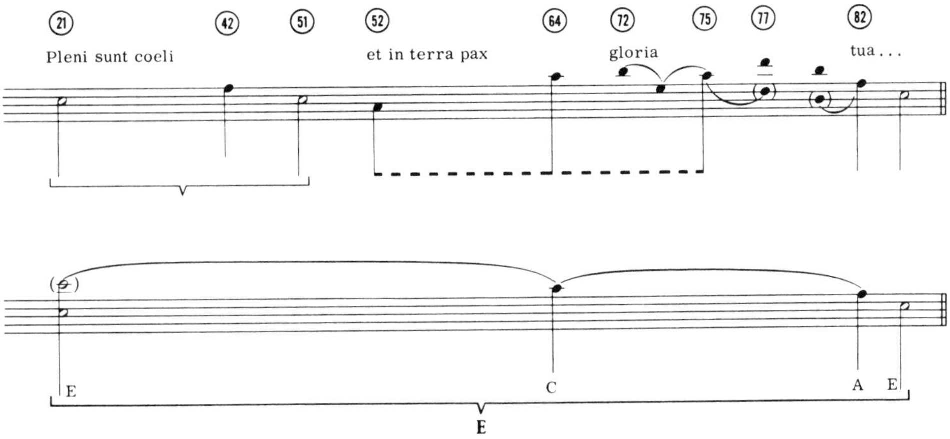

in each unit, is seen as another example of the flexible adaptation of the chant material (Example 20). Maintaining the consistency of the half-step Phrygian opening, one must change the B to B♭ in the third paired statement. The design at bar 10, significantly, is modified, thus not repeating the parallelism of the opening, which would have precluded the use of the leading tone in its most wanted structural parallelism, the V–I motion in the attainment of the crucial C.

The *Benedictus*, set for two voices, is a curious piece whose overall structural unity is, at this point, questionable (Example 21). Its general organization of text and design is clear. The opening motive to the *Benedictus* is stated six times. "Qui venit" has its own motive, stated four times. The remaining section includes not less than ten statements of the same phrase to the words "in nomine Domini." Canon at the fifth is fairly consistently maintained, breaking each time primarily for the purpose of cadence. The fifth relationship still exercises its primary and consistent role in achieving immediate tonal goals. Further, the first large prolongation of A moves in a descending fifth to the tone, D, which serves as the center for the large prolongation for "in nomine." But how is this D to be explained? The return to the "Osanna" for its final repetition to end the movement, commencing on E, cannot be explained tonally except as a large-scale

EXAMPLE 19 *Sanctus: Osanna*

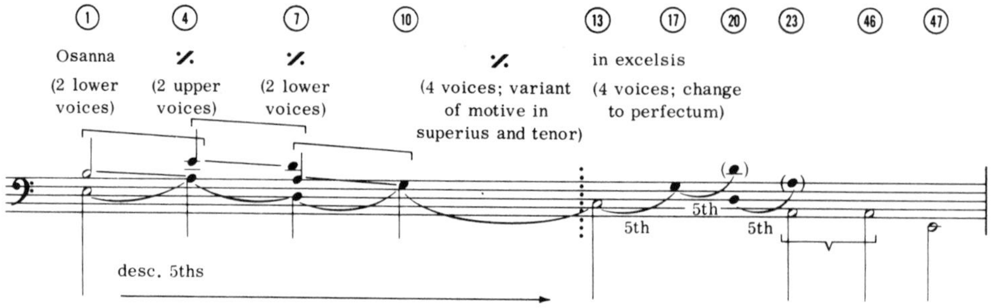

EXAMPLE 20 *Sanctus: Osanna*

EXAMPLE 21 *Benedictus*

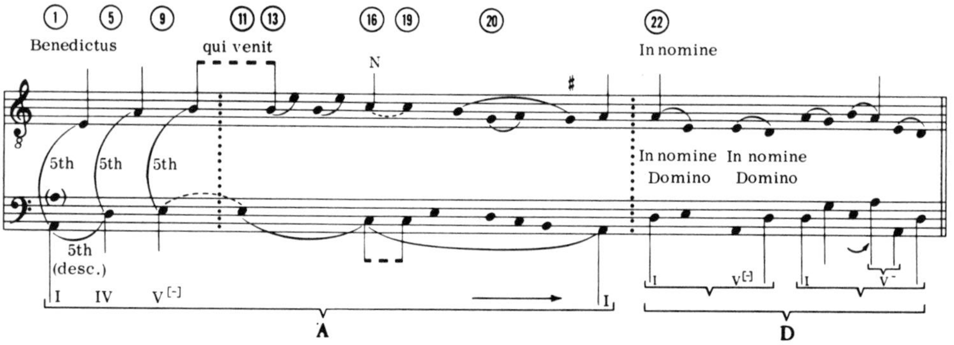

neighboring-tone motion, E–D–E. In so far as the evidence in this Mass is concerned, this technique is completely atypical.

Agnus Dei I emphasizes the structural importance of the same C Ionian in a bold and direct way that makes it unique (Example 22). To adapt the chant material to meet this condition, the imitative process must be changed, and here it is at the unison for altus, bassus, and tenor, and octave for superius. The first two voices immediately establish C prolonged through the modification of the fifth tone of the chant melody from D to C. Imitation at the unison rather than at the fifth, as in the openings of each of the preceding movements, is essential to establish the C-major opening. The tenor and superius, as upper voices, can continue the more exact paraphrase. The carefully worked-out repetitions can be understood in the context of the repeated prolongations of the C-chord. Then, when the more exact paraphrase occurs in tenor and superius, it is treated within these extensions —even, as in bar 6, supported by the dominant.

The ending of each of the movements illustrates Josquin's flair for climax achieved through the reiteration, in each case, of a motive. Sometimes the repetitions are many. More is involved, however, than merely thematic intensification. It is true that the end of the chant melody descends, and thus the polyphonic endings are a paraphrase of it. But Josquin shapes it to suit his own purpose, and in each case goes beyond it to start his descent from C, rather than B, the corresponding tone in the chant from which the descent begins. Thus he achieves a beautiful symmetrical complement to the beginning of each movement's rise from E to C. He does this in two basic ways: 1) a stepwise descent from C to E; 2) a non-stepwise descent, omitting in his upper-voice structure both the B and F, thus paralleling the beginning tones, e.g., in the *Kyrie* and the *Gloria*, which, after the neighbor-note motion above and below E, move to G, A, and then C. It is apparent in the analyses (Example 23) how important the third is, in both direction and prolongation. This is particularly stressed in the end to the *Gloria* and the concluding *Agnus Dei*. Finally, it becomes more than merely apparent that the upper voice is not an "equal" voice in the multilinear expression of musical thought. These endings strongly affirm the central and unifying position and role of E Phrygian. E is the key, and Phrygian is the mode. The upper line's clarity in outlining the motion to

EXAMPLE 22 *Agnus Dei I*

the final E, in the top voice, surely contradicts any possible interpretation of ambiguity. If one remembers the initial starting tone in the movement, one must be led to the possible interpretation of the complete rounding out of the E center through the motion of an upper line which begins on E and returns to E. Two examples of this possibility are given (Example 24). *Kyrie II* illustrates that type of opening which commences from a C in the lowest voice, above which the top-line motion, basically uniform in nearly all of the openings related to this principle, is E–D–C. The ending of the piece completes the descent of the octave. Transfer of register is involved in all of the openings, i.e., the motion from E to D then followed by a resolution to C an octave higher. This has been conditioned by the parallelism to the chant. The opening to the *Gloria*, as shown, is the more usual one, i.e., springing from the imitation at the fifth below, in which the direct motion to the A in the bass sets the stage for the motion to the C. The lower graph (b) of the *Gloria* abstractly represents the complete descent of the octave on the substituted one-register basis, in the version of E prolongation which begins upon E in the bass.

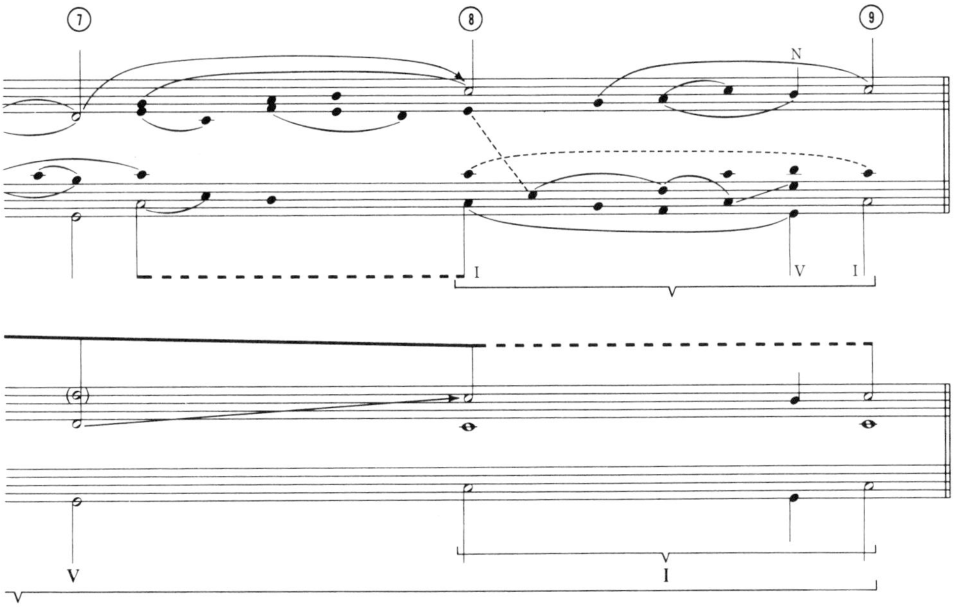

Thus, thematic design, direction, and structural parallelism are fused inseparably to gain climax and organic unity.

ISAAC: MISSA CARMINUM

ISAAC'S *Missa Carminum* (Examples 25 through 37) is a unique composition which projects an original concept of unity of a very high order. Thus far scholars have not been able to establish the identity of all the *carmina* that supposedly pervade the Mass, except, of course, for the very direct duplication of the famous Isaac lied, "Innsbruck, ich muss dich lassen," in its textless (instrumental) version,[10] as a contrafactum for the second "Christe eleison," and the use of the lied, "Die brünlein die do fliessen."[11] *Kyrie I* also has a very strong song quality, and the opening bears a strong resemblance to "Kein frewd."[12] Even "Die brünlein" is buried within the

[10] Printed in *Denkmäler der Tonkunst in Österreich* (Vienna, Artaria, 1907; Leipzig, Breitkopf and Härtel, 1907), Jahrg. XIV/I (hereafter cited as DTÖ XIV^{I}), p. 83 (No. 22).

[11] Discussed by Friedrich Blume in the preface to *Das Chorwerk, No. 7* edition of the Mass, in which mention is made of other possible sources.

[12] Isaac's setting is in DTÖ XIV^{I}, 16 (No. 13).

EXAMPLE 23

Kyrie II

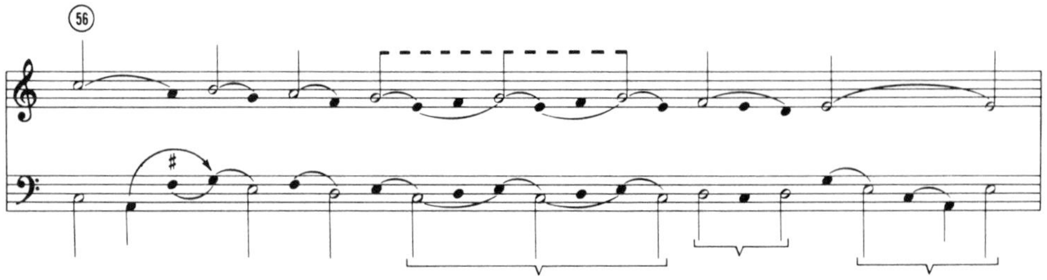

Gloria

Credo

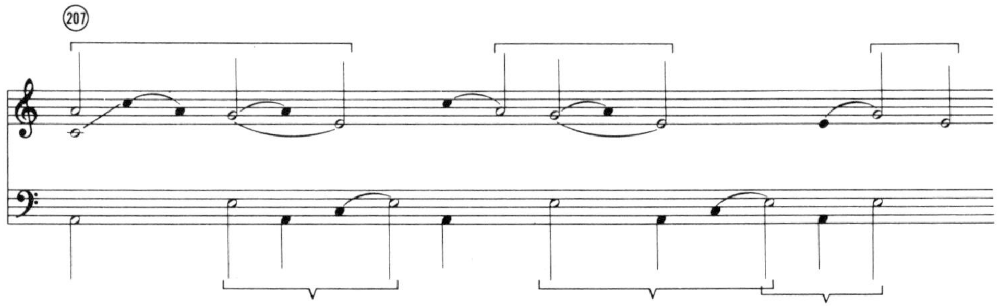

Osanna (finale of Sanctus)

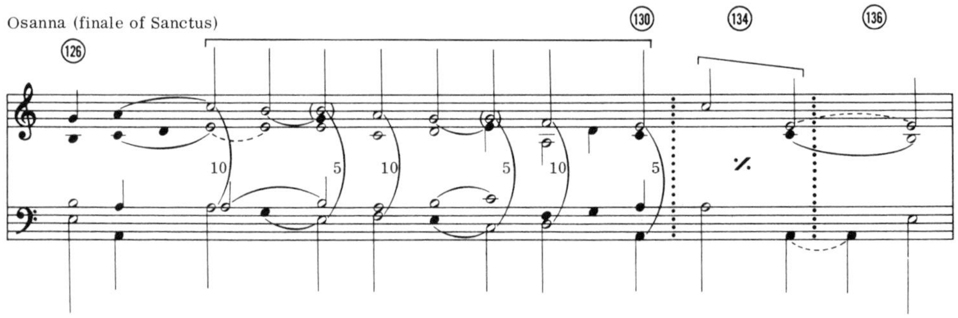

EXAMPLE 23 (*continued*)

Agnus Dei I

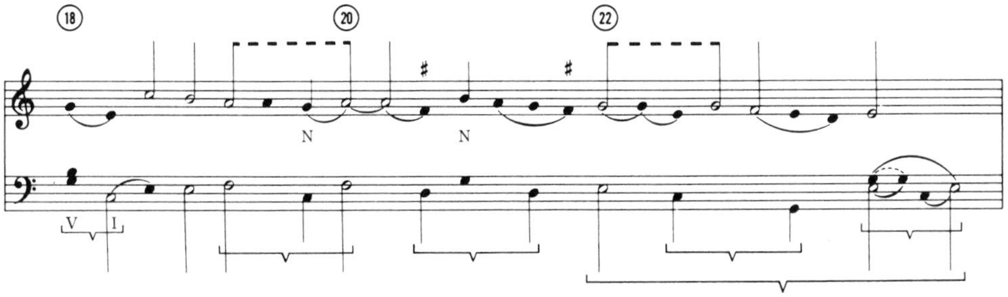

Agnus Dei III

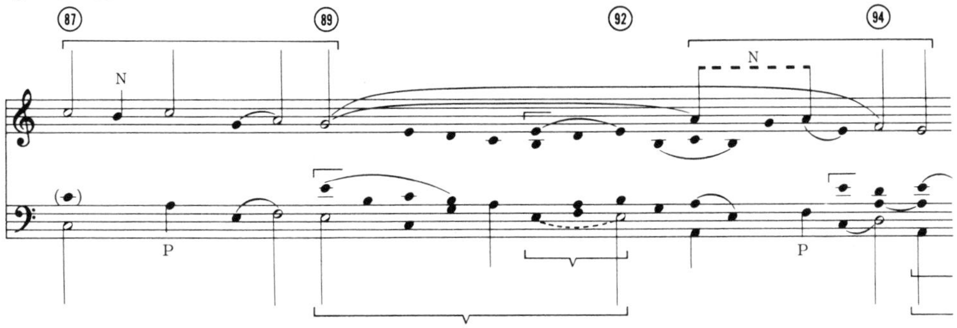

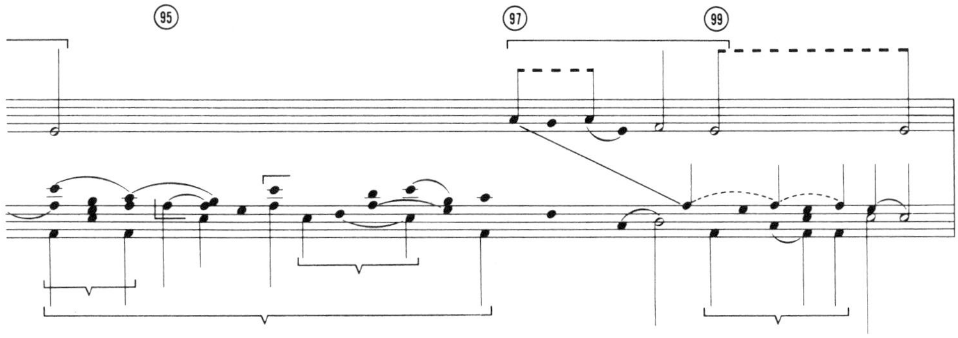

EXAMPLE 24

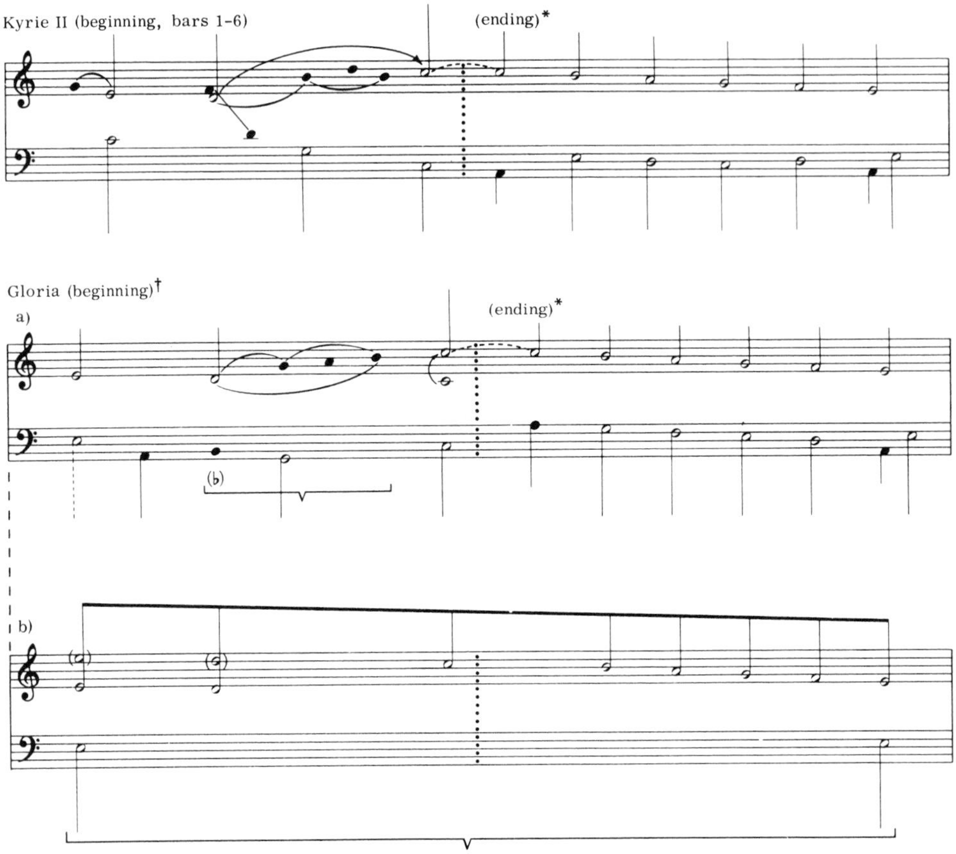

*See also Example 29. †See also Example 10.

interior and is very much lost in the polyphonic flow. While one may hope to discover one day additional song references which lie within, the Mass is truly a "Mass of songs" because it is essentially based upon the structural character of "Innsbruck." If it can be discovered that the openings of any of the movements or sections within the movements bear any resemblance to a specific *carmen*, it will, indeed, be much more than a coincidence that the movements are so closely related. It will be quite conclusive that the songs for the openings were chosen carefully because of their similarities. Again it must be stated that the *Kyrie I* seems to have a song source, and its strong individuality is affirmed by its adaptation for the opening of the *Sanctus*. There is, therefore, a strong structural unity to the Mass, for each of the movements reflects a large, overall reiteration of the structure, not only confined to the basic tonal organization but to the uppermost voice as well. One might be tempted to describe the parallelisms of the top line as an example of paraphrase, or the duplication of the tonal structure as a sophisticated extension of "parody" (*imitatio*) technique, but it is far more subtle and fascinating. The heart of the Mass, then, is the structure of the song "Innsbruck."

The vocal version[13] is given in Example 25. Its basic structure is similar to the instrumental version, the greatest difference being in some of the details created by the latter's emphasis on the canon between the tenor and superius, and the ending in which the upper voice rises to the high G, transferring the same basic motion of the vocal version one octave.[14] It must be emphasized that both the text and textless versions are involved in the Mass. A primary difference between them lies in the emphasis given to the upper voice, above all others, in the vocal version. Of the twenty-two German songs set by Isaac that are published in DTÖ XIV[1], this is the only one in which the melody is not set in the tenor, as is the case in the instrumental version. The unique top-voice setting is enhanced by the division of the melody into phrases separated by incisions of silence. This top-voice emphasis acts as a basis for the character of the upper voice during the entire Mass. The analysis of the structure of the song, given in graph 25a, reveals the emphasis made upon the interval of the fifth in the uppermost voice. While the melody rises a fifth at the outset and remains the highest point for the entire song, the third plays a dominant role, revealing its importance (note the indication of the bracket ┌──┐) in both large and small scale activity.

Another point which must be stressed is the function of the E♭ in the bass, which creates the effect of Mixolydian, but actually occurs in descending stepwise motion from the tonic to the dominant. In the instrumental

[13] "Isbruck, ich muss dich lassen," printed in DTÖ XIV[1], 15 (No. 12).

[14] In terms of actual register, the final F in both versions is the same, since the top voice of the "instrumental" version is set one octave lower than the "song" version, hence the rise of an octave restoring it to the same register.

EXAMPLE 25 *Innsbruck, ich muss dich lassen*

Graph 25a

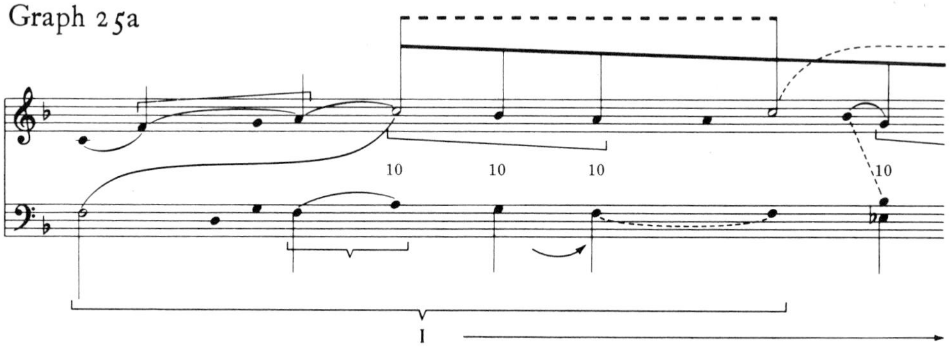

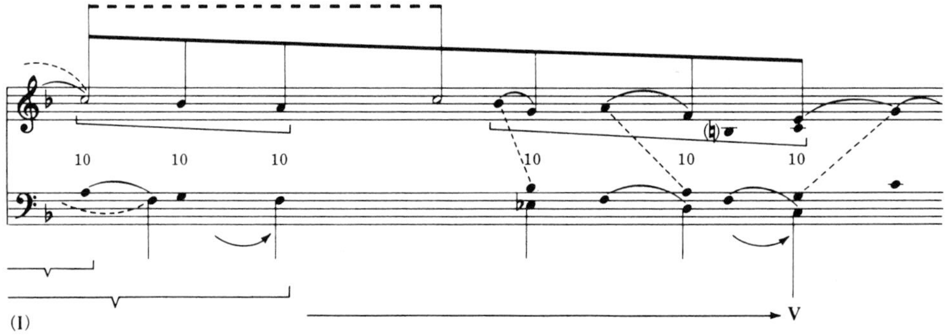

8
mein stras - sen in frem-de land da - hin. Mein freud ist mir
10
10
5
6
IN
V
I
16
ich im e - - lend
1.
bin, wo
2.
bin.
(II6)
I
IV
V
I

EXAMPLE 26 *Missa Carminum: Kyrie I*

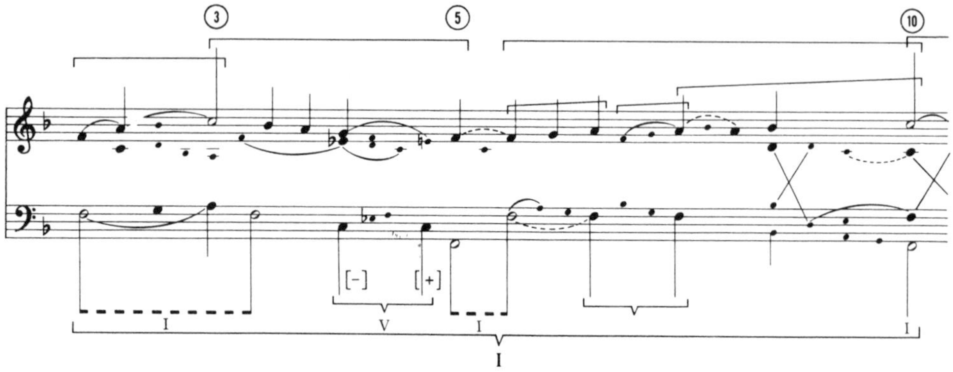

version its function is more directly involved in modal mixture, stated as it is within the prolongation of the dominant.

An analysis of the *Kyrie I* is shown in Example 26. If this stems from another song, its structural similarities with "Innsbruck" are a remarkable coincidence in regard to both the top and bottom lines. Again the motive of the third in the melodic line recurs in both diminution and augmentation. The bass, likewise, is involved in the dominant mixture (E♭). The space of the fifth is emphasized in the top line (as shown by the bracket ┌──┐).

Christe I emphasizes at the outset the opening fifth. The C is prolonged and does not begin its structural descent until bar 23. Within the

EXAMPLE 27 *Kyrie: Christe I*

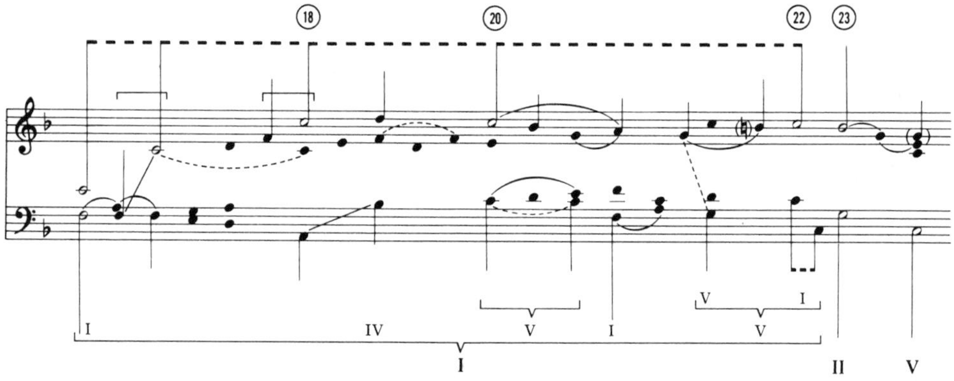

Isaac

extension of the dominant that terminates the movement (an harmonically "open" movement), the theme of the beginning is brought back in the bass, beautifully fusing the repetition of the theme with the final dominant (Example 27).

Christe II is, of course, the instrumental version of the "Innsbruck" tune. *Kyrie II* opens on the third, and the upper voice clearly fills, in the opening measures, the descent from A to F. The path is very different, thereby providing an interesting variation (Example 28).

Simultaneously, the tenor is following the melodic path of *Kyrie I* in rising a fifth to C, and falling stepwise. Immediately afterwards the bass

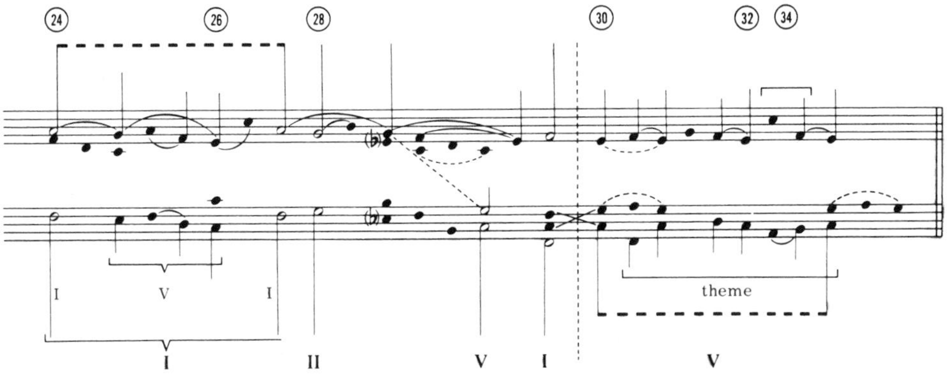

EXAMPLE 28 *Kyrie II*

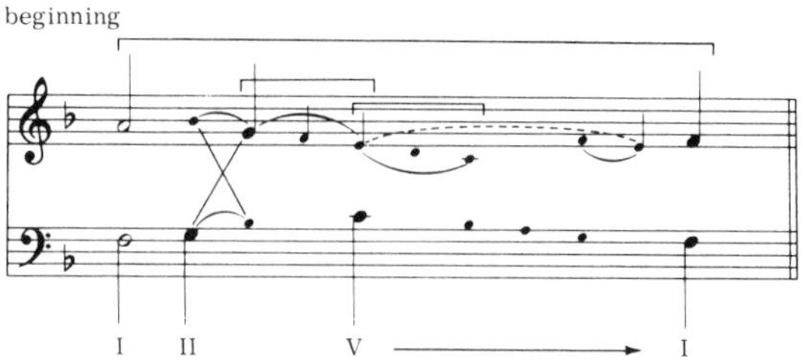

and tenor are in close stretto in which the fifth is intensified, and the descent in both voices is achieved at the end of the movement, thus realizing at the same time a multilinear parallelism of a basic detail of the *Kyrie I* structure. The tenor and the bass of the movement are given (Example 29).

EXAMPLE 29 *Kyrie I*

The tenor appropriately terminates the movement in augmentation of the descending line. The closing section of *Kyrie II* reiterates an "Innsbruck" motive while completing the structure (Example 30).

The polyphonic section of the *Gloria* begins with emphasis on the leap F to C, with an opening stretto of three voices at a combined space of only two measures. The upper voice spins out the same course as in *Kyrie I*, but in a different way. Here the fifth is given greater prominence, and further intensification of the opening leap comes in the section immediately following with the text "Laudamus te." "Benedicimus te, adoramus te, glorificamus te" continues to prolong the top C, moving down a third to A, or down an octave. Finally, on "gratias agimus tibi," the descent to F, supported by

EXAMPLE 30 *Kyrie II*

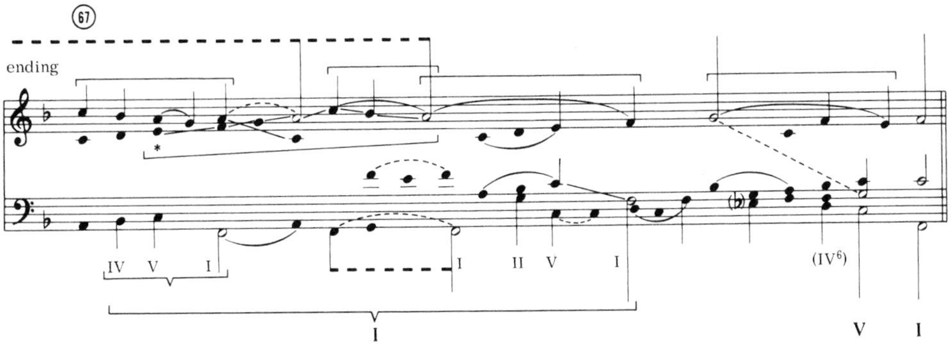

*Innsbruck motive.

the tonic, is completed, clearly marking the end of the section. Beginning with "Propter magnam gloriam," similar prolongations are made, again resolving to F significantly at "Jesu Christe," from which point it is prolonged until the end of the first part of the *Gloria*. An interphonic fivefold statement of a concluding motive structured on the same descending fifth is an impressive climax.

The entire "Qui tollis" section is based on the descending third, the textual subdivisions intimately related to the top-voice structure. The "Qui sedes" section begins the quote of the lied "Die brünlein," first appearing in bar 98 in the bass. Several minor changes are made in order to accommodate the melody within the tonal scheme. The melody is based on the Dorian triad, from a purely monophonic viewpoint synonymous with Aeolian since the tone B does not occur. The prolongation of this large section containing the song is in the dominant (minor), in this respect paralleling the use of mixture in both *Kyrie I* and "Innsbruck." The opening of "Qui sedes" unequivocally projects the rising fifth in alternating paired voices. The final descent to F coincides with the conclusion of "Dei patris." The "Amen," with its play on upper and lower neighbor notes of F (in the top line), acts as a genuine structural coda. The entire final "Cum sancto spiritu" emphasizes the motion through the triad, both ascending and descending, through reiteration of melodic fragments (Example 31).

EXAMPLE 31 *Gloria*

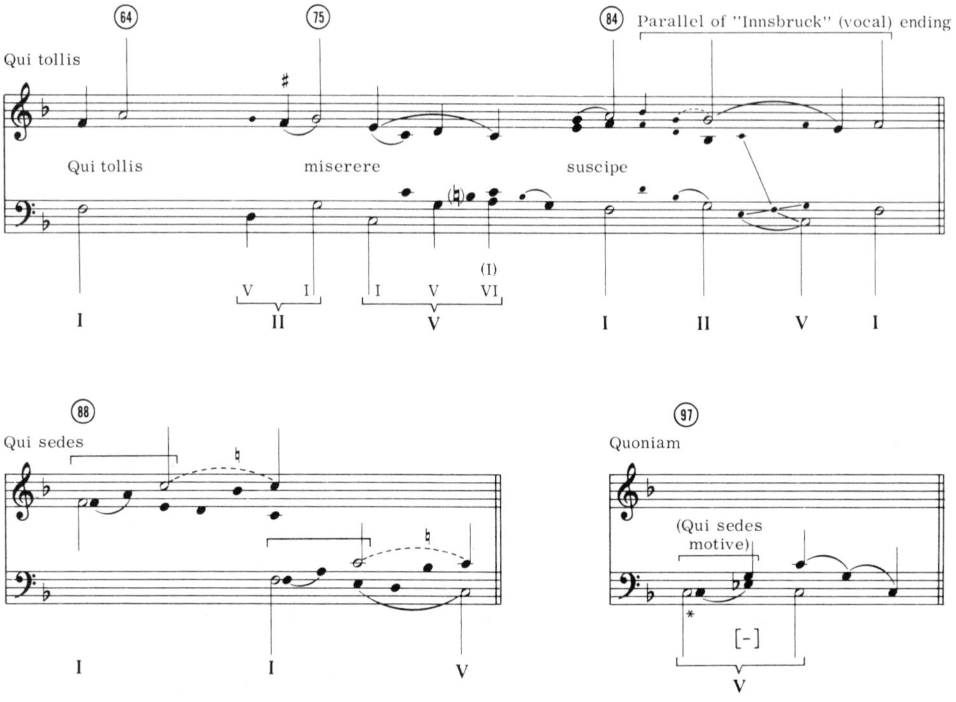

*"Die brünlein" melody begins.

EXAMPLE 31a

The *Credo* begins with another variation of the prolongation of the initial A moving to G, the latter supported by the dominant. In a reiteration of this motion, the G at bar 30 is supported by the II chord. At "Qui propter nos homines" (bar 46), a remarkable section begins. Using the technique of alternating paired voices, each pair in a tight stretto of the same theme, the design is repeated in this alternation, first in the tonic, then in the dominant.

After these four paired statements (actually, eightfold through the partial canon at the fifth below in each paired-voices statement), the theme is stated twice in the tonic, once by the altus, and again by the bassus. Still using alternating paired voices, the second voice in each case simultaneously states the space motive of the unifying theme, a descending fifth, in diminution, once in the tonic, the second time in the dominant, but subservient to the concluding tonic structured by the motion of the lower voice. The control is remarkable, the spatial expansion of the motive drawn from the *structure* of the opening of "Innsbruck," unequivocal.

In "Et resurrexit" is presented another variation of the opening, melodically closely related to the *Credo* beginning. The concluding section, starting at "Et vivificantem," climactically states four times a concluding motive of a rising fifth with a neighbor note (related possibly to the second part of "Die brünlein"), all within the dominant, and concluding with the tonic through the extension of the theme's ending. This ending is preparatory to the climax that is achieved at the end of the *Credo* as a whole which, beginning at bar 156, utilizes the same theme *in extenso*. Appropriately beginning with the text "expecto resurrectionem mortuum," hence the connection with the "et resurrexit" section, the upward leap of a fifth, first within the v, and then in I, is interphonically employed, all four voices moving within these two triads with intensity, the upper voice outlining reciprocally to the ascending fifth the descent through the triad, this being the prime closing device throughout the entire Mass.

The comparison of the *Sanctus* with *Kyrie I* has already been observed. The melody as it appears in the tenor of the *Kyrie* is stated only in part by the tenor of the *Sanctus*, but more fully in the superius (in duplo) and later, similarly in the bassus. The structural parallelism is therefore quite obvious. It has a brief but lovely delay of the final tonic during which the motive, rising through the tonic triad, is stated again, in the altus.

In "Pleni sunt coeli," the clarity of the divisions of the triad-forming schematic structure in the top voice is heightened by the phrasing units, further intensified at some of the points by the bass motion and the emphasis on v and I, as well as repetitions which further call attention to the points of division. Of particular interest is the treatment of A, the third of the triad, as a main point in the top line. Here is another singular variation in the setting, for the A, from bar 46 to bar 60, is supported by a prolongation of the A-minor triad. At first its prolonged form seems to be in the Phrygian environment, i.e., B♭ as a passing note between C and A. At bar 50, B♮ in the altus is a possibility against the F. Its use during the remaining ten measures is strongly suggested by both vertical and linear considerations. Even the use of G♯ as a leading tone at the cadential points is tempting. During this prolongation, the motive of A to C in the top voice is repeated. When this prolonged section is concluded at bar 60, the motion in the bassus to C (bar 61) and then to F (bar 62) completes the return to the tonic in a fashion suggesting in the largest structural sense the outlining

EXAMPLE 32 *Sanctus: Pleni sunt coeli*

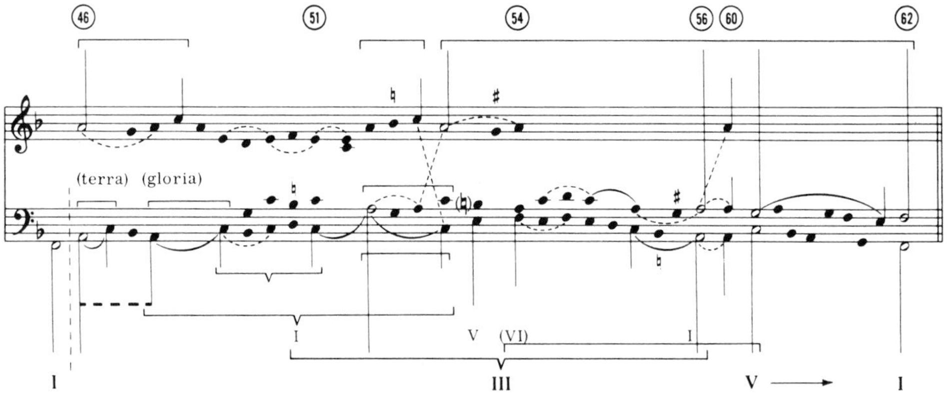

of the motive F–A–C–F (Example 32). The conclusion of the movement brings back with intensified repetition the descent from A to F via the leading tone (bar 62) *and* a variation of the opening structure (beginning in the altus, bar 65), a beautiful climax to a fascinating movement (Example 33). Note the reiteration of bars 4–7 of "Innsbruck."

In "Osanna I" the superius descends a fifth in extended tones, from C to F, and immediately ascends via the same tones back to C, while the tenor does the same, but at the fifth (actually a fourth below), beginning before the superius. These two-line statements are repeated, but the second statement is followed by an extension which now proceeds stepwise down to the F, thereby completing the section in the usual fashion. The procedure of descent within the fifth followed by ascent is a reversal of the path taken

EXAMPLE 33 *Pleni sunt coeli (gloria)*

Graph 33a

previously. Further, the theme is exactly symmetrical, i.e., the descent is succeeded by an ascent in exact retrograde (Example 34). At the end of the section the bass almost climactically sums up the motion through the fifth with I–V–I leaps. Similarly, the bass motion at the end is an exact inversion of the bass motion at the beginning.

EXAMPLE 34 *Sanctus: Osanna I*

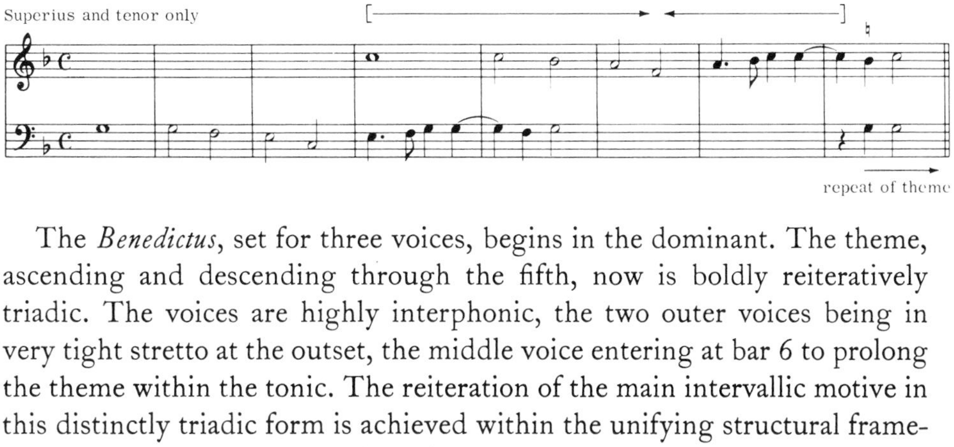

The *Benedictus*, set for three voices, begins in the dominant. The theme, ascending and descending through the fifth, now is boldly reiteratively triadic. The voices are highly interphonic, the two outer voices being in very tight stretto at the outset, the middle voice entering at bar 6 to prolong the theme within the tonic. The reiteration of the main intervallic motive in this distinctly triadic form is achieved within the unifying structural framework, this time emphasis being given to the opening C through the prolongation of the initial dominant. Interesting, as well, is the long extension

EXAMPLE 35 *Benedictus*

103
105
V
V

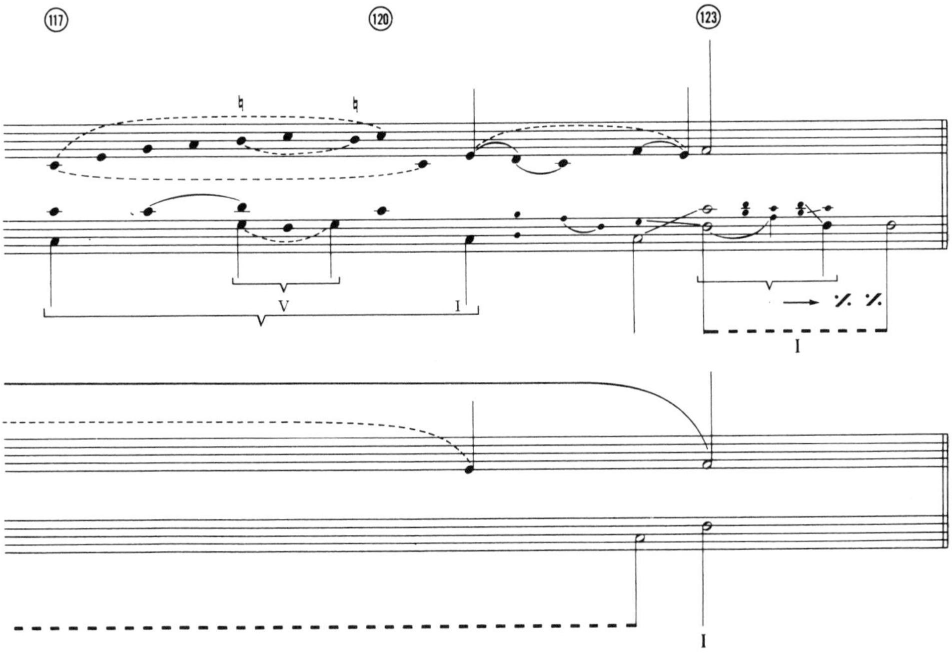
117
120
123
V
I
I
I

of the E, attained at bar 109, until the final tonic is reached. During this extension, the triadic motive, in the dominant as it is at the beginning, is reiterated, this time figurated with both step and neighbor-note motion. The analysis (Example 35) does not show the full manipulations of the triadic motive in the lower voices.

"Osanna II" begins with the upward leap of the fifth, reiterated and then descending to the final F. This is done twice, interphonically (in part) stated as well (bass twice, tenor once). This fragment is drawn from the second part of "Die brünlein." The interphonic statement is beautifully fused with the structural parallelism of the top line and the I–V–I support

EXAMPLE 36 *Benedictus: Osanna II*

(Example 36). The section is very brief, the two statements referred to above constituting seven measures. The remainder of the section, set to the prolonged F in the tenor, acts as a genuine structural coda. Above and below the sustained first degree of the key in the tenor, motion within the IV chord takes place, a technique of extension which later on was to be called a "plagal cadence." The contrapuntal limitations are clearly set, for a theme within the triadic contour of either V or II against the sustained tone is not possible. VI, IV, or, of course, I, are usable, and it is the latter two that are here applied.

The *Agnus Dei*, as a whole, becomes the climax to the Mass. Each section makes intensive use of the source motive, not only in regard to the rising fifth, but also the neighbor note of the fifth, first given prominence in the opening to *Christe I*, in both tenor and superius. The concluding top line, attaining the first degree through the leading tone, is employed in each of the sections of the *Agnus Dei*, but most interesting is the parallelism in *Agnus Dei II*, in which the leading tone is attained through the transfer of the octave. This is the same technique used in the instrumental version of the "Innsbruck" setting, i.e., the same as *Christe II*. This ending is immediately preceded by an interesting variation of the treatment of the descending line in which the E♭, so purposefully used in the bass of the "Innsbruck" setting, is applied to support the fourth degree. This is particularly effective after the pause of all the voices, and in association with the text, "miserere nobis," the only time that this has happened in the entire Mass.

The *Agnus Dei III* is an admirable conclusion, and, in effect, a grand climax. The theme at the outset combines the triadic and neighbor-note motives. First stated in the bass, the theme is brought in successively by the altus, superius, and tenor. Although the entries overlap at different lengths, the manner very much approaches the texture of the fugue, except for the reciprocal relationship of dux–comes tonic and dominant, since all entries are at the unison or octave. But the through-composed unity of the movement, in terms of extension of design beyond the cumulative quasi-fugal beginning, is unequivocal. The theme is reiterated on the first and fourth degrees and appears in all the voices, almost without break, the last statement entering in an upper voice above the sustained first degree, thus fusing the theme with a structural coda, the neighbor note being supported here, as in a previously cited example, by the IV chord. The first step in the extension utilizes the deceptive cadence V moving to VI as a delay of the structural tonic, then slipping down into I at the beginning of the next measure. From the viewpoint of the fugue as a through-composed piece in which a principal idea is reiterated throughout, this *Agnus Dei* is closer to

EXAMPLE 37

its spirit and more significant than the host of contemporaneous examples that are related only to the textural opening of the fugal procedure.

The magnificent climax is achieved through the use of melodic parallelism, i.e., the paraphrase technique (Example 37). But this top-voice paraphrase simultaneously is the song "Bruder Conrad," which was also set polyphonically by Isaac.[15] The "Innsbruck" song and "Bruder Conrad" are thus intimately tied together. But the relationship is more than musical, for the text of "Bruder Conrad," a little, sad song of suffering, contains the phrase, "Ich far dohin"; the identical words are in the "Innsbruck" song! (See Example 25.)

The entire Mass as a very personal reflection of Isaac invites further study. It possibly is intimately connected with his final departure from Innsbruck, as revealed by the texts of the songs and their subtle interrelationships. Of further interest is the use of the E♭ and E♮. This mixture is present not only in the "Innsbruck" song but also in the Mass proper, but is significantly reserved in the Mass for the signal expression of the word "miserere." This affective role can be seen in "Qui tollis," again in "Qui sedes" (immediately preceding "miserere nobis"), and finally in *Agnus Dei II*. Fascinating as well is that the E♭ in the "Innsbruck" song appears to the text: "ich far dahin." The subject of "Die brünlein die do fliessen" is separation from one's sweetheart; Isaac is to be separated from his beloved Innsbruck.

This fascinating subject requires further investigation, but surely its basic significance in this Mass is obvious, and it is an important factor in the overall unity that is achieved in the Mass both in its structure and in its spirit. The principal fount of this spirit is the "Innsbruck" song, whose essential clarity of tonality and structure pervades the entire Mass, absorbing within its interior the appropriate commentaries of several songs, all of which combine to give the title, *Missa Carminum*, double meaning.

JOSQUIN: MISERERE MEI, DEUS

JOSQUIN's motet "Miserere mei, Deus" (Examples 38 through 40), of singular importance as one of the early Psalm settings, and celebrated during

[15] See instrumental setting in DTÖ XIV^{1}, p. 73; the text of the song is provided, *ibid.*, p. 189.

the sixteenth century as perhaps his most famous work, has been described in detail by both Osthoff and Reese.[16] While it has been cited as a composition for five voices, it is, compositionally, for only four voices, the fifth voice being brought in as the added tenor only at specific points to announce the main "Miserere" motive. The motive enters in the fifth voice at the conclusion of each verse of Psalm 50 (Vulgate), except in verse 14, where it also appears at the half-verse, thus, in toto, in twenty-one statements. Commencing on e^{I}, each successive statement is one step lower, thereby descending one octave for the first eight verses. The next eight statements reverse the direction, successively ascending an octave. The last five statements, beginning again on the e^{I}, descend successively stepwise, the last statement being made on a.

The motet, in three *partes*, is divided accordingly to coincide with the direction of the motive statements (Example 38). Each time the motive is repeated to the text, "Miserere mei, Deus." Since the repetition of this text does not occur in the Psalm itself, it represents direct and bold textual emphasis which, of course, is given added character and dimension through its specific musical association. One cannot fail to be impressed and, per-

EXAMPLE 38 *Miserere mei, Deus* Josquin

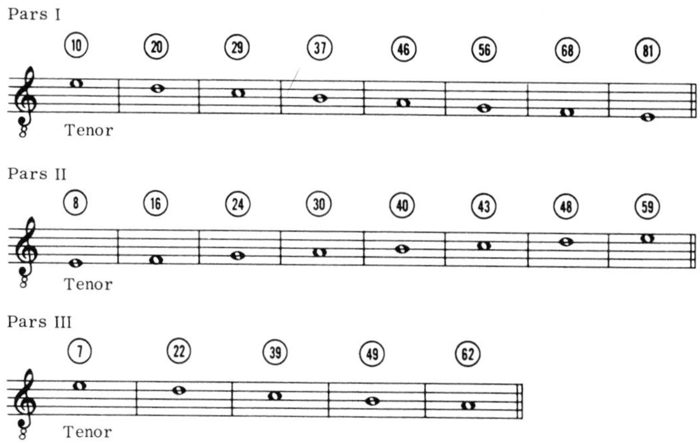

[16] Osthoff, II, 119 ff.; Gustave Reese, *Music in the Renaissance* (New York, Norton, 1954), p. 248.

haps, moved by its recurrence, particularly in the declamatory rendition of all five voices, a strongly sonorous quality contrasting with the weaving, interphonic linearities that always characterize the section that precedes the announcement of the motive.

The ordering of the motive within the ascent and the descents coinciding with the verses, as previously described, represents an overall plan of a very ingenious nature, involving thought given to the structure of the text of the Psalm as a whole, and its relationship to a musical plan which is also governed by a musical order. Since it was necessary to divide one verse into two parts to permit twenty-one statements of the motive, one realizes the care given to the place of division. Occurring in *pars* II, it permits the commencement of that part significantly with the text "Audi," which is handled so dramatically (with word painting) and beautifully in its antiphonal statement by only two voices. *Pars* III appropriately begins with "Domine." The significance of the direction and division of the statements of the motive is of primary importance, and will be discussed later.

The integration of the design is most obvious in the repetition of a textual–musical motive. This is complemented by other details which are not difficult to perceive, such as the use of the third, and the motivic character of the neighbor note, the latter derived perhaps from its importance in the main motive. The third as a constantly recurring melodic interval is related to the intensive use of imitation in close stretto, e.g., the section beginning in bar 39, *pars* I, as well as the three-voiced stretto that follows at bar 59. There are examples too numerous to mention, including the Josquinian terminal third in the superius at the end of *pars* I, and in the altus at the end of *pars* III. Of particular interest is the octave descending-scale motive that becomes prominent in *pars* III and assumes such importance in the entire section, even in the closing statements of the superius and bassus. The organization of the "Miserere" motive in *partes* I and II within the octave e^{1}–e perhaps is the springboard for this octave-scale motive which, in diminution, takes on the function of design climax.

The outline of the direction of the "Miserere" motive, the disposition in *partes* I and II of the octave range, e to e^{1}, and the descent in *pars* III to a finalis on A suggests the true tenth mode, Hypoaeolian, as yet not officially admitted into the modal community. Thus, the organization of *partes* I and

EXAMPLE 39

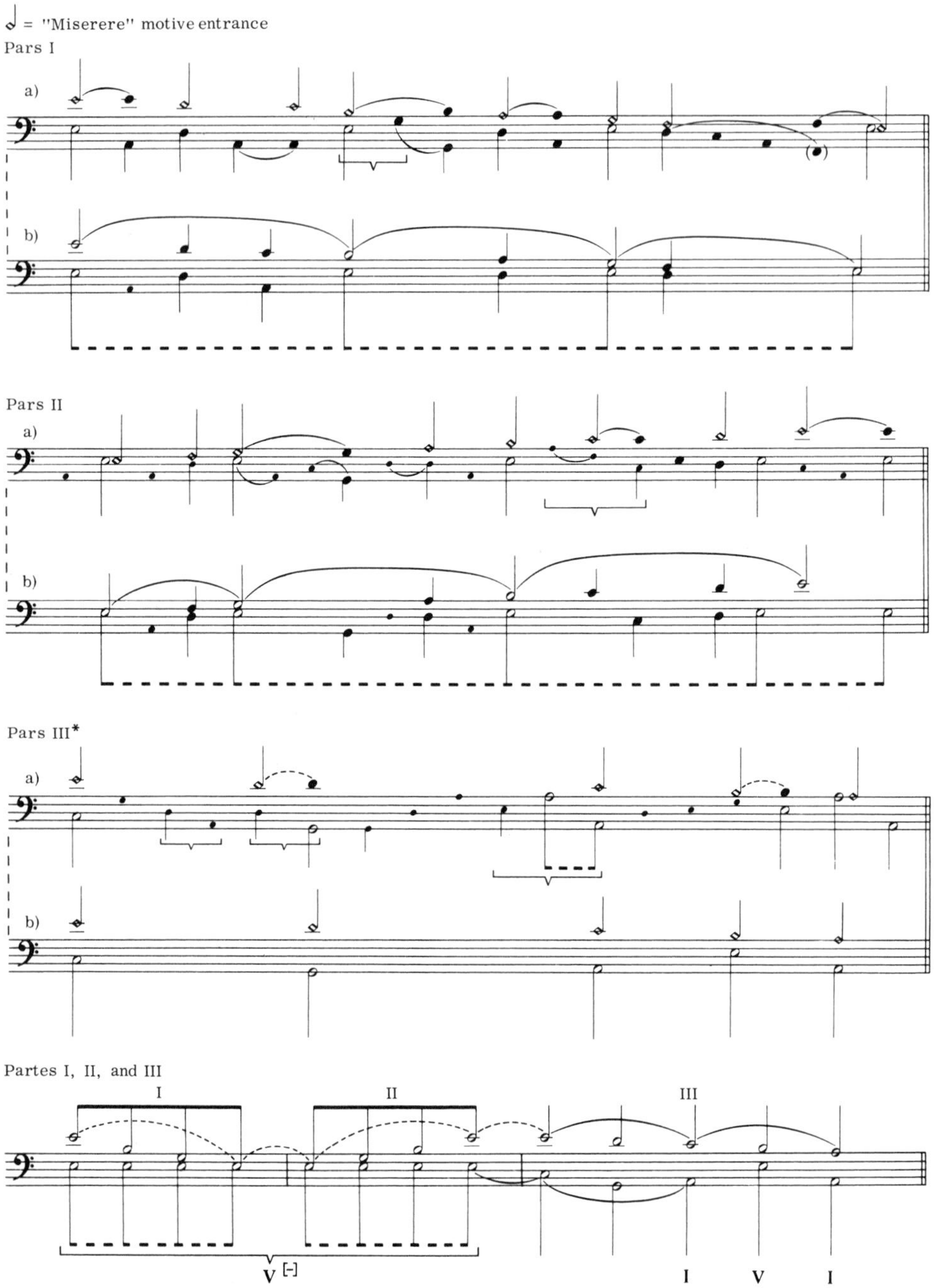

*See also Example 40

EXAMPLE 40 *Pars III*

*Entrance of 5th voice ("Miserere" motive).

EXAMPLE 40 (*continued*)

*Entrance of 5th voice ("Miserere" motive).

EXAMPLE 40 (*continued*)

EXAMPLE 40 (*continued*)

*Entrance of 5th voice ("Miserere" motive).

EXAMPLE 40 (*continued*)

II prepares these sections for the climax and resolution achieved in *pars* III to which, from a structural viewpoint, *partes* I and II are subservient. These two sections are a tonal extension of E, which, during its prolongation, takes on the property of the Phrygian mode. This mode, as seen in the study of the *Missa Pange Lingua*, cannot make use of a v–I function. As in this Mass, the fifth relationship is used frequently within *partes* I and II, as though to compensate for the lack of v–I. While the prolongation of A minor is emphasized at times, intensified by its own cadences, these come within the larger framework of E Phrygian, and *partes* I and II are not to be considered erroneously as A minor (or Aeolian) at those points at which these emphases occur.

The structural climax comes in *pars* III. Though I and II are prolonged within Phrygian E, one cannot dismiss the bass function, and in his own fashion Josquin has equated the Phrygian mode's E in relationship to the final A with the v–I function. The ambivalence of this bass motion via Phrygian or true dominant can be seen in the unquestionable fashion in

Graph 40a

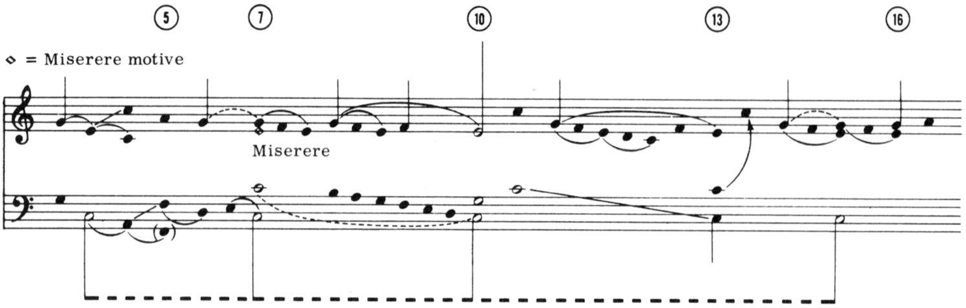

Graph 40b

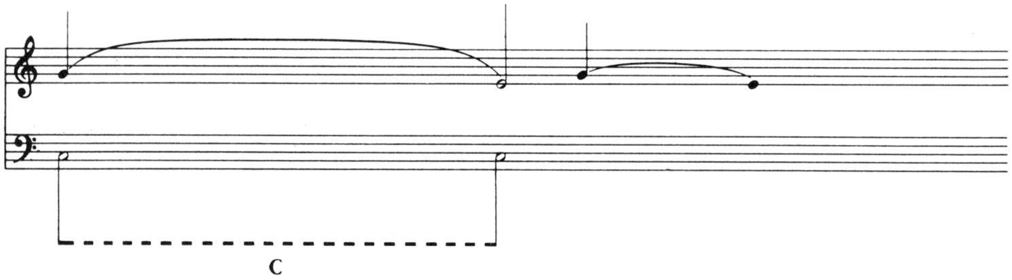

Graph 40a (*continued*)

Graph 40b (*continued*)

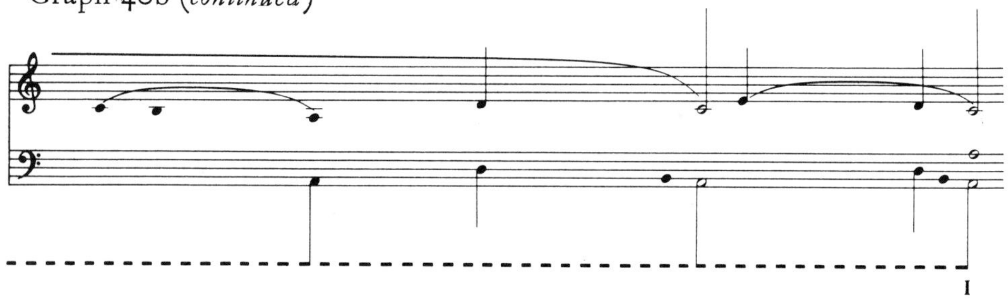

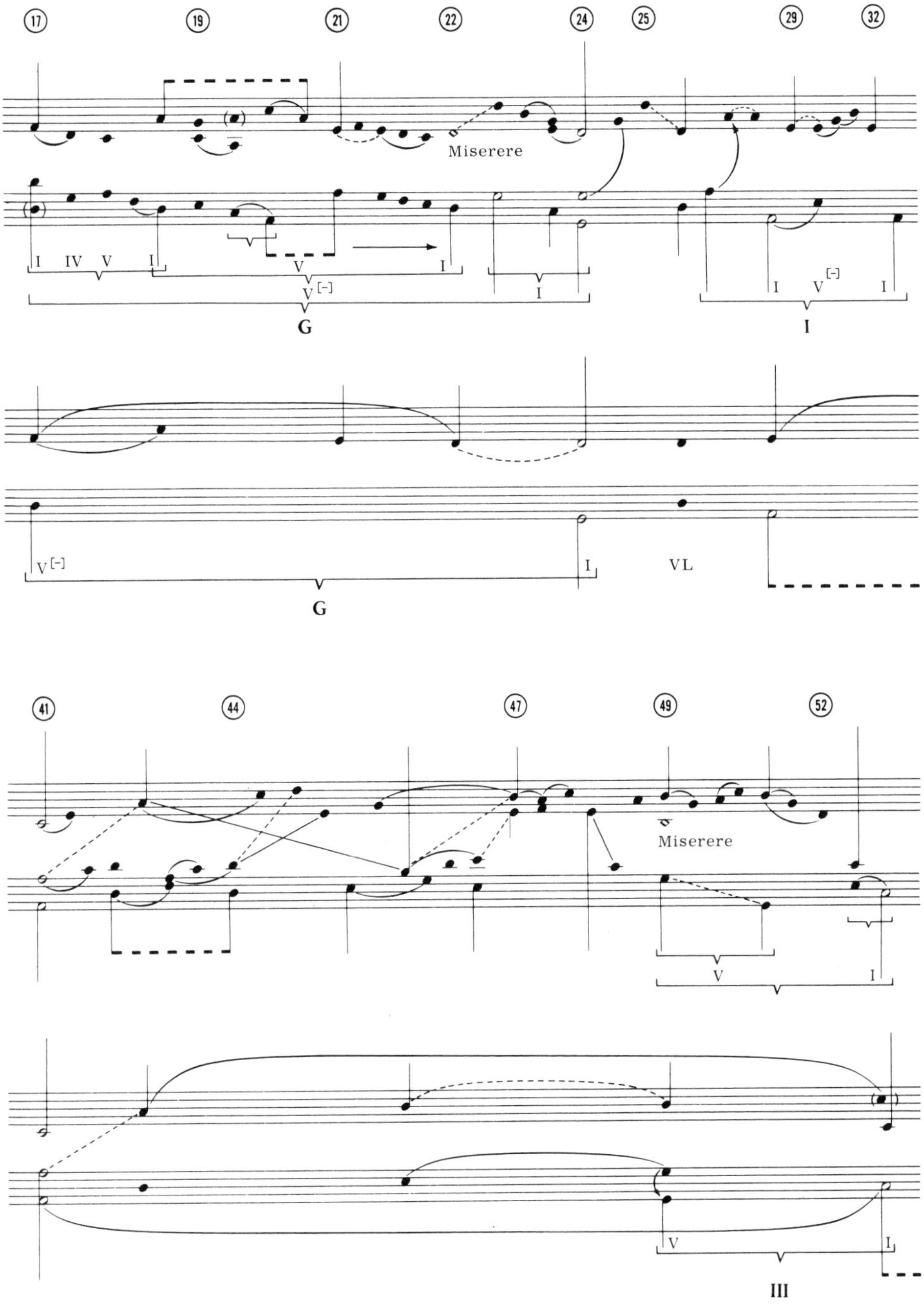
17
19
21
22
24
25
29
32
Miserere
I IV V I
V
I
V[-]
I
G
I V[-] I
I
V[-]
I
VL
G
41
44
47
49
52
Miserere
V
I
V
I
III

Graph 40a (*continued*)

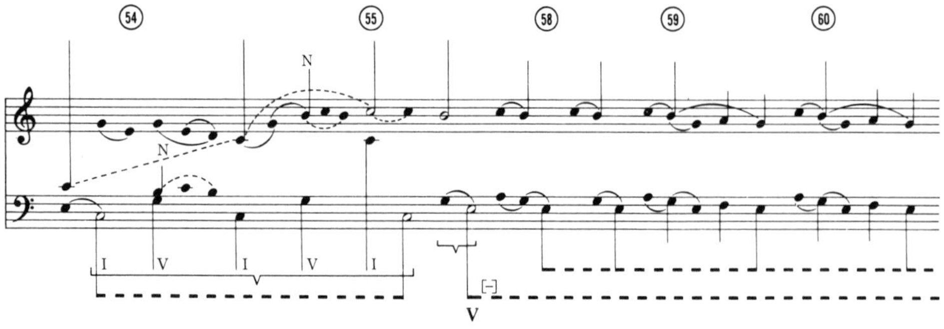

Graph 40b (*continued*)

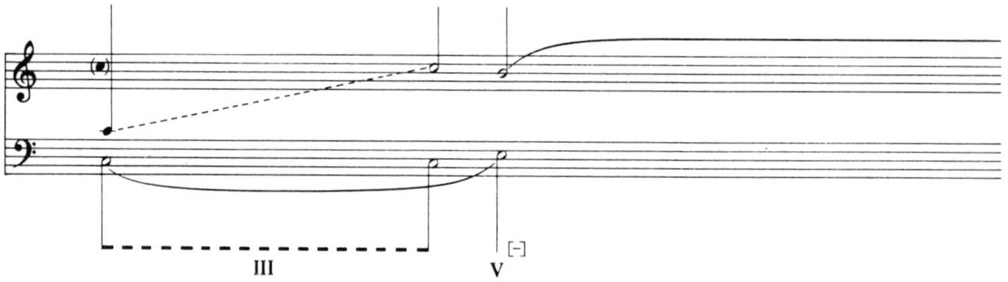

which E frequently is converted into a leading tone chord via the process of musica ficta.

The clarity of the relationship of the path of the "Miserere" motive to the ordered prolongation within the e octave and its resolution to the finalis, A, can be seen in Example 39, an outline of the relationship of each of the entrances of the motive to the bass voice. The choice of the supporting tones in the bass in *partes* I and II establishes the clarity of concept of chord-extension designed to produce a stability of structure representing a vision of unity involving the fusion of thematic design and tonal organization. The spatial extension of this plan is tremendously impressive. It must be emphasized that the tenor organization is not independent of the bass line, for it is the latter that clearly defines the significance of the motivic tenor and determines the role that it plays in the structure of the work as a whole. Finally, it is necessary to note that the motivic tenor is, most often, an inner voice, and that while its procedural role is self-evident, the uppermost voice

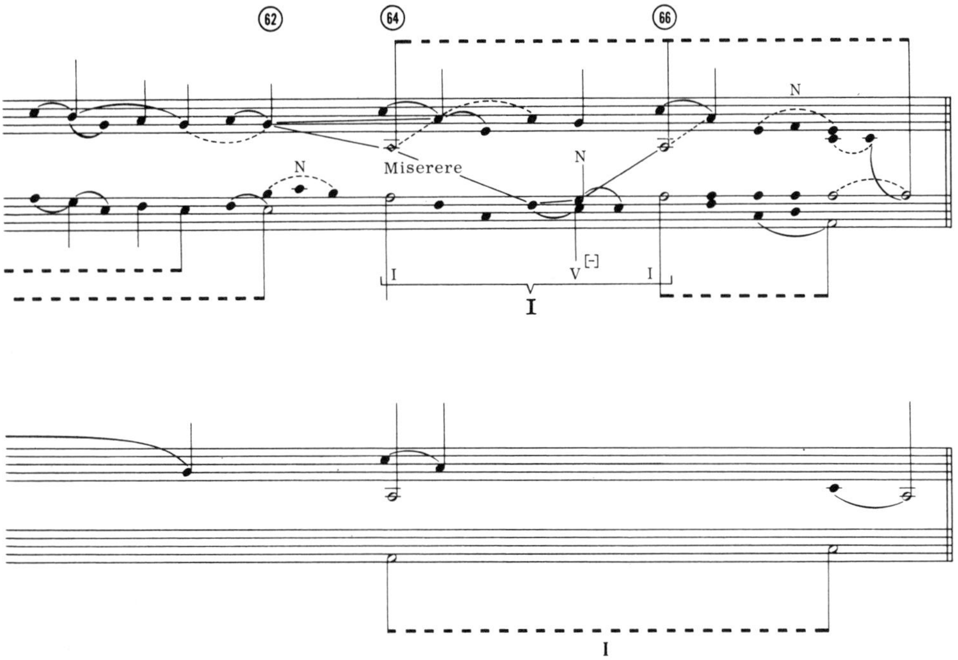

plays a primary part in determining the structural order which can never be fully understood without realizing the nature and function of the outer voices. Yet the motivic tenor rises at critical moments to become a temporary upper voice.

With this view in mind, the final analysis of *pars* III is given, thereby indicating the manner in which the motivic tenor becomes only a part of the total polyphonic structure. In this analysis the role of the bass, in that it is more than a support to the motivic tenor, becomes clear. The strong reiteration of the octave–scale motive can now be seen in relevance to the motions of the bass, in which octave activity is defined in direction, e.g., at the beginning of the section. One can also see the abundant evidence of the importance of the third, the use of the neighbor-note motion, and the involvement of the fifth relationship in the bass. Finally, one cannot dismiss as insignificant or accidental the direction of the bass line which, from bar 39 to the end of the motet, outlines the triad, A–C–E–A (Example 40).

The Prologue to Orlando di Lasso's Prophetiae Sibyllarum

WILLIAM J. MITCHELL

TONAL is an interesting term which seems to be used most widely to describe the organizing properties of the major–minor system. If it is going to continue to have this limited meaning, it would be wise to redefine or redescribe "organizing properties" for these seem to consist, as widely held, in solely harmonic factors which can be summarized in the formula, I–IV (or II)–V–I. There are, to be sure, chromatic extensions which are described in word games such as "V of V of V *lowered*."[1] But no one has yet given serious thought to what a "V lowered," if there is one, would do to the "organizing properties," since these are based, according to the definition, on V–I in part, not on V *lowered*–I. And so it is with many other chromatic elements, such as that form of augmented sixth chord whose reputed root, unheard and unhearable of course, is said to lie a diminished fifth under the lowest audible tone. Such terminological fantasies have the effect of fracturing, if not destroying, the system they set out to describe and bolster. Fortunately, music goes on serenely, unruffled by the assaults of the Roman legions, because, perhaps, the more fanciful and extravagant the descriptive terms become, the less relevance they have to the object described and the objective sought. Eventually no one pays serious attention to them.

Edward Lowinsky[2] has avoided such pitfalls in presenting the case for the

[1] Cf. Example 669 in Walter Piston, *Harmony* (3d ed.; New York, Norton, 1962).

[2] Edward Lowinsky, *Tonality and Atonality in Sixteenth-Century Music* (Berkeley and Los Angeles, University of California Press, 1961), pp. 39–41. The piece also appears in *Das Chorwerk* (Berlin, Kallmeyer, 1937), No. 48, p. 5; and as Example 64 in Richard L. Crocker, *A History of Musical Style* (New York, McGraw-Hill, 1966), pp. 211 f. In Example 1, accidentals apply only to the notes before which they stand. The (♮) of bar 20 is cautionary; the (♯) of bar 24 is suggestive rather than mandatory.

EXAMPLE I *Prophetiae Sibyllarum* Lasso

"triadic atonality" of Lasso's prologue to the *Sibylline Prophetesses.* It is cited as a "magnificent" example of "a music in which extreme chromaticism and constant modulation within a triadic texture of harmony erode any sense of a stable tonal center."

The analysis presented by Lowinsky is, however, a curious mixture of description and pejoration. One can easily be led to the conclusion that Lasso has written both a poor *tonal* piece, and a "magnificent" *atonal* one. If Lowinsky has not succumbed to a "v of v of etc."[3] approach he still clings to a chordal-harmonic assessment of the organizing properties of tonal music. Perhaps the erosion of any "stable tonal center" is less the fault of Lasso, who seems to have made a splendid effort, than of the analysis which is indeed atonal.

It is our contention that descriptive terms like tonal, atonal, and modal, are largely the result of such fractional views of musical processes. So long as the sole concern of the analyst remains the exclusively harmonic evaluation of sonorities, so long will the terms remain vague and elusive, and so long can a piece palpably dedicated to G major, minor, or Mixolydian be considered atonal. The fault lies not with Lowinsky, whose standing as a Renaissance scholar needs no additional kudos, but with the analytic tools that he has inherited and employed.

With no desire to take on the appalling task of setting the world straight on the proper use and meaning of terms, it is nevertheless proposed that the piece be reexamined with a view toward introducing, in fact stressing, linear and broad structural values. Such an approach may, perhaps, help to bring into focus significant temporal factors of organization that have hitherto been neglected analytically.

The relation of certain voice-leading techniques to structural analysis must be clarified before we proceed. Lasso, in this piece, as well as elsewhere, makes frequent use of crossed parts as an immediate means of avoiding parallel fifths or octaves, and of satisfying chromatic half-step motions. Some of these are illustrated in Example 2. The usual procedure

[3] For example, the C♯-chord of bar 4, as the piece is presented, could easily be called a "vi of v of v of v," or a "ii of v of v of v of v," but both are irrelevant.

EXAMPLE 2

of regarding the structural top voice as a composite formed by the crossed parts will be followed here.

The most problematic parts of the prologue are in bars 1–9 and, perhaps, bars 20–25. The opening presents a recurrent challenge.[4] How are we to evaluate the solo g, the C-chord, and the succeeding chord on g, all forming a small unit? In a context such as this, the tenor's g relates persuasively to the following G-chord, thus placing the C-chord in a position of dependence, as suggested in Example 3 and confirmed by the continuation of the prologue. Such imaginative beginnings seem insuperably difficult to

EXAMPLE 3

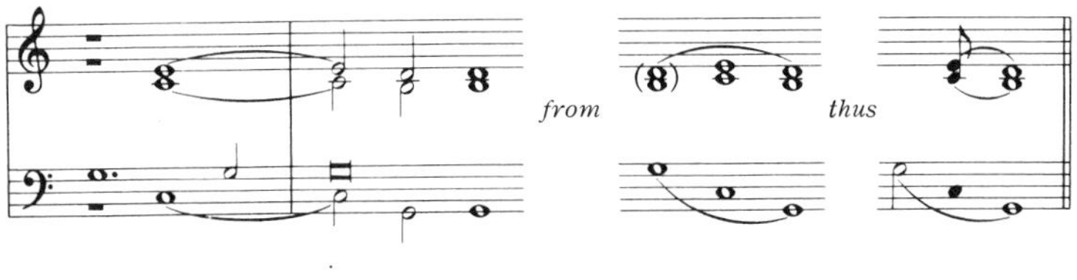

the harmonic analyst,[5] since they do not advertise their chordal components. Certainly it is not unreasonable to state, on this linear basis, that an embellished G-chord is represented in bars 1–2.

4 Similar beginnings were discussed in *The Music Forum,* I (New York, Columbia University Press, 1967), 176–79.

5 See, for example, the difficulties faced by Ernst Kurth in his *Romantische Harmonik und ihre Krise in Wagners "Tristan"* (2d ed.; Berlin, Hesse, 1923) because he ignored the value of the opening notes in the *Tristan* Prelude.

The C♯-minor chord in bar 4 must be evaluated linearly if it is to make sense, for it is not a normal member of the community of chords that comprise the harmonic elements of g. The questions to be answered are directed at the ways in which a c♯ and a g♯ must behave in order to relate to the tonal center, g. The simple answers, which provide us with a significant clue to the structure of bars 1–9 are: The c♯ should move to d; the g♯ should move to a, as in Example 4.

Example 4a sketches a common way of employing a 5–6–5 technique to bring such chromatic tones into the sphere of g. Example 4b is more closely related to the technique employed by Lasso whereby the chromatic tones are shifted to other positions to consummate their motions, following which they return to their original places. The appropriateness of these colors and shifts is related to the word "chromatico" which they accompany in a delightful kind of tone-painting.

EXAMPLE 4

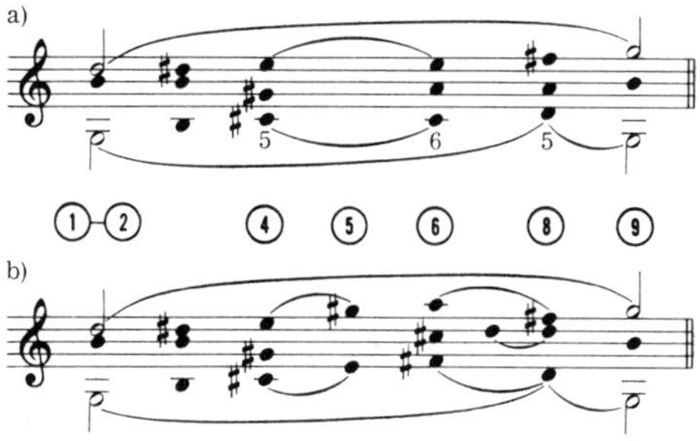

EXAMPLE 5

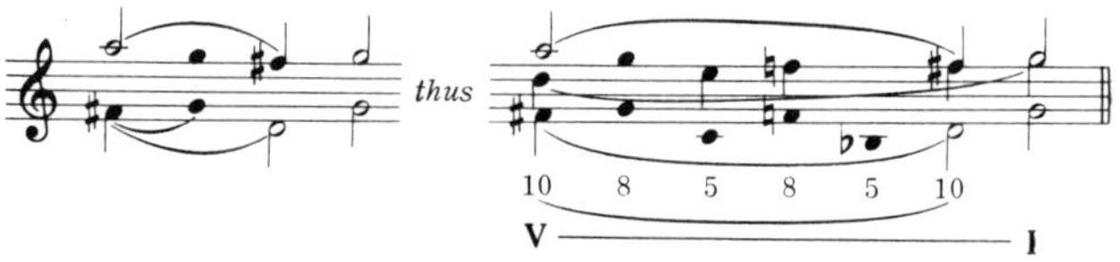

Note that the G-chord that is included in Example 4b is that which appears in bar 9. The earlier one in bar 6 is part of a prolonging motion

EXAMPLE 6

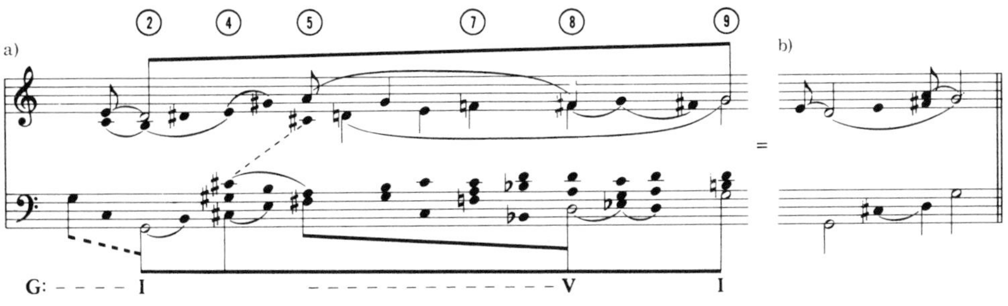

which joins a (bars 5–6) to f♮–♯ (bars 7–8). The accompaniment to these bars is fashioned out of descending fifths as indicated in Example 5.

With the ordering of the linear details behind us, we are in a position to present an inclusive sketch of this remarkable section. As graphed in Example 6b the main ingredients are: 1) The opening up of a G-chord by means of a harmonic support in the bass; 2) The joining of d and g in the upper part through a stepwise motion, d–e–f♯–g; 3) The parallelism created by d, graced by e at the beginning, and g, which also has before it a gracing upper neighbor a, but much extended. Note that extending techniques employed by Lasso bring in their wake a twofold attempt to move from d to g in the forms of d–d♯–e (bars 2–4) and d–e–f–f♯–g (bars 6–9).

Bars 9–12 are simple and need not detain us. As graphed in Example 7, the structural intent is to continue the ascent of the top part to the tone b (bar 12), following the d–g of the earlier bars. The bass is readily understandable, and all techniques of motion are direct.

As can be gathered from Example 7, bars 1–12 form a broad unit, the function of which is to open up the G-chord in such a way that the initial d of bar 2 ascends through g (bar 9) and on to the high point b (bar 12). The thirteen bars that follow also represent a unit which can be subdivided into a second, more elaborate ascent from g (bar 13) to b (bar 20), and then a concluding descent from this b, down through g (bar 21), and on to the concluding d of bar 25, as represented in Examples 8 and 9.

EXAMPLE 7

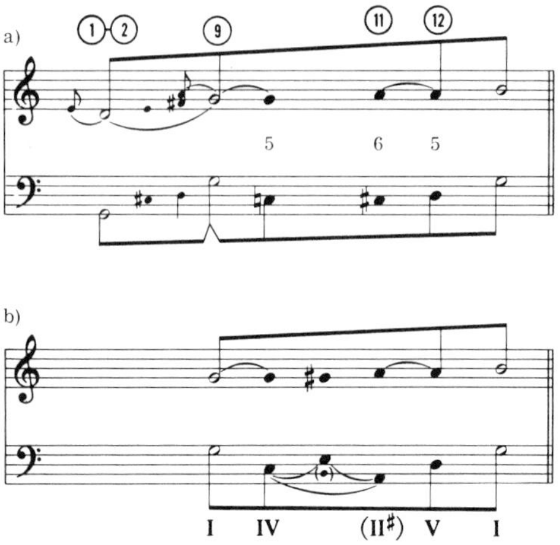

EXAMPLE 8

EXAMPLE 9

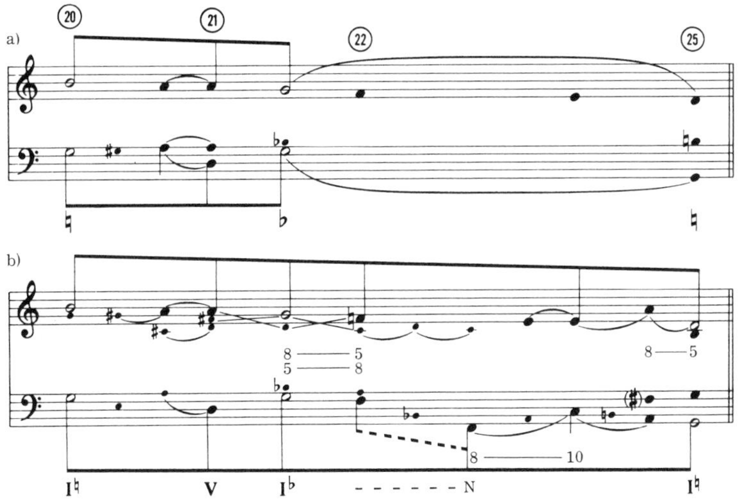

The motions of the top part are direct, but considerable interest attaches to the structure of the bass and to prolongations of the inner parts. So far as the bass is concerned, it takes its departure from g (bar 13), passes through e (bars 13–15), and on down to c (bar 18), from which it moves up again through e♭ (bar 19) to g (bar 20). It forms, thus, a plagal arch with the critical tones g–c–g reached by means of successive thirds, g–e–c and c–e♭–g. The immediate techniques of connection are descending fifths (bars 13–18) and the voice-leading technique, 5–3–5 etc. (bars 18–20).

A veiled parallelism appears in bars 13–15, 15–17, and 19–20. In each case the motion of a third has been indicated by downward stems and beams in Example 8b. The second of these is the clearest, and the third in bar 20 is the most elaborate, being spread in artful duplication over an octave.

The remaining bars, 20–25, are given over to a stepwise descent of the upper part from b through g to d, thus counterbalancing the ascending sixth of bars 1–12. There is yet another balancing element: the tenor and bass, g–c–g of bars 1–2, are answered by a corresponding f–b♭–f in bars 22–23.

EXAMPLE 10

a)

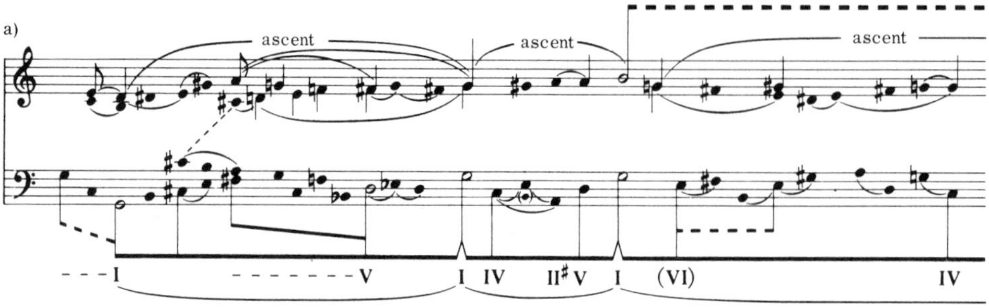

b)

The third of the upper part, b–a–g, in bars 20–21 has a simply fashioned bass that moves by fifths. The descent from g to d is more complicated. We can hear in it a harbinger of coda procedures of times to come as the descent touches on f in bars 22–23. However Lasso's accompaniment is quite unique, for the extension of the F-chord gives it a structural priority over the more usual C-chord of bar 24. Under the conditions that precede it, c can be reckoned only as a fragment of the F-chord, used in this case to provide consonant support to the passing e of the top part. In the broad view, however, the four concluding bars represent only the working out of the prevailing G-chord, as indicated in Example 9a.

Note that the G-minor chord of bar 21 is caused by an application of "mi supra la." Should the tenor's written f in bar 24 be raised to f♯ as an aspect of musica ficta? Probably it should, in which case the encompassing f in the bass of bars 22–23 must be thought of as momentarily inflected in its return to g.

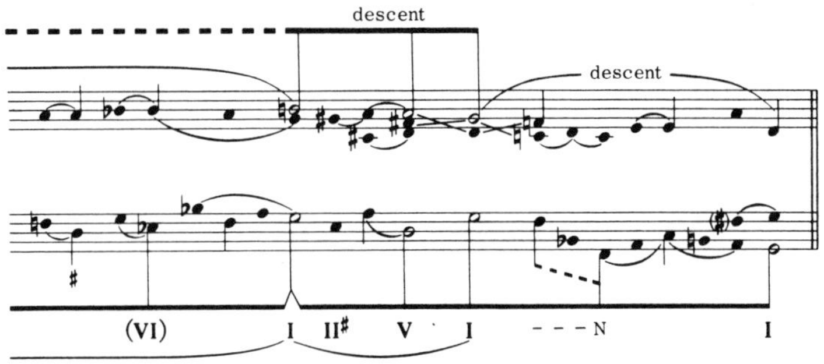

Finally, Example 10 brings together a total view of the prologue in an attempt to reveal its comprehensive linear drives and its contrapuntal as well as its harmonic accompaniments. Certainly, if doubts have existed about its tonal qualities, about its imaginative employment of enlarged organizing properties, the evidence that led to them should be rigorously retested.

The Sarabande of J. S. Bach's Suite No. 3 for Unaccompanied Violoncello, [*BWV 1009*]

HEINRICH SCHENKER

Translated by Hedi Siegel

THE EYE can follow and encompass the lines of a painting or architectural structure in all their directions, breadth and relationships; if only the ear could hear the background of the fundamental structure (*Ursatz*) and the continuous musical motion of the foreground as profoundly and as extensively. We would then envisage the twenty-four bars of this Sarabande as a gigantic structure, whose many broad and striking events, while seeming to have a private, autonomous existence, all bear a profound and exacting relationship to the whole.[1]

The graphs of Example 1,[2] which include the foreground graph (*Urlinie-Tafel*), may serve to guide us through the enchanted world Bach has created in this composition.

The fundamental line (*Urlinie*) traverses the entire octave, thus giving the C-triad its primary melodic expression. (See the fundamental structure in Example 1a.) The arpeggiation up to the fifth, G, in the bass is another

[1] This essay has been translated from Heinrich Schenker, *Das Meisterwerk in der Musik* (3 vols.; Munich, Drei Masken, 1925, 1926, 1930), II, 97–104, with permission of the publisher.

[2] *Ibid.*, Anhang VI. Hereafter, unless otherwise indicated, the footnotes are Schenker's. Most of them originally appeared as part of the text. The references have been amplified, and English translations are referred to where possible.

expression of the same triad. Then the G itself is arpeggiated, G–D–G, thus transforming the $\hat{4}$ of the fundamental line, basically a passing seventh, into a consonance.[3] The return to the G completes the arpeggiation of the dominant triad; the tonic follows, thus closing the original arpeggiation of the principal triad. Finally, the last three notes of the fundamental line are set in motion above the tonic.

The first c^1 of the fundamental line, functioning as a 1, could move up to $\hat{3}$ or $\hat{5}$. This course is obviated by the constraints imposed upon it as the seventh of the neighboring chord, $D^{7}_{\sharp 3}$. Thus the c^1 must function as the $\hat{8}$ of a descending line (see Example 1b). This technique of causing a descent in the upper voice through the use of a seventh becomes the essential characteristic of the primary level of diminution of the Sarabande. It appears again when the $\hat{5}$ moves to the $\hat{4}$ through the applied dominant (*Hilfsklang*) $A^{7}_{\sharp 3}$, and when the $\hat{4}$ moves to the $\hat{3}$ through the G^7. (See the brackets, ┌───┐, in Example 1b.)

The motion of the bass from C to D and from G to A poses the threat of parallel fifths. In the first progression Bach avoids them through the 5–6–5 technique, and in the second through the interpolation of the seventh. The unprepared seventh that precedes the $\hat{3}$ is justified by the fact that a leap from 5 to 7 in a dominant chord can also be heard as 8–7.[4]

The bass tones under the $\hat{7}$–$\hat{6}$–$\hat{5}$, $\hat{4}$–3–2, and $\hat{3}$–$\hat{2}$–$\hat{1}$ provide the $\hat{6}$, 3, and 2, originally dissonant passing tones, with a consonant setting (see Example 1b).[5] At the $\hat{6}$, a C precedes the entrance of the D in the bass. (The D itself occurs as a divider of G.) This permits the introduction of another characteristic seventh ($^{6}_{5}$) that, within the narrower confines of the cadence, requires a subsequent descent.

The diminution grows richer at the next structural level (see Example 1c). The c^1 fulfills its implications and moves down through a fourth to g. This is only a temporary move, however, since it is clear that the c^1 will soon be regained. While the upper voice fills in the fourth, the middle voice moves to the neighboring tone thus: 3–4⌢4–3. This motion of the

[3] Cf. *ibid.*, p. 195, "Erläuterungen," Fig. 4.

[4] Cf. C.P.E. Bach, *Essay on the True Art of Playing Keyboard Instruments*, William J. Mitchell, tr. (New York, Norton, 1949), p. 274, "The Chord of the Seventh II," section 1.

[5] Cf. Schenker, II, 195, "Erläuterungen," Fig. 4.

EXAMPLE I

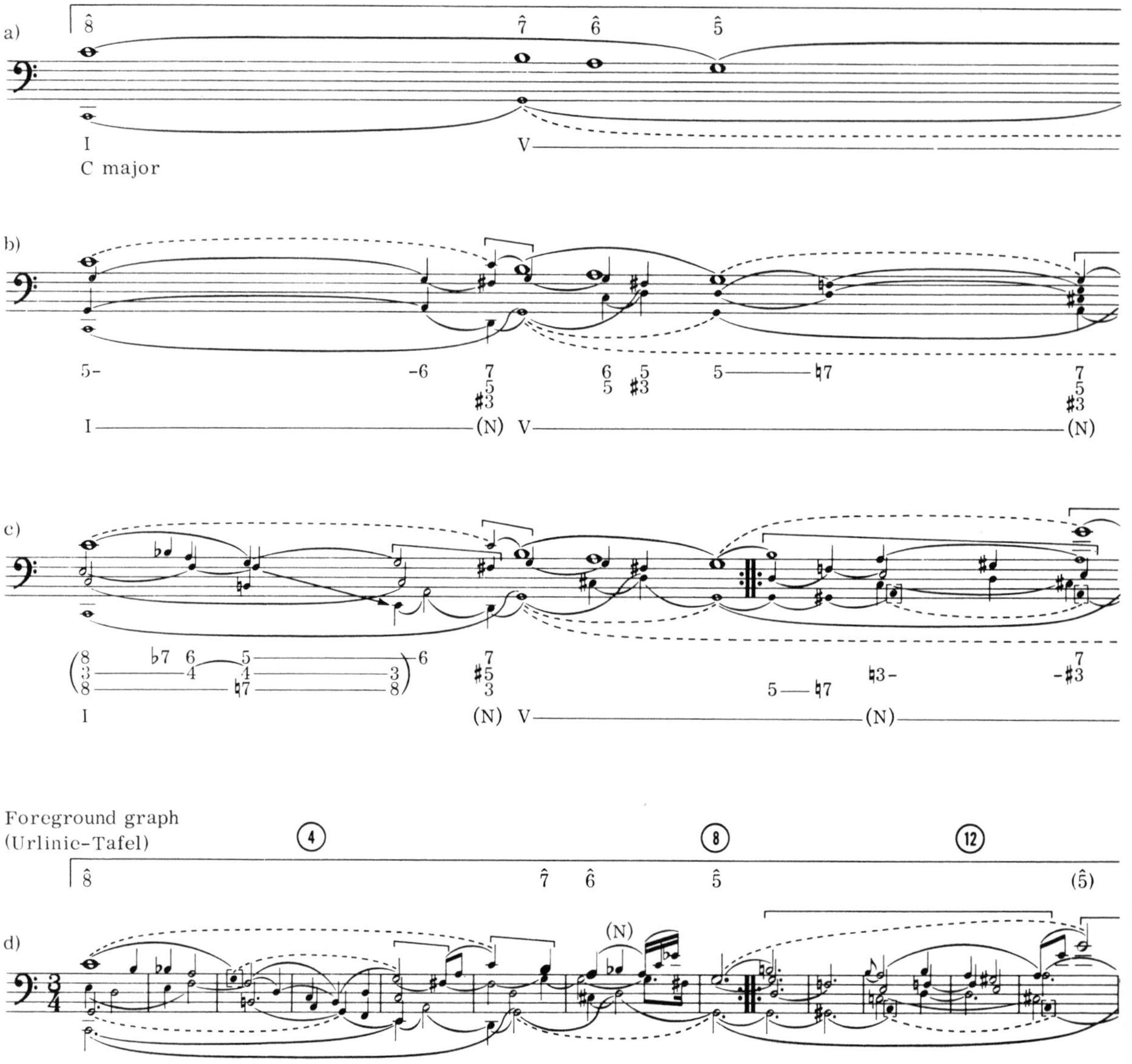

4̂
3̂ 2̂ 1̂
(Div.) V I
5
7
3
(Div.) V I II V I
♮3 - ♯3
(Div.) V I II V I
16
20
24
4̂ 3̂ 2̂
3̂ 2̂ 1̂

middle voice to f accounts for the lowering of the passing seventh in the upper voice. The lower middle voice also moves to the neighbor (8–7–8). Only when the 7 and 5 combine with the 4 does the suspension become effective.

The resolution of the f, the suspended 4, is transferred to the lower octave. (See the arrow in Example 1c.) This makes it seem as though the bass moves accidentally to E, to the 6 position of the tonic chord. The next bass tone is A, predetermined by the voice leading shown in Example 1b. Thus the bass does not leap directly from C to A; the E serves as a connecting link. This results in a beautiful transformation of the original 5–6–5 technique (see Example 1b).

The g in the upper voice, the final tone of the descending fourth-progression,[6] forms a seventh with the bass tone, A; therefore the g must resolve down to the f♯. The c^1 can be regained only by means of superposition (*Übergreifzug*). (See the first two brackets in Example 1c.) The dotted line indicates the continuity between the two c^1's, showing that the first c^1, even though it initiates the descending fourth-progression, is unaffected by it and retains its independence.[7]

After the double bar, the $\hat{4}$–3–2 is transferred up an octave; superposition helps bring about the transfer. The octave-coupling [indicated by the dotted line, which marks the continuity between the two g's][8] exploits the resources of the instrument, which, in almost human fashion, likes to express itself fully; if the requirements of the fundamental structure are satisfied, why should the instrument be denied like satisfaction? The brackets in Example 1c immediately after the double bar clearly depict both superpositions. In the first of the two progressions, the upper voice moves from b to a, while the bass passes from G to A through the chromatic tone G♯, introduced under the seventh, f. The voice leading seems to demand that an A-minor triad should follow. However, in order that the triad fulfill the auxiliary role indicated by the voice leading in Example 1b, its third must be raised so it may assume the character of a dominant. The c is not immediately altered to c♯; a neighboring sonority intervenes. As the c♯ is

[6] "*Quartzug*," a linear progression through a fourth. Schenker's "*Quintzug*" and "*Terzzug*" will be translated as "fifth-progression" and "third-progression," respectively. (Translator's footnote.)

[7] Schenker, II, 15 ff.

[8] Translator's comment.

attained, the g^1 is superposed in the upper voice, thus introducing the $\hat{4}$–3–2 succession.

The voice-leading scheme of Example 1b now dictates that the divider D must move down a fifth to G. To reinforce the inevitability of this descent, the third over the D is raised (f to f♯). Additional tension is created by the seventh, c^1, which is part of the descending fifth-progression in the upper voice. One more step in the progression would take us to the seventh, f, which in turn would lead to the $\hat{3}$. Bach, however, adheres strictly to the voice-leading scheme shown in Example 1b, and approaches the f from the d below. Only after the middle voice has moved through the fourth between d and g does the seventh, f, appear. This fourth-progression in the middle voice is accompanied by a similar progression in the bass, ending on the C.

The voice-leading scheme in Example 1c is sufficiently detailed to exhibit the surface key changes. The first superposition, $_{g\text{–}f\sharp}{}^{c^1\text{–}b^1}$, could already be considered a modulation to G major. But on no account may we regard the succeeding superposition, $_{b\text{–}a\ -}{}^{g^1\text{–}f^1}$, as a modulation to D minor; rather, the b, followed by the seventh, G♯–f, effects a modulation back to C major from G major. The determining factor here is that the superposition begins with b♮–a, not with b♭–a. (The latter alone could have effectively suggested the IV in D minor.) Furthermore, the next sonority is an A-minor triad, not an A-major triad which would have served as the dominant of D minor. Up to the point at which the third of the A triad is raised, there is nothing in the voice leading that in any way predetermines D minor. The passage can thus on no account be read as a D-minor cadence: $\text{IV}^{\flat 3}$–(II–) $\text{V}^{\sharp}$–I. Hence we have no choice but to adhere to the basic feeling of tonic expressed in the voice leading of Example 1b. In Example 1c, therefore, we acknowledge a single modulation only, the modulation to G major, which leads us to question whether the assumption of even this modulation has any validity. In other words, the voice leading shown in Example 1c is, in spite of its advanced stage of development, so permeated with the feeling of tonic that it is incompatible with any concept of frequent key change.

In the foreground graph presented in Example 1d, we find a diminution that is ornamented with motives. The fresh beauty and independence of these motives cause us to forget that they are subsidiary elements in the final synthesis. As such, however, they interact in hidden ways, now as cause, now as effect (*eins dem andern Schicksal und Erfüllung*).

In the first two measures, the 3–4⌢– motion of the middle voice is melodically reinforced by the lower neighbor, d, which creates the tension of a syncopation on the second beat of the first measure. A rare surprise awaits us in bar 3; the final tone of the fourth-progression is omitted! The voice leading unmistakably causes us to expect the g in bar 3, so Bach masterfully delays its entrance while he introduces a descending four-note arpeggiation from the f at the $\substack{7\\5\\4}$. (See the parallel place in Example 1c.) Bach chooses the solution of transferring the suspended ⌢4, f, as the seventh of the built-in four-note arpeggiation, to the bass. The g is reached in bar 5, through an ascending arpeggiation that begins with the b on the second beat of bar 4. The motive b–d–g, seemingly an incidental product of the voice leading, becomes an essential characteristic of the diminution. This new motive is used at the first superposition, where the f♯–a–c^1 replaces the $\substack{c^1\\f\sharp}$ of the preceding structural level. Thus this arpeggiated motive, as it first appears, is a by-product of two voice-leading techniques. In its first appearance it results from the transfer of the seventh into another voice; in the second it is part of the superposition. Likewise, the motive a–c^1–e♭^{1}, found on the third beat of bar 7, is subservient to the octave-coupling [g–g^1] that follows, since the e♭^{1} carries the line higher than the two preceding motives and effectively prepares for the g^1 in bar 13.

In bars 11–12, the upper neighbor, b, is added to the upper voice, whereas in the parallel place in Example 1c we find only the lower neighbor, g♯. This leads to a richer chord succession, which has the apparent function of a I–II–V–I in A minor. As in bars 5–6, the arpeggiated motive a–e^1–g^1 replaces the $\substack{g^1\\a}$. The upper voice reaches its highest point at the g^1. In bar 14 the neighboring tone, b♭, helps to enrich the chord, and to a certain extent it suggests the D-minor tonality that the ear was denied in bars 9–12.

The arpeggiated motive f♯–a–c^1–e^1(–d^1) in bars 17–18 connects the third of the D-major triad with the d^1 in the upper voice in bar 19, which is linked to the d^1 in bar 16. Bars 20–22 (23) of the foreground graph depict the elaboration of both fourth-progressions.

The metrical organization of the piece is also represented in the foreground graph. The composition is divided into eight-bar phrases. The appropriate segment of the fundamental line (*Urlinie-Stück*) is shown above each cadence.

The foreground of the piece [*Ausführung*][9] reaps a rich harvest from the background and the middleground. The entrance of the f in bar 3 is slightly delayed; it is preceded by an ascending third-progression from the d. There is no doubt that this progression is derived from the d–e–f of the middle voice in bars 1–2. The d–e–f pattern is restated at the end of bar 3, thus intensifying the upward thrust of the melody, leading to the arpeggiated motive in bar 4, the characteristic motive of the diminution in the foreground graph. In bar 7, the customary $^{6-5}_{4-3}$ suspension is used over the D of the cadence, but with the minor sixth, b♭. This alteration, together with the e♭ of the arpeggiated motive, is an indication of the mixture of major and minor.

In bar 9, the details of the diminution clearly emphasize the leap from the fifth to the seventh (cf. Examples 1b and 1c.) The fact that the b♭ occurred in bar 7 as part of the detailed diminution emphasizes the return to the b♮ in bars 9 and 10. This confirms our earlier assertion that this section of the piece is in C major and that there is no modulation to D minor. The diminution in bars 11 and 12 is usually misunderstood; a misinterpretation of the f♯ and g♯ in bar 12 can easily lead to a reading different from that shown in the foreground graph. There, the passage is still governed entirely by diatonic principles, in this case those of A minor. Thus we find f in the middle voice in bars 11–12 (see Example 1d). The chromatic change occurs when the vertical sonorities are transformed into the consecutive tones of the melody. A literal transcription of the middle voice shown in the foreground graph would contain an augmented second, as shown in Example 2. In order to avoid the unneeded augmented second, Bach changes the f to f♯. This also necessitates the use of f♯ on the first beat of the measure.

The sixteenth-note diminution in bars 17 and 18 harks back to that in bar 5. On the third beat of bar 22, the d^1 is touched on briefly as part of the diminution. There is a temptation to hear this as the continuation of the d^1 of bars 16 and 19. In that case the d^1 in bar 22 would have the function

[9] Translator's comment: see the Sarabande itself.

EXAMPLE 2

of a $\hat{2}$ which resolves to the $\hat{1}$, c^1, in bar 24. This appearance, however, is deceptive. The disposition of the fundamental-line segments over the cadence in bars 6–8 and 13–19 absolutely requires that, for the sake of symmetry, the $\hat{3}$–$\hat{2}$–$\hat{1}$ first appear in bars 23–24 (see above). Nevertheless the d^1 in bar 22 does maintain the level necessary for the position of the closing c^1, which is the same as that of the opening of the Sarabande.

The interpretation of a composition depends to a great extent on the dynamic motion. By varying the degree of light and shade, the performer can bring the phrases and motives to life, thus enabling the ear to hear their relationship to the various structural levels.[10] The principal determinants for the dynamic motion in this piece are the tensions created by the raised third of the applied dominants in bars 5 and 13. The immutable rule that chromatic alterations be emphasized is strictly observed.[11] After an initial piano, a crescendo begins in bar 5, leading to the chromatic tone, f♯. This is followed by a contrasting diminuendo in bars 7 and 8. The chromatic tone, neighboring tone, and cadence in bars 13–16 are subject to similar dynamic motion (< >). Parallel events in the last section call for a crescendo during the approach to the seventh, f, in bars 20–22. There is a diminuendo at the cadence in bars 23–24. Thus we have the basic shadings determined by the voice leading shown in Examples 1b and 1c. Merging with these are more subtle shadings, dictated by the many connecting ties, neighboring tones, and suspensions which are found in the diminutions of the foreground graph and in the piece itself. However, these must be executed with restraint, so that they do not distort the basic dynamic motion. Any other interpretation and execution will surely founder, for the immutable forces that govern this Sarabande do not admit an arbitrary interpretation of any part of the composition.

[10] Cf. Schenker, I, 71 ff.

[11] Cf. C.P.E. Bach, pp. 162 ff., section 29.

Chopin's Nocturne in C♯ Minor, Opus 27, No. 1

FELIX SALZER

In his Nocturnes, Op. 27, written in 1835, Chopin has presented us with two fascinating versions of ternary form. In these works the composer has achieved contrasting solutions, neither one representing the usual A–B–A^{1} form. This is obvious in the case of Op. 27, No. 2, where a first impression may lead to the assumption of rondo-like organization.[1] In the C♯-Minor Nocturne, on the other hand, the surface design is more that of an A–B–A^{1} form. And as we are accustomed to looking for thematic, rhythmic, and textural changes, as well as those of tonal movement, in order to recognize form sections, we might be led to the following scheme: A (bars 1–28), B (bars 29–83), and A^{1} (bars 84–101). This would present us with an asymmetric form, in itself by no means an unusual occurrence.

The degree of asymmetry becomes more evident, however, when we realize that, out of the twenty-eight measures of section A, only ten (1–7, 24–26) are taken over into the A^{1} section. After bar 94, just the broken chords of the left-hand part remain, for the melody no longer echoes the opening section; instead it augments and varies in a most imaginative way the D♭-major (C♯-major) passage of bars 65 ff., with its characteristic descending sixth and the ensuing neighboring motion over the subdominant chord (Example 1).

From this it seems to follow that the D♭-major (C♯-major) passage and the conclusion of the work may stand in a more meaningful relation than superficial hearing can disclose. The impression of a coda (beginning in bar

[1] See my analysis of Op. 27, No. 2, in *Structural Hearing: Tonal Coherence in Music* (2d ed.; New York, Dover, 1962), Example No. 506.

EXAMPLE I

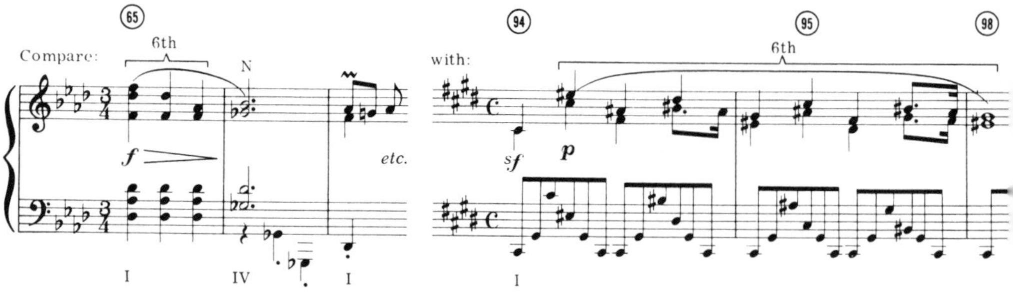

94) is awakened; if, however, a coda *does* begin in bar 94 the assumption that section A^1 begins in bar 84 becomes questionable. Furthermore, if we realize that the entire bass cadenza of bar 83 constitutes a prolongation of the structural dominant (no dominant follows this one!), then the form of the composition no longer seems to correspond to a normal A–B–A^1 scheme, in spite of the obvious similarities between the beginning of the work and bars 84 ff. and the indication of "Tempo primo." It becomes appropriate to revise our hypothetical interpretation of the form.

In works of this kind, the form can be recognized only after the voice leading and the thematic–motivic and rhythmic design have been clearly understood. The totality of the voice leading will be presented in stages, from the basic graph (Example 2) to the final foreground graph of Example 5. The basic graph, together with the main prolongations (Examples 2 and 3), clearly delineate the tonal plan of the whole and are shown first.

If we compare the music with these analytic reductions, we will realize that the work as a whole is based upon the division of structure caused by *interruption*, the pre-interruption segment being largely in minor whereas the post-interruption segment is dominated by the major mode. For the purpose of underscoring this contrast of mode, we have used C♯ major in the graphs of Examples 2 and 3 instead of Chopin's D♭ major (bar 65). In the pre-interruption section, the significant melodic prolongation caused by the embellishing G♯ should be noted; as we shall see later it stems from the opening measures. The same is true of the important inner-voice motion from C♯ to the Phrygian D♮, which later moves on to D♯ and E; this originates in the left-hand part of bars 4–6. Between the dividing v and the resumption of the structural progression in bar 65 (tonic with third in the

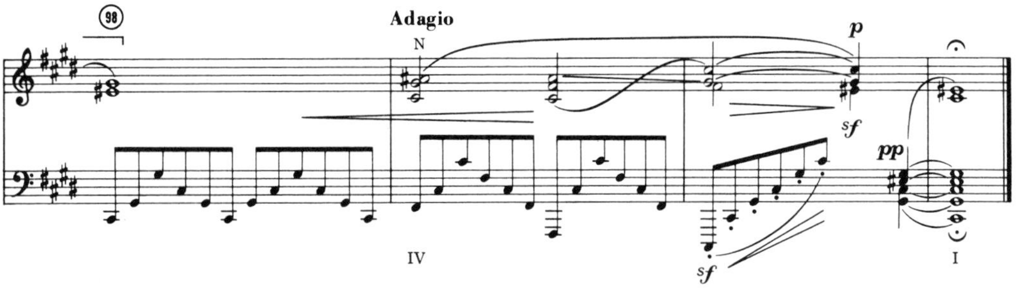

EXAMPLE 2

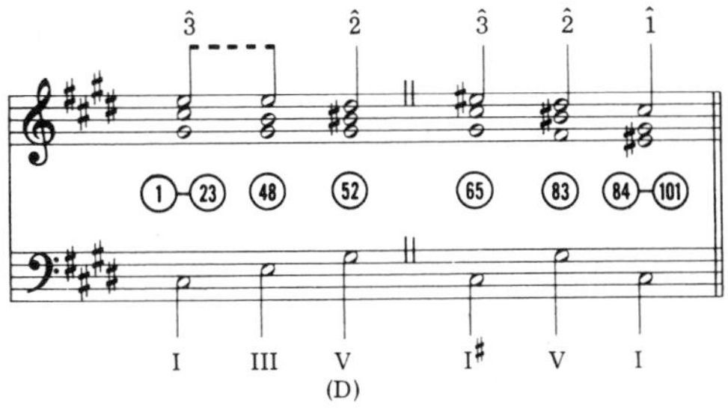

EXAMPLE 3

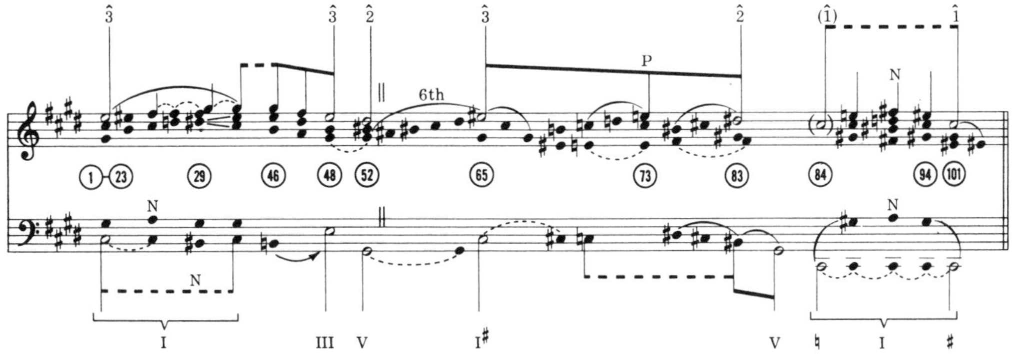

top voice), we hear a passage prolonging the v by means of a melodic sixth clearly aimed at the major $\hat{3}$ of bar 65.

Most fascinating is the way Chopin reaches the v in bar 83. The C-major chord, a passing chord, gives emphasis and support to the passing tone E♮, which connects E♯ (F♮, bar 65), with D♯. The bass tone, C, subsequently becomes B♯, the inner voice (third) of the v; the root of this chord appears in the cadenza (see Example 4). Within the final prolongation of I (bars 84 ff.), the minor mode makes one last appearance, but, from bar 94 on, it is evident that the major mode has the final word.

The outer·form of this work is indicated in Example 4. As in many other works, the ternary form develops out of the binary division caused by *interruption*. In studying Example 4, we find that the extended prolongation of the initial I constitutes section A. The motion from I via III to v (bar 52) fills section B. Unlike many other pieces in ternary form, the entire motion from I to the dividing v takes place in this second section, which has been endowed by Chopin with an exuberant expressiveness. One should note that the motion to the mediant of bar 48 has been foreshadowed by the embellishing mediants of section A which, however, true to their contrapuntal nature, do not proceed to the dominant but drop back into the somber C♯-minor sonority.

From an understanding of the total voice leading—and in particular of *interruption*—an important fact emerges concerning the third section of the Nocturne. What is usually referred to as section A¹ (bars 84–101) reveals itself to be the imaginative conclusion of a section in C♯ major beginning in bar 65 after an extended dominant preparation (bars 52–65). In terms of structure, this conclusion prolongs the final tonic, which follows the structural dominant of bar 83 expanded in the form of a cadenza. The so-called plagal cadence of bars 98–101, like most plagal endings, follows the actual cadence; it is typically found, as here, in a coda. As shown in Example 1, it is a varied echo of the neighboring subdominant chord of bars 65 ff.

Although the thematic design and the tonal structure clearly point to a ternary form, some aspects of this composition move counter to the ternary scheme. These counterforces add significantly to the individuality of the work. One of them has led us to indicate a "quasi-A¹" at bar 65. For in contrast to most works in three-part form, there occurs at this point no resumption of the thematic material of section A. It is as if the major mode demanded a different thematic content. This "no return" to the dark atmosphere of the beginning was evidently dictated by a need to maintain and increase the energetic momentum achieved at the end of section B with the arrival at III and V—hence the boisterous passage of bars 65 ff. However the work was not to end in this way. Once more the opening mood is evoked; then the exalted character of the passage in major appears again in a subdued variation that suggests the resignation found in many of the beautiful codas of the literature. The whole piece lies under the spell of the transformation from the minor of the first section to the major prepared for in the middle section and achieved in the final one.

Another element working against the ternary form scheme can be observed in the measures leading into section B; these create a veritable blurring of formal contours. Section B begins in bar 29, but the motion leading to bars 29 and 30 commences with the last phrase of section A. Example 5 will show this in greater detail, but already at this point we can recognize that, starting in bar 23, E (top voice) moves via E♯ to F♯ and later, in section B, to G♯. The F♯ is transferred down an octave and is joined by its lower third, D♮. The motion is arrested at the broken third D–F♯, which then melts into D♯–F♯ and continues to C♯–E with G♯ taking over the top voice. Thus an overlapping of sections occurs that tends correspondingly to increase the dividing effect of the coming dominant. In summary, the following forces work against the impression of a clear-cut and stable ternary organization: the all-important change from minor to major, with its starkly contrasting melodic–rhythmic material, obliterates one of the characteristics of three-part form; the overlapping of sections A and B intensifies the drive to the V and makes the latter chord a strong articulating force; these two factors create a tendency to divide the piece into two halves (bars 1–52 and 53–101). This, of course, corresponds exactly to the background binary form caused by interruption that underlies the ternary form of the foreground (see Examples 2 and 3). This underlying binary structure is also emphasized by the symmetric changes of tempo and meter. The pre-interruption segment moves from slow duple meter to the agitated triple meter with its dactylic rhythms. The post-interruption segment begins with the lively triple meter (now omitting the dotted rhythmic pattern) and returns to the original slow tempo and duple meter.

In Example 4 the reader may already have noticed the interrelation of

EXAMPLE 4

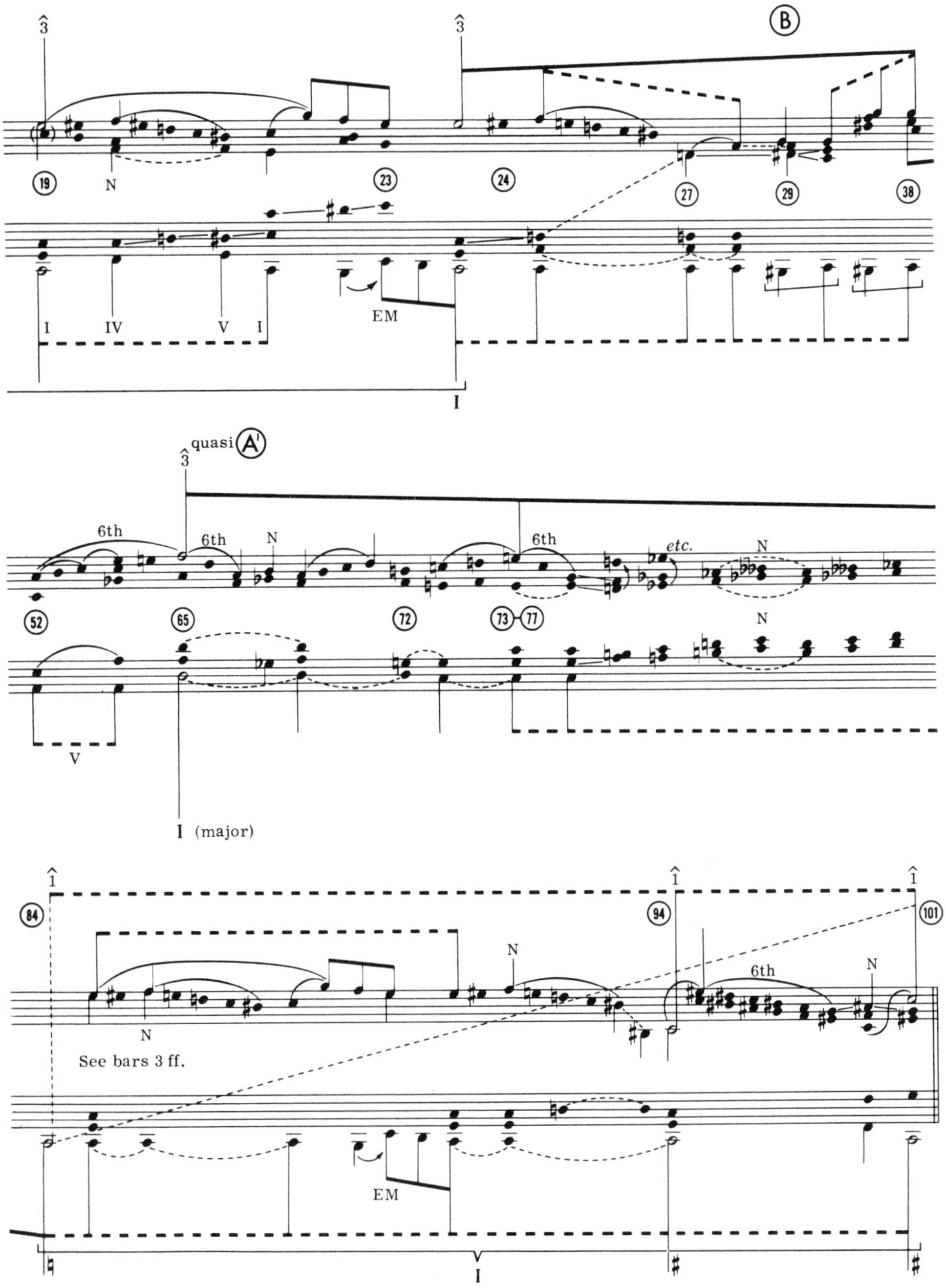
B
N
19
23
24
27
29
38
I
IV
V
I
EM
I
quasi A'
6th
6th
N
6th
etc.
N
52
65
72
73-77
N
V
I (major)
84
94
101
N
N
6th
N
See bars 3 ff.
EM
I

EXAMPLE 5

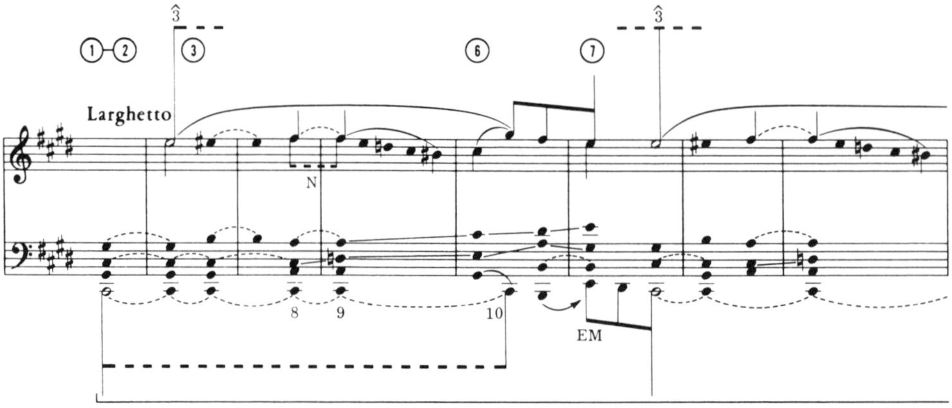

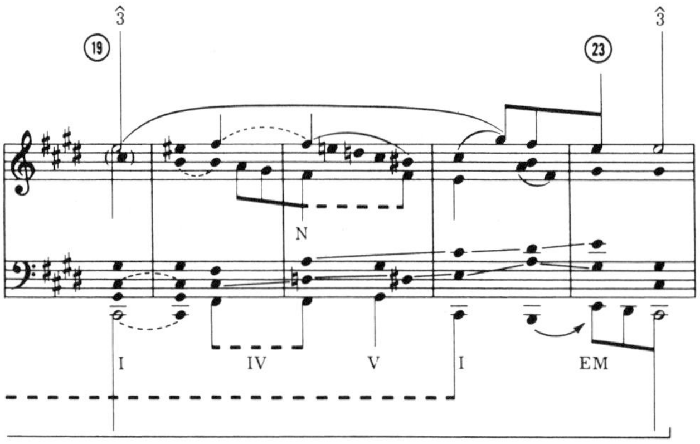

continued on page 292

thematic–motivic design between sections A and B; he will also have gained insight into the specific tonal techniques employed in the pre- and post-interruption segments. Final clarification, however, will come by way of Example 5, which constitutes the detailed foreground graph of the entire work.

The events of section A can now be fully grasped. Bars 1–7 contain the nucleus of coming developments. In the top voice the line moves from the structural E to F♯ and then on to the embellishing G♯; in a broader sense the F♯ also acts as a neighboring note to E. The graph attempts to show these two events: E–F♯–E are stemmed downward and E–F♯–G♯ are stemmed upward. Within these measures we hear the unfolding of a

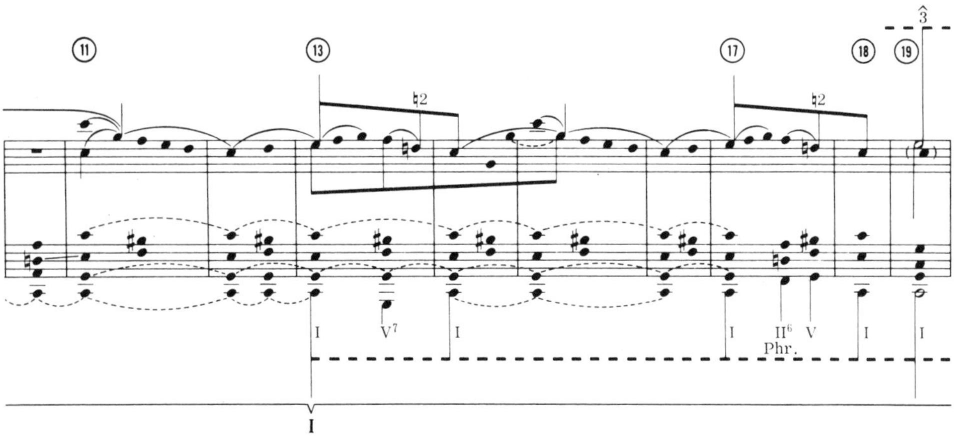

EXAMPLE 5a

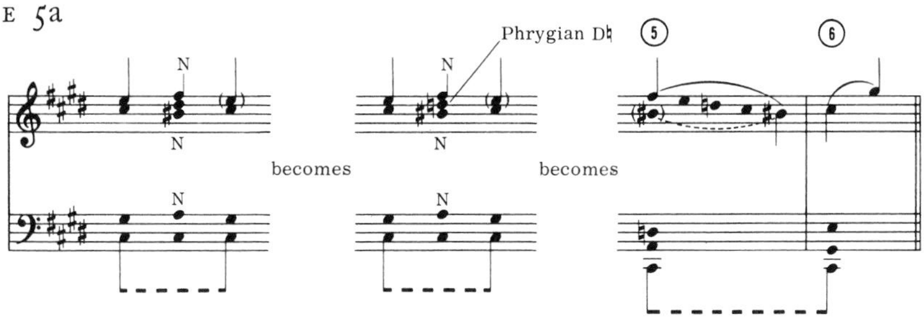

neighboring diminished seventh with the Phrygian D♮ replacing D♯; this leads to an unfolding of the tonic (illustrated in Example 5a).

We now realize that these motions, together with the embellishing mediant in the bass, play a major role throughout the work—especially in section B where the top voice shows a heightened drive to the embellishing G♯; the contrapuntal III of section A becomes a harmonic III in section B. Another motion up to G♯ occurs in bars 7–11, in which the unfoldings are suddenly interrupted by a rest; this same effect takes on enhanced meaning when the broken third, D♮–F♯ (bars 27–28), becomes $^{\text{F}\sharp}_{\text{D}\sharp}$ (bar 29). In bars 13–18 the characteristic D♮ also becomes part of a descending linear progression, E–D♮–C♯, thus offering the colorful Phrygian anticipation of

EXAMPLE 5 (*continued*)

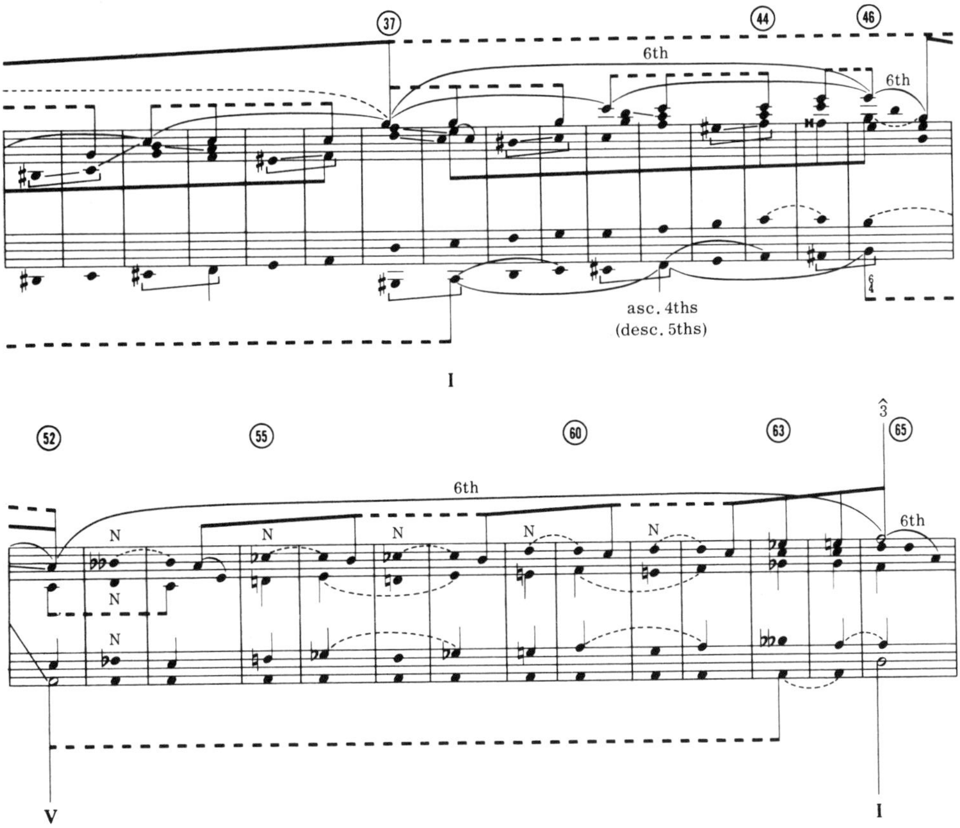
37
44
46
6th
6th
asc. 4ths
(desc. 5ths)
I
52
55
60
63
3̂
65
6th
N
N
N
N
N
N
N
6th
V
I

EXAMPLE 5b

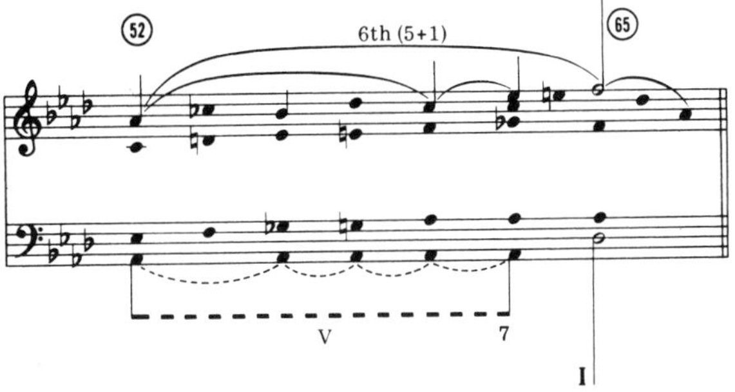
52
6th (5+1)
65
V
7
I

EXAMPLE 5 (*continued*)

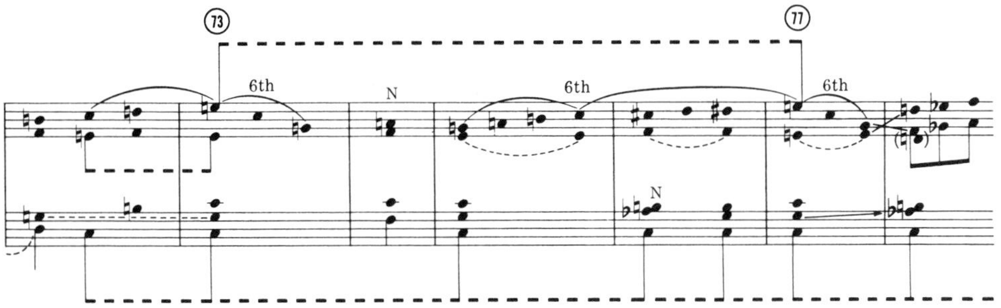
73
77
6th
N
6th
6th
N

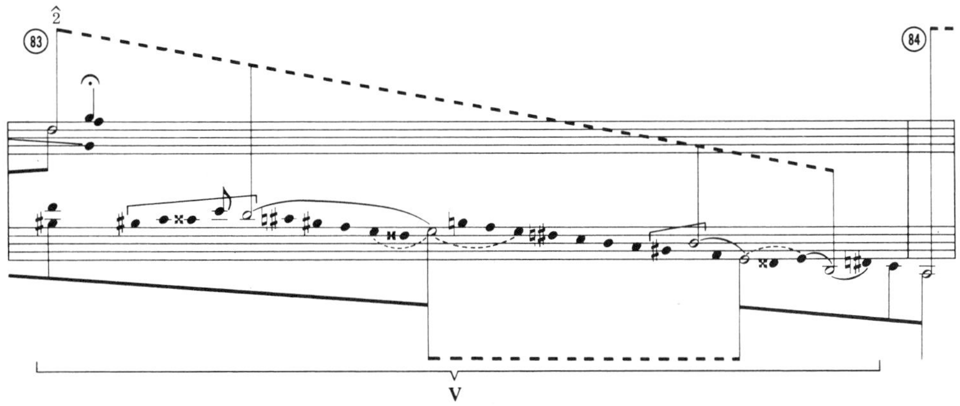
2̂
83
84
V

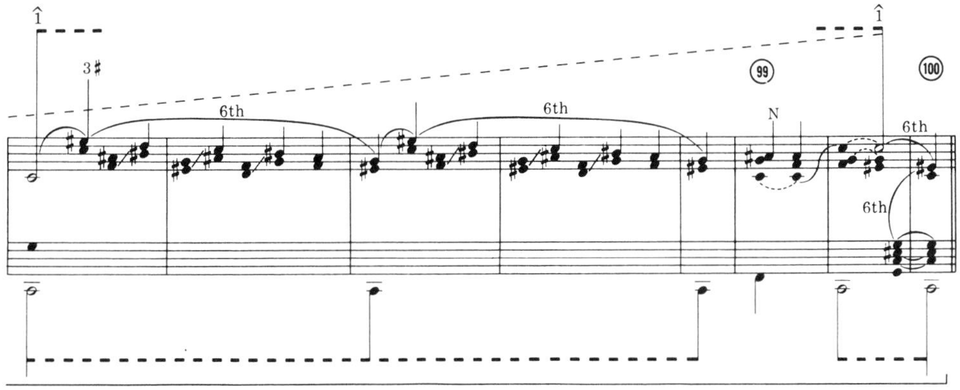
1̂
3♯
6th
6th
99
N
1̂
100
6th
6th

the structural diatonic line, E♯–D♯–C♯. Observe also the ascending third to G♯ between bars 13 and 15 and its diminution within the unfoldings of bar 13. Finally note the increase in harmonic activity; the first Phrygian D is supported by a v^7, creating a subtly affective dissonance; the second one is supported by $I–II^6$(Phr.)–V–I. Section A is rounded out with a varied repetition of the contents of bars 3–7 but with greater harmonic involvement (I–IV–V–I).

What follows, though still part of section A, is the beginning of a motion which section B continues and brings to a conclusion on the dominant; this overlapping of the two sections was mentioned earlier. Example 5 gives a detailed account of these measures with their imaginative augmentation of the opening ascent of the top voice from E via F♯ to G♯. After F♯, the motion seems to slacken; the F♯ is transferred down an octave and the left hand's musing over the Phrygian D♮–F♯ almost causes the forward impulse to cease. Suddenly, with the *piu mosso* in triple meter, directed motion resumes; G♯ is in the top voice but in the lower register. The ensuing decisive motion to the upper register (bar 37) finally fulfills the ascending third begun with E in bar 23. And now, after an intensified repetition of bars 29–36 in the higher register (bars 37–44), the melodic line is catapulted to the high E (bars 45–46). Instead of ascending yet another third to G♯, the line moves by arpeggio down a sixth to G♯; thus the original register is maintained.

At this point the tonal events become drastically compressed; they follow each other rapidly or occur simultaneously. The descending sixth that moves within the domain of the retained tone, G♯, represents the first announcement of this descent which is to assume so great a significance in the final section. The descending third, G♯–F♯–E, occurs simultaneously with G♯–F♯–G♯; thus the structural tone, E, is "covered" by the embellishing G♯, which veils the descending third; this third, incidentally, is the beginning of an octave descent of G♯ into the middle-voice region (G♯–F♯–E–E♭–C♮–B♭–A♭) while the structural top-voice tone, E, proceeds to the structural E♭ (D♯) over the dividing V (bars 51–52).

The ensuing *agitato* passage is a dramatic transition to the tonic and the top-voice tone F(E♯) by means of an ascending major sixth over a dominant pedal (see also Example 5b). This ascent has its origin in the arpeggiated ascending minor sixth of bars 37–46, and appears again in a condensed version just after the tonic (bar 65) has begun the post-interruption phase of this work (bars 67–69). The motion from the passing tone, E, of the top voice (over the C-chord, bar 73) to the final v is of some complexity. If we carefully compare the graphs of this passage (as indicated in Examples 4 and 5) we will understand that the structural v, with D♯ as top voice, is reached by what can be traced back to a chromatic motion out of the inner-voice tone G♮ of the C-chord (see Example 4). In the actual composition, the sixths of bars 78–80 are inverted thirds. This means that the inner voice as indicated in Example 4 has been shifted above the top voice of the underlying voice leading; the motion of this voice culminates on G♯. Once again (see bar 48) the structural top voice has been covered by G♯. The interpreter must take care in bars 81–83 to bring out clearly B♯–C♯–E–D♯; the E, of course, is an appoggiatura.

These tones—the denouement of the preceding motion—are taken up immediately afterward by the bass cadenza. The idea of expressing the dominant in the form of a unison cadenza with polyphonic implications is most original; D♯ remains the top-voice tone. The transfer of register downward achieves the fascinating result that all the voices conclude in a veritable breakdown on the single tone C♯; over this tone, the several bars of section A appear once more retrospectively. By means of another transfer of register, now directed upward, the C♯ is gradually brought back to the original register of the work.

In *Structural Hearing* I have grouped several works under the title of "Individual Forms"; Chopin's Opus 27, No. 2, is one of these. It now appears that the first Nocturne of Opus 27 also represents a work in which the composer has molded the framework of the outer form in response to the demands of his material. A preoccupation with stereotyped and static conceptions of form often makes us insensitive to the imaginative outlook which great composers time and again demonstrate in the formal organization of their works.

Tonal Coherence in the First Movement of Bartók's Fourth String Quartet

ROY TRAVIS

THE Fourth String Quartet of Béla Bartók has been characterized as "the summit of his constructive genius" by Halsey Stevens, who regards it as "close to being, if it does not actually represent, Bartók's greatest and most profound achievement."[1] It was to the Fourth Quartet that Milton Babbitt turned for characteristic examples in his discussion of "The String Quartets of Bartók."[2] My own high esteem for the work has led me to believe that a search for its tonal coherence might yield some valuable insights into the structural problem of creating a large-scale tonal entity out of nontriadic materials. In the essay that follows I have summed up the results of my analysis of the first movement.

The purpose of this analysis is not merely to demonstrate that this movement is tonal—that fact has been intuitively grasped by many who have heard the piece. Rather, the purpose is to inquire into the exact means by which the overwhelming impression of tonality is achieved. If, in the search for these means, a rather simple, underlying structure eventually emerges, I should like at the outset to forestall a misunderstanding that may easily arise: my purpose is not merely to uncover some simple underlying progression *per se*; rather it is to give meaning to that progression by demonstrating the complex hierarchy of relationships which ultimately participates

1 Halsey Stevens, *The Life and Music of Béla Bartók* (rev. ed.; New York, Oxford University Press, 1964), p. 191.

2 Milton Babbitt, "The String Quartets of Bartók," *The Musical Quarterly*, Vol. XXXV, No. 3, pp. 377–385; see also Allen Forte's discussion of the third movement of the Fourth Quartet, "Bartók's 'Serial' Composition," *The Musical Quarterly*, Vol. XLVI, No. 2, pp. 233–45.

in its articulation. If one is really to understand the means by which this piece is heard as a single, overarching movement through time, then he must hear the structure in terms of the details, and the details in terms of the structure.

To lead the reader step-by-step through the dialectical process by which I eventually arrived at the conclusions set forth in the following pages would take far too much space. Therefore I present my analysis from the general to the particular, rather than *vice versa*.

Anyone who has heard this movement must have been struck by the extraordinary finality of the last few measures. It is not just the *pesante* indication, the triple and quadruple stops, the fortissimo dynamic, or even the especially forceful presentation of the principal motive. These elements, even taken together, can only partially account for the conviction of this ending, which so clearly confirms a kind of C-tonality. Yet how can this be reconciled with the equally definite—and even systematic—use of chromatic and whole-tone clusters, melodic doublings of the second and ninth, glissandi, etc., elements commonly associated with the vocabulary of atonality?

In my analysis I shall attempt to demonstrate that the final measures do in fact complete a structural denouement which is tonality-defining for the entire movement, providing that one is prepared to admit the possibility of a dissonant tonic sonority.[3]

In bar 1 the sonority first appears as a three-tone chord, C–E–F♯, in a spacing which suggests the overtone series. It is the outer-voice interval, C–F♯, which is significant, however, and we shall see that a number of chord-forms in a variety of spacings are used to project the interval. This tritone, C–F♯, is ultimately defined by a top-voice structure which descends in whole steps from F♯ to C, supported by a quasi I–IV–V–I progression in the bass. Throughout the movement the interval of the tritone is ubiquitous as a unifying element. Thus it happens that the penultimate structural member in the bass, G, is all but replaced by a neighboring A♭ (resulting in the outer-voice relationship of a tritone, A♭–D).

[3] In two earlier articles I have discussed several examples involving dissonant tonic sonorities. See "Toward a New Concept of Tonality?" *Journal of Music Theory*, Vol. III, No. 2, pp. 257–84, and "Directed Motion in Schoenberg and Webern," *Perspectives of New Music*, Vol. IV, No. 2. pp. 85–89.

EXAMPLE I

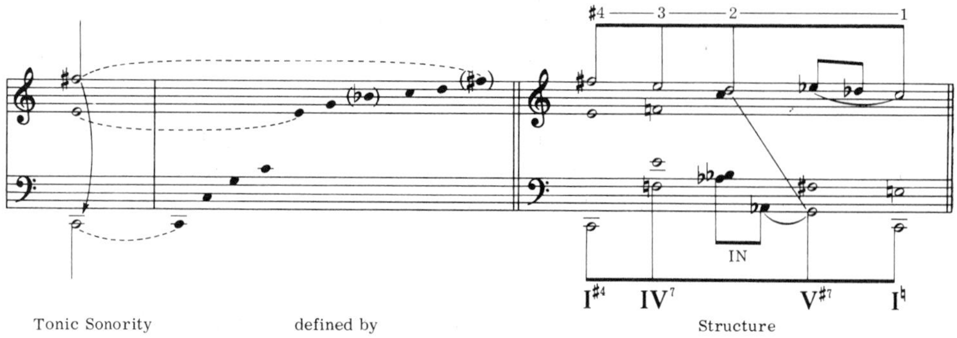

EXAMPLE 2a

Structure, formally articulated

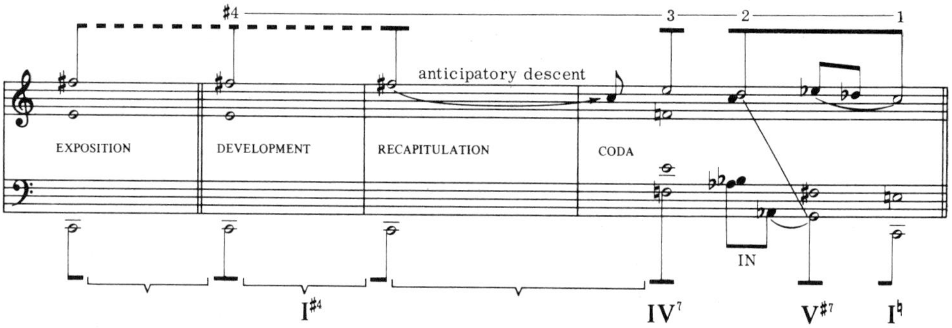

EXAMPLE 2b

Structure and chief prolongations, formally articulated (background graph)

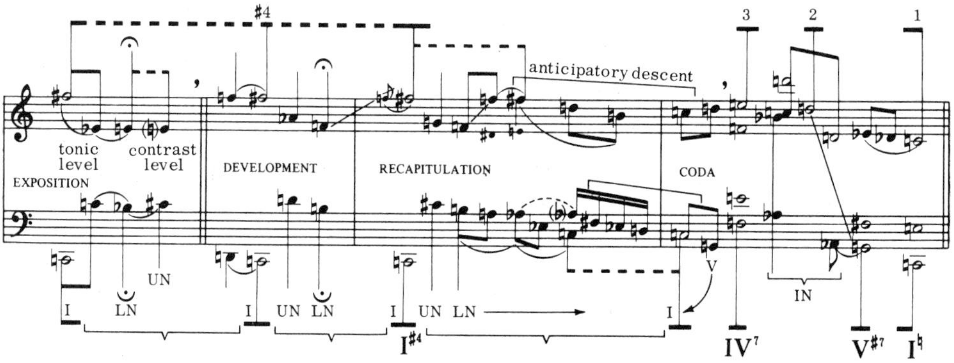

That the movement is in sonata allegro form has already been recognized, at least implicitly. According to Leo Treitler, for example, the second subject begins at bar 15, and the exposition ends at bar 49.[4] There can be little doubt that the recapitulation begins at bar 93, and the coda at *piu mosso*, bar 126. What has not been explained, however, is the relationship—essential to any sonata allegro design—which obtains between tonal and formal articulation.

Let us speculate for the moment on the possibility for winning a large-scale formal design from the simple structure set forth in Example 1. In many triadic compositions, the structural descent, like the denouement of a good play, occurs toward the end. By far the greater portion of time may be concerned with a gathering of tension around the initial member of the structural top voice, although anticipatory descents may often occur. It is therefore quite conceivable that the exposition, development, and recapitulation sections could all be concerned with various motions which, in the last analysis, could be understood as prolonging the initial structural member, in this case the tonic sonority with F♯ on top. The structural descent, E–D–C, which would release the tension gathered around this tone, might well be withheld until the coda, however. Example 2a shows the relation between formal sections and structure as described above; in Example 2b, possible neighboring prolongations of the tonic have been added. Note how the top voice, in making its anticipatory descent to C just before the coda, leaves the initial structural tone, F♯, hanging in the air. At the same time, the bass, in returning from the lower neighbor B♮ to C, traverses the space of a subdivided major seventh. The octave C so reached is itself prolonged by a retroactive dominant whose upper tone, D, carries the ear to E, the top voice of the second structural member, IV^7.

In Example 3, a much more detailed graph is presented. Here, each of the prolongations added to the structure in Example 2b has been extensively elaborated. Let us consider these elaborations as they occur, section by section. Although a detailed coordination of graphic analysis to the music must await Examples 6a to 6d, bar numbers have already been introduced in the present example. I shall therefore use these as convenient reference

[4] Leo Treitler, "Harmonic Procedure in the Fourth Quartet of Béla Bartók," *Journal of Music Theory*, Vol. III, No. 2, pp. 292–98.

EXAMPLE 3 *Middleground Graph*[5]

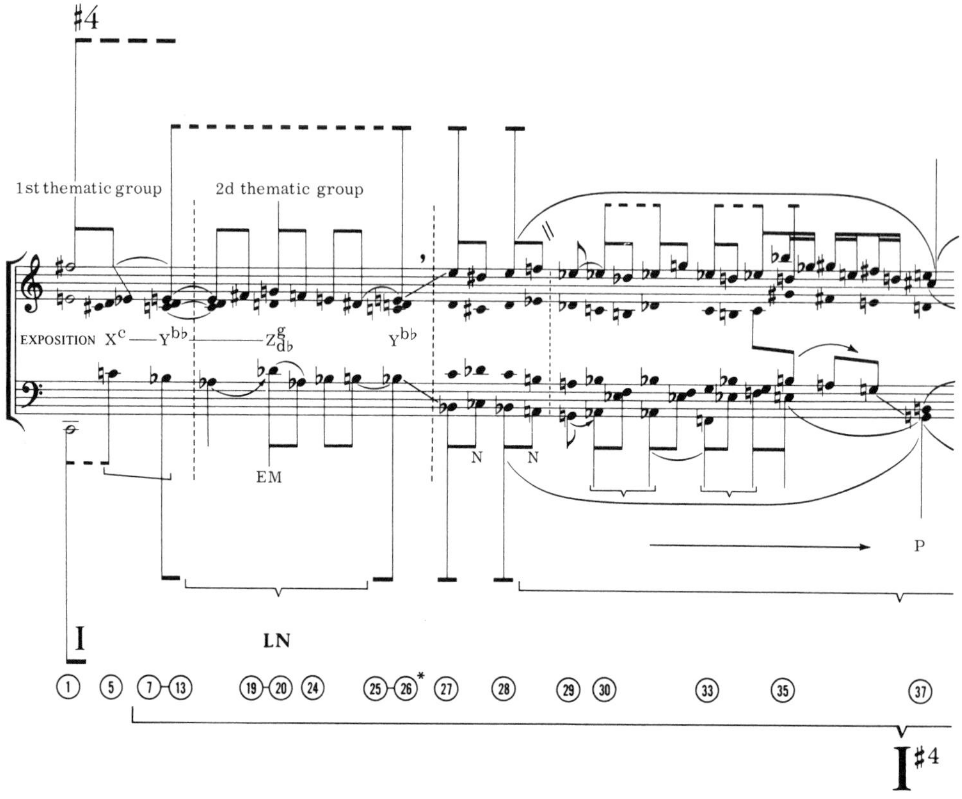

*For a further clarification of the motion of bars 26–43, see Example 4.

[5]For purposes of comparison with Examples 6a–6d (foreground graph), Example 3 is also presented as a fold-out following the index.

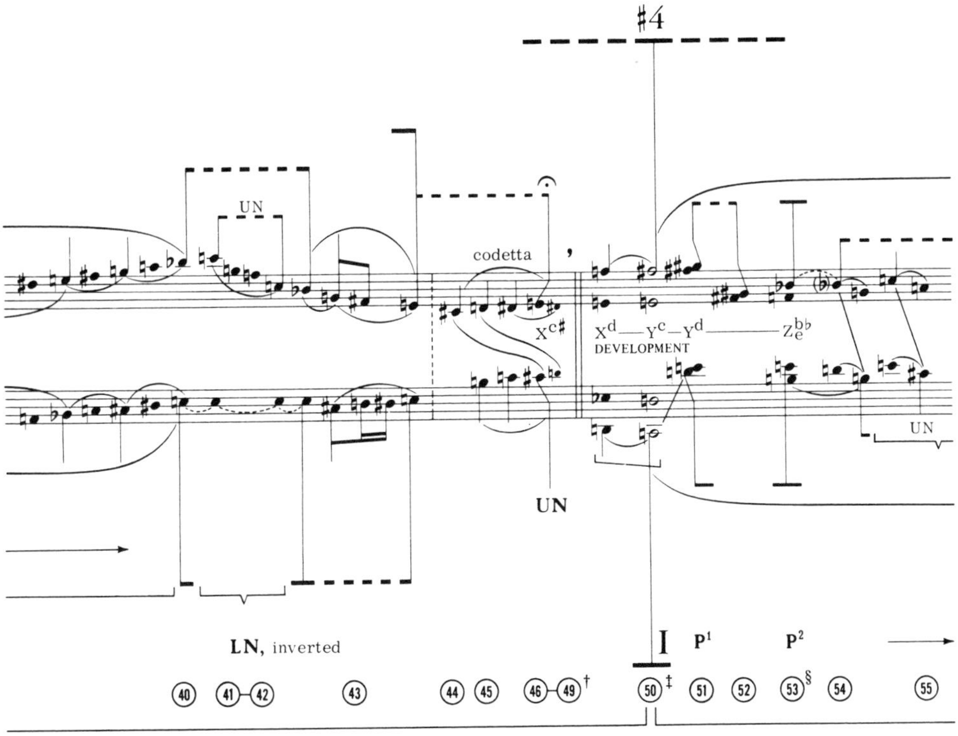

†Compare X^{c}–$Y^{b\flat}$ progression of bars 5–7 with X^{d}–Y^{c} progression of bars 49–50.

‡Compare motion of bars 26–40 with that of bars 50–63; in each case there is an exchange of outer parts. (See Example 5.)

§Also, compare motion of bars 19–25 with that of bars 53–61; in each case there is a descent from one tritone to another a minor third below.

EXAMPLE 3 (*continued*)

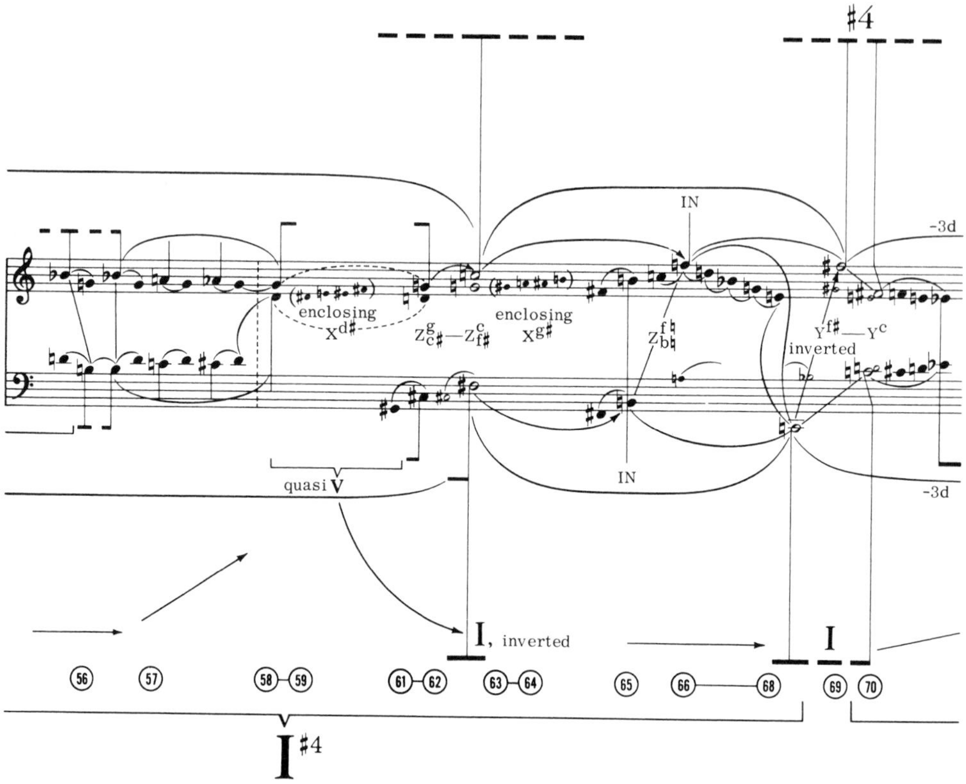

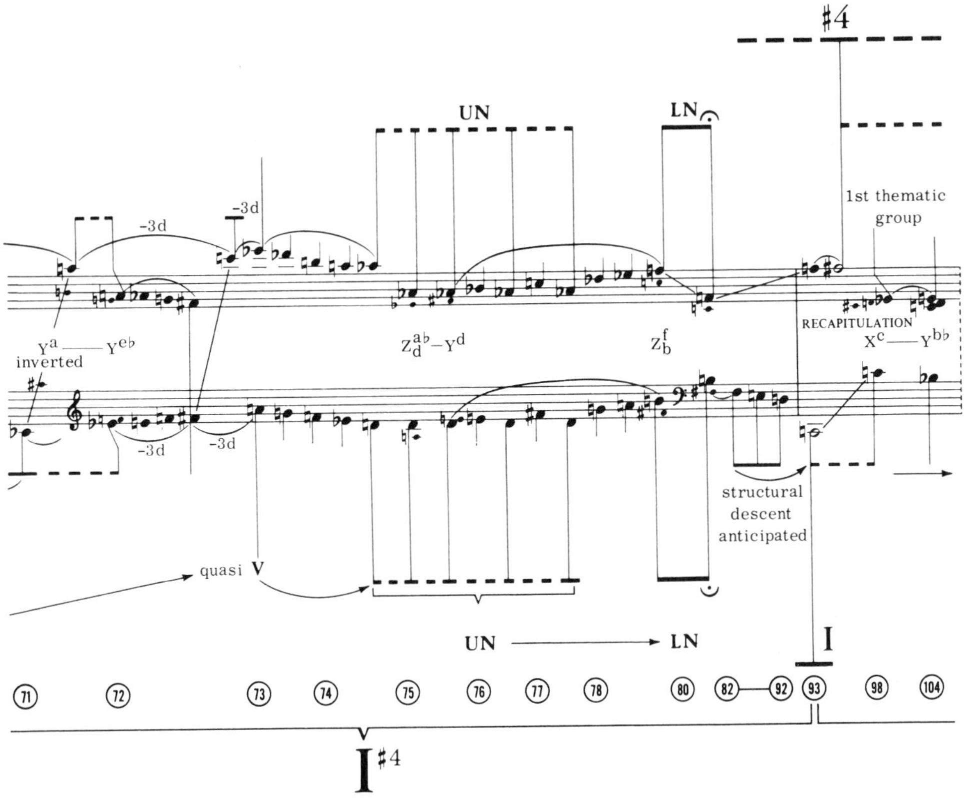
♯4
UN
LN
-3d
-3d
1st thematic group
Ya inverted —— Yeb
Zab d – Yd
Zf b
RECAPITULATION
Xc —— Ybb
-3d
-3d
structural descent anticipated
quasi V
UN → LN
I
71 72 73 74 75 76 77 78 80 82 92 93 98 104
I♯4

EXAMPLE 3 (*continued*)

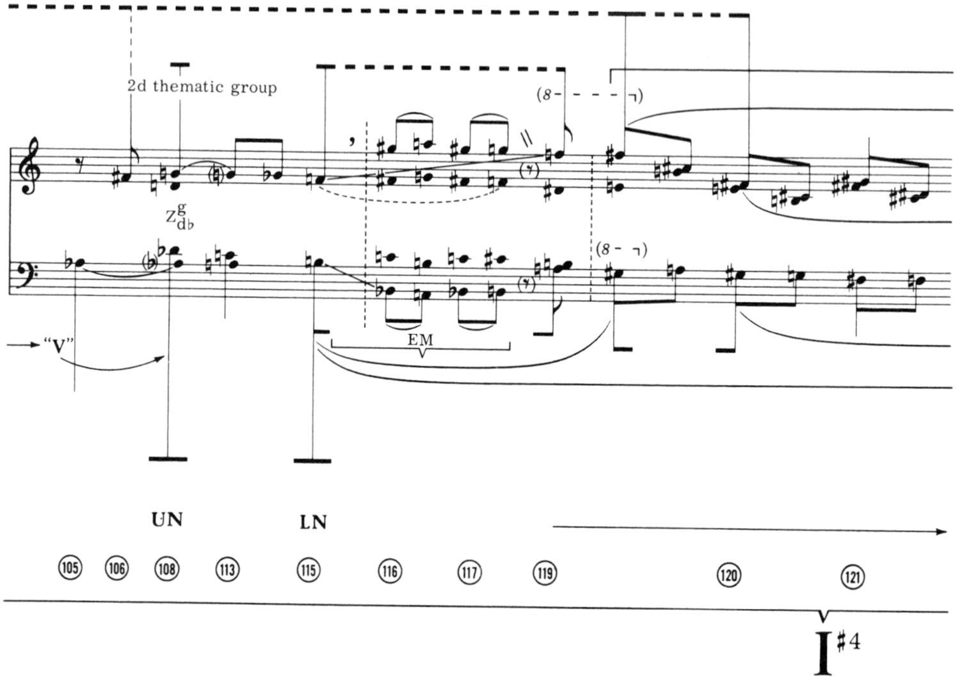

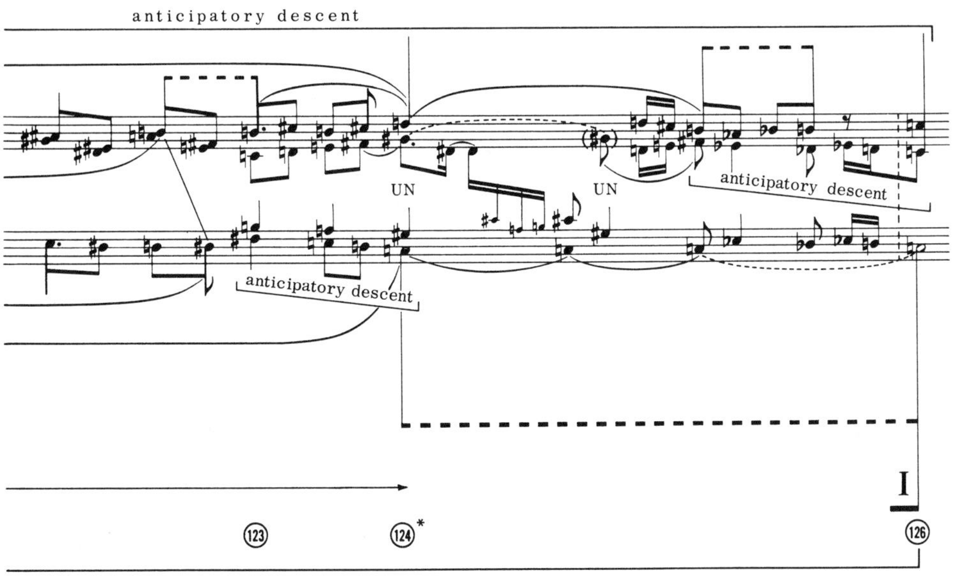

*Compare bars 124–126 with bars 41–43.

EXAMPLE 3 (*continued*)

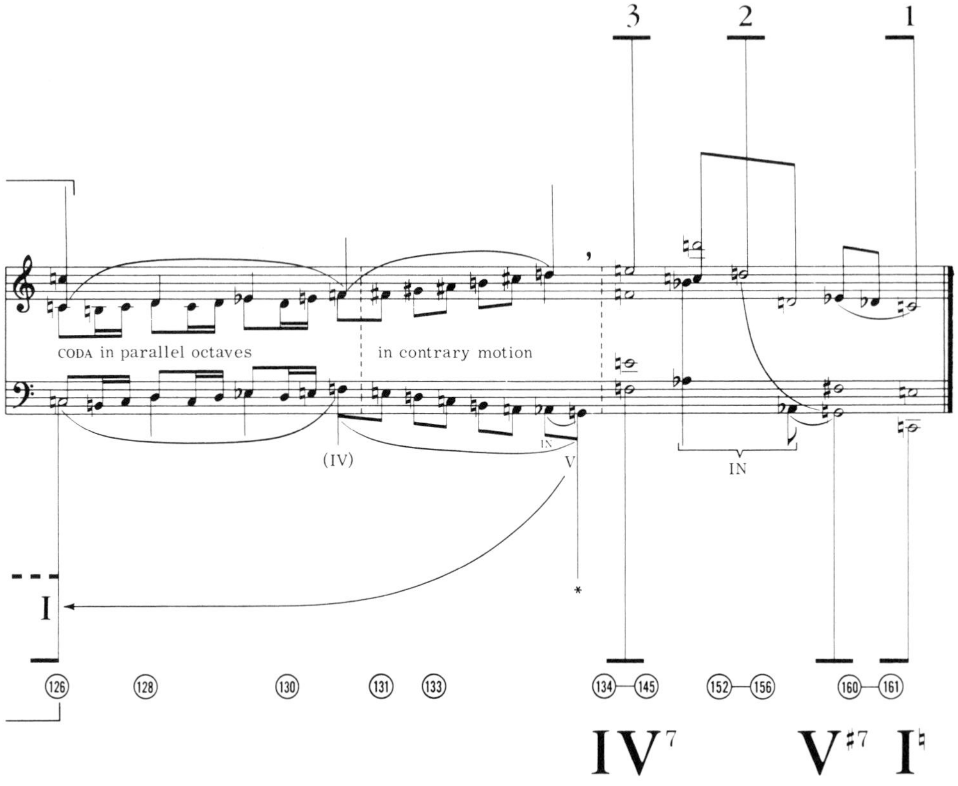

*We have already seen anticipations of the structural melodic fall, F♯–E–D–C, in the bass motions of bars 83–93 and bars 123–124. Here, in the canonic prolongations of bars 126–134, we find an anticipation, I–IV–(N)V, of all but the final member of the structural bass progression. As at bars 27–29, the principal canonic voices relate to each other obliquely rather than vertically.

points. Please note that Example 3, which is the middleground graph of the entire movement, is explained in the verbal text which follows. Examples 4 and 5 are illustrations of detail.

The first thematic group of the exposition (bars 1–13) is concerned with a movement from the tonic tritone C–F♯ to the lower neighboring tritone B♭–E. The latter interval delimits a whole-tone cluster, B♭–C–D–E, which is approached indirectly by means of an expanding chromatic cluster, C–C♯–D–E♭. George Perle has pointed out the importance of this progression, which he called "x–y," to the vocabulary of this movement.[6] I have borrowed his terminology, identifying a given transposition of either chord-form by reference to the lowest note in the cluster. Thus the appoggiatura chord in this progression is designated x^{c}, and the lower neighbor chord, $\mathrm{y}^{b\flat}$.

The second thematic group (bars 14–43) is concerned with various prolongations of $\mathrm{y}^{b\flat}$, which chord turns out to be the contrasting tonal level of the exposition. The first of these prolongations (bars 13–26) involves a motion to and from an embellishing chord, A♭–D♭–D♮–G♮, a familiar Bartók sonority which Treitler, in his addendum to Perle's contribution, has called "z."[7] Since this chord can readily be described as two perfect fourths whose roots lie a tritone away from each other, I shall identify a given transposition of it in terms of the two roots, in this case, $\mathrm{z}^{g}_{d\flat}$.

The other prolongation of $\mathrm{y}^{b\flat}$ consists of an exchange of tones in the outer voices, so that the interval B♭–E♮ at bar 27 is inverted to become E♮–B♭ at bar 40. This exchange is effected by means of a descent of a subdivided tritone in both voices, plus an intervening change of register. Thus the bass moves from B♭ (bar 27), via G (bar 37), to E (bar 40), while the soprano moves from E (bar 27), via C♯ (bar 37), to B♭ (bar 40). After a further upper neighbor prolongation of the B♭ (bars 40–42), the soprano descends another tritone, having thus traversed an octave from E to E. At this point the top voice merges with the bass, which has remained on E, at the unison of bar 43. Examples 4a through 4d illustrate a step-by-step derivation of

[6] George Perle, "Symmetrical Formations in the String Quartets of Béla Bartók," *Music Review*, Vol. XVI, No. 4, pp. 300–12.

[7] Treitler, in *Journal of Music Theory*.

the details of this prolongation. In comparing Example 4c with 4d, note the transfer of register which occurs between bars 37 and 40 in the latter.

EXAMPLE 4

Prolongation of $\text{Y}^{\flat\flat}$, (Example 3, bars 26–43): step-by-step derivation of details

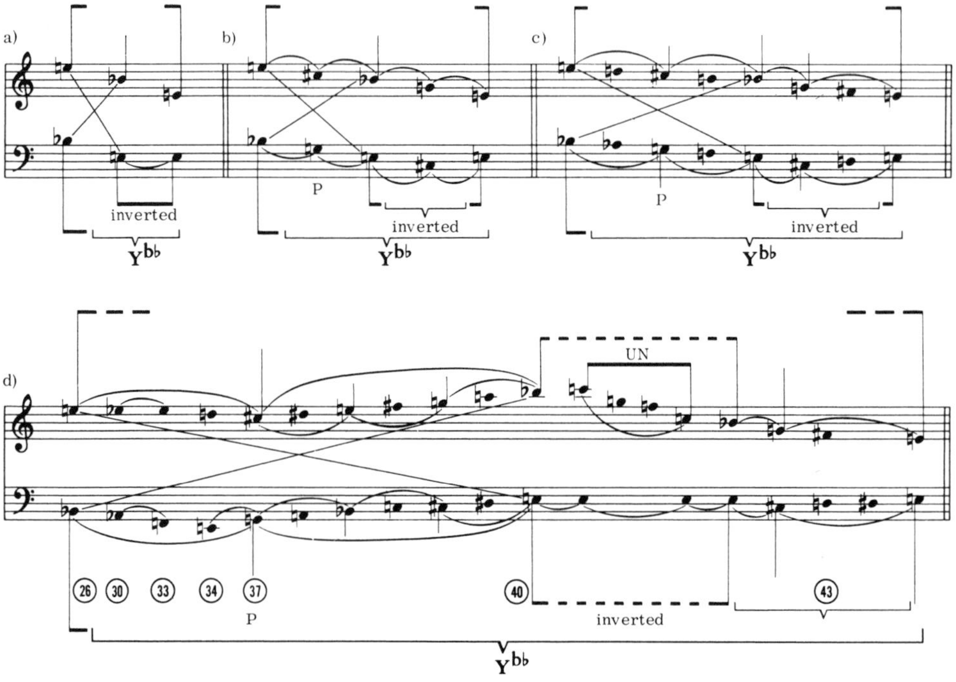

Thus the $\text{Y}^{\flat\flat}$-chord has been considerably emphasized by means of two prolongations which extend from bars 13 to 43. In fact it is just this emphasis which led me to state earlier that $\text{Y}^{\flat\flat}$ constitutes the contrasting tonal level of the exposition (analogous to the dominant or mediant levels so often reached in the second thematic groups of triadic expositions). In larger context, however, the $\text{Y}^{b\flat}$-chord serves as an extended neighbor to the initial tonic sonority (see Example 2b).

The exposition is closed off by a brief codetta (bars 44–49) during which the four-tone chromatic cluster $\text{X}^{c\sharp}$ is unfolded. The top voice, E, of this sonority is retained from the foregoing lower neighbor chord, while the bass, C♯, can be understood as an upper neighbor to the bass, C, from which the movement began.

The development section begins with a precipitous return to the tonic tritone, now expressed as a Y^{c} chord, thus completing the overall neighboring motion of the exposition. This return is accomplished by shifting the X–Y progression of bars 5–13 up a whole step. Here, however, the X–Y progression has been considerably compressed, occupying only a single measure of time (see bars 49–50). The sequential parallelism implied by this transposition is made strikingly explicit by the prolongation of Y^{c} which follows. Just as the tritone B♭–E was prolonged by an exchange of outer parts in bars 26–40, so here is the tritone C–F♯ prolonged by such an exchange in bars 50–63.

EXAMPLE 5

Large-scale parallelism between exposition and development sections

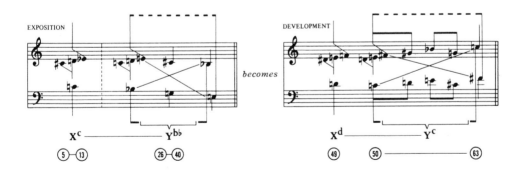

As Treitler has pointed out, the X^{d}–Y^{c}–Y^{d} progression of bars 49–51 leads into a $\text{Z}^{b\flat}_{e\natural}$-chord at bar 52. The change of chord-form, however, in

no way impedes the stepwise ascent from C–F♯ to its inversion; the principal voices continue to move in parallel tritones. Furthermore, the approach to the goal of motion F♯–C is intensified by means of a z-chord a perfect fourth below, which can be regarded as a quasi-dominant ($z^{g}_{c\sharp}$). Note how smoothly the outer voices B♮–B♭, retained from $z^{b\flat}_{e\natural}$, converge upon the upper perfect fourth of this quasi-dominant (see Example 3, bars 54–62).

At bar 69, the original form of the tonic tritone C–F♯ is regained. It is first expressed as an inverted $Y^{f\sharp}$-chord, then as a Y^{c}-chord. The descending natural succession (in z-chords!) which led into the inverted form of I, $z^{c}_{f\sharp}$, at bar 63, carries forward into an incomplete lower neighbor chord, $z^{f\natural}_{b\natural}$, at bars 65 and 66. A descent in thirds, from the top-voice F♮ of this chord, eventually leads into the bass of the tonic tritone, reached just before bar 69. Thus, bars 50–69 of the development section can be understood as a single large-scale prolongation of I (see Example 3, bars 50–70).

The remainder of the development section (bars 69–93) is concerned with another prolongation of I, in this case an upper and lower neighboring motion. The upper neighbor, D–A♭, is reached at bar 75. It is prefaced by its own "dominant," A–E♭, which makes a quasi-Phrygian stepwise descent from V to I in bars 73–74. The quasi V, A–E♭, is itself reached by means of an ascent in minor thirds, beginning at the tonic sonority of bar 68 (see Example 3, bars 68–75). A stepwise ascent through a major sixth (from bars 75–80) leads to the lower neighbor z^{f}_{b}. This chord, which is sustained from bars 82–92, is an analogue to the dominant pedal so often attained at the end of triadic development sections. Note the bass descent, F♯–E–D–C, which anticipates the structural melodic descent of the entire movement. The point of recapitulation is, of course, signaled by the arrival on C in the bass at bar 93, and the immediately subsequent emphasis on F♯, the top voice of the tonic tritone (see Example 3, bars 75–93).

The recapitulation is concerned with yet another neighboring motion around the tonic tritone. The upper neighbor chord, $z^{g}_{d\flat}$, is reached at bar 108; the lower neighbor, B–F, is reached at bar 115. At bar 119, the top-voice F♯ of the tonic tritone is strongly reaffirmed. In the meantime, the bass has moved from B (bar 115), via A♮ (bar 119), to G♯ (bar 120). The outer parts continue in contrary motion, the bass eventually descending a major seventh, from B (bar 115) to C (bar 124), the top voice ascending a minor sixth from F♯ (bars 119 and 120) to D (bar 124). The latter tone is characteristically supported at the tritone by an inner voice, G♯; the soprano does not complete its anticipatory descent into the tonic until bar 126.

The octave C reached here serves as the point of departure for the coda. It is within the latter section, of course, that the structural descent takes place. There is only one minor addition here—a subdominant in bar 130 has been interpolated between the tonic of bar 126 and its retroactive dominant in bar 134 (see Example 3, bars 93–161).

If the reader will turn to Examples 6a to 6d, he will find a detailed documentation for the structural reading summed up in Example 3. Relationships which were merely sketched in the latter example will here be found to have been greatly expanded and elaborated. It is therefore suggested that the reader continually refer back to Example 3 whenever he feels himself to be losing his bearings. A piano reduction of each of the four main sections of the movement appears at the top of Examples 6a to 6d, and a graphic analysis appears immediately below. Where it has seemed necessary to do so, I have added brief verbal comments. Otherwise I have preferred to suggest the implicit hierarchy of structural values by means of various stem lengths, slurs, and prolongation symbols.[8]

In his biographical study of Bartók, Halsey Stevens mentions a meeting of Bartók and Henry Cowell in London in December, 1923: "Both were house guests in the same home, and Cowell, then investigating the possibilities of tone clusters, was playing some of his own music one Sunday morning when Bartók, attracted by the strange sounds, appeared and asked if he might listen. Bartók himself had occasionally piled up adjacent notes in something approaching clusters, but Cowell's development of a tone-cluster 'technique' was quite new to him. . . . Early the next year Bartók wrote to Cowell asking whether the latter would object to his using tone-clusters in his own music; the letter with this modest request has disappeared, but the piano music which Bartók wrote in the next few years shows the effect of his accidental encounter with the young American."

[8] I have adopted many of the graphic procedures used by Felix Salzer in his analysis of twentieth-century music in *Structural Hearing* (2d ed.; New York, Dover, 1962).

In referring to a characteristic complex of tones in the second movement of the Fourth Quartet, which was composed five years after Bartók's meeting with Henry Cowell, Mr. Stevens states that such a passage "cannot be considered a cluster since each of the seven (chromatically adjacent) notes is arrived at through the most logical of melodic progressions in the preceding bars; the piling-up of adjacent notes is therefore a contrapuntal, not a harmonic, procedure."[9]

As we have seen, the x- and y-chords of the first movement have been treated with similar contrapuntal logic. Whether one should therefore not call them "tone-clusters" I am not prepared to say. The fact remains, however, that in this movement, out of a relatively meager vocabulary of non-triadic materials, Bartók was able to create and elaborate a new and complete tonal system, true on every level to its primordial tonic sonority.

[9] Stevens, pp. 67 and 190–91.

FOREGROUND GRAPH OF THE FIRST MOVEMENT OF BARTÓK'S FOURTH STRING QUARTET, WITH PIANO REDUCTION

EXAMPLE 6a *Exposition* (bars 1–49)

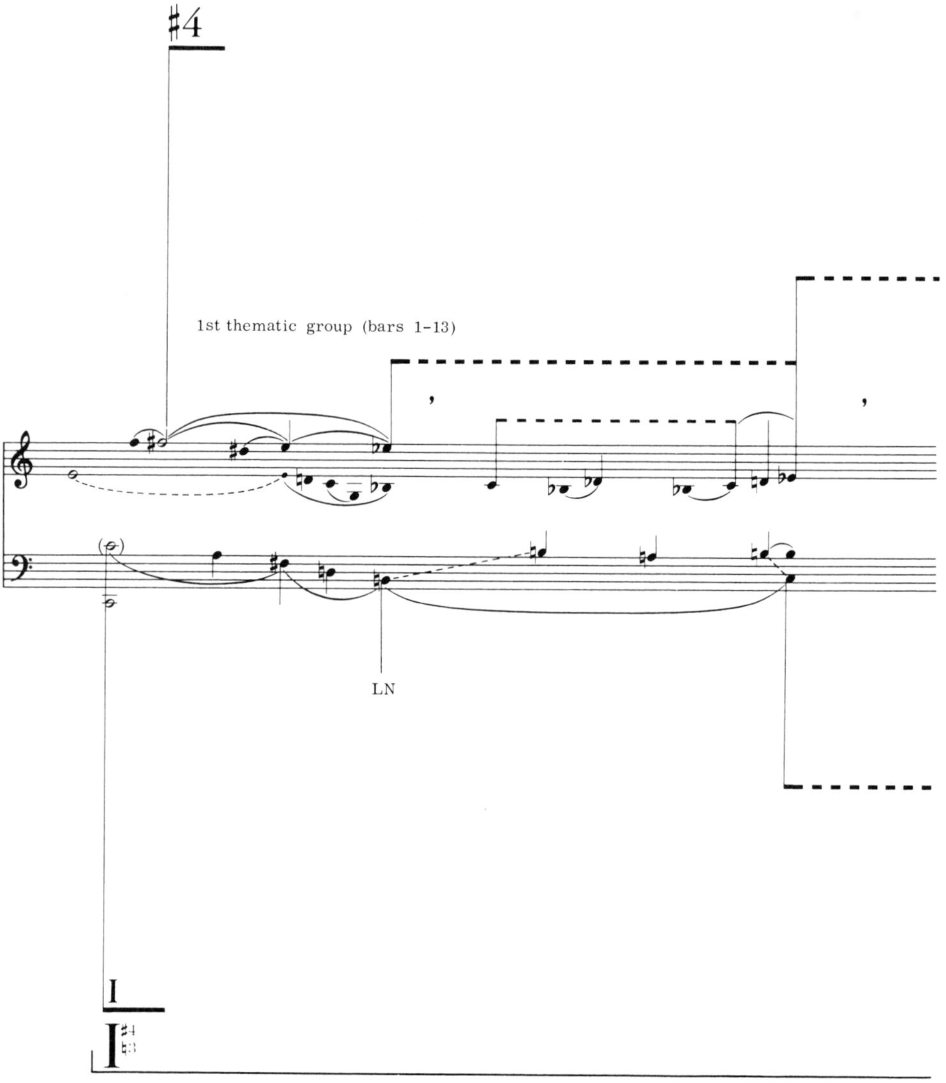

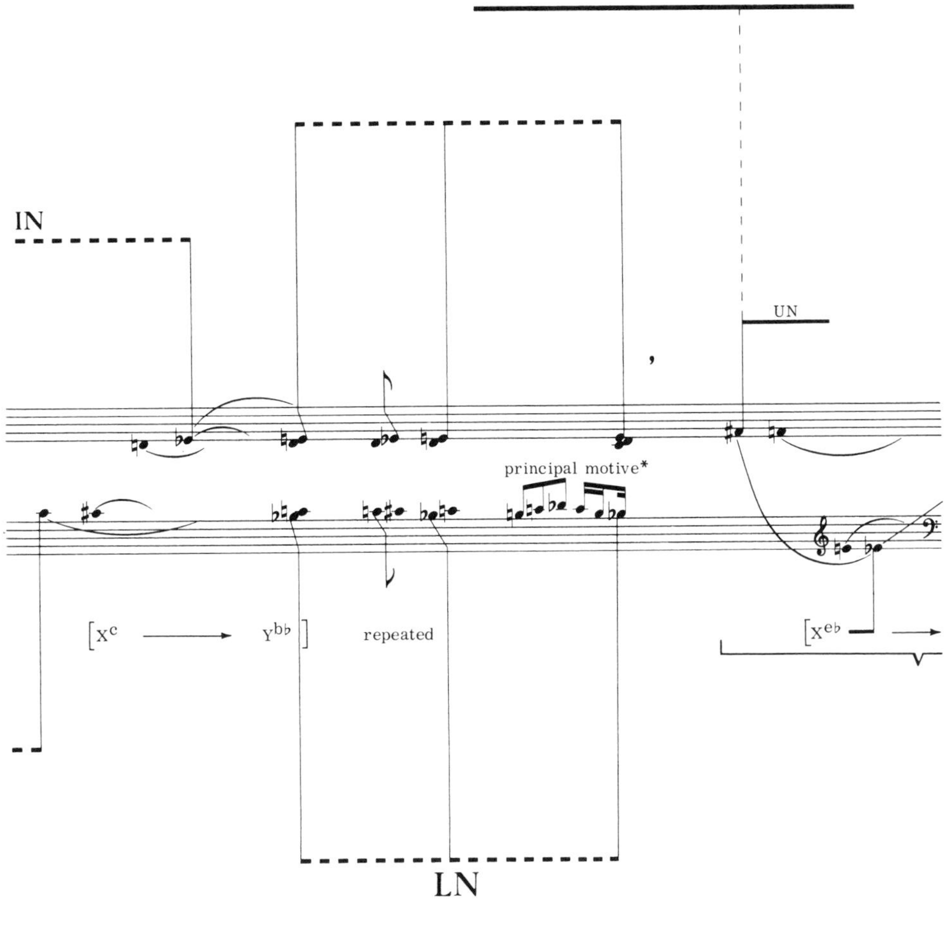

*As George Perle has already pointed out, the principal motive can be regarded as a melodic statement of an X-chord (in this case, X^{bb}).

EXAMPLE 6a (*continued*)

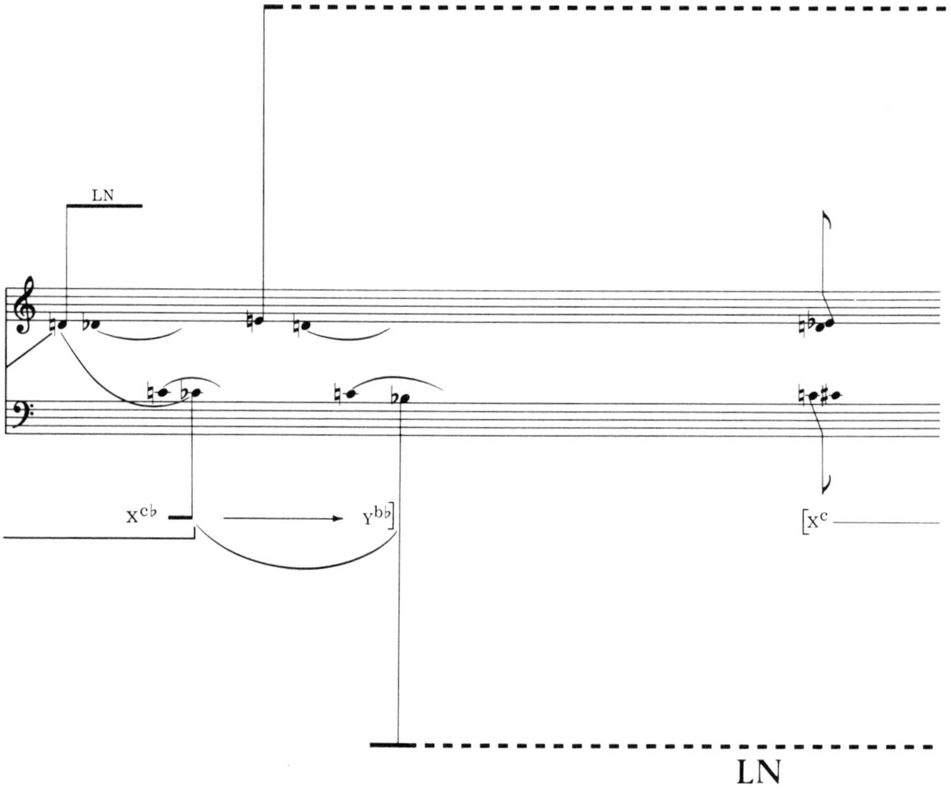

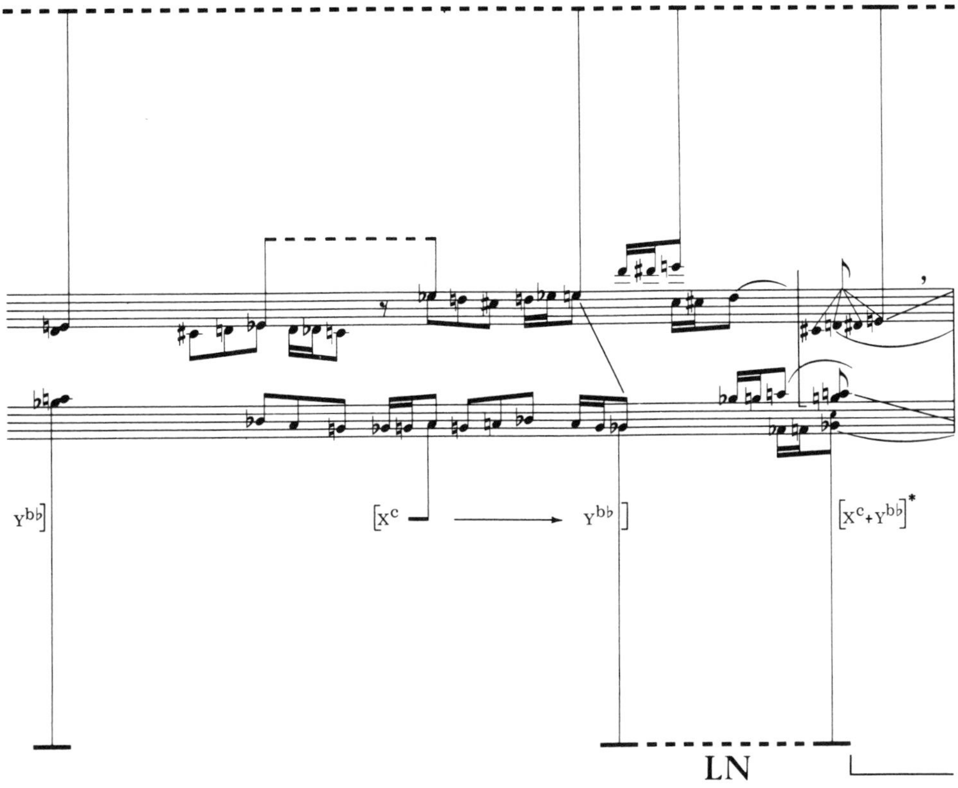

*Summary of bars 5–13 in a single chord.

EXAMPLE 6a (*continued*)

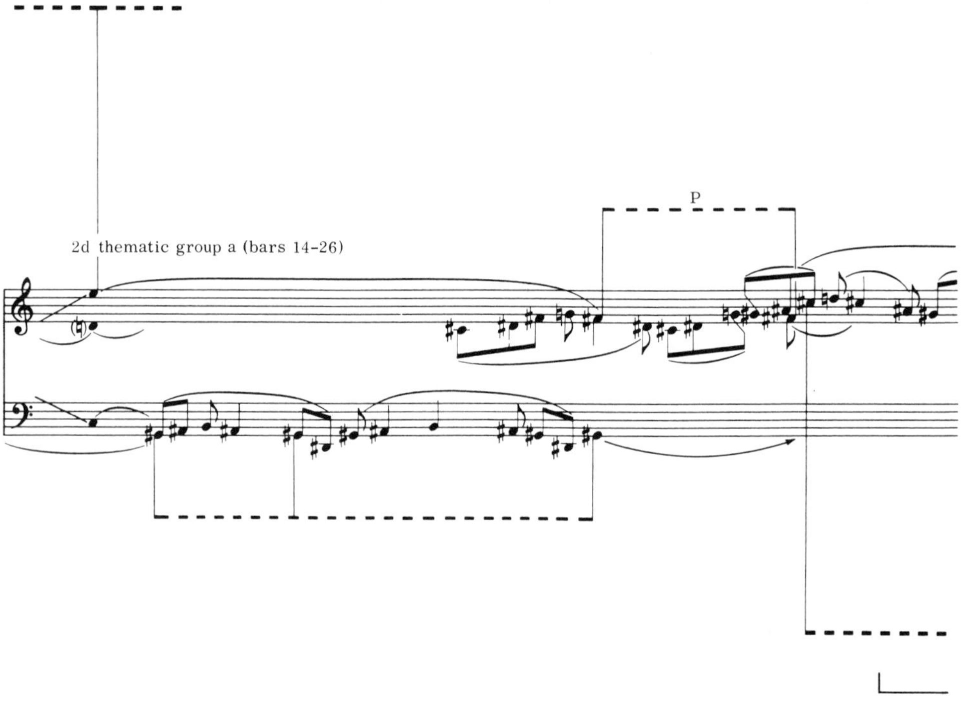

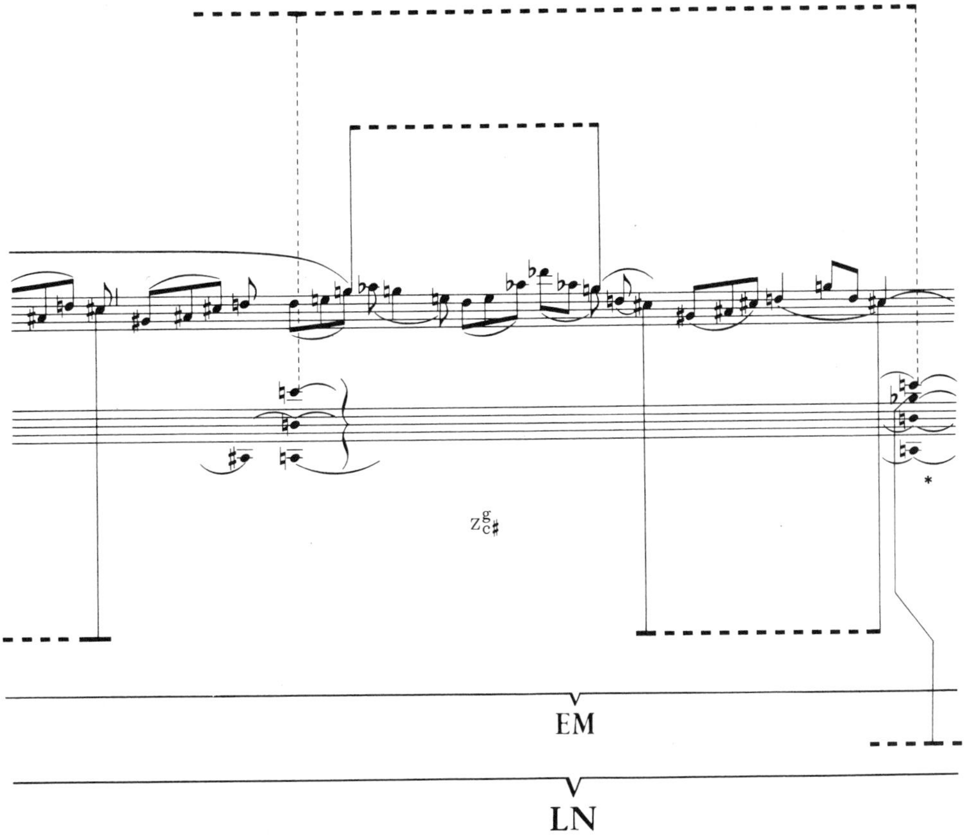

*Note that the three upper tones of Y^{bb}, unfolded by the viola ostinato beginning in bar 14, are transferred to the cello in bar 19. The remaining tone, B♭, of the sonority, now inverted, is contributed by the 2d violin in bars 22–24.

EXAMPLE 6a (*continued*)

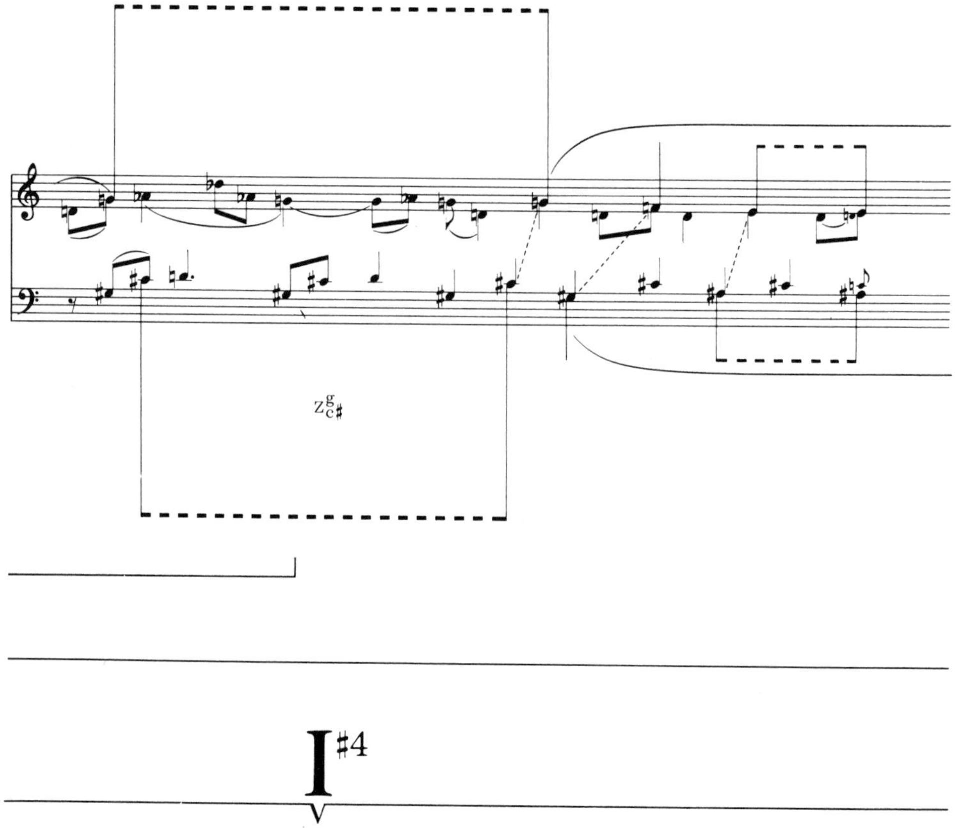

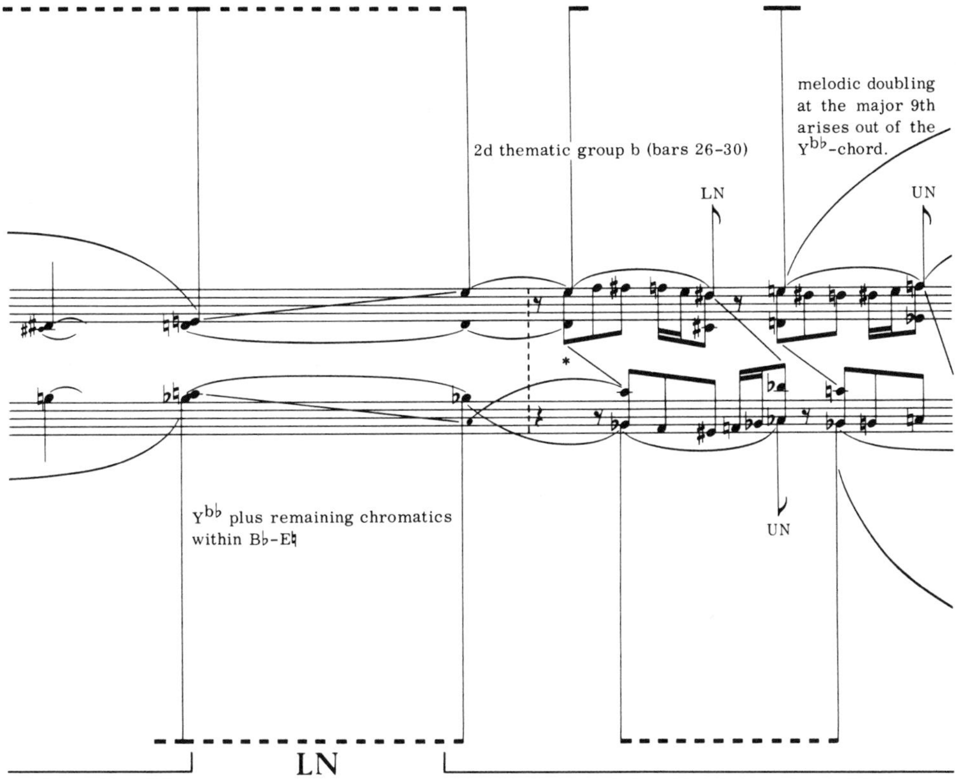

---

*As a result of the imitation, the two pairs of voices are related to each other obliquely rather than vertically.

EXAMPLE 6a (*continued*)

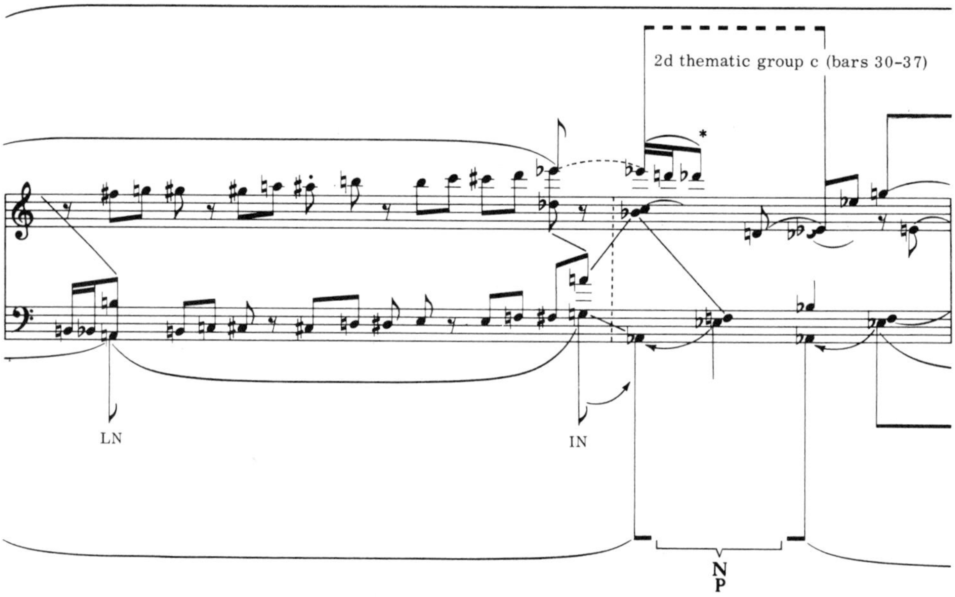

*  is a fragment from , the principal motive transposed.

sf

EXAMPLE 6a (*continued*)

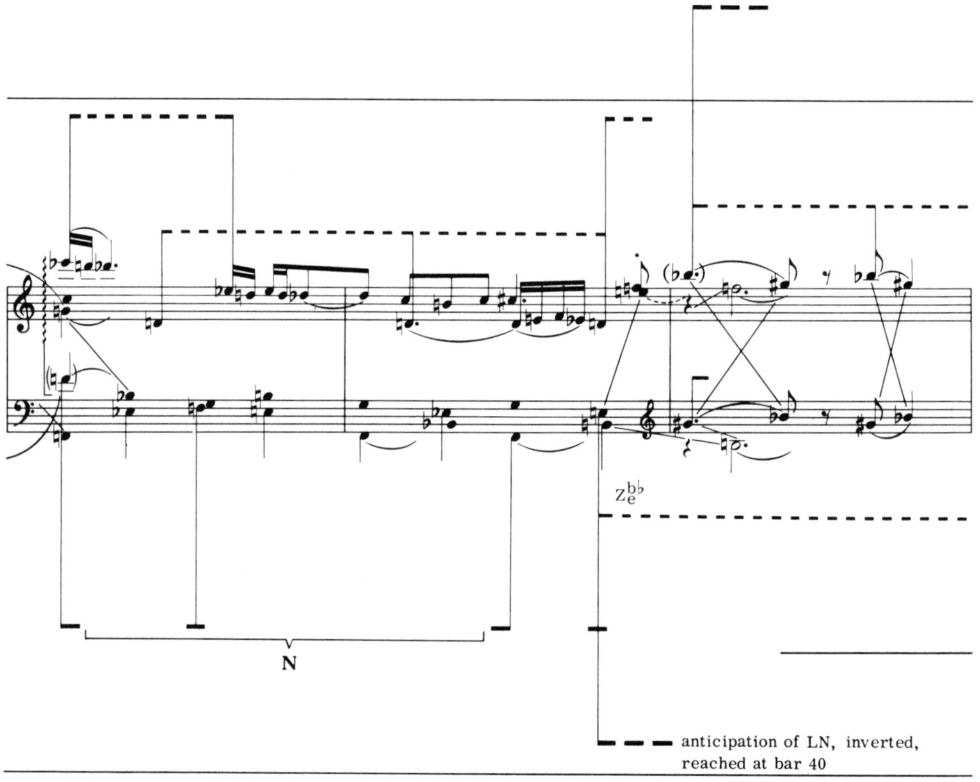

sf
f pesante

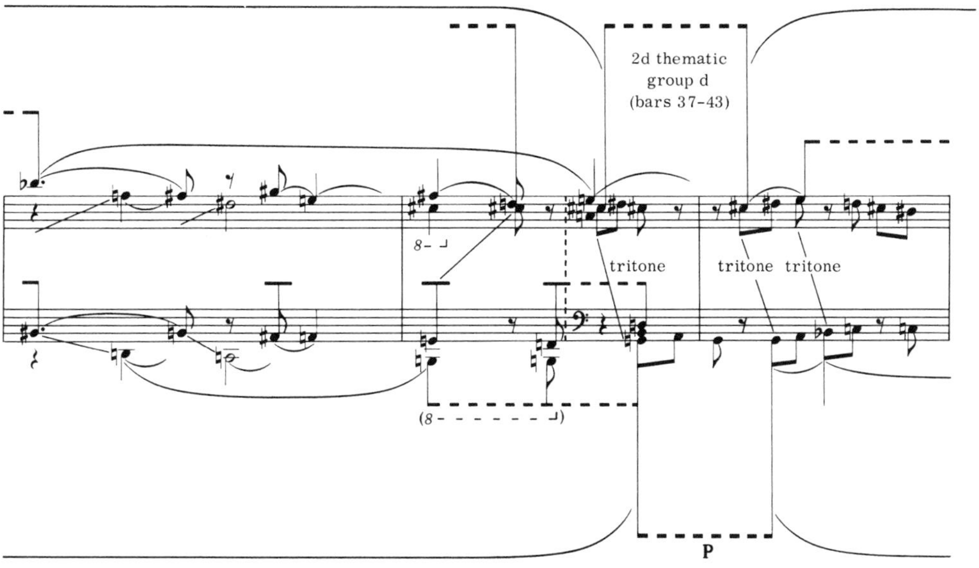
2d thematic
group d
(bars 37-43)
tritone
tritone tritone
P

EXAMPLE 6a (*continued*)

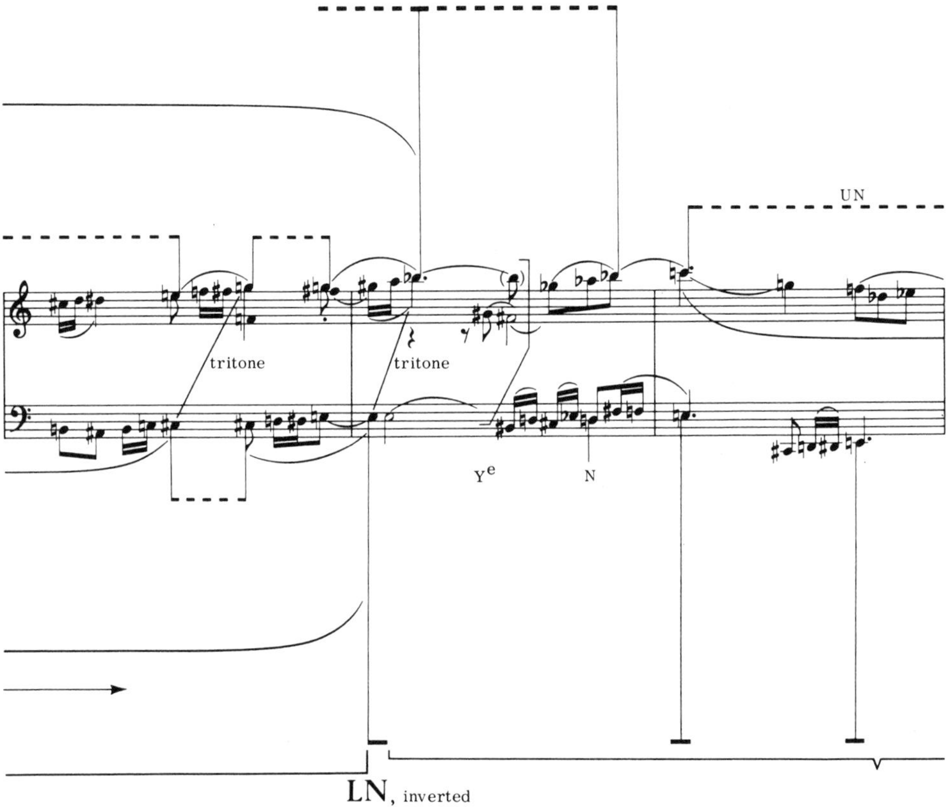

Codetta (bars 46-49)

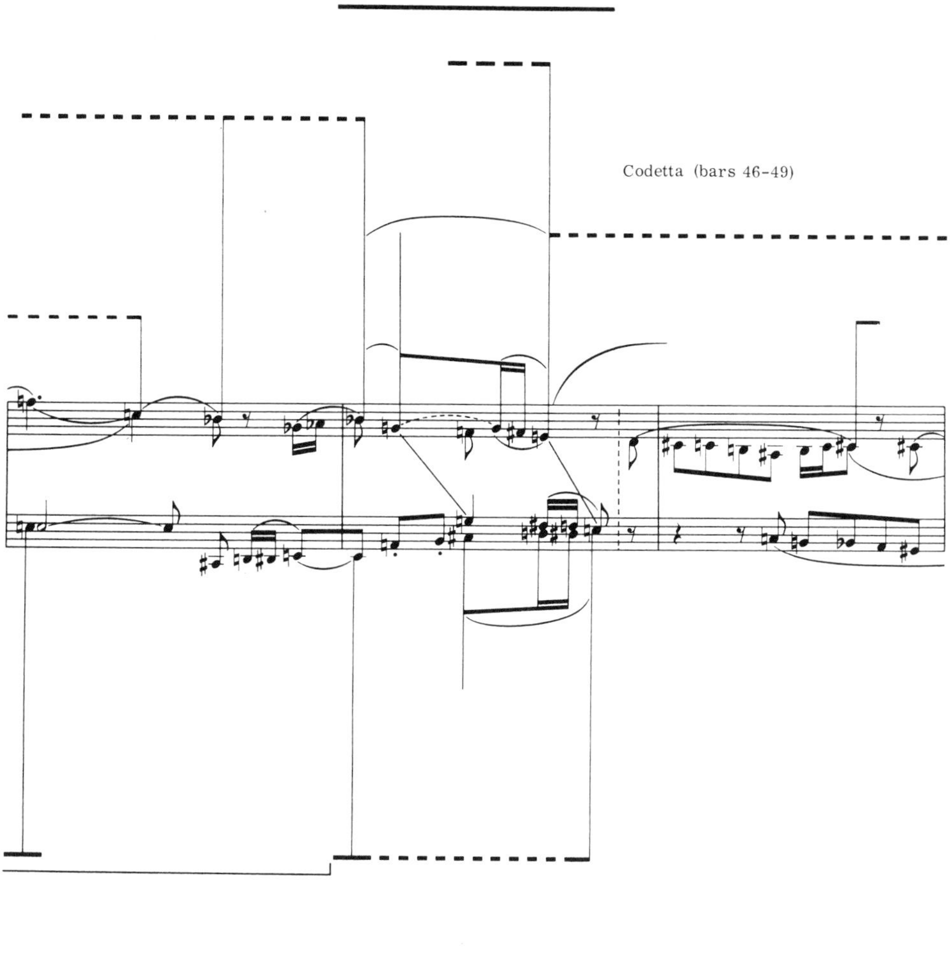

EXAMPLE 6a (*continued*)

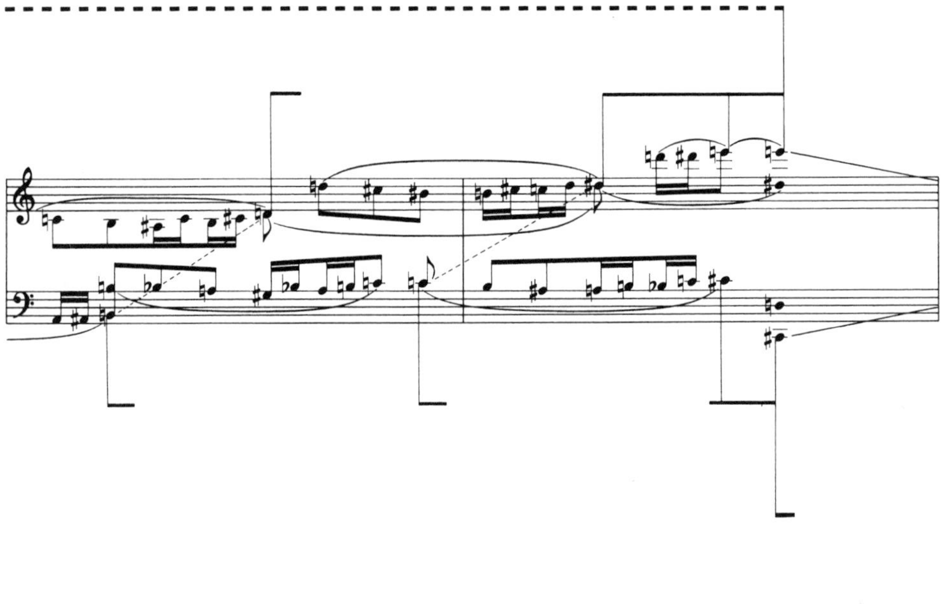

3
3
3
3
Ped ten.

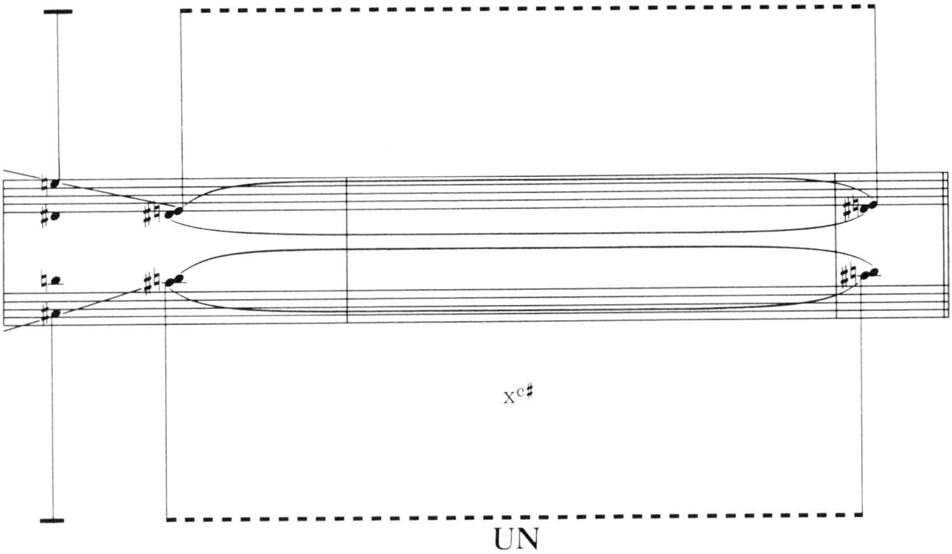
x c♯
UN

EXAMPLE 6b *Development* (bars 49–93)

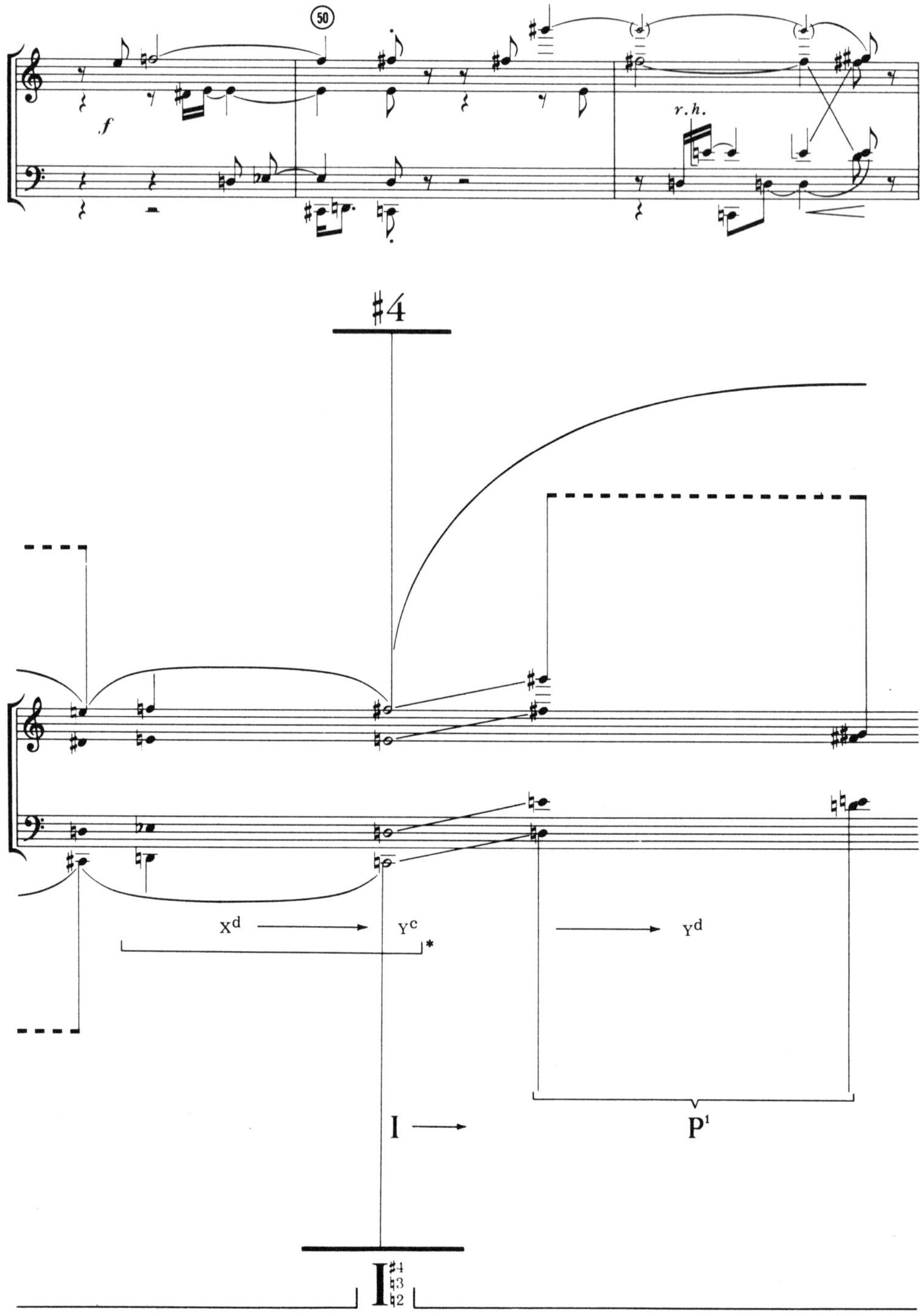

*Compare with bars 5–7.

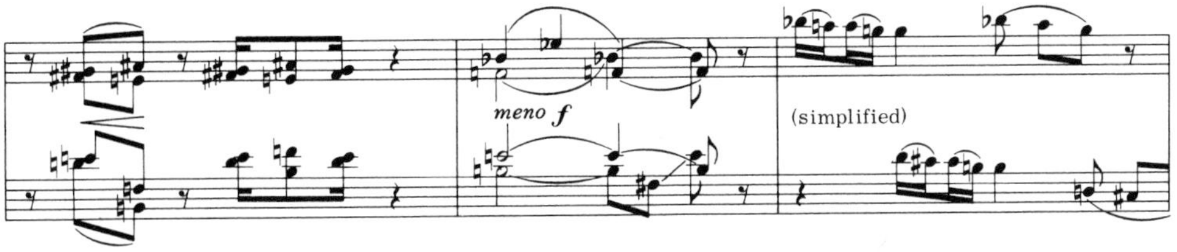

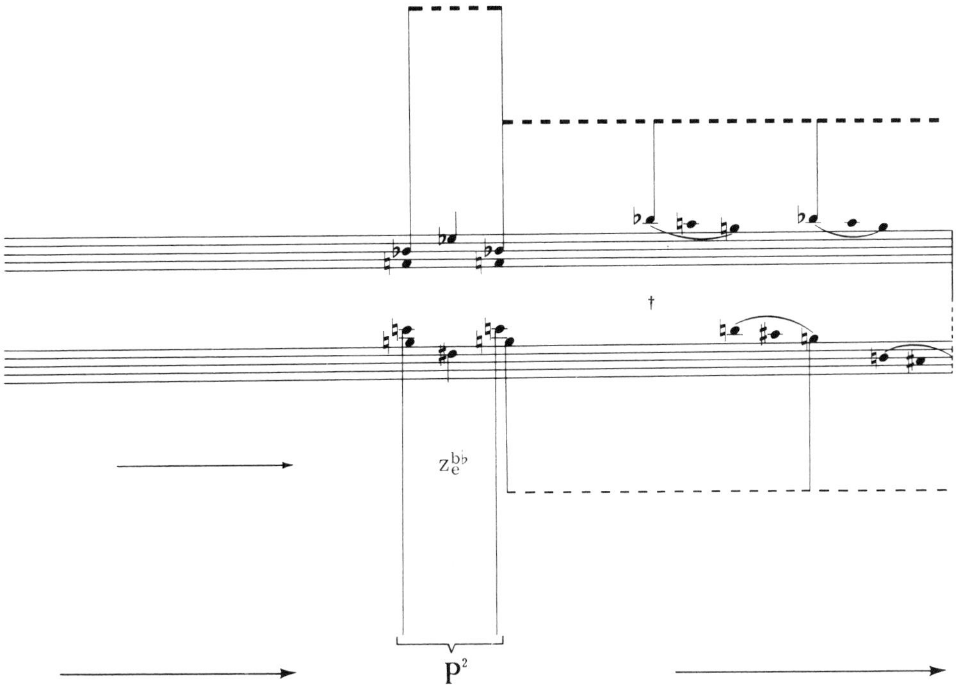

†The tones B♮–B♭, retained from $z^{b\flat}_{e\natural}$ at bar 53, converge on the perfect fourth, D–G, at bar 57. The tones of $x^{d\sharp}$, which chromatically fill in that fourth, are projected as inner voices from bars 54–62. At bar 60, D–G becomes the upper fourth of $z^{g}_{c\sharp}$.

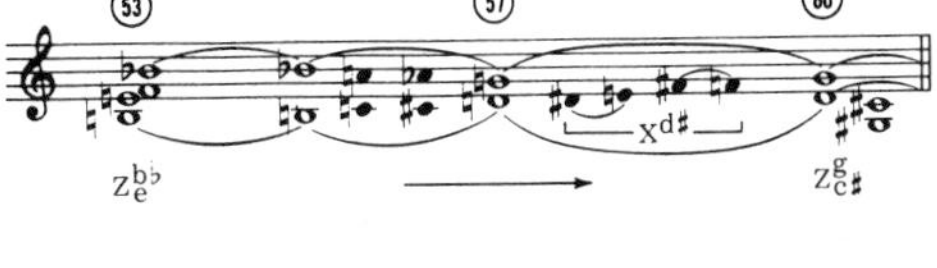

EXAMPLE 6b (*continued*)

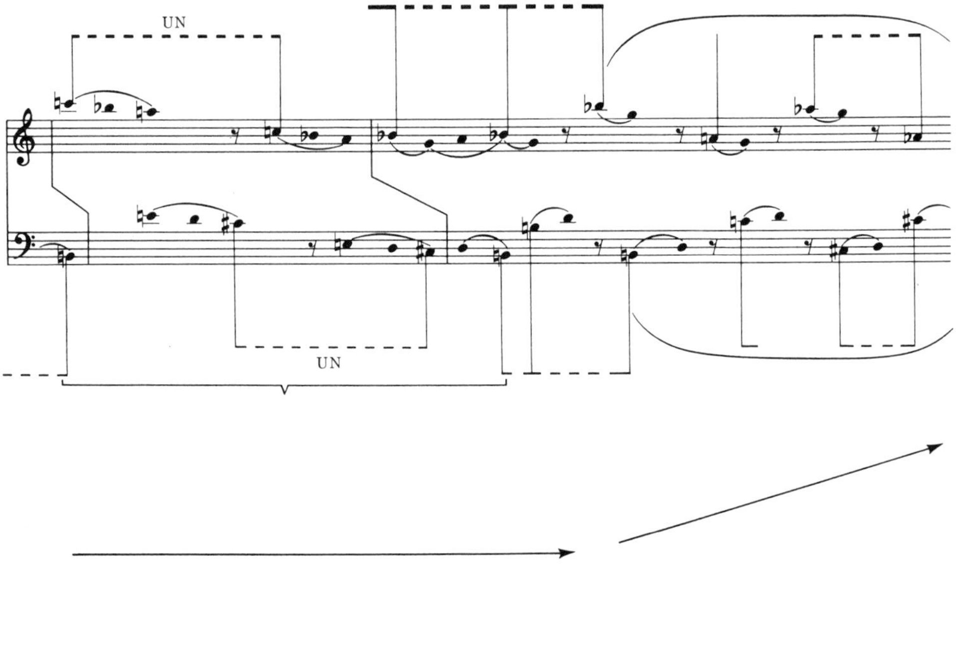

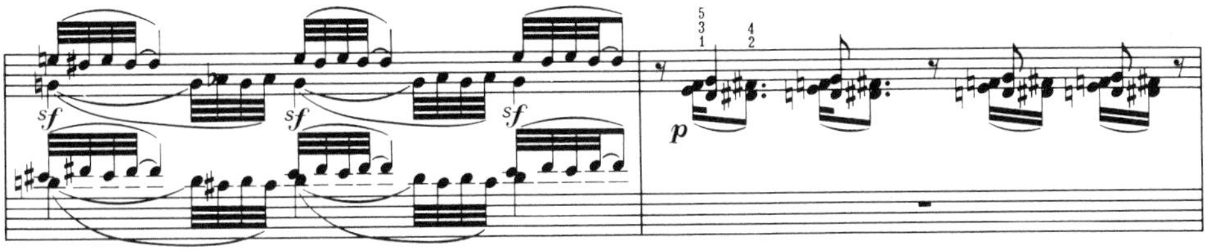

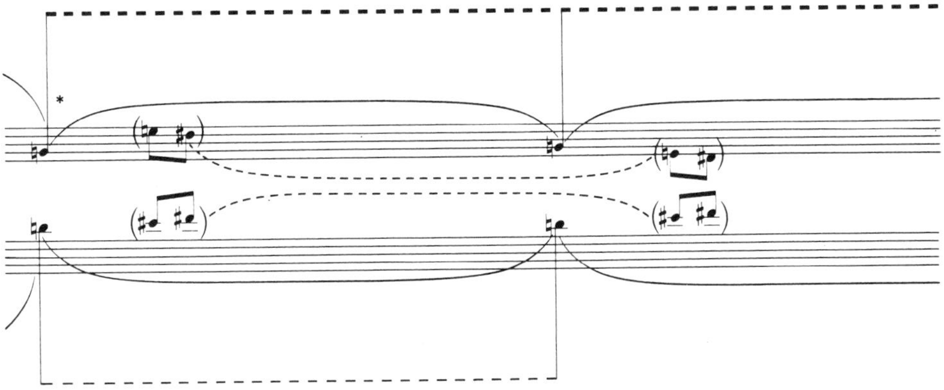

I♯4

*See example footnote on p. 333.

EXAMPLE 6b (*continued*)

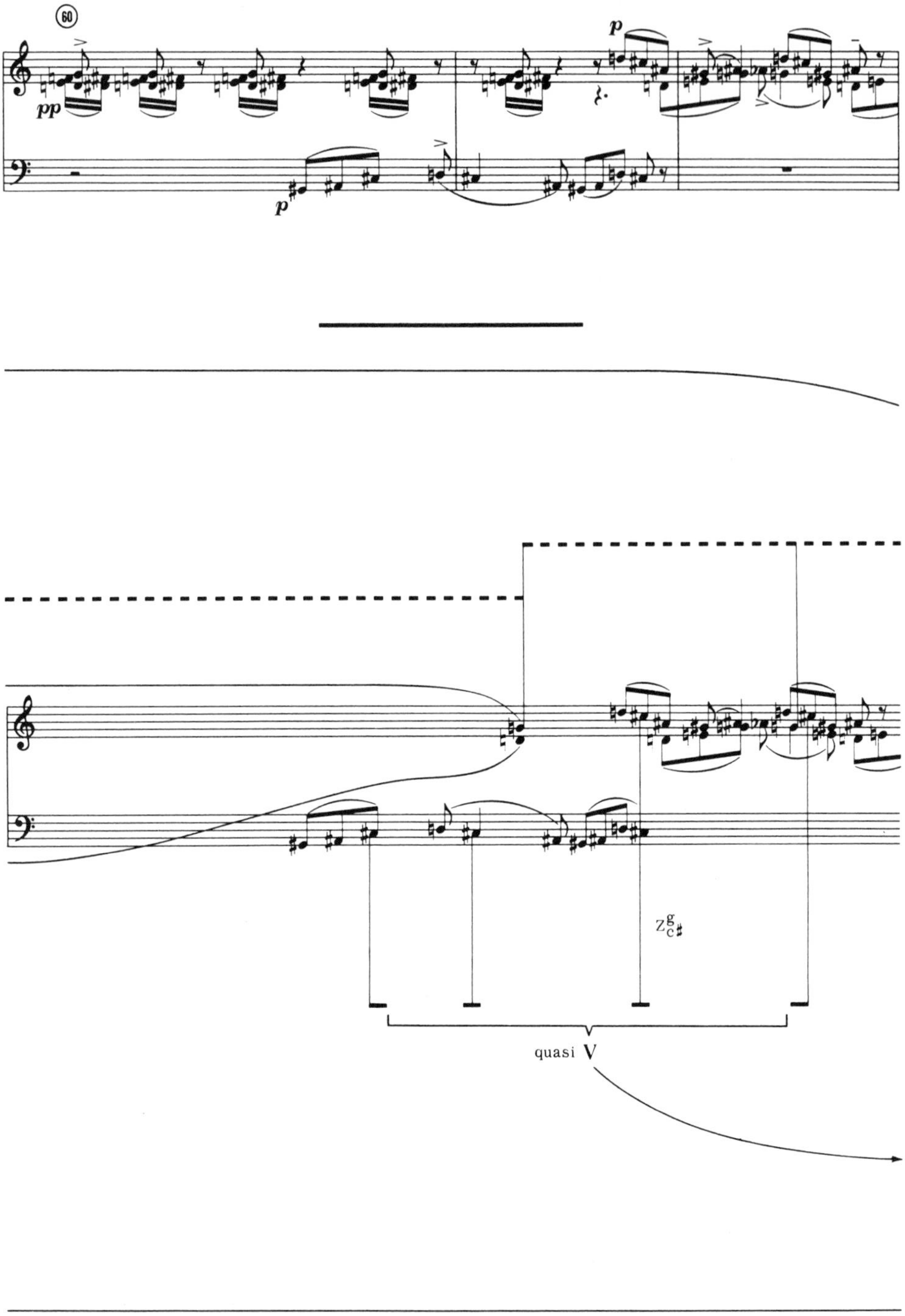

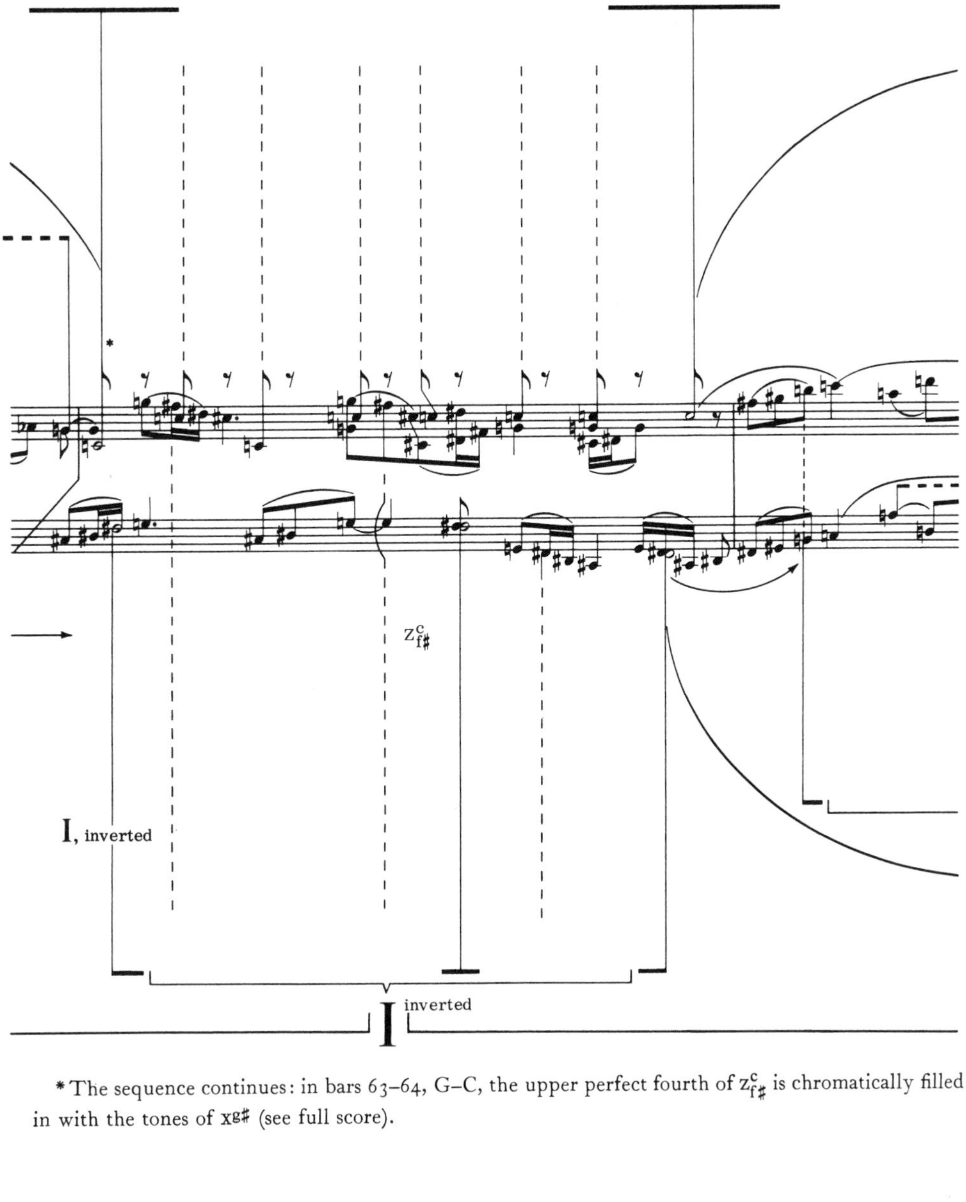

* The sequence continues: in bars 63–64, G–C, the upper perfect fourth of $z^{c}_{f\sharp}$ is chromatically filled in with the tones of $x^{g\sharp}$ (see full score).

EXAMPLE 6b (*continued*)

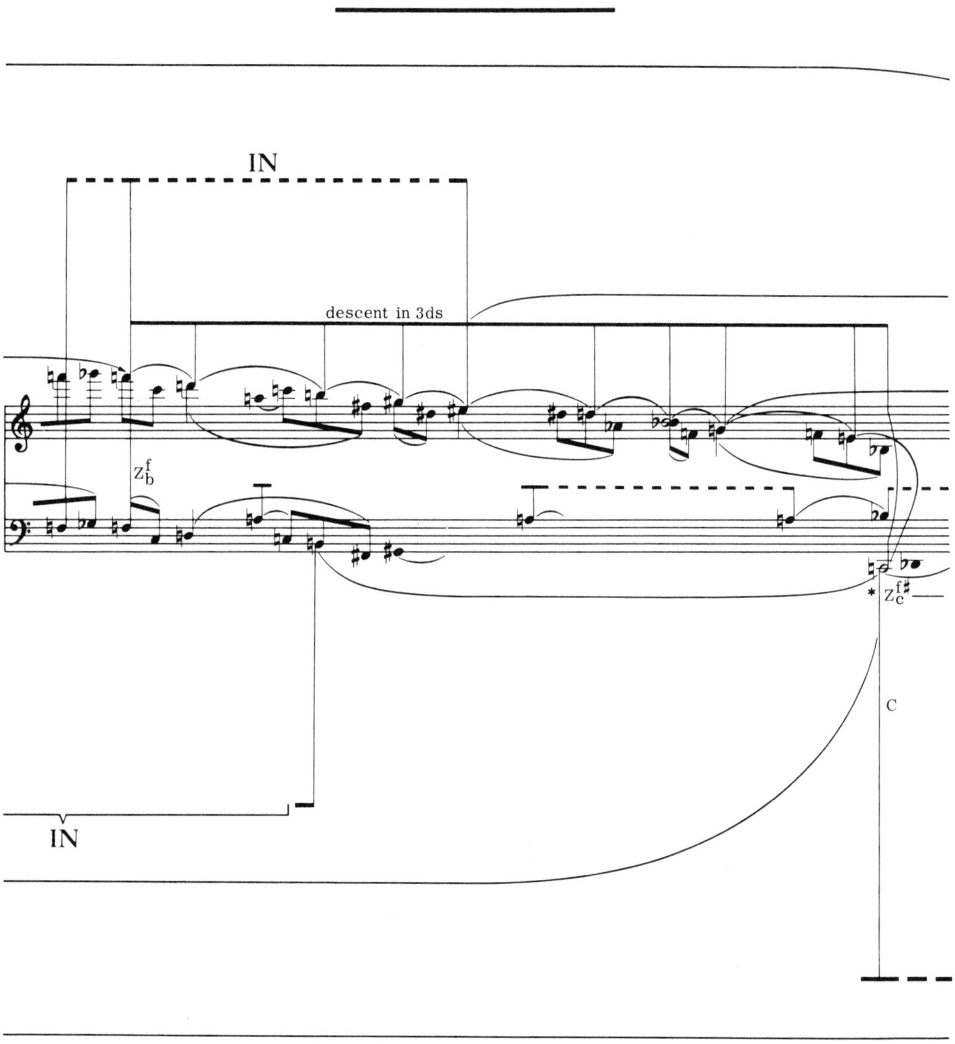

*In bar 69, the voices move melodically in terms of z-chords, but vertically (or rather, obliquely) in terms of parallel y-chords, inverted. This is sequentially continued at bar 71.

70
pp
mf

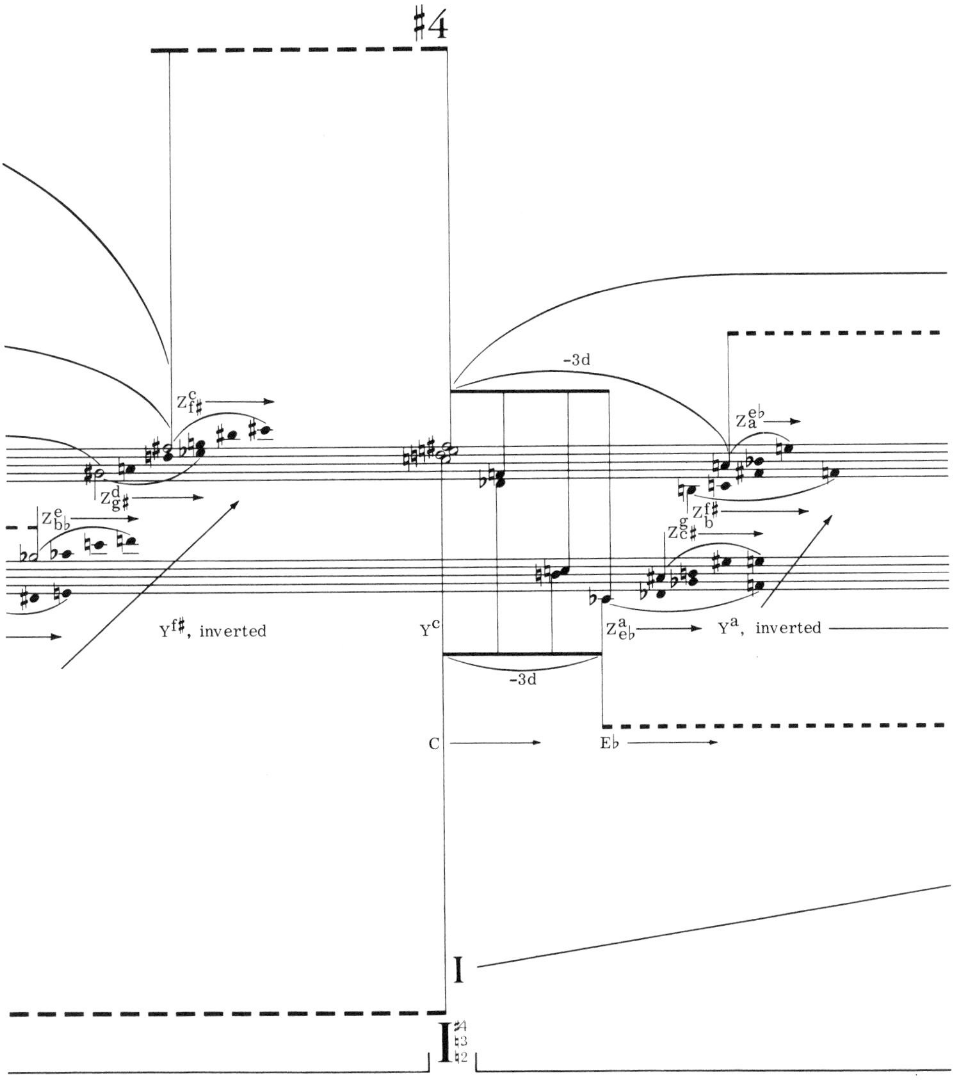
♯4
Zc f♯
Zd g♯
Ze b♭
Yf♯, inverted
Yc
-3d
-3d
C
E♭
Zeb a
Zf b
Zg c
Za e♭
Ya, inverted
I
I ♯4 ♮3 ♮2

EXAMPLE 6b (*continued*)

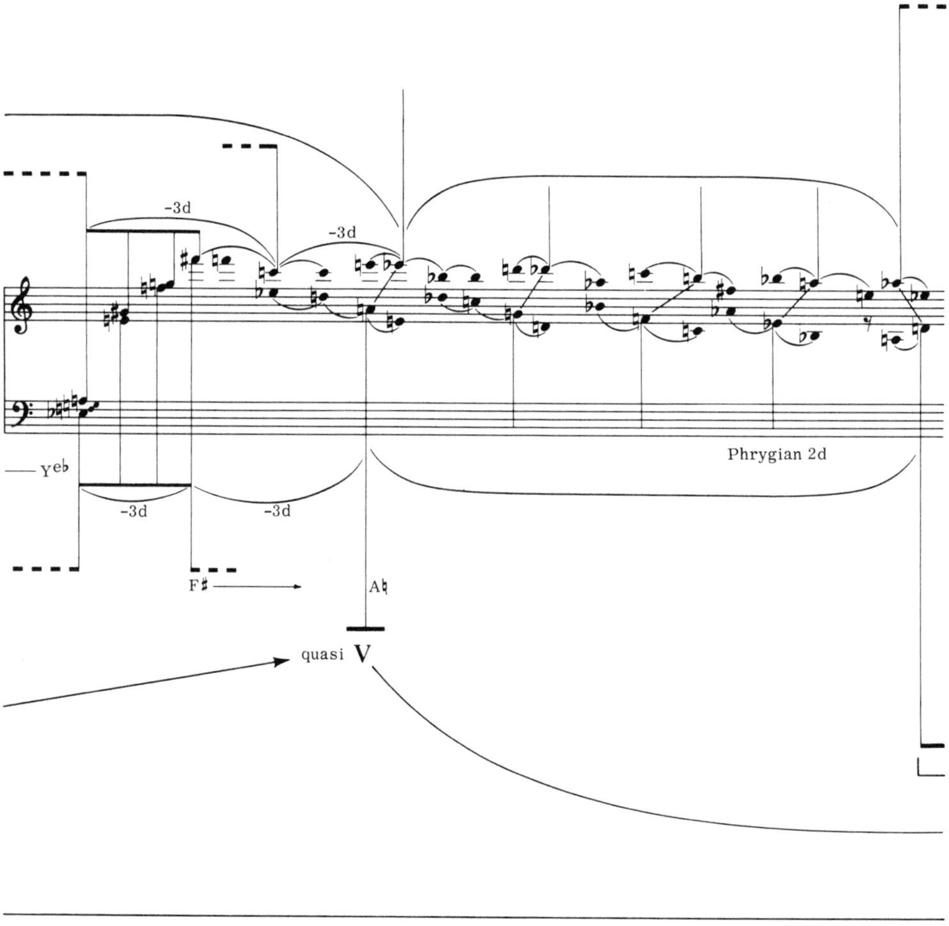

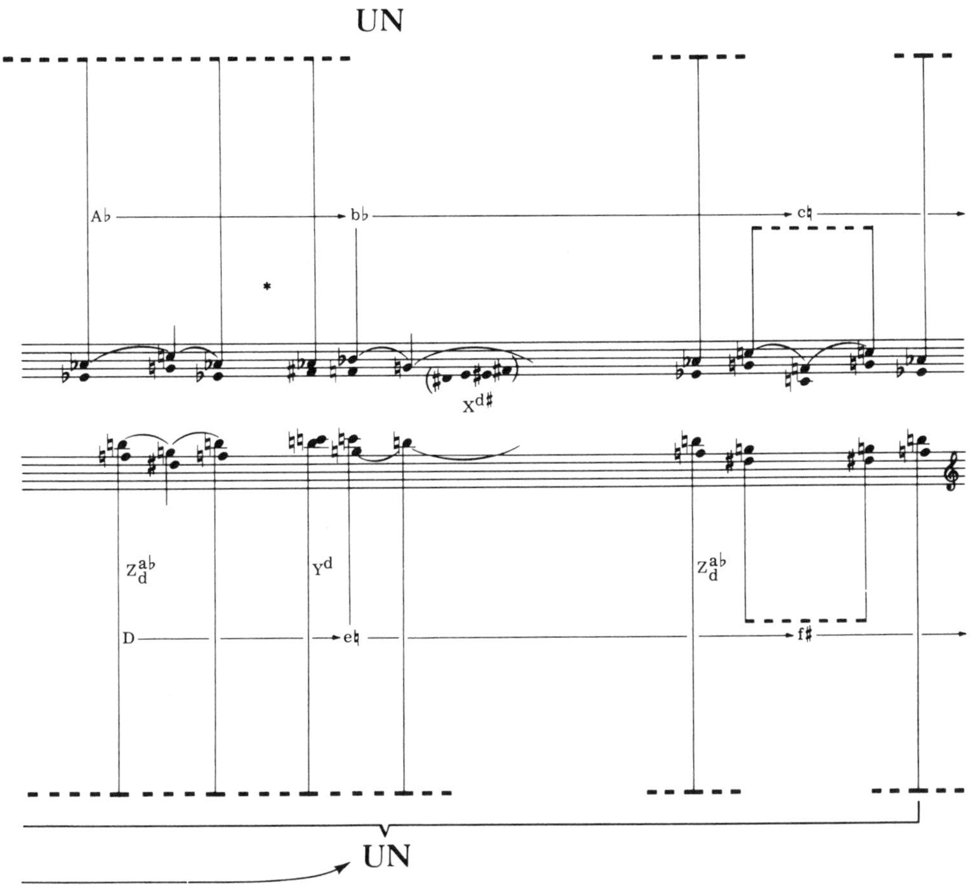

*Here is an example of the same tritone, D–A♭, expressed first as a Z-chord and then as a Y-chord.

EXAMPLE 6b (*continued*)

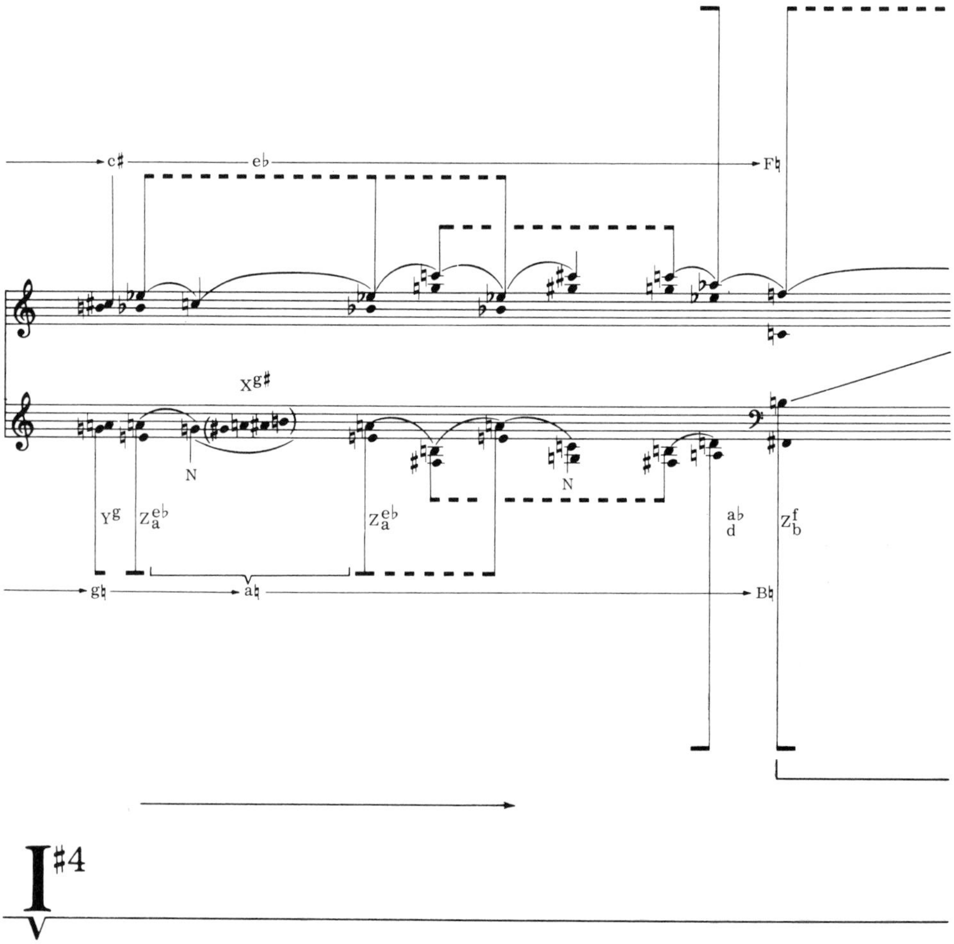

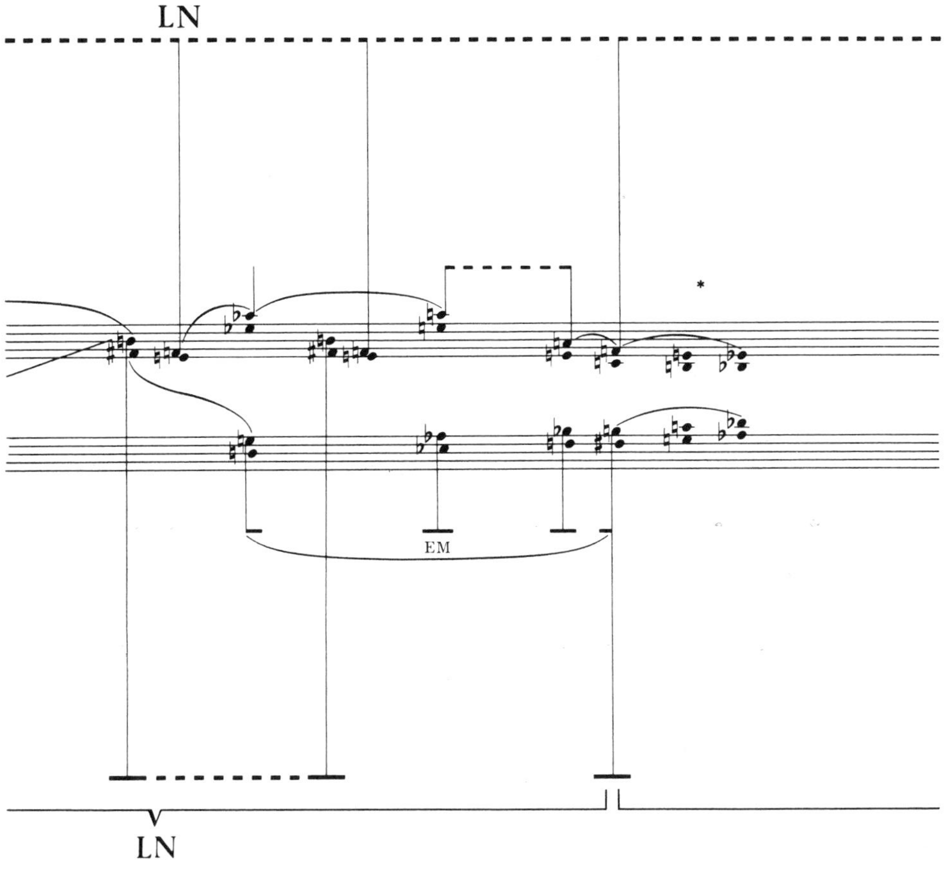

* 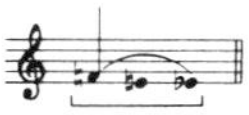 foreshadows  in bar 94.

EXAMPLE 6b (*continued*)

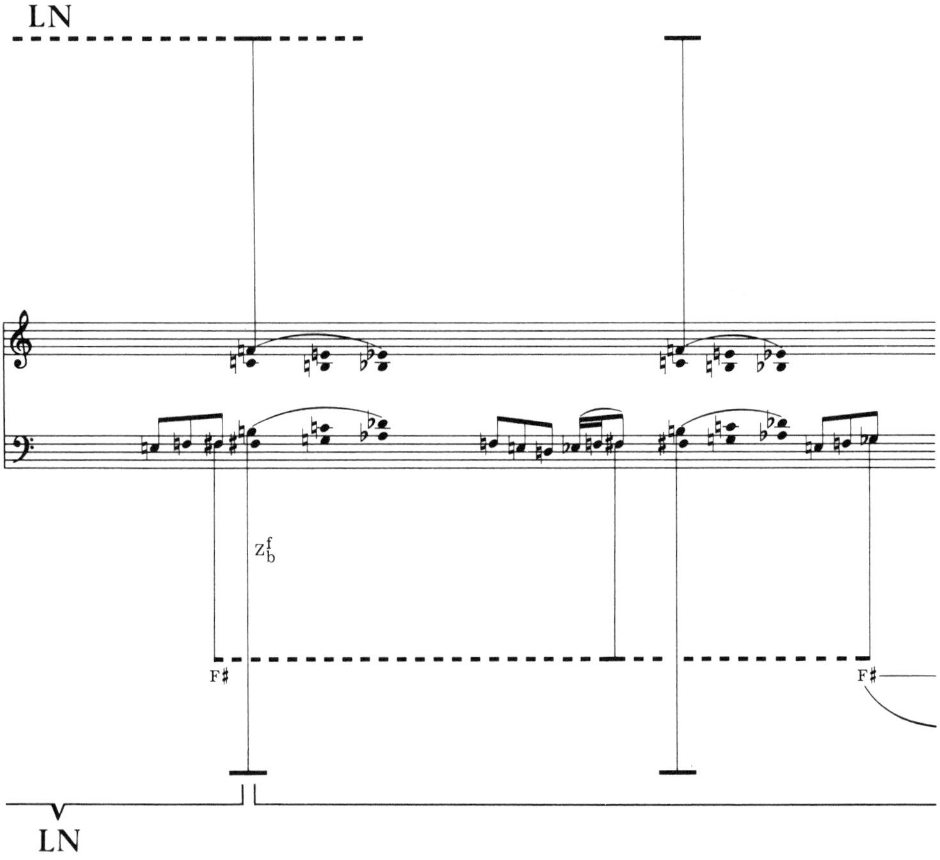

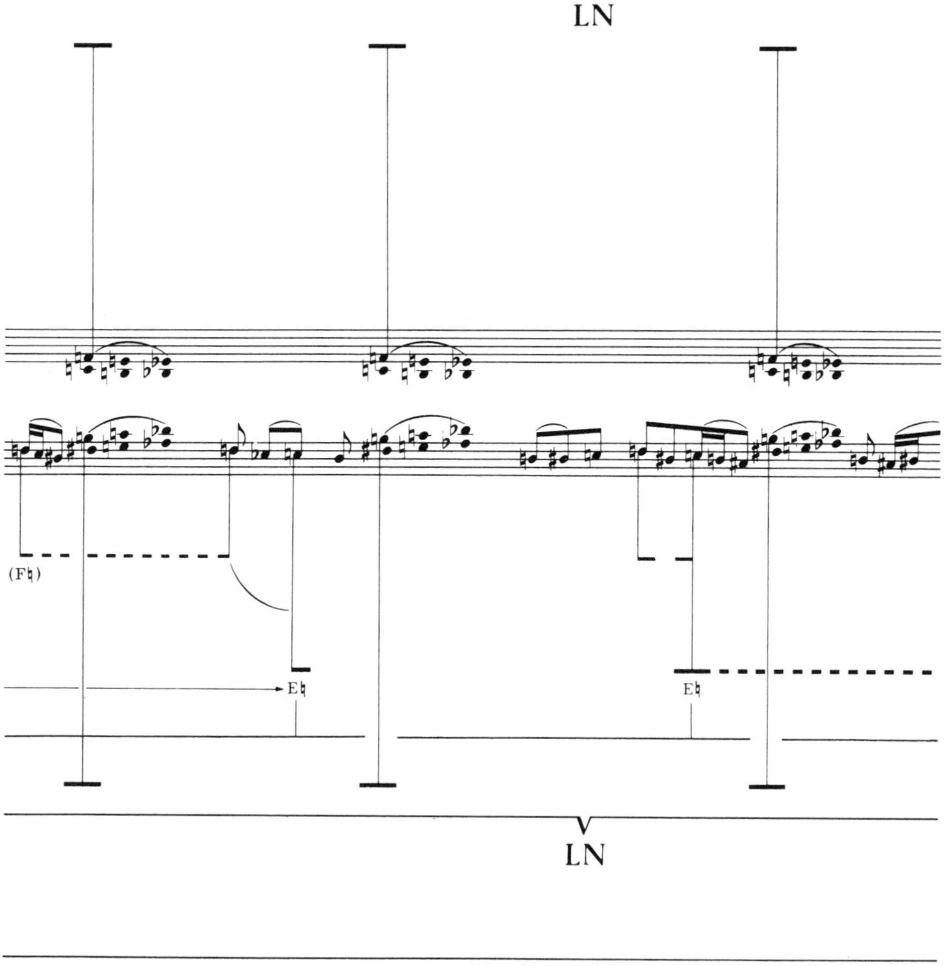
LN
(F♮)
E♮
E♮
LN

EXAMPLE 6b (*continued*)

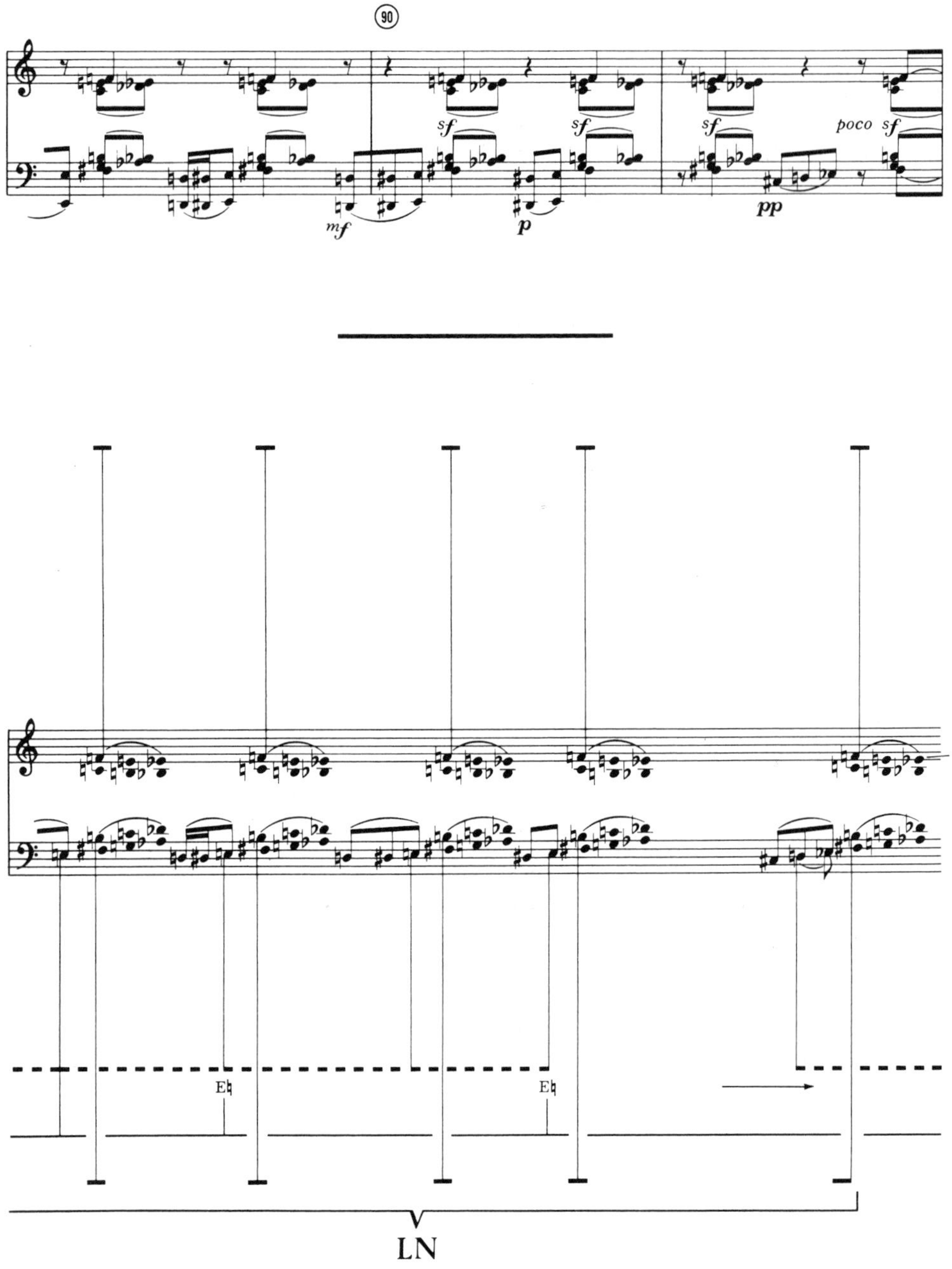

EXAMPLE 6c *Recapitulation* (bars 93–126)

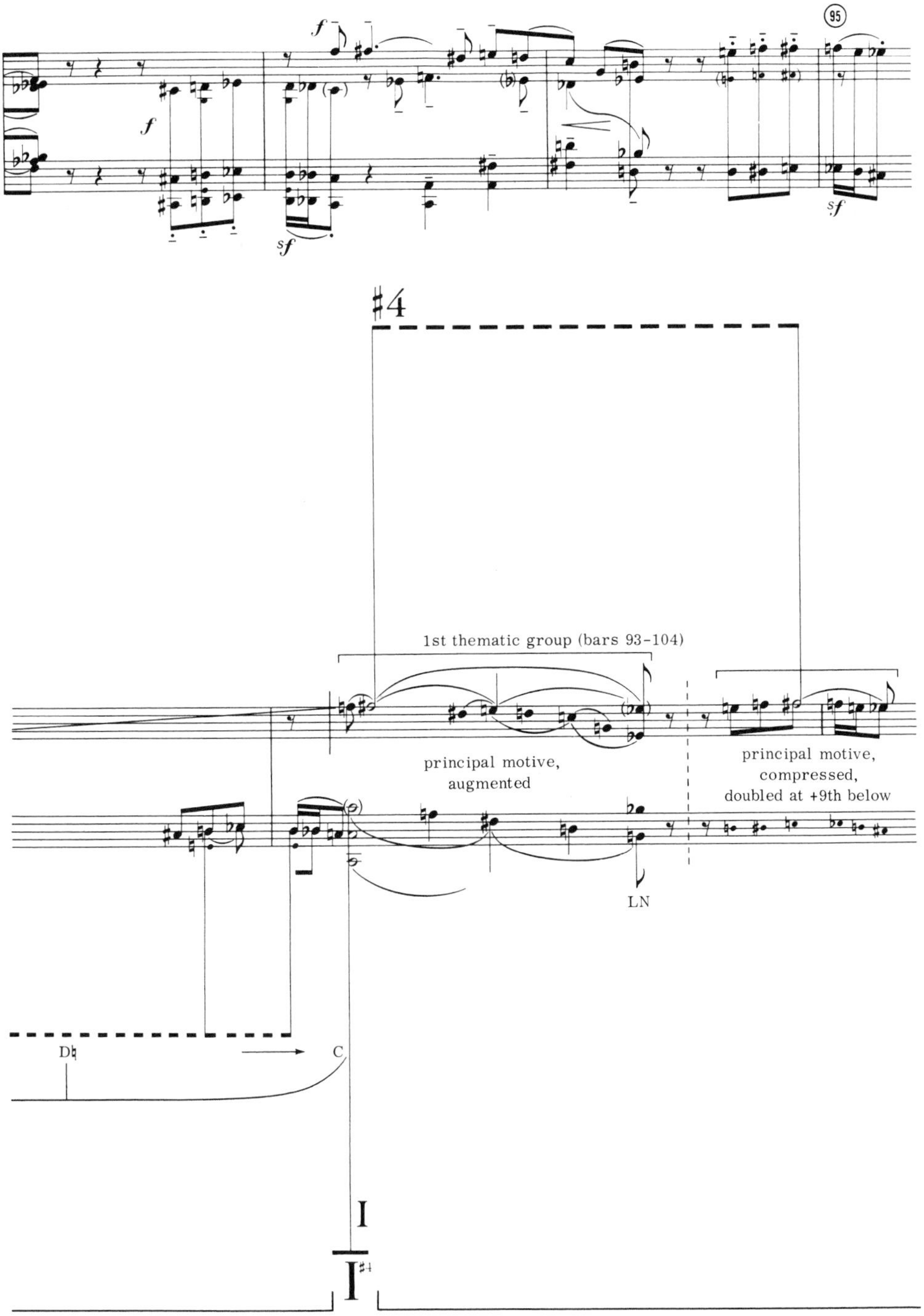

EXAMPLE 6C (*continued*)

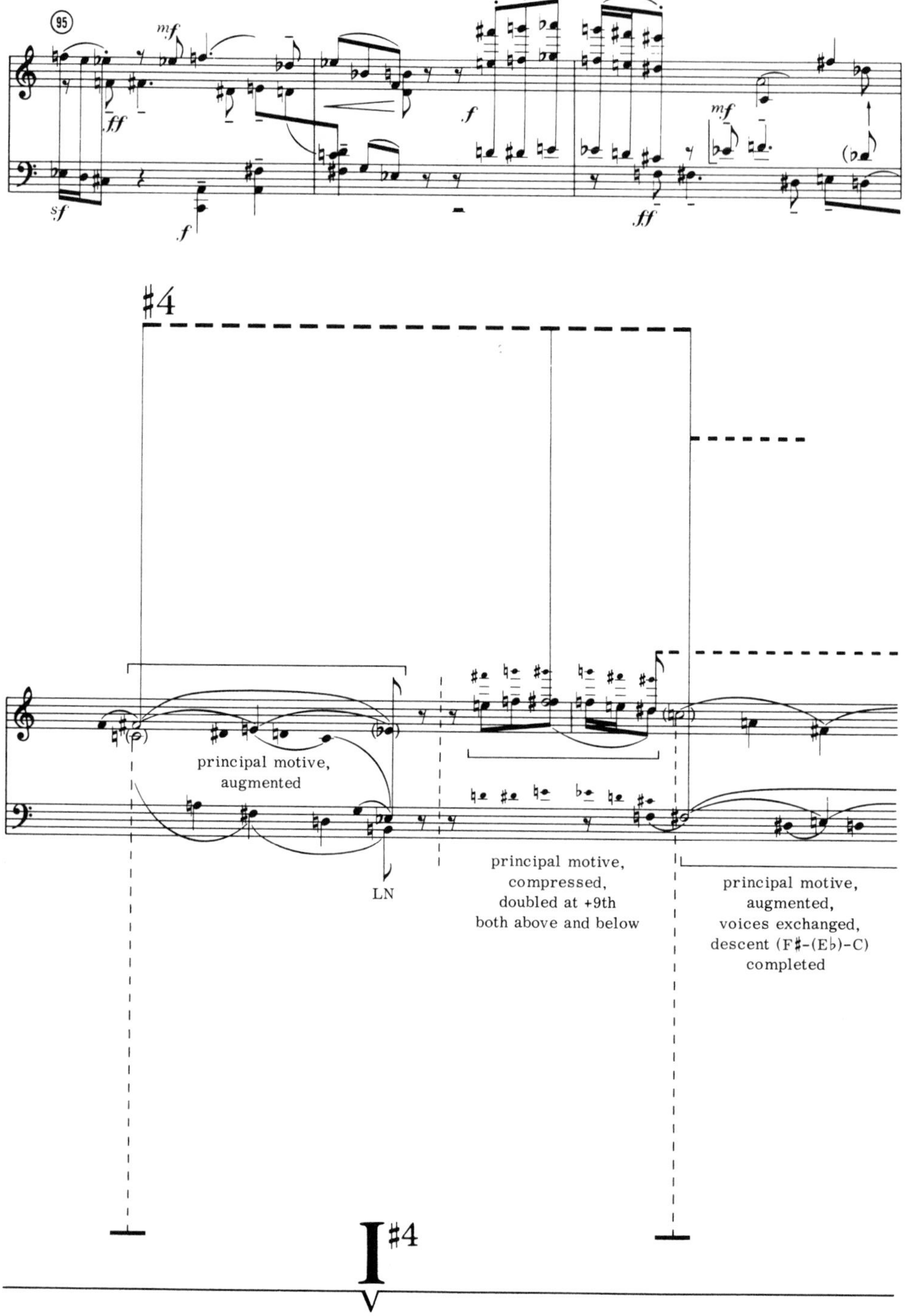

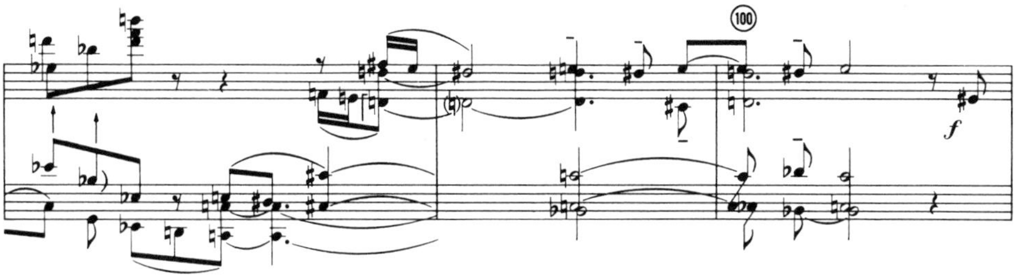
100
f

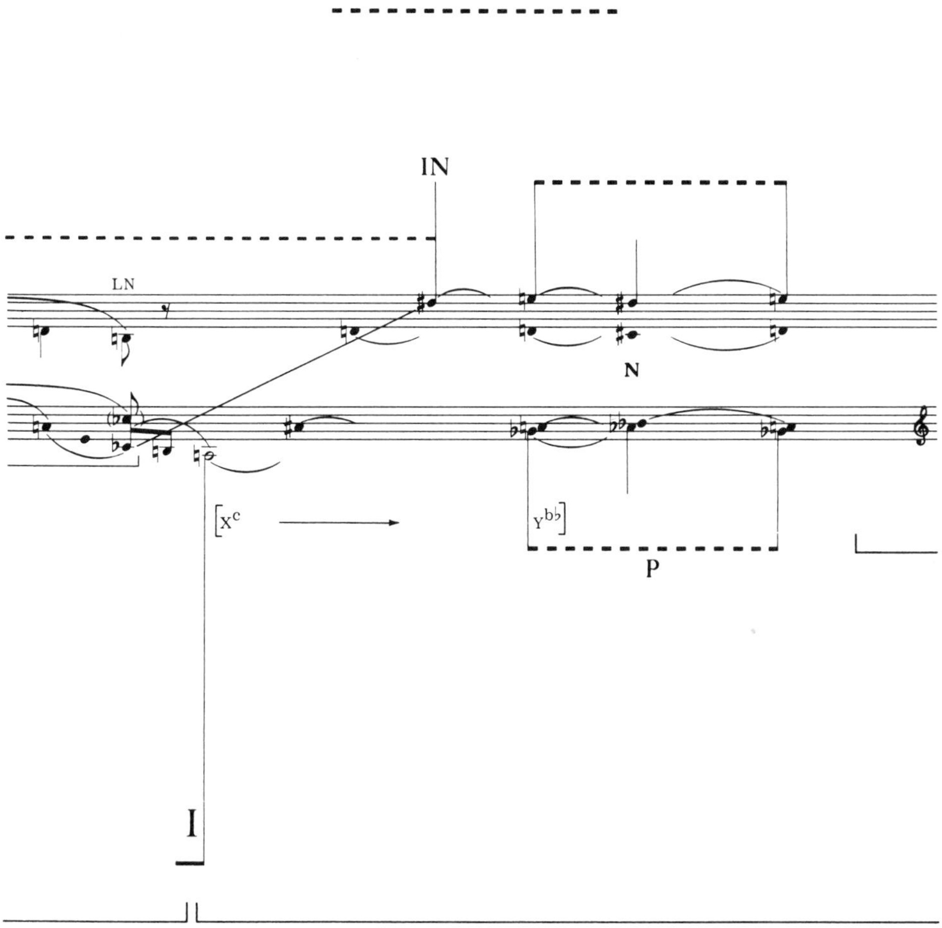
IN
LN
N
[X^c
Y^bb]
P
I

EXAMPLE 6c (*continued*)

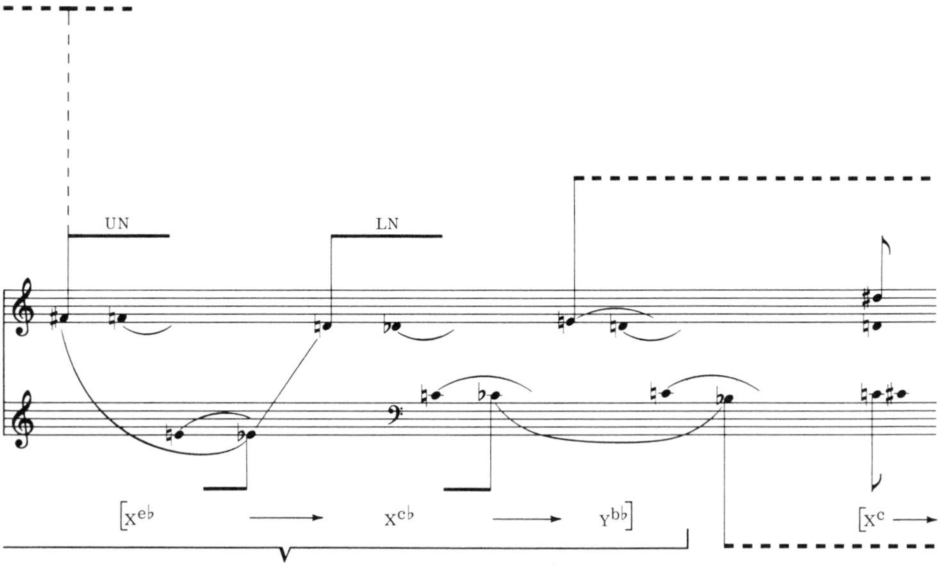

105
p

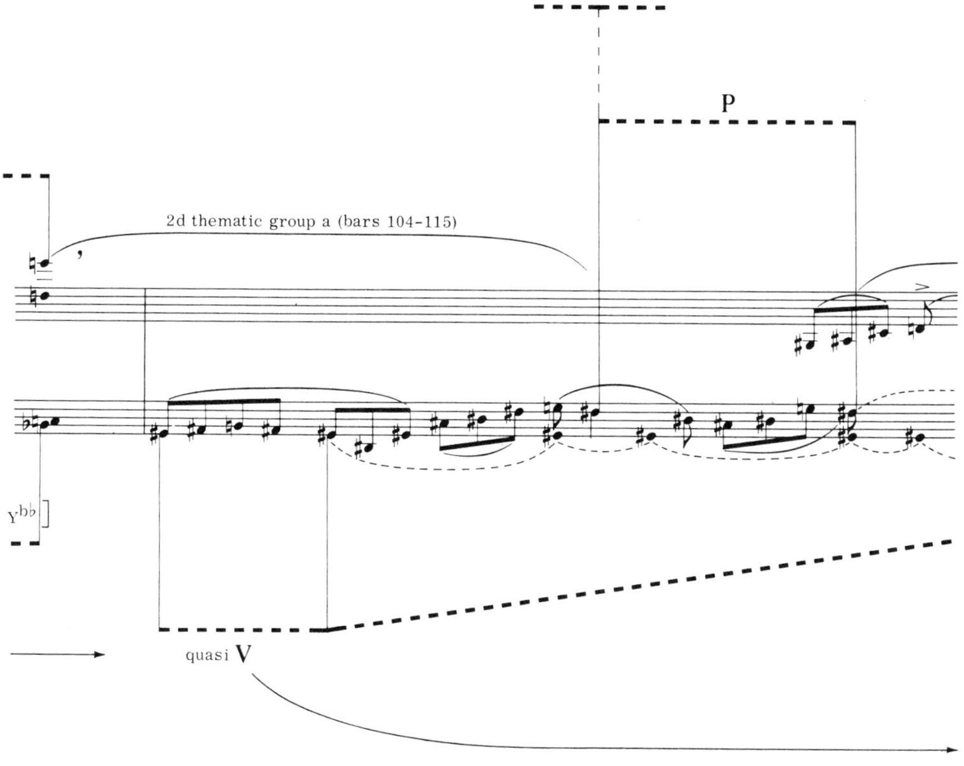
P
2d thematic group a (bars 104-115)
Y^{bb}
quasi V

EXAMPLE 6C (*continued*)

110

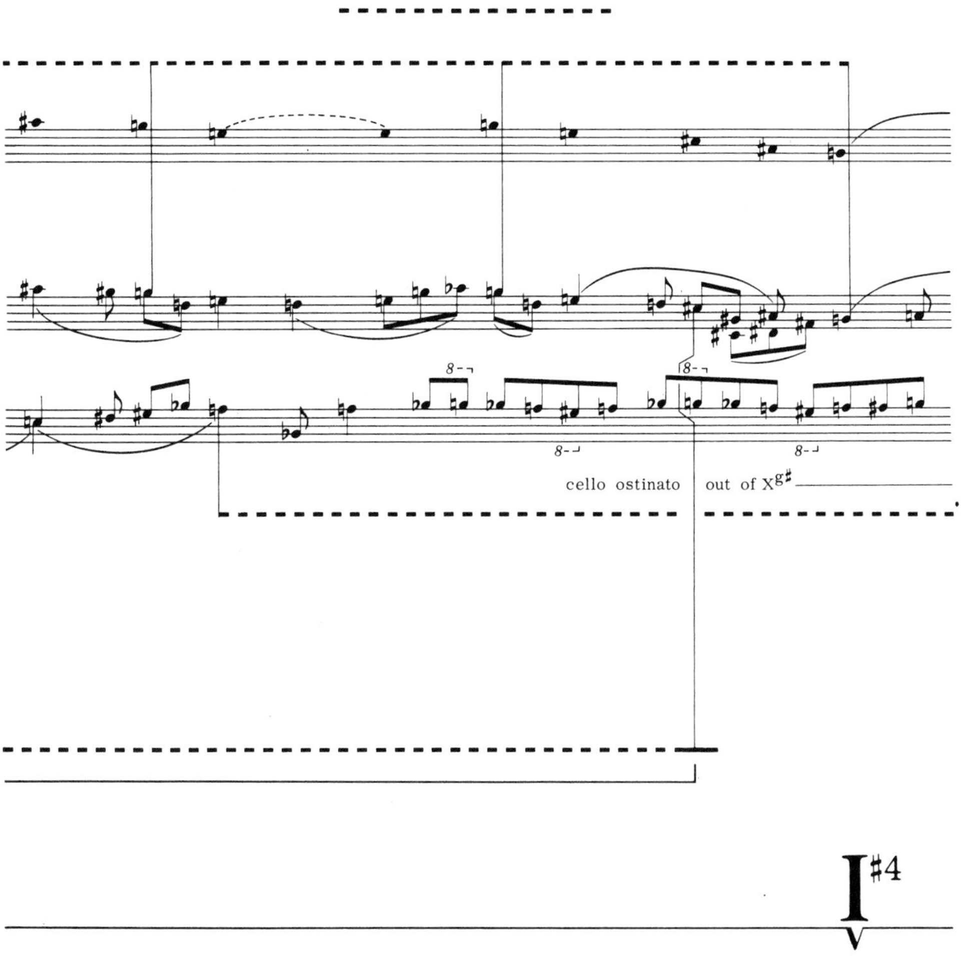
cello ostinato out of Xg♯
I♯4
V

EXAMPLE 6C (*continued*)

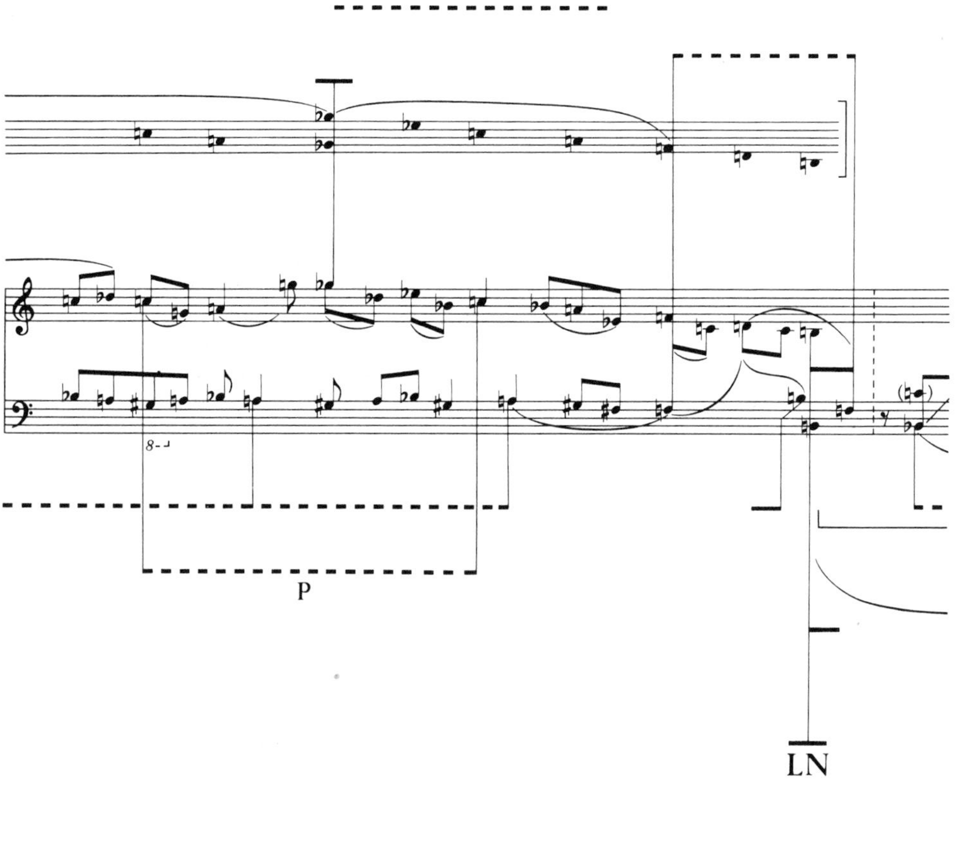

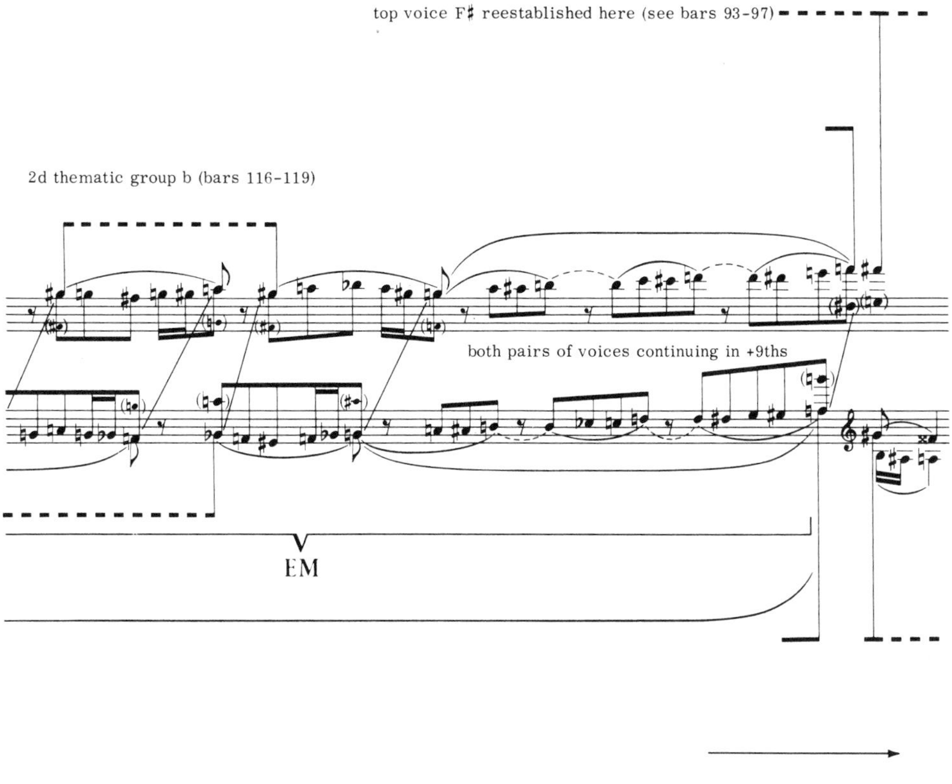
top voice F♯ reestablished here (see bars 93-97)
2d thematic group b (bars 116-119)
both pairs of voices continuing in +9ths
EM

EXAMPLE 6c (*continued*)

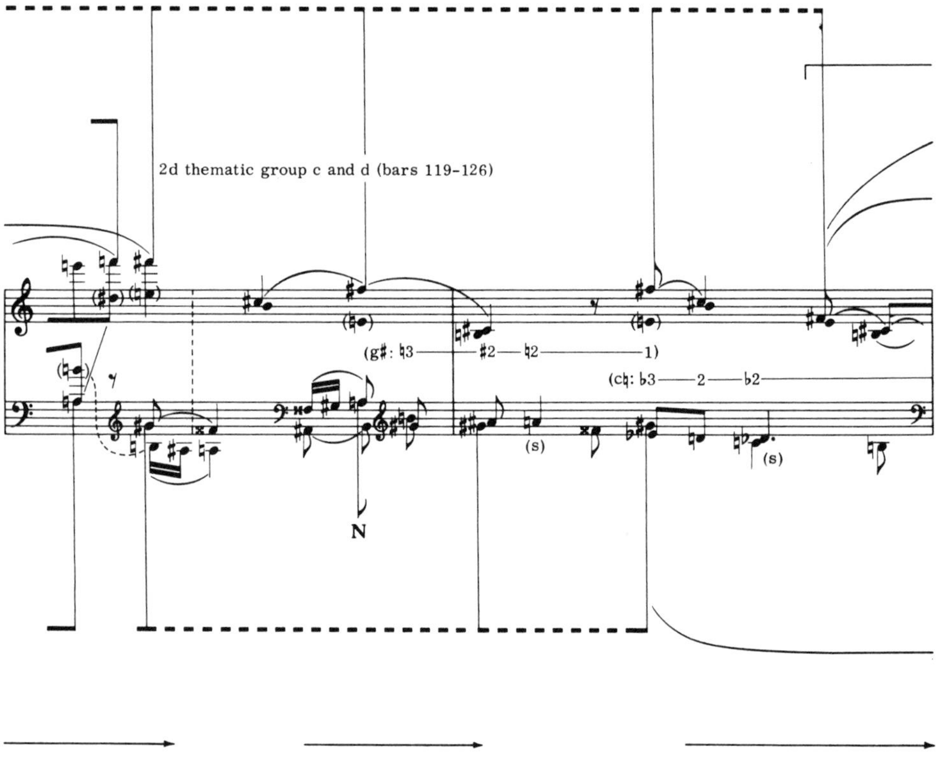

(s) = suspension.

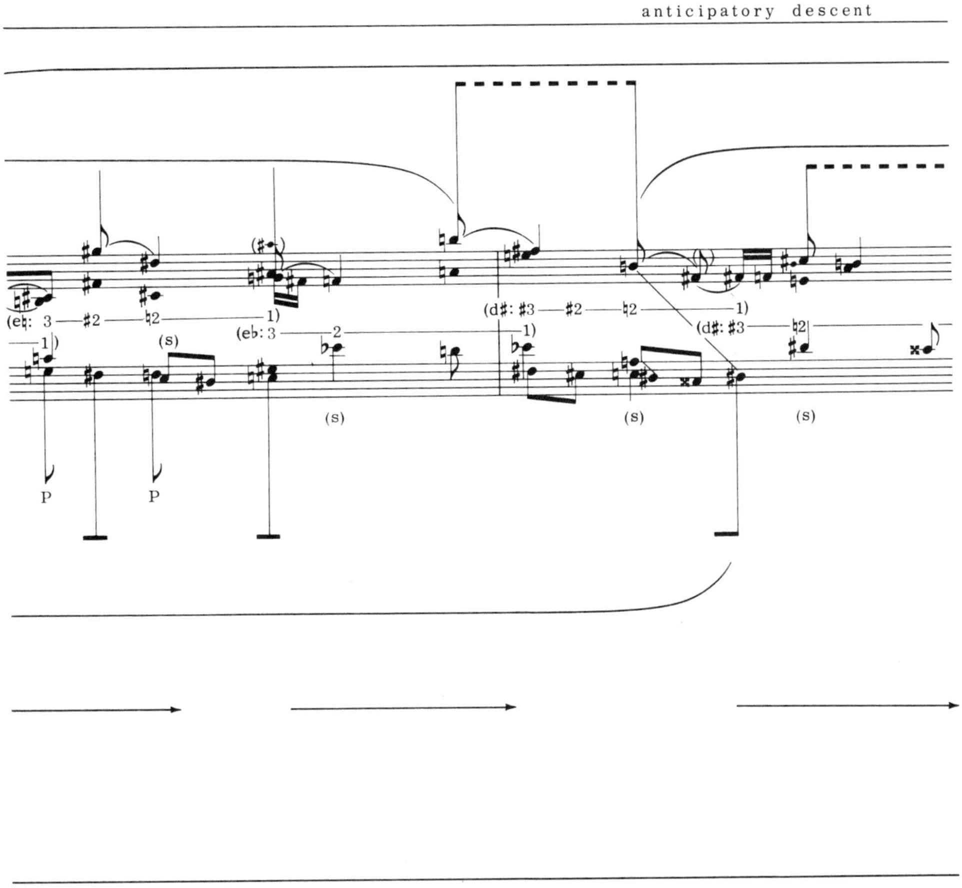
anticipatory descent
(e♮: 3 — ♯2 — ♮2 — 1)
(e♭: 3 — 2 — 1)
(d♯: ♯3 — ♯2 — ♮2 — 1)
(d♯: ♯3 — ♮2
(s)
P
P

EXAMPLE 6C (*continued*)

125
sf
sf

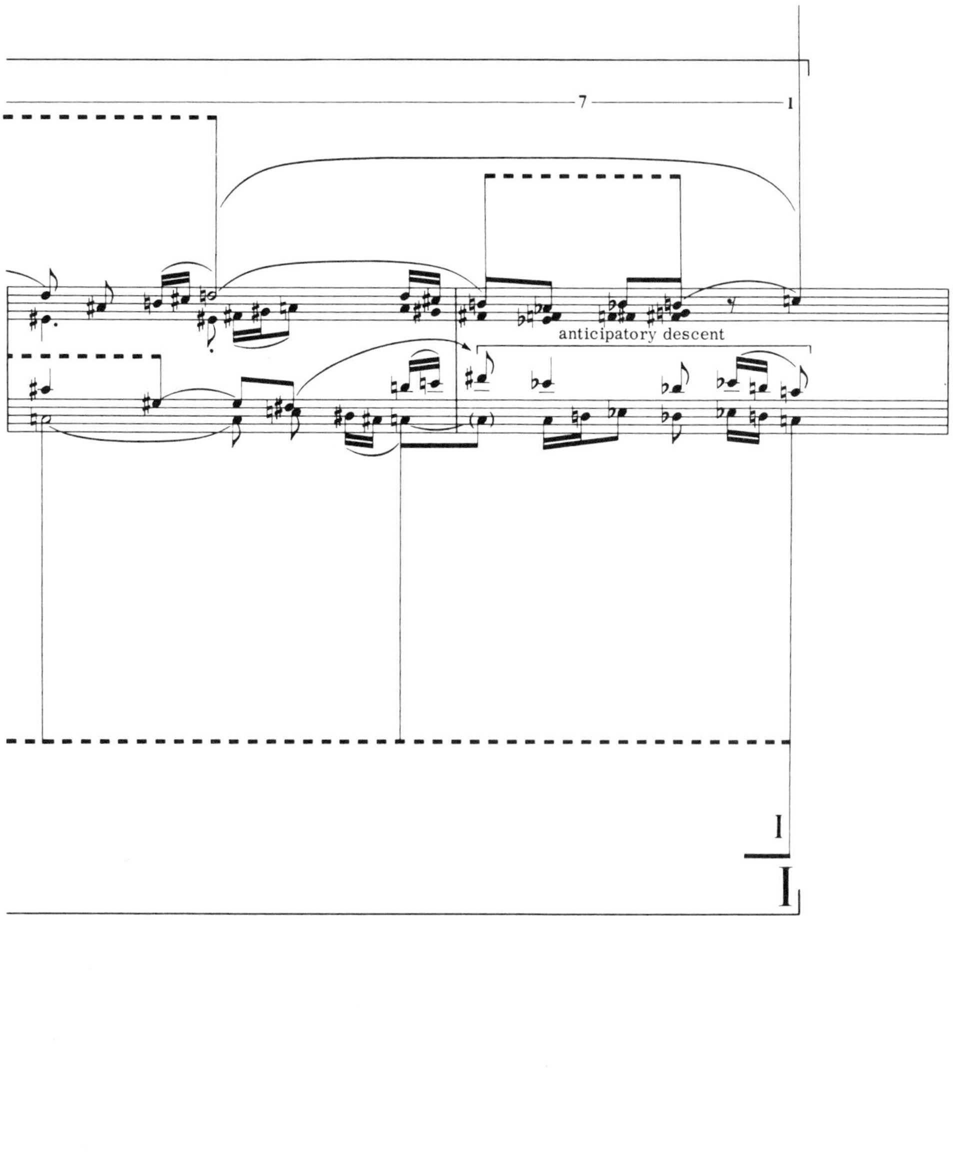
7
1
anticipatory descent
I
I

EXAMPLE 6d *Coda* (bars 126–161)

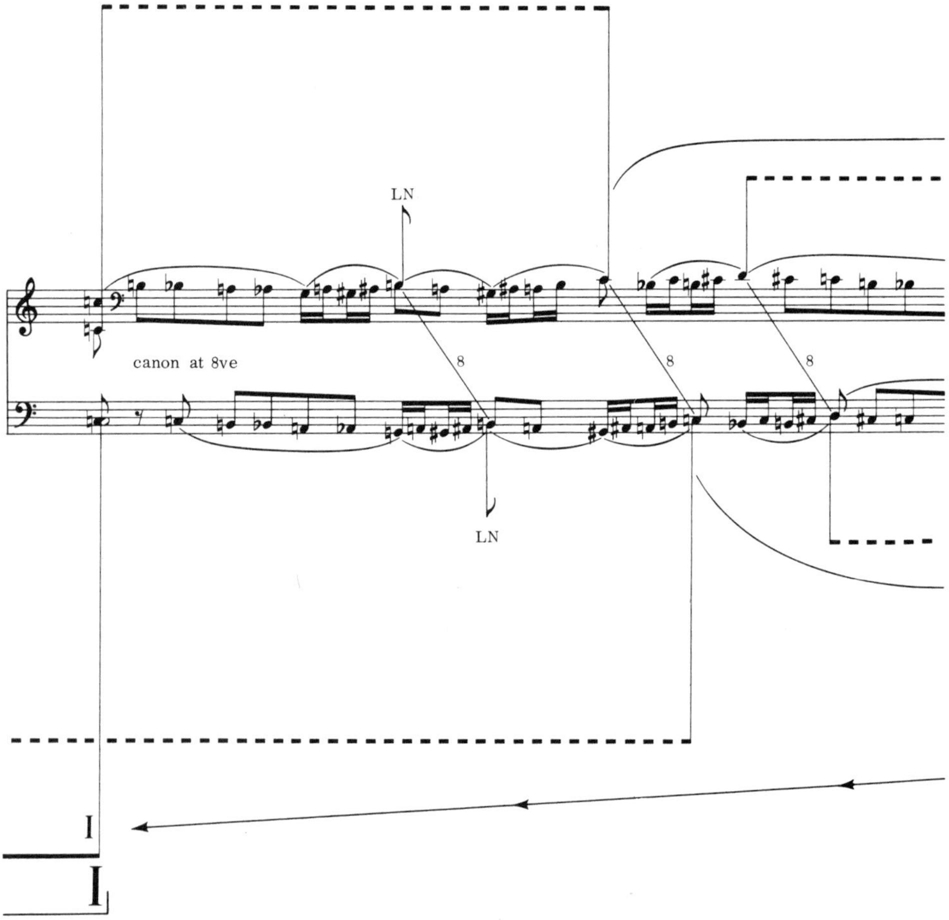

130
sf
sf
sf
sf

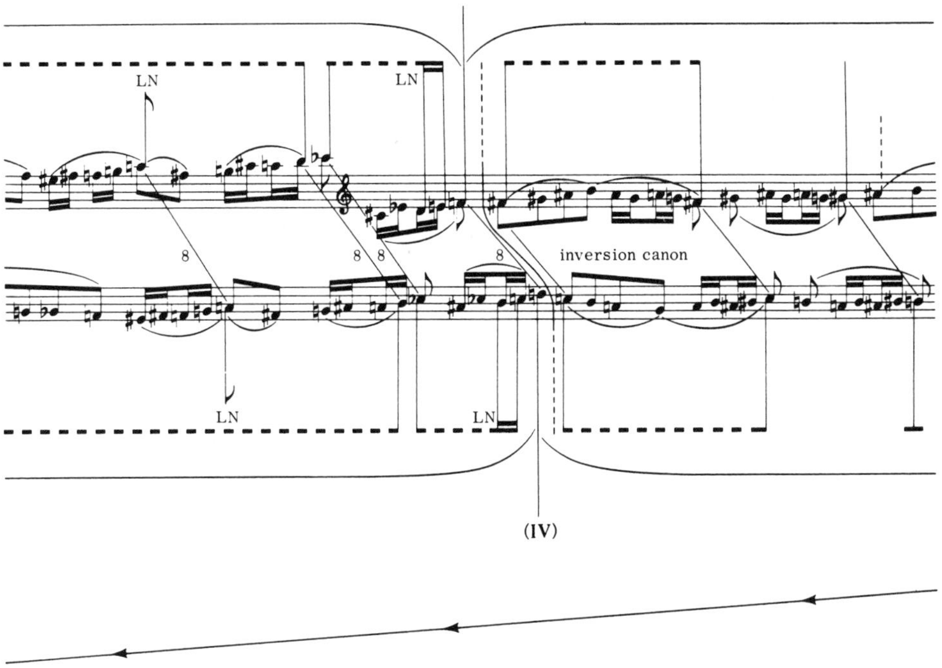
LN
LN
8
8 8
8
inversion canon
LN
LN
(IV)

EXAMPLE 6d (*continued*)

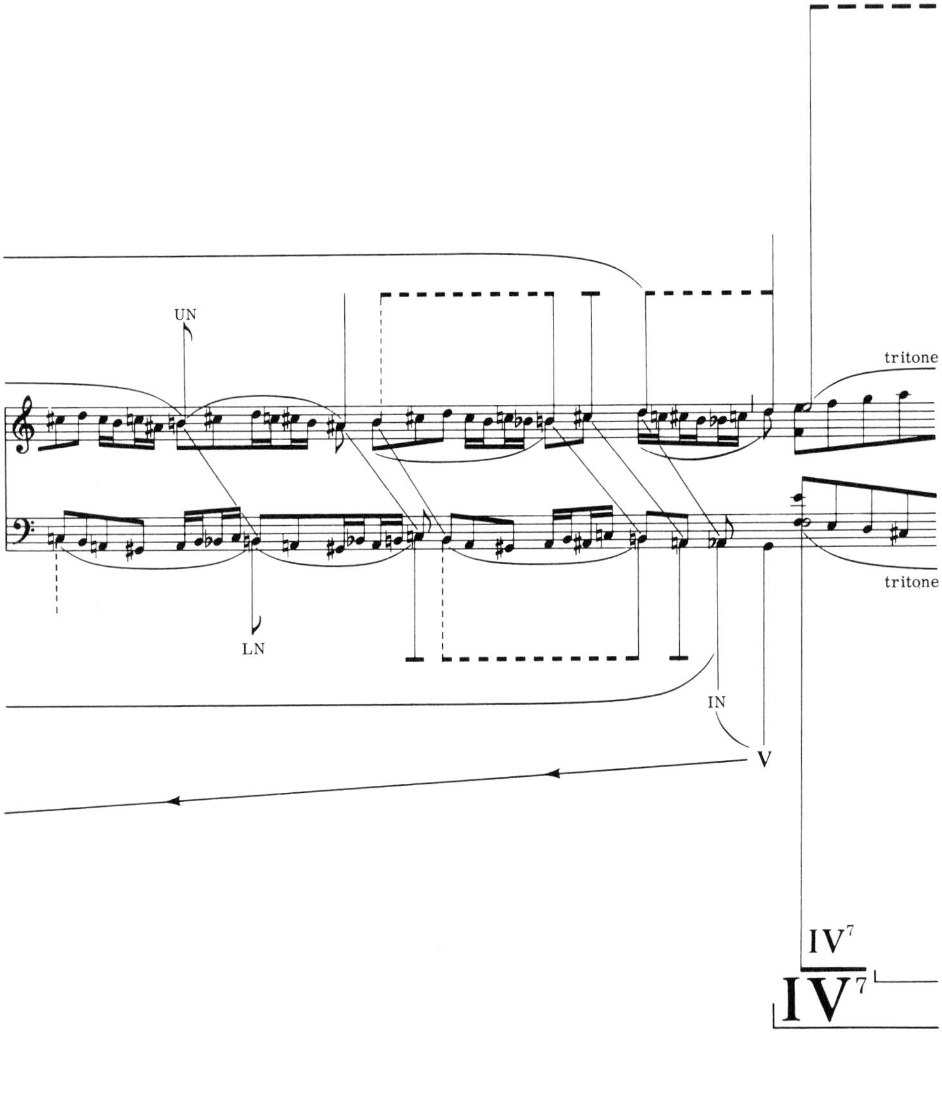

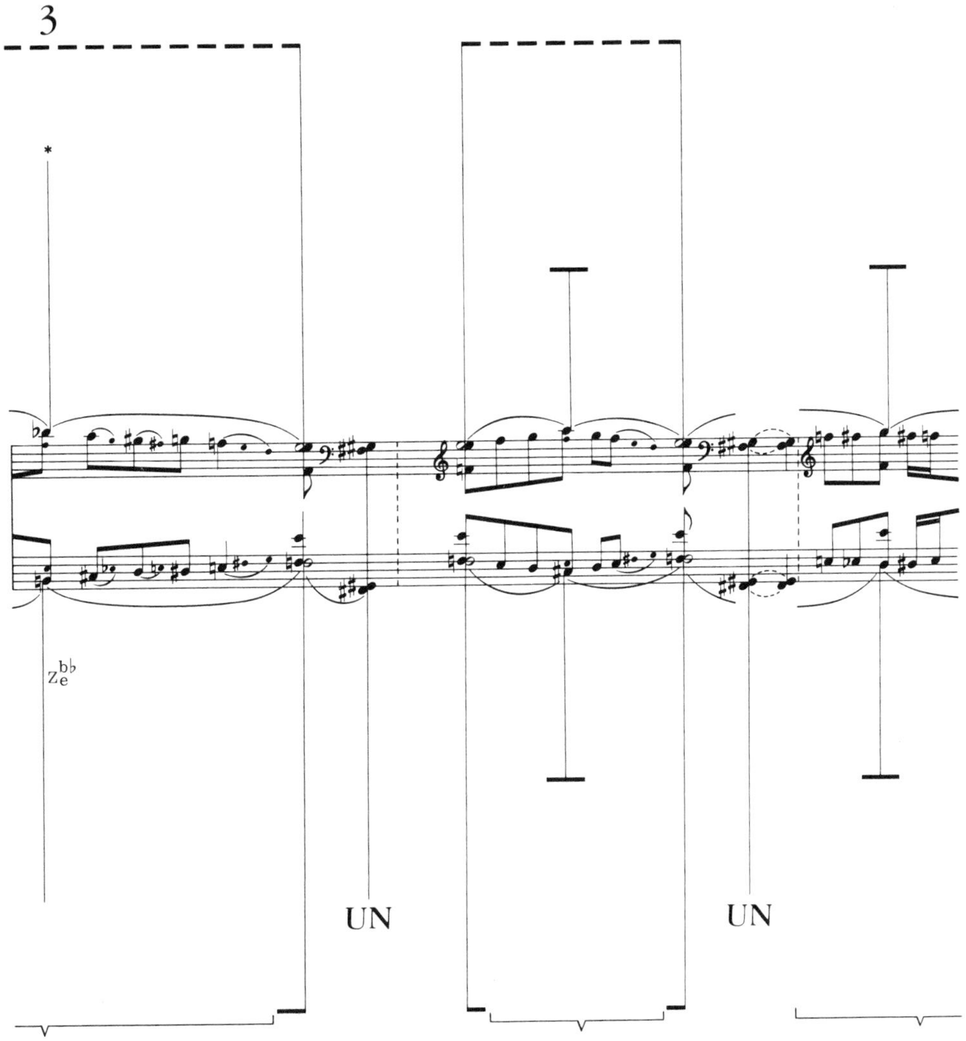

*Note that each successive embellishing chord of IV7, beginning with the z_e^{bb} of bar 135, tends progressively closer in its outer voices to the F–E of the principal chord (see bars 134–145).

EXAMPLE 6d (*continued*)

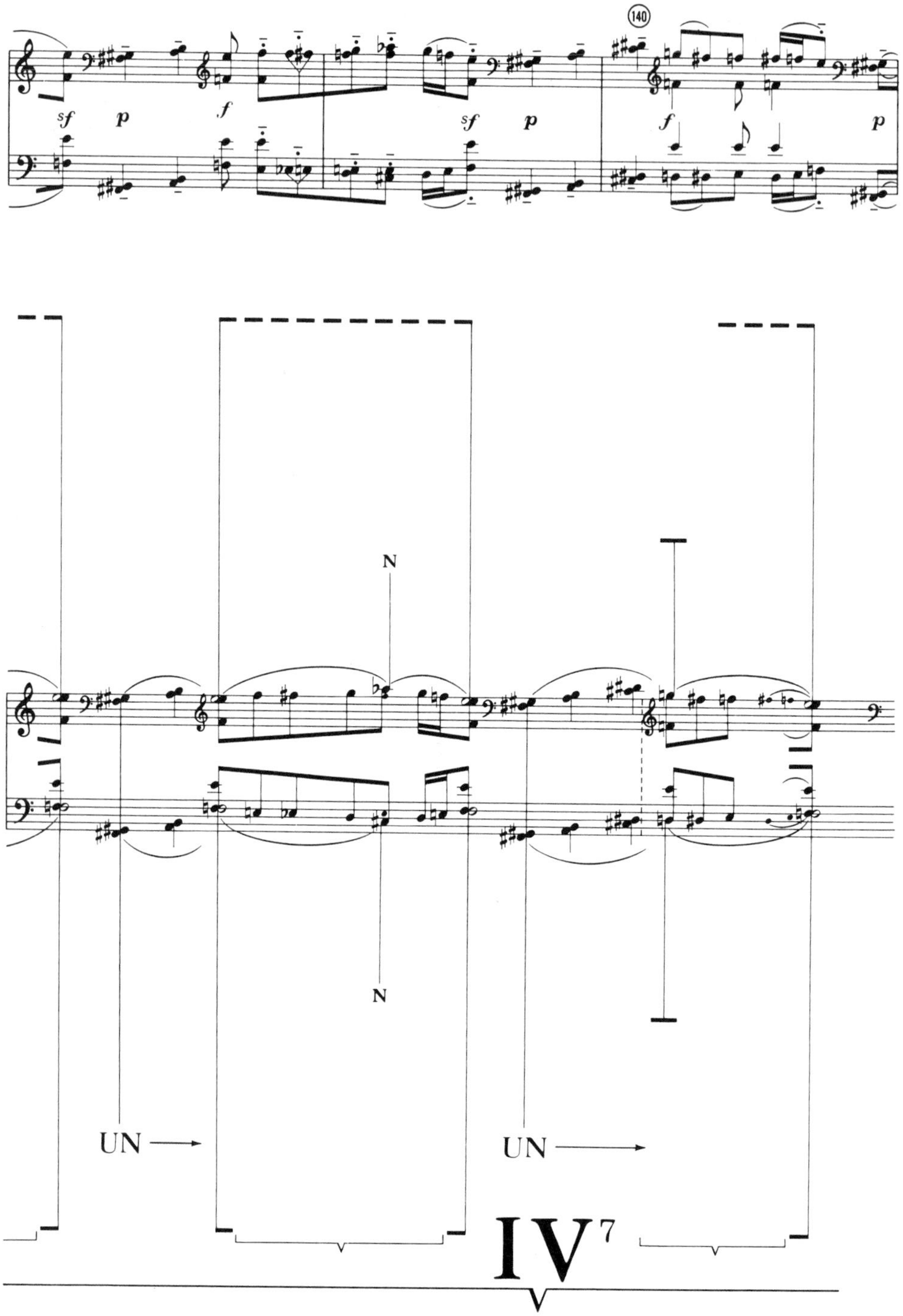

f
p
f
p

UN
UN
UN

EXAMPLE 6d (*continued*)

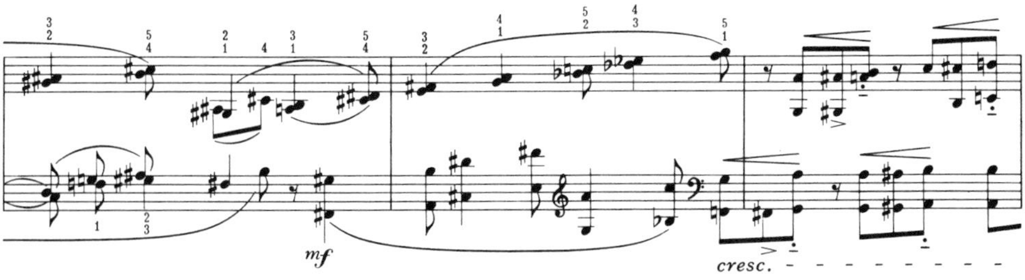

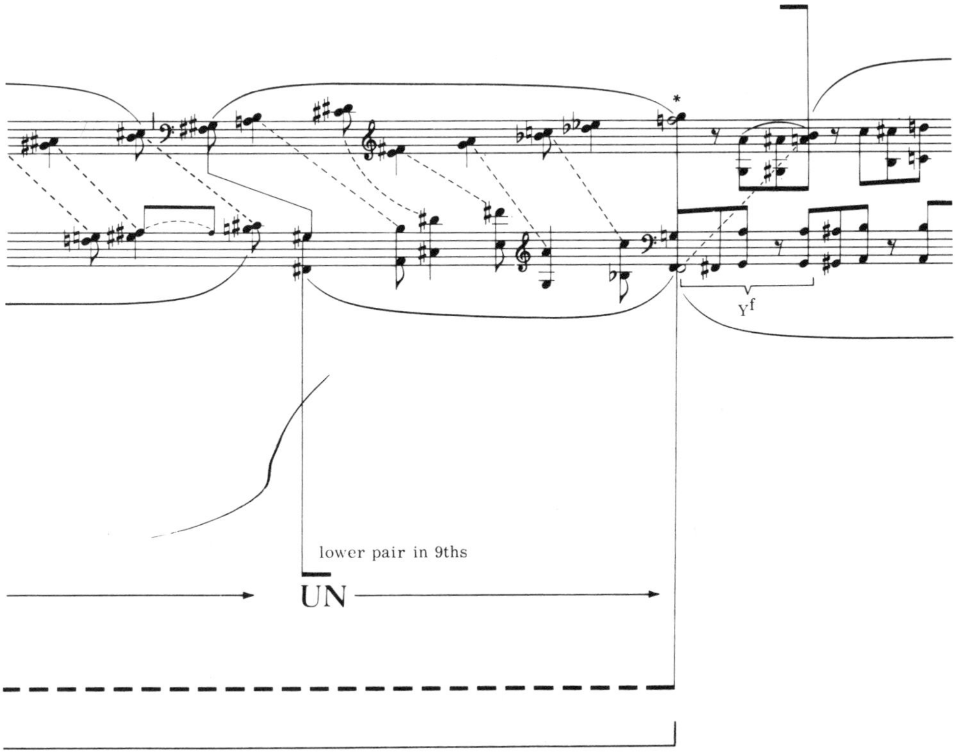

*This two-octave ascent in parallel major seconds (or ninths) finally brings the upper neighbor, F♯, introduced in the bass just before bar 136, back to its principal tone, F♮.

EXAMPLE 6d (*continued*)

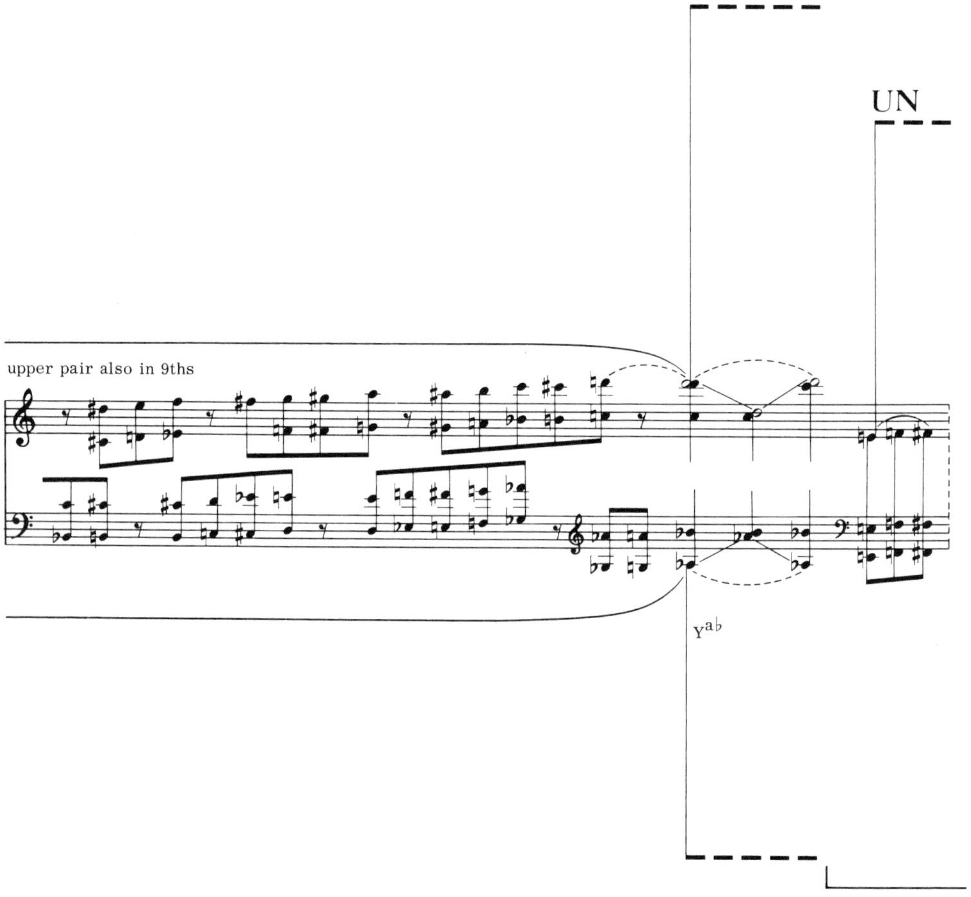

155
sf
sf
sf
sf
sf

2
UN
UN
LN
IN

EXAMPLE 6d (*continued*)

*Similarly, the ascent of a seventh here brings the upper neighbor, E♮, introduced in the soprano at bar 152, back to its principal tone, D♮.

160
sf
ff
sf
sf

2
1
V♯7
I♮

Index